Power in World Politics

The concept of power is central to the study of world politics. It enables us to identify pertinent actors and relationships in the international system, to locate sites of political activity and holders of responsibility for shaping our lives. And in a changing world giving rise to new phenomena of conflict and cooperation, students of international relations cannot ignore that 'power' has multiple meanings.

This book gives substance to the view that we need to break with the habit of defining power exclusively in terms of military capabilities of states. Featuring contributions from distinguished and upcoming scholars it explores facets of power in international politics through a variety of conceptual lenses. Drawing on insights from social theory and placing a particular focus on the phenomenon of 'soft' power, fifteen chapters assess the meaning of power from the perspectives of realism, constructivism, or development studies, with discussions ranging from conceptual analysis to practical application.

Power in World Politics attempts to broaden theoretical horizons and enrich our understanding of the distribution of power in the world we live in, thereby also contributing to the discovery and analysis of new political spaces. This is essential reading for all advanced students and scholars of international relations.

Felix Berenskoetter is a Ph.D. Candidate at the London School of Economics and Political Science, Department of International Relations. His research interests include international political theory, history of ideas, German–American relations, and European Security.

M. J. Williams is Head of the Transatlantic Security Programme at the Royal United Services Institute for Defence and Security Studies in London, where he is also the Director of the RUSI Project on Civil-Military Relations. His research interests include the changing character of war, NATO, US-European relations, security cooperation and US Foreign Policy.

Power in World Politics

Edited by
Felix Berenskoetter and
M. J. Williams

Routledge
Taylor & Francis Group

LONDON AND NEW YORK

First published 2007
by Routledge
2 Park Square, Milton Park, Abingdon, Oxon OX14 4RN

Simultaneously published in the USA and Canada
by Routledge
270 Madison Avenue, New York, NY 10016

Routledge is an imprint of the Taylor & Francis Group, an informa business

© 2007 Felix Berenskoetter and M. J. Williams, selection and editorial
matter; the contributors, their chapters. Thanks to Millennium: Journal of
International Studies

Typeset in Times New Roman by
Taylor & Francis Books
Printed and bound in Great Britain by
Antony Rowe Ltd, Chippenham, Wiltshire

British Library Cataloguing in Publication Data
A catalogue record for this book is available from the British Library

Library of Congress Cataloging in Publication Data
1. Balance of power. 2. World polities. 3. International relations.
I. Berenskoetter, Felix. II. Williams, Michael J., Dr.
JZ1310.P69 2007
327.1'12–dc22
2007006058

ISBN13: 978-0-415-42113-3 (hbk)
ISBN13: 978-0-415-42114-0 (pbk)
ISBN13: 978-0-203-94469-1 (ebk)

Contents

Contributors

Felix Berenskoetter is a Ph.D. candidate at the Department of International Relations and the London School of Economics and Political Science. His research interests include international political theory, history of ideas, German foreign policy, transatlantic relations and European security. He is a former editor of *Millennium: Journal of International Studies*.

Janice Bially Mattern is Associate Professor of International Relations at Lehigh University. In addition to a number of articles on the logic and transformation of world order, she is the author of *Ordering International Politics: Identity, Crisis, and Representational Force*. Her current research examines how transnational criminal practices can be expressions of sovereignty and citizenship.

Thomas Diez is Professor of International Relations at the University of Birmingham. He has published widely on discourse analyses of debates about European integration and its relationship with conflict transformation. *The European Union and Border Conflicts*, co-edited with Mathias Albert and Stephan Stetter, will be published by Cambridge University Press in 2007. He is currently working on projects assessing the role of human rights in conflict transformation and problematising the securitisation of migration in Europe after 9/11.

John Gaventa is Professor at the Institute of Development Studies, University of Sussex and the Director of the Development Research Centre on Citizenship, Participation and Accountability. He has written extensively on issues of power, participation and citizen action, including his books *Power and Powerlessness: Quiescence and Rebellion in an Appalachian Valley* (1980) and *Global Citizen Action* (2001, co-edited with Michael Edwards). He received his doctorate from Oxford University.

Joseph M. Grieco is Professor of Political Science at Duke University. He is the author of *Cooperation among Nations: Europe, America and Nontariff Barriers to Trade*, and *Between Dependency and Autonomy: India's Experience with the International Computer Industry*; and the co-author (with G. John Ikenberry) of *State Power and World Markets: The International Political Economy.*

Stefano Guzzini is Senior Researcher at the Danish Institute for International Studies and Professor in the Department of Government at Uppsala University, Sweden. He is the author of *Realism in International Relations and International Political Economy* (Routledge, 1998) and is currently working on *Power and International Relations* (Cambridge University Press). Together with Milan Brglez, he edits the *Journal of International Relations and Development.*

Wolf Hassdorf is a Tutorial Fellow in International Political Economy at the London School of Economics and Political Science. His current research interests include the political economy of international financial regulation in transition economies, constructivist approaches to financial market behaviour and the role of national identity in economic developmental strategies in East Asia.

Richard Ned Lebow is the James O. Freedman Presidential Professor of Government at Dartmouth College and Fellow of the Centre of International Relations at the University of Cambridge. His most recent books are *The Tragic Vision of Politics: Ethics, Interests and Orders,* (Cambridge, 2003) and *Conflict, Community and Ethics* (Routledge, 2006). He is the co-editor of *The Politics of Memory in Postwar Europe* (2006), *Unmaking the West: 'What-If' Scenarios that Remake World History* (2006) and *Social Inquiry and Political Knowledge* (2007).

Ronnie D. Lipschutz is Professor of Politics and Co-Director of the Center for Global, International and Regional Studies at the University of California, Santa Cruz. His most recent books are *Globalization, Governmentality and Global Politics: Regulation for the Rest of Us?* (Routledge, 2005) and a text co-authored with Mary Ann Tétreault, *Global Politics Because People Matter* (Rowman and Littlefield, 2005). He is editor of *Civil Societies and Social Movements* (Ashgate, 2006).

Steven Lukes is Professor of Sociology at New York University. Among his publications are *Emile Durkheim: His Life and Work, Individualism, Liberals and Cannibals: The Implications of Diversity* and *Power: A Radical View,* recently published in a revised and expanded edition. He is currently completing a book on moral relativism.

Ian Manners is Senior Researcher and Head of the European Union Internal Dynamics Unit at the Danish Institute for International Studies. Together with Sonia Lucarelli he has recently co-edited *Values and Principles in European Union Foreign Policy* (Routledge, 2006). His current working project is *The Normative Power of the European Union in World Politics.* His research interests include EU politics and policy-making, with a particular interest in normative theory and politics in the EU.

Joseph S. Nye, Jnr. is Distinguished Service Professor and former Dean of Harvard's Kennedy School of Government. He has served as Secretary of Defense for International Security Affairs, Chair of the National Intelligence Council and Deputy Secretary of State for Security Assistance, Science and Technology. In 2004, he published *Soft Power: The Means to Success in World Politics*, *Understanding International Conflicts* (5th edn), and *The Power Game: A Washington Novel*.

Erik Ringmar is Professor of Cultural Sociology and Political Economy at the National Chiao Tung University, Hsinchu, Taiwan. His most recent book, *Why Europe Was First*, discusses the origins of European modernity. His new project, *The Fury of the Europeans*, deals with imperialism in China in the nineteenth century.

Brian C. Schmidt is Associate Professor in the Department of Political Science at Carleton University, Canada. He is the author of *The Political Discourse of Anarchy: A Disciplinary History of International Relations* (SUNY Press, 1998) and *Imperialism and Internationalism in the Discipline of International Relations*, co-edited with David Long (SUNY Press, 2006).

Rosemary E. Shinko is Visiting Assistant Professor of International Relations at Bucknell University. She has published articles on Palestinian identity and statehood, Kosovo, as well as approaches to the teaching of IR theory. Her research interests include exploring the theoretical points of contact and disjuncture between postmodernism, realism and liberalism, exploring the ethical aspects of postmodern agonistic politics and investigating postmodern conceptualisations of subjectivity.

Jennifer Sterling-Folker is Associate Professor of Political Science at the University of Connecticut. She specialises in international relations theory, international organisation, and neo-classical realism and has published articles and book chapters on a variety of subjects. She is also author of *Theories of International Cooperation and the Primacy of Anarchy* and editor of *Making Sense of International Relations Theory*. In 2008 she begins a five-year term as co-editor of *International Studies Review*.

M. J. Williams is Head of the Transatlantic Security Programme at the Royal United Services Institute for Defence and Security Studies in London, where he is also the Director of the RUSI Project on Civil-Military Relations. His research interests include the changing character of war, NATO, US-European relations, security cooperation and US Foreign policy. He is the author of *On Mars and Venus: Strategic Culture in US and EU Foreign Policy* (LIT 2005) and *From Kosovo to Khandahar: the Evolution of an Alliance* (Routledge 2008). He is a former editor of *Millennium: Journal of International Studies*.

Acknowledgments

This volume started life during our time as editors of *Millennium: Journal of International Studies*. Ideas were debated at a conference at the LSE in October 2004 and lead to a special issue of *Millennium*, Volume 3, Number 3, where a number of contributions contained in this volume originally appeared. The articles selected for this book have been revised by their authors, some of them substantially, and complemented with original essays by John Gaventa, Joseph Grieco, Joseph Nye, Jnr., Erik Ringmar as well as Ian Manners joining Thomas Diez as a co-author.

As it is with such things, this book is the result of a great many people's input, and we are indebted to all who assisted us in bringing it to life. At *Millennium* we would like to thank everyone of Team 33, including Rashmi Singh and Dorethea Kast. We are also grateful to the LSE's International Relations Department, in particular Chris Brown, Michael Cox and Mark Hoffmann for supporting *Millennium* and encouraging us to pursue this book project. Among those people who provided stimulating ideas in and around 'power', Stefano Guzzini, Olya Gayazova and Christopher Coker deserve special mention.

At Routledge we would like to thank Craig Fowlie for taking this project on board and everyone involved in the production process. Thanks also to Kate Clouston for helping us compile all kinds of odds and ends and to the contributors for their patience and receptiveness to rounds of editorial comments.

Finally, we each would like to thank our parents for all their support (enabling, empowering and otherwise) allowing us to survive as graduate students in London. This book is dedicated to them.

F.B.
M.J.W.
London, August 2007

1 Thinking about power

Felix Berenskoetter

'What holds the world together in its core?' This famous question is posed by Goethe's *Faust*, who after years of tireless studying realizes that he still has not grasped the essence of the world. Frustrated with the limit of his own knowledge, he enters a pact with the devil in the hope to find the answer. Although scholars working in the field of International Relations (IR) generally do not harbour *Faust's* ambitions the question of how to grasp 'world politics' remains a formidable challenge. Perhaps the most prominent and most enduring answer is to focus on 'power', that is, to conceive of the world of politics as one that is held together by power relations. Yet doing so does not provide analysts with an essence. As the literature tells us, 'power' is an essentially contested concept, with different interpretations held together more by a family resemblance than a core meaning. And because the meaning we choose determines which relations we consider relevant and where we locate political spaces – in short, how we conceptualize 'world politics' – it is pertinent to be aware of the different ways 'power' can be defined. In short, we need to think about power.

In the field of IR, thinking about power was long considered the domain of realism. Hans Morgenthau famously declared that, anchored in a human desire to dominate and/or the need for self-protection, 'statesmen think and act in terms of interests defined as power' (Morgenthau 1960: 5) and that power is 'the immediate aim' of all states (1960: 27). Ever since, realist scholars successfully monopolised 'power' as an analytical device to make sense of international politics, defined it primarily in terms of military capabilities and used it for classifying states and explaining their behaviour. Ironically, attempts to establish alternative readings of international politics often reinforced this marriage. Exceptions aside, critics of realism gained their academic currency by either refining or rejecting realism's focus on power, instead of forcefully articulating an alternative reading of it. Thus, while the past two decades produced significant discussions over the meaning of other core concepts of IR, such as security or sovereignty, the so-called linguistic turn did not really spark much interest in debating 'power'. This volume is an invitation for scholars of world politics to do so.

To be sure, with its aim of engaging the meaning of power in IR, this book stands not alone. It builds on David Baldwin's repeated calls to pay closer attention to the concept used so often (Baldwin 1979; 1989; 2002) and is inspired by the agenda of critically examining orthodoxy and moving attention to analytical silences (Enloe 1989; 1996), as well as by Stefano Guzzini's nuanced and differentiated readings of 'power' (Guzzini 1993; 1998; 2000c). Furthermore, it is worth noting that most alternative conceptions of power found in the silences of the discipline are not new but merely forgotten voices. To bring them back into memory and place the contributions of this volume in context, this introduction will present an overview of the debates about 'power' in social and political theory and their echoes in IR.

By doing so, it provides a critical complement to Baldwin's approach aimed at refining the measurement of power. It also puts into perspective a recent publication by Michael Barnett and Raymond Duvall (2005a), which tries to systematically capture different conceptions of 'power' and explore connections between them. Although valuable in raising awareness of the richness and complexity of 'power', both sets of authors neglect the theoretical contexts in which the concept has been embedded. Most strikingly, their texts do not discuss the power debates in social and political theory, including the 'three faces', or 'three dimensions' as Steven Lukes (1974; 2005) originally called them. Baldwin's (2002: 179) statements that this debate is of no importance to IR scholars could be explained with his belief that power is a phenomenon that can be measured with 'increased precision' (Baldwin 1979: 162). Taking the behavioural lens of the 1950s Chicago School as his main point of reference, it appears that for Baldwin the portrait of 'power' is not painted by theory and, therefore, cannot be modified by it. Abstract theoretical debates at best are repetitions on the theme and at worst obscure the true nature of power.[1] Somewhat differently, Barnett and Duvall only pretend to ignore the 'three faces'. While dismissing the debate on the peculiar ground that it lacks 'elements of a systematic typology' (2005a: 43, n. 13), their own typology carries a striking similarity and is backed with references to its key representatives. Barnett and Duvall also do not touch on the link between different conceptualisations of power and different approaches to theorising world politics, which allows them to blend out that connections between multiple forms of power may be difficult to establish across meta-theoretical divides.

The view put forward here is that IR scholars cannot ignore theoretical debates when thinking about 'power'. Being aware of the work done in social and political theory not only serves as an inspiration and minimises the risk of reinventing the wheel. Even more so, it allows us to see how, different concepts of power are embedded in different theoretical frames and everything that comes with it, including our understandings of 'causation' and of 'politics'. Moving towards this point, the following discussion will first give the topic some grounding by reviewing the definition of power in and around the writings of Max Weber. It will then adopt Lukes' typology of the 'three dimensions' as a vehicle for tracing conceptions of power found in political and social theory into IR. Here two caveats must be made: first, loosely associating the three dimensions with the familiar IR tripartite of realism, institutionalism/regime theory and constructivism/ postmodernism, is, of course, only one way of organising the debate, and by no means a perfect one. Insights and issues do cut across.[2] Second, despite the seeming temporal development in the narrative below, it does not intend to tell a story of theoretical progress. Rather, as Steven Lukes (2006: 164) reminds in response to his critics, the reader should keep in mind that every way of seeing is also a way of not seeing.

Foundations and dimensions

From Hobbes to Foucault, philosophers have always found 'power' inter-twined with the human condition, with Nietzsche suggesting that the feeling of power [*Gefuehl der Macht*] has become both the greatest love of and a 'demon' to humans.[3] Contemporary writings most frequently refer to Max Weber, whose insights influenced a number of important works on 'power', including those of Robert Dahl, Hans Morgenthau, Raymond Aron, and Michael Mann.

Weber defined power, the German *Macht*, as the 'opportunity [*Chance*] to have one's will prevail [*durchsetzen*] within a social relationship, also against resistance, no matter what this opportunity is based on' (Weber 1976: 28, author's translation).[4] This definition is remarkably rich. First, and most obviously, it points out that power is a relational phenomenon that cannot be grasped without first identifying a social relationship. Weber (1976: 13) defines a social relationship as a phenomenon where the meaning frame within which the individuals' will is formed and behaviour takes place is 'mutually adjusted and oriented towards each other'. Hence, identifying whether and how individuals stand in a power relationship requires the identification of the meaning context, that is, a shared system of values. Second, as an opportunity, or potential, which does not have to be realised, the definition suggests that identifying power has much to do with identi-fying the position someone is placed in vis-à-vis others, which allows seeing power as both 'capability' and 'effect'. Third, the qualification that meeting and overcoming resistance is not a necessary feature can be interpreted that power means accomplishing one's will not only against but also with others, thus encompassing phenomena of both resistance and cooperation. Thus Weber also allows for the notion of empowerment, or 'power to', and leaves open the possibility that a power relationship is not necessarily hierarchical, as implied in the notion of 'power over'. Although, by making power a strictly social phenomenon, his definition does not cover empowerment understood as individual development.

Weber is clear that the concept is amorphous. As he puts it, the position of having one's will prevail can arise due to 'all thinkable human qualities and [in] all thinkable constellations' (1976: 13; author's translation). Weber spoke of different facets of power more specifically in the context of a particular phenomenon, namely that of *Herrschaft*. Usually translated into English as authority, domination, rule, or governance, *Herrschaft* is defined by Weber as 'the opportunity to find obedience amongst specified persons for a given order' (Weber 1976: 28, author's translation). Such obedience, Weber suggests, is based on a belief in the legitimacy of the command motivated by rational cost–benefit calculation, custom or personal affection.[5] Therefore, he argues, for *Herrschaft* to be considered legitimate the relationship between the actor giving the order and the one following it must be 'institutionalised' (with institutions understood in a broad sense) in one of three types: (i) a legal or contractual arrangement in which both are members and are following agreed-upon rules, such as in a bureaucracy; (ii) a belief in tradition which designates clear hierarchies through standing/ rank, such as between the patriarch and the servant; (iii) the charismatic quality of the person issuing the order obtained, for instance, through extraordinary acts that create bonds of personal affection, such as between leader and disciple (Weber 1992: 151–66). In crude terms, these three types attribute the willingness to follow orders to a technical, a habitual and an emotional relationship.[6]

Finally, and quite importantly, Weber's *Herrschaft* describes ways of having one's will prevail without using force (physical violence) and, thus, describes power as a psychological phenomenon. This distinction between power as 'civil obedience' (de Jouvenel 1952) and the application of physical violence is echoed by most theorists, although they maintain that power remains linked to violence in one way or another (see below).[7] Few would go as far as Hannah Arendt, who makes a fundamental distinction between power and physical violence, noting that 'out of the barrel of a gun grows the most effective demand, resulting in the most instant and perfect obedience. What can never grow out of it is power' (Arendt 1970: 51). This juxtaposition is informed by a conception of power as 'the human ability not just to act but to act in concert' (Arendt 1970: 44), which sits uneasily with Weber's definition of *Macht* and is formulated in opposition to his notion of *Herrschaft*. More precisely, while Arendt echoes Weber's emphasis on power as a social phenomenon and its need for legitimacy – which, for Arendt, is derived from the group coming together – power is not being expressed in obedience. Instead, Arendt sees power as *creative*, as something productive, as a phenomenon of empowerment emerging through togetherness exemplified in non-violent resistance movements.[8] This communal, or consensual, conception of power, also found in Parsons, shifts the focus away from Weber's emphasis on the 'prevailing will' to the extent that 'acting in concert' creates something new that has not been there before.

The first dimension: winning conflicts

When tempted to specify 'power', IR scholars usually adopt Robert Dahl's definition of 'A getting B to do something B would otherwise not do' (Dahl

1961; 1968). Yet Dahl (like Baldwin) built on the work by Harold Lasswell and Morton Kaplan (1950), which reads like a transmission of some of Weber's conceptual insights to an American audience in the behavioural gown of the Chicago School. Like Weber, Lasswell and Kaplan understand power as a phenomenon of interpersonal relations. They define it as the production of intended effects on other persons, more precisely as A affecting B through the shaping and distribution of values within a shared 'value pattern'.

Lasswell and Kaplan further differentiate between 'power' and 'influence'. Whereas the former is understood as 'actual control' of shared value patterns under the threat of sanctions (1950: 76), influence is defined as a potential contained in a superior position and lacks the coercive character of 'power' (1950: 58f). While this view is shared by most scholars, there is disagreement over how to relate the two concepts. Lasswell and Kaplan treat 'power' as a subcategory of 'influence', whereas others see the two as analytically distinct (Mokken and Stokman, 1976; Morriss 2002), or understand 'influence' as a specific form of 'power' (Barry 1976; Oppenheim 1976; Baldwin 2002). Because deciding for one or the other position either narrows nor expands the meaning of power, this is more than semantic bickering. Lasswell and Kaplan's narrower qualification of power as a coercive phenomenon presupposes conflicting interests and effectively defines power as winning conflict manifested in 'observable acts', that is, in A's participation in the making of policy affecting B's values (Lasswell and Kaplan 1950: xiv). Stressing that the means allowing such control could be 'many and varied', they follow Weber in emphasising the importance of *context* for understanding power, arguing that analysts must take into account 'weight' (degree of participation in the decision), 'scope' (the values shaped) and 'domain' of power (the specific persons involved).

Robert Dahl complement Lasswell and Kaplan's theoretical discussion by focusing on the measurement of 'power' in decision-making. He responded to voices in the late 1950s claiming that American politics was dominated by a small group of elites and, criticising the lack of empirical evidence behind this claim, he aimed at showing that 'power' was held more broadly ('distributed pluralistically') across society. To do so, his study sought to identify who was most successful in advancing preferences in a series of decisions in the community of New Haven, Connecticut. Adopting the emphasis on context, Dahl recorded conflicting preferences for the outcome of a given decision among the actors involved and then analysed whose interests prevailed by recording successes and defeats (through vetoes) in these decisions (Dahl 1961). Although he does not provide new theoretical insights, Dahl's study is valuable for sharpening the analytical edge of power as a zero-sum game and fuelling the debate on 'who governs' (see also Polsby 1980).

The understanding of power as prevailing in observable conflict is popular in IR scholarship. It resonates particularly well with the realist assumption of states as competing entities and of power as the ability to win wars. To be sure, as Brian Schmidt reminds in his contribution to this volume, realist scholarship was never unified, or unidimensional, in its thinking about power. Yet from the complex (or: broader) discussions found in the writings of Carr (2001), Morgenthau (1960), and Raymond Aron (1966), including the view that economic resources serve both as a prerequisite for military power and as a independent means of influence (Hart 1976; Gilpin 1981), to the simpler (or: narrower) views expressed by Kenneth Waltz (1979) and John Mearsheimer (2001), the realist baseline takes the distribution of military capabilities as the indicator for measuring 'power'. Over time, this bestowed IR with two truisms: first, assuming the primary indicator for power to be the ability to win wars, power relations among states designate positions of (in)security, that is, having power (or not) is synonymous with being safe (or not). As a result, power analysis is security analysis. Second, assuming the distribution of power to be a zero-sum game, the security dilemma turns 'power to' automatically into 'power over', as one state's increase in military capabilities is perceived by other states as a potential for domination.

In the context of the Cold War arms races, the key question for many IR scholars was how to know which side would prevail in a conflict, specifically whether power lies in the possibility (potential) of using military instruments or in their actual use (exercise). This is closely related to the question whether power should be measured in terms of resources (properties) or outcomes (effects) and to what extent either can be measured objectively.

Understanding power as control over resources leads to the question to what extent different 'types' of resources (e.g., industry, military, population size, etc.) can be aggregated into a single indicator of 'power' and to what extent resources can be used effectively across policy realms. For those scholars agreeing on the importance of context and the low fungibility of power resources, operating with a 'lump concept' of power is of little analytical value (Baldwin 1979, 1989; Keohane and Nye 1977; Guzzini 1993). Furthermore, the actor controlling resources also must have the will of using them, with some suggesting that 'will' is a power resource in itself (Hart 1976: 290). Although this point is rejected by realists emphasising that states (should) operate under the assumption of worst-case scenario, as scholars writing on deterrence have pointed out, defining power as control over resources runs the danger of losing sight of the relational dimension, specifically the fact that resources need to be recognised by others (Jervis 1976). Regardless of A's intentions, for there to be a power relationship, B needs to be aware not only of the existence of A's resources but also needs to know that and how they could be used. In short, resources and their potential effect must be communicated through, for instance, military parades or the 'testing' of weapons (Carr 2001: 103).

When the American experience in Vietnam demonstrated that a greater arsenal of military resources does not automatically translate into winning wars, scholars shifted towards an understanding of power as 'control over outcomes' (Hart 1976). Yet here it is important how 'control' is being measured. If identified backwards from the outcome (winning the war), the argument quickly becomes tautological. This is most obvious in the problem of the 'freerider' or the 'benefit fallacy', also mentioned by Lukes, namely, that just because A benefits from the outcome of the war does not mean that A had any influence in bringing victory about. Furthermore, as the latest Iraq war exemplifies, one must be careful of defining the 'outcome' by asking *when* conflict is actually won. And then there is the (somewhat problematic) argument that losing wars is not necessarily an indicator of weakness but merely a consequence of 'conversion failure', that is, of not fully using the resource available, which Baldwin (1979) calls the 'paradox of unrealized power'.[9]

Given these problems of measuring power as 'war-winning ability', it is not surprising that some arguments central to realism remain slippery. As the contribution by Joseph Grieco reminds, this is the case for the meaning of and impact of 'polarity' (also Guzzini 2006). The same ambiguity bedevils the 'balance of power' proposition and the question whether and how balancing occurs, memorably captured by Ernst Haas (1953) and occupying scholars to this day (Little 1988; Levy 2002; Brooks and Wohlforth 2005).

The second dimension: limiting alternatives

Dahl's approach of measuring power by looking at who wins a conflict of preferences in a given decision is criticised most effectively by Peter Bachrach and Morton Baratz (1963; 1970). They argue that the focus on the formal decision-making process does not take into account that decisions differ in their significance and, most importantly, that certain decisions may not take place at all. Thus, Bachrach and Baratz put forward a second dimension of power which involves the analysis of 'non-decisions'. More specifically, they suggest that power analysis has to address the question why some alternatives are not part of the debate and, consequently, who has the authority to exclude issues from the discussion. The answer lies in what has become known as agenda-setting power, namely, the ability of actors 'to create or reinforce barriers to the public airing of policy conflicts' (Bachrach and Baratz 1970: 8). In other words, power is exercised by actors who can mobilise the system-inherent bias ('rules of the game') built into institutions to their advantage and, thus, limit choice about which decisions can be taken.[10]

This angle puts more emphasis on structure. Rather than assuming a power relation as being two autonomous individuals facing each other and taking victory as the indicator for identifying the powerful, it moves attention to how their environment structurally (dis)advantages one side. Differently said, whereas the previous dimension focuses on the direct relationship between A and B, here power works more indirectly through both actors being positioned in an institutional setting and the ability of A to influence this setting 'against' B. This observation can be found in the famous analyses of bureaucracies by Weber, Robert Michels or Graham Allison and also echoes in Michael Mann's notion of the states 'infra-structural power' through controlling the provision of public goods and services (Mann 1993).

In IR, the second dimension can be found in the regime and institution-alist literature, as well as the literature on globalisation. It emerged out of discussions surrounding the phenomenon of interdependence in the 1970s, where scholars began pointing towards the impact of the market on deci-sion-making and, thus, on state sovereignty. Robert Keohane and Joseph Nye (1977; 1989) were among the first to argue that asymmetrical economic interdependence affects the autonomy of the state and provides sources of influence different from those emphasised by realists.[11] They conceptualise interdependence in terms of 'sensitivity' and 'vulnerability', the first refer-ring to the degree to which A is affected if B shifts its policy in a specific issue area (such as oil production), and the second referring to A's (in)ability to switch to an alternative source (such as nuclear energy). Keohane and Nye suggest that international regimes ('rules, norms, procedures') function as a intervening factors through which interdependence among states is channelled and shows its effects. Consequently, they identify the ability to make and change these regimes as a source of power, an argument further explored in Stephen Krasner's (1985) discussion of 'meta power' (also Carporaso 1978; Beck 2005).

The analysis of agenda-setting power is not confined to the economic realm but is also relevant to the study of international law. Studying the influence of supranational legal institutions such as the European Court of Justice (ECJ) or the International Criminal Court (ICC) and under-standing how international law 'works' requires looking at who controls ideas of 'legitimacy' and 'justice' and, thus, leads back to Weber's question of the foundations of legal authority.[12] Agenda-setting power also matters in the realm of security policy, ranging from forums like the UN Security Council or the North Atlantic Treaty Organization (NATO), where states deliberate and decide on security problems and appropriate responses (Haftendorn *et al.* 1999) to the control of information by intelligence services (Herman 1996), including non-state actors (Leander 2005). Finally, increasing attention is being paid to the role played by international media consortia and the Internet in influencing and setting agendas for public opinion.[13]

An important question for IR scholars is whether international regimes increase or decrease vulnerability of states and, related, to what extent institutional structures enable or constrain those acting within them. The answer hinges on who has the power to write the rules of the game, which can be boiled down to the question of whether 'regimes' can exercise agenda-setting power independently from their members. Some institutionalists, like Krasner or Keohane, see states as the primary actors which delegate tasks to institutions but remain in control. In this case, the question is which state controls the regime's agenda, its channels of communication and flows of information, and decides about membership, and thereby enables or prevents participation in the decision-making process. The contrasting view holds that international regimes have a significant life of their own and take decision-making autonomy away from states. This perspective can be found in the neofunctionalist/supranationalist argument prominent among theorists of European integration (Haas 1964; Sandholz and Stone Sweet 1998), the work on 'structural power' informing dependency theory and transnational empire (Galtung 1971; Strange 1988), the argument that international organisations produce effects unintended by their creators (Barnett and Finnemore 1999), and studies on the ability of non-state actors to advocate norms across state boundaries (Risse 2002).

Much of the answer to whether the emergence of new participants on the scene is weakening the state depends on whether the international distribution of 'power' is seen in plus- or zero-sum terms. Whereas those who in the 'globalisation' debate in the 1990s proclaimed the state 'dead' seem to have assumed the latter, now the view has taken hold that the relationship between state and non-state 'actors' is intertwined and cannot be neatly divided into 'winners' and 'losers'. For instance, Michael Mann (1997) argued that not only do effects of economic globalisation differ from state to state but that there generally is a positive relationship between the rise of transnational networks and what he calls the infrastructural power of states (also Weiss 2005).

Thus, the second dimension moves research away not only from the realist focus on war and military capabilities but also from state-centrism by deterritorialising the spatiality of power relations (Agnew 2003; Beck 2005). Even if the notion of 'indirect' power remains analytically limited to resources activated by and effects brought upon humans, the second dimension invites taking into account a number of ways humans influence their environment that may, eventually, affect them. As such, the second dimension makes a double-move of expanding both the meaning of power and the parameters able to influence agendas, a phenomenon sketched out systematically by John Gaventa in his chapter. It is undeniable that opening the door into space makes power relationships much more difficult to pin down. Who, for instance, controls the global economic structure: the consumer or, reviving the argument originally criticised by Dahl, a network of the 'capitalist elite'? Is agenda-setting necessarily a conscious exercise and, if not, how should we think about non-intentional power (Strange 1988)? These are tricky questions. And one may even go further by suggesting that institutions not only exclude certain interests from the debate but actually play a role in shaping them. This facet of power is explored in the third dimension.

The third dimension: shaping normality

Building on Bachrach and Baratz's argument that power also (indeed, more significantly) operates by creating silences, the third dimension revolves around the view that power is not only at work where there is a *conflict* of interests but also where there is (an apparent) *consensus*. Moving conceptually into the 'influence' terrain mentioned earlier, this dimension highlights the forces giving and controlling the meaning of 'normality'. Two authors, Steven Lukes and Michel Foucault, have been particularly influential in illuminating this angle.

Engaging Bachrach and Baratz, Lukes (2005) introduced the 'third face' of power by arguing that the absence of conflicting interests does not necessarily indicate the absence of a power relationship. Indeed, he argued, 'the most effective and insidious use of power is to prevent such conflict from arising in the first place' (Lukes 2005: 27). This view was derived from a Gramscian perspective and contains the argument that actors may have the ability to shape the interests of others. In a similar vein, Foucault (1988; 1995; 2002) put forward the notion of 'productive' power, which, derived from his analysis of the constitution of the subject, highlights forces constituting identities through discourses of normality. Also using concepts like 'disciplinary' or 'pastoral' power, as well as 'governmentality', Foucault focused on what he called the power–knowledge nexus, that is, on the mechanisms by which expert knowledge is (re)produced.[14]

Lukes and Foucault both see power dynamics in terms of shifting intensity rather than a zero-sum distribution. Furthermore, because both approach the study of power from a critical perspective, they see it primarily as having an oppressive/dominating (or 'power over') effect, leaving open when, or to what extent, the process of shaping interests and identities has a supportive/ enabling (or 'power to') effect. Although their arguments do not rule out the latter, they sit uneasy with the positive notion of 'empowerment' found in Arendt and, discussed in sophisticated terms by Morriss (2002).[15]

This shared ambiguity regarding 'empowerment' actually rests on rather different philosophies (see also Lukes, this volume). As critics have pointed out, Lukes's approach is more agency-oriented, allowing the analyst to dichotomise between 'powerful' and 'powerless' agents while containing a thin conceptualisation of structure (Hayward 2000; Guzzini 1993). Also, his theoretical discussion gives few insights on how the powerful actually go about shaping the interests of the powerless.[16] By contrast, Foucault's approach focuses on tracing historically entrenched mechanisms or 'techniques of subjectification' which circulate, in the words of Judith Butler (1997: 6), 'without voice or signature'.[17] Foucault sees productive power not as something that is (or can be) centrally controlled by an Orwellian Ministry of Information, but as something that works through diffuse 'capillaries' contained in seemingly neutral practices of people working in institutions such as hospitals or prisons. The difference is not merely methodological. Lukes's perspective requires the assumption of 'real' interests, the unconscious deviation from which can be attributed to the third face of power, and it contains the possibility that people recognise them. This begets the question of how to determine these 'real' interests and, further, whether helping people to overcome their 'false consciousness' (what Lukes calls 'rational persuasion') is an exercise of power in itself – crucial questions which Lukes remains vague about (Lukes 2005: 35f, 144f).[18] Foucault takes a different track. While agreeing that productive power mechanisms can be made visible through historical analysis and acts of resistance, he emphasises that they cannot be overcome. This different stand is also reflected in the fact that, whereas Lukes focuses on interests, Foucault analyses the construction of identities, of which there are no 'real' ones; there are only identities (or, rather, subjects). Consequently, according to Foucault, there is nothing such as '(il)legitimate' government, there is only, and always, governmentality (Foucault 1988, 2002; Gordon 2002).

IR's engagement with the 'third dimension' is still a story in the making. Crudely speaking, scholars have approached it from two perspectives, a positive and a critical one, both underwritten by normative concerns. Although the gospel of the security dilemma by and large prevented realism from moving the focus on how to win over others towards the question how to *win others over*, the bandwagoning phenomenon has always been a puzzle (Jervis 1999). As Schmidt reminds in his contribution to this volume, classical realists discussed the power to shape opinion through propaganda or public diplomacy, and the competition for allies during the Cold War spurred analysts to think about the power of carrots in the terminology of 'non-coercive' power (Hart 1976) and 'nonpower influence' (Knorr 1975). Economic influence bestowed Germany, Japan, and the EC with 'civilian power' status (Maull 1990), while others traced the power of ideology and knowledge through the practices of epistemic communities (Adler 1987; Haas 1990), synthesized in Joseph Nye's (1990) suggestion that 'soft power' is the basis for successful US leadership in a post-Cold War world (see also Krause 1991). The blur between the positive and normative use of these concepts was in part aided by the fact that none of these grew, at least not explicitly, out of an engagement with the 'power' scholarship in social and political theory.[19] And while the rise of constructivist scholarship in the 1990s produced a wave of studies looking at effects of 'socialization' and the influence of culture, language, ideas, and identity, it rarely framed these as phenomena of power, thereby writing *in* but not *about* the third dimension.[20] Only since in recent years the 'soft' and 'normative' power terminology entered the popular vocabulary, scholars were tempted to take a closer look at their meaning (Nye 2004; Manners 2002). It is in this current that the present contributions by Lukes, Mattern, and Nye intend to clarify the concept of 'soft power', the chapters by Lebow and Hassdorf each look at phenomena of persuasion, and Diez and Manners review the concept of 'normative power Europe'.

Critical scholarship concerned with resistance to the forces upholding the order of things engaged the third dimension of power more thoroughly. Johan

Galtung's (1969, 1971) exploration of the notion of structural violence can be seen in this tradition, and many IPE scholars writing about American hegemony have picked up on Lukes' insights (Ashley 1986; Cox 1987; Gill and Law 1989). More recently, research in IR has begun to adopt Foucault's notion of governmentality to illuminate issues of globalization and of empire (Hard and Negri, 2000; Merlingen 2007), including Lipschutz in this volume. Combining Foucault with a Marxist reading of the dynamic of economic relations, these studies tend to trace power relations to class divisions in the capitalist order, thus maintaining a material basis of the power structure and treating ideology as a derivate thereof. Consequently, they have difficulties explaining how discursive power resources are accessible and represented across socioeconomic divisions. Phenomena of the latter kind have been highlighted by analysts of 'identity politcs', including feminist and postcolonial studies concerned with deconstructing socially dominant categories of gender and race.[21] However, with the exception of Enloe (1989, 1996) or Tickner (1988), despite having another reading of power to offer, as Koehane (1989) recognised, feminist IR long remained reluctant to positively engage the conceptual grammar of a male-dominated discipline, as Weber's (1994) reply to Keohane illustrates. In a less 'critical' vein, the power games of identity politics have also been discussed by scholars analyzing the stabilizing as well as the conflictual/transformative potential of symbols, myths, and memories embedded in discourses of nationalism or religion (Kubik 1994; Campbell 1998; Hall 1999). Again, common to most of these studies is an underlying normative promise emphasizing prospects for change through processes of empowerment and the creation of new participatory spaces, as discussed in the contributions by Ringmar, Gaventa, and Shinko.

The main challenge faced by all third-dimension research is a familiar one: how to study discursively transmitted meaning structures and the manipulation thereof.[22] Few would disagree, for instance, over the symbolic impact of the 9/11 attacks, yet observing and evaluating the power of a brand like Al Qaida is difficult. To get an analytical grip on value systems and delineate discursive contexts, scholars have turned to Jürgen Habermas's discussion of communicative rationality (Risse 2000), Niklas Luhmanns's auto-poetic systems (Guzzini 2004b), or Pierre Bourdieu's view that societies are divided into distinct, though possibly overlapping, cultural spaces (fields), each held together through an internal logic of practices, or *habitus*, and in which power relations are manifested through the distribution of symbolic capital (Hassdorf, this volume).[23]

Power and causality

Using a certain concept of power not only means making an ontological choice about actors and their relations, it also colours our understanding of causality. Scholars writing on power regularly point towards a close relationship between the two, and it is not difficult to see why.[24] Just as George

Sabine noted some time ago that a 'statement of what may roughly be called a causal nature' (Sabine 1969: 12) is a key element of any political theory, 'power' is often found at the centre of an argumentative web. Both concepts give meaning to relationships and are logically linked to effect. Most obviously, if power is the ability to make a difference, that is, if it is *because of* 'power' that things turn out one way rather than another, then identifying 'power' is analytically indistinguishable with identifying a 'cause'.[25] This is significant because it also means identifying who/what is responsible for the way things are, or are likely to be. Power analysis reduces uncertainty and provides ontological security. As a result, it blends positive and normative theorising, a prominent example being the link between polarity and war/peace examined in Grieco's chapter. To assess the usefulness as a positive concept, the challenge lies not merely in empirically validating 'causality' but, more fundamentally, in recognising the internal logic of the power argument and the broader theoretical frame it is embedded in. And then thinking about power in terms of causality faces a number of challenges.

First, if making a difference means that 'it could have been otherwise', power can be made analytically responsible for phenomena of both change and continuity.[26] The second dimension identifies power in A preventing B from choosing otherwise through non-decisions and, thereby, just as the third dimension, points to mechanisms conserving the status quo. Hence, the challenge is to accommodate the insight of power as maintaining continuity with the view that causal statements, as traditionally understood, are about identifying change. Following Oppenheim (1976: 114), one could do so by seeing maintaining the status quo as a form of hypothetical causation: putting in place sufficient conditions for B not doing X means effectively preventing B from the possibility of doing X, regardless of B's intentions. Or, vice versa, one could tie up 'causation' with the exercise of resistance by arguing that B prefers the status quo and resists A's attempts to change it.

Second, there is the question of how and where to attribute causation in phenomena of 'indirect' power and 'unintended' effects. The latter is often captured by noting that it does not matter to the grass whether elephants above make love or war. It is easy to establish the causal arrow here (from the elephants activity to the trampled grass), and it is a phenomenon of power considered from the 'receiving side' (the 'B' in Dahl's definition). But problems arise when responsibility is being attached to the exercise of non-intentional power, examples of which include the security dilemma as well as studies of 'empire'. Things get even more difficult with indirect power, that is, when relations are extended and/or fragmented in time and space. For instance, where to locate 'power' when assessing how A's current activities affect the living conditions of some distant or future B or, going one step further, when considering A's attempts to rule out the very possibility that its lifestyle has an agenda-setting effect on B? It requires considerable analytical sensitivity to carve out complex causal chains, including notions of circular causality as developed, for instance, in cybernetics. But it also begets the question when one should stop seeing relations, and where there is power in chaos.

This flows into the third challenge how to think about causality in mutually constitutive power relations, whether these are Weberian *Herrschaft* relations or other forms of material or ideational interdependence. In a meaning system in which vulnerability is defined in terms of identity, or what Anthony Giddens (1984) has called 'ontological security', even the status of a great power (Agnew 2003) or global civil society (Lipschutz, this volume) relies on 'significant others' recognising its status and enables them to exercise 'representational force' (Mattern, this volume). In particular where hierarchies are difficult to identify, traditional notions of causality are of little value. Hence, research trying to grasp the power of socialisation highlighted in the third dimension cannot escape the distinction between 'causal' and 'constitutive' explanations attached to positivist and non-positivist research, according to Steve Smith 'the main meta-theoretical issue facing international theory' (Smith, 1995: 26).[27] Rather than assuming a unidirectional relationship between temporally separated 'dependent' (Y) and 'independent' (X) variables that can be observed from without, researching how actors are mutually empowered and meaning is intersubjectively constituted requires a different understanding of causal relations.

Here we arrive at the final challenge, namely, whether different conceptualisations of power can be subsumed under the same research design. This is what Barnett and Duvall (2005a) advocate by suggesting that different dimensions of power can be applied to different stages of the argumentative chain and, thus, can be combined analytically.[28] Certainly, it seems worthwhile to re-engage the question of fungibility and search for connections between 'hard' and 'soft' power, as highlighted by various contributors in this volume. However, while it is fruitful to explore how value systems overlap and different kinds of resources and actors affect each other *within* a dimension, one must be careful not to be seduced into applying multiple *concepts* of power within the same argument and, thereby, conducting multi-explanatory research. Following Guzzini (1993), there are at least two plausible reasons that speak against such a strategy.

First, doing so may result in the 'overload fallacy'. Connecting different readings of an essentially contested concept embedded in different theories designed to answer different questions is challenging, to say the least. Second, without delving into what is better left to philosophers of science, if different dimensions of power operate with different conceptions of causation, then they are incommensurable. Seeking to find a pattern in conflict outcomes among actors with fixed value systems simply is different from trying to understand how interests and identities emerge and change through interaction. And the mapping and comparing of resources done by much first-dimension research does not fare well with the emphasis on reflexivity highlighted in the contributions by Guzzini and Diez and

Manners. Thus, it seems that alternative conceptions of power are precisely that, alternatives. Choosing a dimension is an ontological choice which allows telling one story with one set of actors and one type of relation rather than another one. While stories may be told in parallel, as demonstrated in the chapter by Jennifer Sterling-Folker and Rosemary Shinko, and may be seen as analytical devices for practitioners to explore different ways of increasing voice, as proposed by John Gaventa, one must guard against the idea that there may be a way of conceptualising power which enables capturing the totality of social relations.

Hence, instead of trying to subsume distinct concepts of power under one research design, it may be more fruitful to pick up on what can be found in all three dimensions, namely, to take a closer look at the *process* by which power relations are established. Whether understanding power through exercise of delegation, manipulation, (dis)empowerment, socialisation, emancipation, recognition, legitimisation, or resistance – all these see power as something unfolding in a process. This links back to strands of pragmatism visible in the writings of Laswell and Kaplan (1950) and Blau (1964) and currently rediscovered by IR scholars.[29] Although one must be careful not to confuse theory with method here, the process perspective connects 'capability' with 'effect' and emphasises the relational aspect of power, thus providing a corrective to the conceptual dichotomy as either agent capacity or structural 'governance', as suggested by Guzzini (1993). Whereas he presents a frame for power analysis which thinks of poles first and relations after, a process perspective sees power as an 'emerging property' which only exists in interaction (Blau 1964).

Power and politics

Having sketched out the different dimensions of power in IR, the question whether observing international politics through the power glass is a 'realist' practice should appear redundant. Unfortunately, it is not. At least since Morgenthau appropriated Weber (and, by extension, Nietzsche), who in his lecture on 'Politics as a Vocation' suggested that the one who does politics 'strives for power, either as a means in serving other aims ... or as "power for power's sake"' (Weber 1999: 7, my translation), realists have laid analytical claim on the link between power and politics. Interests understood in terms of power made it possible to see politics as an 'autonomous sphere of action' and were therefore declared 'the main signposts' (Morgenthau 1960: 5) through the landscape of international politics, meaning *realist* signposts. However, leaving aside the problem of pressing past thinkers into a tradition, linking the study/meaning of politics to the study/meaning of power cannot be confined to realism. Even the broadest definition of realism cannot accommodate the above three dimensions, and if all IR scholars studying power relations would have to label themselves realist, the paradigm would surely lose its meaning.

The more interesting question is, therefore, what the different dimensions of power mean for our understanding of the political. Like power, the 'political' arises in, or out of, a relationship. Karl Deutsch (1967) describes political relations as power relations, as a relationship of *obedience* based on the interplay of habits and threats. More precisely, he sees political relations characterised by 'the more or less incomplete control of human behavior through *voluntary habits* of compliance in combination with *threats of probable enforcement*' (Deutsch 1967: 232, emphasis added). The two qualifications are worth looking at more carefully. Deutsch contrasts them with obedience obtained through the use of physical violence, which he argues falls outside the realm of politics (Deutsch 1967: 235). While this parallels Arendt's view of power and physical violence as opposites, it still defines politics through an understanding of power intimately tied up with the threat of physical violence. This, again, could be traced to Weber (1992: 80), who suggests that political formations (*Gebilde*) are formations of violence (*Gewaltgebilde*), and who famously defines one such formation, the state, as the community claiming the monopoly over the legitimate use of physical violence within a certain space (Weber 1999: 6). Thus, while political relations do not involve the direct application of physical violence, in the case of the Weberian state, politics is still fundamentally about who has the ability and the right to do so.

However, as Weber pointed out in his discussion of *Herrschaft*, the threat of using force is not necessary to exert influence, a point Deutsch takes up when he speaks about 'voluntary habits'. Politics as or managing people's habits can have a seemingly neutral character, with Weber's concern of the bureaucratisation of the state echoing in Foucault's notion of governmentality. If influencing habits is seen as a form of identity politics, then one can also engage the more agent-oriented version of Carl Schmitt's (1996: 26) definition of the political manifested in the ability to make the distinction between friend and enemy. Because such acts of identity constructions draw lines of inclusion and exclusion, they can be seen as exercising 'structural' violence (Galtung 1969: 168f), or 'symbolic' violence as Bourdieu calls it (Lukes 2005: 140f), which points to a kind of *Gewaltgebilde* which makes Morgenthau's (1960: 5) distinction between the political 'sphere of action' and the sphere of economics, ethics, aesthetics or religion difficult to uphold.

Such an expanded understanding of political relations cannot simply be grasped in terms of obedience. Neither did Weber, who in his above-mentioned lecture defined politics as 'striving for a share of power or to influence the distribution of power' (Weber 1999: 6f, my translation). In the same vein, Carr (2001: 97) referred to the 'political' as 'issues involving a conflict of power' and, thus, as involving opposition. Understood as the ability to decide 'who gets what, when, and how', politics is the *contestation* over the allocation and distribution of resources and values in a society (Deutsch 1967: 234). If for something to be 'political' means to be potentially changeable, to have an alternative, an otherwise, then politics as a struggle for power can be seen as a contest between alternative visions, a contest about shaping and being responsible for the future (and the past, at least in the case of identity politics). An empowerment perspective can also entertain the notion of politics as contestation if expressed in terms of resistance or emancipation. If, however, pursuing one's will is read with Ringmar as a creative process enabling individuals (or groups) to realise their potential in a plus-sum relationship, this would suggest an understanding of politics more in the classical Aristotelian sense of seeking the (common) good and happy life, or in Rousseau's notion of realising the *volonté générale*.

The crucial point is that the meaning of the political is intertwined with the question of where and how we see power relations. For many IR scholars, certainly for realists, the state remains the only place within whose boundaries expect 'proper' politics is possible, that is, where meaningful debate about rights and justice can occur (Wight 1966).[30] However, if one acknowledges different dimensions of power then one cannot but see a greater variety of political spaces in world politics reaching beyond the state and into the 'glocal' (Ferguson and Jones 2002; Beck 2005). As the contributions by Gaventa and Sterling-Folker and Shinko demonstrate, this makes research more exciting and more difficult at the same time, posing questions such as whether different power relations create different 'publics' and to what extent it is possible to think of 'politics via markets' (Lipschutz, this volume). Moreover, as Phillip Darby notes, an expansion of the political needs to refrain from seeing global interaction in the binary modes of domination and resistance and instead 'recognize the ambiguity and mobility of the processes and parties involved' (Darby 2004: 26).

In the end, the question of which power relations to focus on implies a choice – and it is a crucial choice. One does not have to be a radical constructivist to recognise what Guzzini calls the performative aspect of power analyses, namely, that identifying political spaces and making the distinction between inside (where power is) and outside (where it is not) is itself a political act (Walker 1993). As Steven Lukes put it,

> our aim is to represent [power] in a way that is suited for description and explanation. But our conception of it may result from and be shaped by what we are trying to explain [...] how we think of power may serve to reproduce and reinforce power structures and relations, or alternatively it may challenge and subvert them [...]. To the extent that this is so, conceptual and methodological questions are inescapably political.
>
> (Lukes 2005: 63).

Hence, systematic clarity does not help to 'tie down' (Dahl) the concept of power, at least not in the sense *Faust* would like to have it. Power will remain a contested concept, which means analysts will have to choose. If this book contributes to increase awareness of different facets of power and to encourage critical checking of our theoretical toolbox, it has partly achieved its objective. Yet IR scholars should not stop there if they recognise that thinking about power is as much about refining explanatory frameworks as it is about devising a theory of world politics.

Overview of contributions

Although there are no strict thematic lines dividing the chapters of this volume, it is possible to see them as composing three clusters. The first three contributions, including this introduction, provide the reader with a more generic overview of different approaches to the study of 'power' in IR. After problematising its use in realism, a number of chapters present ways of conceptualising what could broadly be called 'soft power'. In the second half of the book, the discussion then gradually moves away from state relations and brings into focus different sites of power, with a particular focus on the ability to create and to induce change. The volume concludes with a reminder by M. J. Williams that theoretical perspectives greatly affect political practice the different facets of power at play in the current 'war on terror'.

Following this introduction, Stefano Guzzini presents a constructivist analysis of the concept of 'power' or, rather, discusses what such an analysis entails. He argues that research must be sensitive to the theoretical context within which each concept is embedded and must be aware of the performative aspect of 'power' analysis, that is, it must show how a specific understanding of 'power' shapes the way we think and act. On this basis, Guzzini stresses both the importance of conceptual history and the necessity for the analyst to be reflexive when doing so by recognising that identifying power relationships is a political act in itself.

A different approach to conceptual analysis is taken in the second contribution where Brian Schmidt reviews realist understandings of power. Taking up the notion of realists as theorists of power politics, Schmidt disentangles the myth of a singular realist conception of power. He categorises the writings of prominent realists into classical, structural and modified approaches and shows that significant differences exist regarding the definition, location and supposed effects of 'power'.

An important realist argument concerning the effects of 'power' is examined by Joseph Grieco. In his chapter, Grieco assesses Kenneth Waltz's claim that the distribution of 'power' among states has an effect on the likelihood of inter-state war and shows that there are both empirical and theoretical problems with this argument, including (i) Waltz' vague conception of polarity, in particular the question of how nuclear weapons feature in this calculation; and (ii) the logical shortcomings of the suggestion that certain power constellations reduce uncertainty and 'miscalculations' among states.

Moving away from the realist focus on military capabilities, the next five chapters focus on the phenomenon of 'soft power'. The cluster begins with a contribution by Steven Lukes, who grounds the analysis of power in sociological terrain and reminds that the identification and evaluation of a power relationship is intrinsically linked to an understanding of the interests of the actors involved. Contrasting the agent-centred thrust in Joseph Nye's discussion of 'soft power' with Foucault's 'ultra radical' conceptualisation, Lukes calls for a more careful engagement with the concept and workings of 'soft power', concluding that we need to think harder about what it means to 'succeed' in winning the hearts and minds of others.

The chapter by Richard Ned Lebow takes a look at a central mechanism of soft power, persuasion, through Ancient Greece. Drawing on insights from writers like Thucydides and Sophocles, Lebow discusses the social basis of influence by highlighting the complexity of human needs and the ways communal bonds anchored in these needs may be strengthened or weakened. The chapter's basic argument is that the creation of a common identity through honest dialogue is the most enduring foundation for persuasive leadership. Lebow notes that contemporary foreign policies often pay insufficient attention to this insight, with visible costs.

In her contribution, Janice Bially Mattern presents a slightly different perspective of the dynamics of 'soft power'. Suggesting that IR has long neglected the concept of 'attraction' in world politics, Mattern draws on Lyotard and argues that soft power is exercised by applying 'representational force'. This argument builds on an understanding of international politics as a sociolinguistic realm where 'reality', and the identities embedded in it, is produced through communicative exchange. Consequently, Mattern suggests, attraction rests on the ability to provide a narrative of reality which sustains the others' subjectivity, an ability which can be used coercively and, therefore, may be not so 'soft'.

The chapter by Wolf Hassdorf provides a third reading of soft power and, importantly, of its limits. Hassdorf applies Bourdieu's notion of 'symbolic power' to investigate the ability of state authorities to influence international financial markets. Analysing British currency strategy during the 1992 European Exchange Rate Mechanism crisis, he demonstrates how the Major Government exercised symbolic power inherited from Thatcher to construct credibility for an unsustainable exchange rate commitment. Hassdorf argues that the fungibility of this resource faced an increasing gap between rhetoric and reality and found its limits when contested by the German *Bundesbank*.

Responding to points made by some of the previous contributors, Joseph Nye outlines what he sees are pertinent themes for a 'soft power' research agenda. Among them, Nye calls for careful and context-sensitive analyses of how cultural and economic resources are channelled and received, as well as how they interact with military capabilities. While its diffused and long-term effects make it difficult to grasp, Nye highlights that 'soft power' can be seen both as a positive concept for social scientists and a normative one central to strategic thinking among foreign policy-makers.

Complementing the concept of 'soft power', the co-authored chapter by Thomas Diez and Ian Manners examines the meaning and performance of the term 'normative power Europe'. Merging an agenda to establish it (Manners) with a critical analysis of the same (Diez), the chapter looks at 'normative power Europe' from three angles: (i) discussing its conceptual links with 'civilian power'; (ii) assessing whether the EU can be considered a unique 'normative power'; and (iii) asking to what extent the discourse on 'normative power Europe' is itself a practice of European identity construction, emphasising the importance of reflexivity on both the geopolitical and the academic level.

Erik Ringmar's contribution argues for replacing the 'power over' perspective popular among IR scholars with the 'power to' perspective and, thus, to focus on *potentia* rather than *potestas,* on phenomena of empowerment rather than domination. Placing Foucault's notion of productive power on a liberal track close to Lukes, Ringmar sees *potentia* as a structural facet of power which enables individuals to discover potentialities through reflection and gives them the opportunity to actualise their projects. His argument emphasises the role of institutions in empowering and disempowering actors and, consequently, calls for analyses of which institutions enable or disable reflection, action and compromise.

This agenda is close to the one laid out in the chapter by John Gaventa, which suggests ways for identifying sites of 'power' in a world characterised by phenomena of 'globalisation' and new forms of governance. Coming from a development perspective, Gaventa argues that analysts and practitioners of change must think not only along the three dimensions (outlined above), but also in terms of levels (from local to global) and spaces of participation (from closed to claimed). He emphasises that these three continua interact, captured in the concept of the 'power cube'. Awareness of these interconnections, Gaventa suggests, improves understanding for bringing about change, which he illustrates through the Jubilee 2000 campaign for debt relief.

Another approach for analysing power relations in a globalising world is presented by Ronnie Lipschutz. In his contribution, Lipschutz focuses on the specific relationship between global civil society and modes of political rule which shape and govern global markets. Applying Foucault's notion of governmentality, he proposes a dialectical reading of this relationship which sees global civil society not as a challenge to but as a product of a global neo-liberal regime and, thus, as co-constituting global neo-liberal order. This, Lipschutz argues, seriously limits the potential of global civil society groups for bringing about change.

Possibilities for change are also explored in the chapter by Jennifer Sterling-Folker and Rosemary Shinko, which presents two different ways of framing and reading 'power' into the 'China–Taiwan' relationship. This is done through a debate between a realist (Sterling-Folker) and a postmodern voice (Shinko), with the former emphasising state-centrism and focusing on the triangular relationship between the US, China and Taiwan, and the postmodern narrative employing a 'power to' perspective and stressing the potentiality of the people to rethink Taiwan's identity vis-à-vis the Mainland. In traversing the realist–postmodern divide, the chapter is exemplary in showing how, despite their incommensurability, the two perspectives can enter into dialogue with each other.

Acknowledgements

For their helpful comments I would like to thank Chris Brown, Stefano Guzzini, Kimberly Hutchings, Oliver Kessler, Anna Leander, and Erik Ringmar.

Notes

1 His critique of Waltz in Baldwin (1993, 2002) is telling.
2 For other perspectives in social theory, see Barry (1976); Morriss (2002); Haugaard (2002), and for IR see Baldwin (2002); Guzzini (1993); Barnett/Duvall (2005a, 2005b).
3 Nietzsche, *Morgenroete* (1881: 23, 262). For overviews of the treatment of power in Western thought, see Haugaard (2002), Lukes (2005: 163–68).
4 Many English texts use the translation found in Dahl, namely 'the probability that one actor within a social relationship will be in a position to carry out his own will despite resistance, regardless of the basis on which this probability rests.' I find this translation problematic, for two reasons: (i) it understands the German *Chance* as 'probability' whereas Weber more likely meant 'opportunity' or 'possibility' and (ii) it ignores that Weber did not make overcoming resistance a necessity when he wrote 'auch gegen Widerstreben' (Weber 1976: 28).
5 Legitimacy is defined by Seymour Lipset as involving 'the capacity of the system to engender and maintain the belief that the existing political institutions are the most appropriate ones for society' (cited in Kubik 1994: 8). It should be noted that, faithful to the ideal of a 'value free' social science, Weber's notion of legitimacy is not bound to a specific form of governance. Rather, he sought to outline different ideal-types of institutions in which orders were accepted. In this sense, it is a 'behavioural' perspective.
6 Weber also outlines the limits for each power relationship, that is, the factors weakening the ability to command and willingness to abide in all three cases.
7 The distinction is found in, for instance, de Jouvenel (1952); Morgenthau (1960); Lasswell and Kaplan (1950); Oppenheim (1976); Aron (1966); Hart (1976); Baldwin (1979).
8 However, when Arendt mentions Gandhi as an example, the dividing line between her understanding of power and Weber's *Herrschaft* becomes blurry, as Gandhi seems to fit quite comfortably with the notion of the charismatic leader. Hence, a Weberian phenomenon of *Herrschaft* could be seen as compatible with Arendt's notion of legitimacy in the moment of group formation.
9 One could argue with Guzzini (1993: 462) that agenda setting and mobilization bias are not the same, with the former putting more emphasis on agency and the latter on structure.

10 The 'conversion failure' argument is difficult to reconcile with the definition of power as winning conflicts. It is also dubious because it suggests that failure, for example through lacking 'political will,' is ex-post fixable. Thanks to Stefano Guzzini for pointing this out.

11 Although, as criticized by Baldwin (1979), Keohane and Nye maintained the primacy of the realist focus on military capabilities.

12 Claude (1966); Beyers (1999). For an insightful critique of Beyers, see Orford (2000).

13 See the contributions in Millennium, 32/3, 2004.

14 For empirical studies inspired by Foucault, see Said (1979); Hayward (2000).

15 On Foucault, see Honneth (1991); Gordon (2002). One could argue there is a shift in how Foucault conceives of productive power, with his later lectures toning down the theme of domination and being more sympathetic to both its enabling effect and the possibility of resistance (thanks to Kimberly Hutchings for pointing this out). In his original argument Lukes explicitly sets his argument in contrast to Arendt (and Parsons). Yet his new edition attempts to incorporate a 'power to' argument Lukes (2005). For a discussion, see Political Studies Review (2006).

16 For empirical studies, see Gaventa (1980), also Kubik (1994).

17 Which has lead Hayward (2000) to suggest that Foucault's approach is 'de-facing' power relations. See also Guzzini's (1993) notion of 'impersonal power.'

18 For a critical discussion, see Bradshaw (1976).

19 There are exceptions, of course, such as Ruggie's (1975) discussion of institutional authority, which draws on Weber, and Little's (1989) take on 'consensual power,' which draws on Arendt.

20 Alexander Wendt recognizes that the proposition of international politics being shaped by power relations 'cannot be a *uniquely* realist claim.' Yet his promise to present an alternative understanding of 'power constituted primarily by ideas and cultural contexts' rather than 'brute material forces' remains unfulfilled (Wendt 1999: 97, emphasis in original). Wendt does not discuss the meaning of power, let alone provide a 'rival' conceptualization of it, but only offers a corrective for the neorealist reading.

21 Butler (1997); Enloe (1989, 1996); Orford (2000); Darby (2004); Agathangelou and Ling (2005).

22 For theories of discursive power, see Holzscheiter (2005)

23 See also Leander (2005); Bourdieu (1977, 1993).

24 Deutsch (1967: 239); Oppenheim (1976); Baldwin (1979); Guzzini (1993).

25 Obviously, there is no difference between 'power' and its effect because 'power' is defined through what it does.

26 This implies that a full grasp on any power phenomenon requires counterfactual reasoning (Guzzini 1993: 447).

27 For a discussion, see Hollis and Smith (1990); Wendt (1998).

28 Barnett and Duvall's (2005a) complex definition of power can be read as asking for a three-tiered analysis.

29 On process, see Jackson and Nexon (1999); on pragmatism, see the contributions in Millennium 31 (3), 2002.

30 For a critique of this view, see Walker (1993, 1995); Brown (2002); Darby (2004).

2 The concept of power

A constructivist analysis

Stefano Guzzini

It has become more commonplace to stress the centrality of the concept of power for constructivist meta-theory and theorising (see, in particular, Hopf 1998, Guzzini 2000a). Moreover, constructivism has put some order into its own power concepts, which usually come as variations on the theme of 'Lukes-plus-Foucault' (Guzzini 1993, Barnett and Duvall 2005a). Therefore, this article will take a slightly different tack. Rather than exploring once again what the concept of power can mean for constructivists, it analyses the implications of constructivism for doing a conceptual analysis, here of power.[1] It will try to show that besides an analytical assessment ('What does power mean?'), a constructivist conceptual analysis also includes a study of the performative aspects of concepts ('What does "power" do?'), which, in turn is embedded into a conceptual history or genealogy ('How has "power" come to mean and be able to do what it does?'). Indeed, by stressing the reflexive relationship between knowledge and social reality, such a conceptual analysis is itself part (but only part!) of a more general constructivist power analysis.

After a short preface on my take on constructivism, the following article exposes in some detail the results of such a threefold analysis. Turning to the classical focus of conceptual analysis on the meaning of power, the first section disputes the viability of attempts to find a neutral meaning across meta-theoretical divides. Although such attempts clarify thought, and would undoubtedly facilitate scientific communication, as well as enhance our capacity for the construction of variables, the meaning of most central concepts in the social sciences is dependent on the theoretical or meta-theoretical context in which they are embedded. When applied to concepts in explanatory theories, this results in explanatory perspectivism. As long as we have to live with our meta-theoretical dilemmas, such as the agency–structure debate, concepts cannot be neutral.

Moving to the performative analysis of the concept of power, the second section discusses how conceptual analysis, instead of digging deep in order to find a neutral meaning of a concept, starts from the usage of concepts and from there moves backwards to their meaning. From there, constructivist analysis asks what the concept of power 'does'. Following William Connolly and

Steven Lukes, it is possible to show that using 'power' has a certain role in our political discourse (Connolly 1974): it tends to 'politicise' issues. Connected as it is to the idea of the 'art of the possible', attributing 'power' to an issue immediately implies that 'we could have done things otherwise'. In other words, attributing power to an issue immediately raises the stakes for political justification of action or non-action. Hence, the plethora of newer and wider power concepts in international relations (IR) reflect the attempt to draw more aspects of international life into the realm of politics – and its resistance has the opposite effect. The definition of power thus becomes part and parcel of politics itself (Guzzini 1994).

Finally, a short, indeed too short, third section deals with the historical or genealogical component of how 'power' has come to mean and to do what it does. Such an analysis in its entirety is of course well beyond the scope of this article. Yet, if the argument of the second section is accepted – namely, that the use of power discourse tends to be connected with a certain definition of politics (its realm and its justification) – a genealogical analysis would investigate under which definitions of power and politics such an effect has become historically possible. Here, one could hypothesise that only in contexts where politics is defined in a way to privilege manipulative features in the 'art of the possible', rather than the notion of a common good, does 'power' have this effect in political discourse. I will argue that, historically, this more manipulative definition of politics has moved from domestic politics to IR.[2]

A preface on constructivism

Constructivism is perhaps best understood as a meta-theoretical commitment (see also Kratochwil 2000: 101). I assume that constructivism is based on three characteristics (for this definition, see Guzzini 2000a, Adler 2002). First, it makes the epistemological claim that meaning, and hence knowledge, is socially constructed. It is constructed, since concepts are the condition for the possibility of knowledge. Our senses are not passive receptors of 'given' facts. The very identification of facts out of the ongoing noise is dependent on pre-existing notions that guide our view of the world. 'When Aristotle and Galilei looked at swinging stones, the first saw constraint fall, the second a pendulum' (Kuhn 1970: 121). This knowledge is, moreover, socially or intersubjectively constructed. Concepts are part of language. Language can neither be reduced to something subjective nor objective. It is not subjective, since it exists independently of us to the extent that language is always more than its individual usages and prior to them. It is not objective, since it does not exist independently of our minds and our usage (language exists and changes through our use). It is intersubjective.

Second, constructivism makes the ontological claim that the *social* world is constructed. As in Searle's famous example about a money bill, it is only our shared beliefs that this piece of paper is money which 'makes' it money (Searle 1995). As all people who have had to go through periods of hyper-inflation would recognise, the moment that this shared belief ceases to exist, the bill is literally no more than a piece of paper. This assumption does not entail that everything is constructed, but it covers that part of reality in which the social sciences are usually interested. Hence, the physical type of support for money (paper, plastic, etc.) is usually not the most relevant for social analysis. What is most relevant is the social or institutional fact; the ontological result of 'our making'.

Third, since constructivism distinguishes and problematises the relation-ship between the levels of observation and action, it is finally defined by stressing the reflexive relationship between the social construction of knowledge and the construction of social reality. In other words, it focuses on reflexivity; that is, on how the social construction of knowledge can itself affect the construction of social reality and vice versa. On the micro-level, reflexivity has to do with what Ian Hacking (1999: 34) calls the 'looping-effect'. Categories we use for classifying/naming people interact with the self-conception of those people. Whereas it makes no difference to stones how we classify them, it makes a difference to people. Identification and identity thus become crucial terms for constructivism.[3] Max Frisch's novel *Stiller* opens with the sentence: 'I am not Stiller!' (Frisch 1954). It tells the story of a Mr White who travels to Switzerland and is taken to be a Mr Stiller who had left that same country many years ago. Although he tries to shrug off this identity in which the environment casts him, the main char-acter does increasingly come to accept a new (or rediscover a previous) identity of his. He becomes 'Stiller' (and the other way round).

On the macro-level, reflexivity refers to 'self-fulfilling prophecies'.[4] As earlier peace research insisted, whether or not the 'law of the jungle' best describes the international system, if we all believe it does, it will quite certainly come to look like one (or be impervious to social learning).[5] The concern in the response to Samuel Huntington's (1993) 'Clash of Civilisa-tion' thesis had much to do with this reflexive relationship between knowl-edge and the social world. Whether or not the main fault lines of conflict really have to be thought in this way, if all people assume they do and act accordingly, the world would indeed become one of inevitable clashes of civilisations. Assuming the claim to be true, our actions would tend to pro-duce the very reality the claim was only supposed to describe. But the rela-tionship between social reality and the social construction of knowledge also works from social facts to knowledge, a component perhaps less tou-ched upon in recent constructivist writings. This involves the questions about the sociology of knowledge which have arguably pushed Thomas Kuhn to his constructivism (Kuhn 1970). It also involves wider questions about the political economy of expertise or knowledge production (e.g., the organisation of learning and education, or the role of think tanks, just to name two); questions which are not specific to constructivism, but which it too needs to account for.[6] With this understanding of constructivism in mind, the remainder of the article assesses what constructivism implies for conceptual analysis.

Analytical conceptual analysis: what does 'power' mean?

The first characteristic of a constructivist conceptual analysis becomes visible by contrasting it with an ideal type of positivist conceptual analysis. In the latter, conceptual analysis is but a means to an end. It should allow better and stable communication. If we never shared at least similar meanings about words, no pertinent discussion would be feasible. In turn, clear understandings of concepts permit the exact definition of variables, which can then be used in scientific explanations. In this context, conceptual analysis is a crucial first step for variable construction and for the transferability of analytical results. Drawing on examples of such conceptual analyses of power, this section will argue that they are useful tools for clarifying thought but eventually fall short of doing justice to the richness of conceptual analysis and, if their methodology is not revised, of even elucidating the meaning of the concept they look at.

Conceptual analysis as a means: descriptive neutrality for better explanation and communication

In its most common version, an instrumental approach to conceptual analysis aims at reconstructing a 'descriptive', i.e. theoretically neutral, meaning of a concept(s) in order to avoid incoherent usage and misunderstandings. This reconstruction is meant to make the concept(s) usable for philosophical discourse and/or scientific inquiry. Since Felix Oppenheim explicitly applies this approach to a conceptual analysis of power, his work provides an appropriate inroad for us into this kind of approach.

For Oppenheim, precisely because social sciences lack a full-fledged theoretical system, academics are put before the choice either to leave political concepts unexplained, a choice of little appeal, or 'explicating them independently of any theories with the purpose of clarifying whatever isolated generalizations have been made or may be asserted' (Oppenheim 1981: 189), thus preparing the day when a theory in the stronger sense will be developed. To construct such a neutral term, Oppenheim wants to carefully include the findings of earlier conceptual analysis so that his proposal be widely shared and acceptable. In the end, he sticks to an understanding of power close to causation (as in the work of Robert Dahl 1968, 1976), without necessarily including the idea of intentionality (as already proposed by Dennis Wrong 1988). As a result, Oppenheim's definition of power refers to the causal relation between one action and another. Oppenheim is careful to define action widely – it includes also 'not doing an action' – so as not to be caught in a behaviouralist fallacy. He also avoids any reference to preferences, intentions or interests, which, in the wake of Lukes's (1974) discussion, have been shown to be contestable and not neutral concepts. He shows cases where none of them is needed. As a result, he approaches power in terms of a probabilistic causation. '[T]o assert that R's action x was influenced by some action y of P is not merely to describe what R did, but also to provide at least a partial *explanation* of P's conduct. (Why did R do x? Because P influenced him to do x)' (Oppenheim 1981: 33).

The probabilistic causation of power is expressed in conditional sentences. Concepts of power can differ in the extent to which Action X is either sufficient, or necessary and sufficient, for Action Y to happen or to be prevented. For instance, a possible condition for the coercion of an Actor B is that Actor A possesses a revolver and the skill to use it. Acquiring both does not yet cause anything, and hence it is not an exercise of power. If Actor A points the revolver at Actor B (Action X), and the latter is induced (1) to do an action which B had not thought of doing before, or (2) to refrain from an action B had thought of doing (Action Y), we have a causal nexus. Here, we have an exercise of power. Action X is a sufficient condition for Action Y. If one can presume that there are other ways to cause B to do Y, this condition is not necessary for causing Action Y.

There are obviously good arguments for being neutral in the construction of concepts. Indeed, it comes as no surprise that the most widely used approach in empirical theorising is to see concepts as synonymous with 'variables' whose content needs to be fixed in order to allow for a rigorous and reproducible analysis. This conception of an artificial, almost mathematical, language is in the tradition of positivism and the condition for the possibility of the quantification of hypotheses.

Yet, whenever the analysis is concerned with the richer concepts of our political vocabulary, this instrumental strategy faces a dilemma. So do concepts like democracy and development, for instance, hardly offer an uncontentious definition in need of only just a bit more careful phrasing. A result of this indeterminacy is that corresponding variables may not always fit from one analysis to another, and communication is impaired (Rueschemeyer 1991). Since discussions about democracy keep on using different meanings which are not easily reducible to each other, the analyst is tempted to replace or narrow the concept with something less contentious (cf. Collier and Levitsky 1997). Hence the dilemma: faced with the difficulties of pinning down a concept, scholars decide to go for its more easily operationalisable aspects, but they thereby incur the risk of neglecting its most significant aspects, which would void the concept of the very significance for which it had been chosen in the first place.

Trying to keep a certain conceptual coherence despite lacking neutrality, a slightly different tack consists in presupposing that the different usages have a common core, which does not necessarily imply a full-fledged taxonomic definition, nor even a neutral one. Steven Lukes, for instance, uses a distinction, taken from John Rawls, between a concept and its different conceptions:

What I propose to do instead is to offer a formal and abstract account of the concepts of power and authority respectively which inhere within the many conceptions of power and authority that have been used by particular thinkers within specific contexts, in development from and in reaction to one another. Any given conception of power and of authority (and of the relation between them) can be seen as an interpretation and application of its concept.

(Lukes 1979: 634)

Here, all concepts must ultimately have a common core.[7] Otherwise, communication would not work. A term like 'anarchy', for instance, might mean the 'law of the jungle' in one context, in another 'rule without government', and in another still 'social organisation without hierarchy'. Yet to be able to refer to all as interpretations of anarchy presupposes a common core. Although this move ensures communicability on a very general level, Lukes's approach is not intended to and does not solve the dilemma for the positivist. By having climbed up the 'ladder of abstraction' to such daring heights, these concepts no longer function as 'data-containers' viable for positivist analysis (Sartori 1970; see also Collier and Mahon 1993). Hence, scholars in this tradition of conceptual analysis face a dilemma (at least when some concepts are concerned): they can either assure communicability or more rigorous variable construction, but not both.

Impossible neutrality and the meta-theoretical dependence of explanatory concepts

Showing the dilemmas of a conceptual analysis conceived in terms of variable construction is but a first step in undermining the positivist understanding of conceptual analysis. As I will try to show in the following section, it is often impossible to isolate concepts from the theories in which they are embedded and which constitute part of their very 'meaning'. As a result, the analysis of concepts such as power cannot be used as a mere means for explanation, wherein they would neutrally assess the salience of competing theories. When Max Weber (1976) put a lengthy introduction to 'basic sociological concepts' at the start of his *Economy and Society*, this was not just a technical and definitional basis for his theory but already part of it, the result of much of his earlier analysis. The relation between these concepts provided the framework of his sociological work. As Martin Bulmer writes, 'concepts such as the "protestant ethic" or "marginal utility" derive their meaning from the part they play in the theory in which they are embedded, and from the role in that theory itself' (Bulmer 1979: 658). As a result, a conceptual analysis which isolates one concept necessarily slides into the task of assessing a whole theory.

I will illustrate this point by discussing the positivist attempt to produce a neutral or descriptive concept (Nagel 1975). That any definition of power can be neutral or descriptive has been contested in mainly two ways. First, some scholars have argued that 'power' belongs to a family of 'essentially contested' concepts. I will take up the discussion of this in the next section, since it will serve as a springboard for a more pragmatic understanding of conceptual analysis. Second, any neutral definition of power seems elusive, precisely because one can make sense of concepts only in their meaning world; a claim with 'strongly holistic implications' (Skinner 1989: 13) which became prominent in the aftermath of Kuhn's analysis of paradigms. This applies as much to the relationship between concepts and social philosophies as it does to the more narrow purposes of explanatory theories, where concept formation and theory formation stand in a mutually constitutive relationship.

Oppenheim opposes this view. He claims that his definition of power does not exclude particular ways of conceiving a social theory. He rests his case with the persuasiveness of his definition: 'I have no better justification than to point to the results of this study' (Oppenheim 1981: 189). And yet, that such a meta-theoretical dependence eludes the search for a neutral concept across the individualist-intersubjective divide can be shown by briefly comparing Oppenheim's claim of a neutral concept with a radically holistic theory and its embedded concept of power; namely Niklas Luhmann's system theory.[8] Luhmann defines power as a symbolically generated medium of communication which reduces complexity and allows calculus. Power resides in the communication, not in action. It is not causal, but functions by attributing causality to a particularly steered communication. I will explain this definition step by step.

Luhmann's social theory is a theory of systems and their autopoietic (internally self-generated) reproduction, not a theory of action. Communication plays a major role in this theory: it consists in the linking-up of systems (coupling) wherein the 'external' is included into the internal reproduction processes. This process can be conditioned by particular media of communication. A medium of communication is a code of generalised symbols that steer the transmission of inputs into the respective selection processes of systems. Power is such a medium of communication.

Media of communication, like power or money, are seen by Luhmann to have developed as a response to the rising complexity of modern societies. As throughout his entire theorising, Luhmann is interested here in the ways systems have been able to cope with (and, in turn, generate) increasing complexity. With the development of written communication and the greater complexity it allows, symbolically generated media of communication became necessary in order to reduce complexity, i.e., to reduce the uncertainty of selection processes (Luhmann 1975: 12–13). They create tacit incentives for the acceptance of certain meanings, thus avoiding the communication to become too complicated, or even impossible.[9] Communication exists only if the reproduction of systems is affected in its ongoing 'selections' – what an individualist approach would perhaps call 'choices' or 'decisions', but which lack the conscious or explicit component of the latter two concepts. Media of communication steer communication and, through this, transmit 'selection impulses'. Power as a medium of communication organises alternatives so that it becomes clear to the communication partners which are those to be avoided. For Luhmann, the code of power communicates an asymmetrical relation, a causal relationship, and steers the transmission of selections from the more powerful to the less powerful system (Luhmann 1975: 22; 1990: 157).

At this point, it might be helpful to pull out the differences between Luhmann's and Oppenheim's concepts of power. For Luhmann, power is not in action, but in communication. 'Will' and motives, i.e., traditional attributes for the explanation of action, are not important for the assessment of action or for power. 'Will' is not prior to power, in the sense that an act of power would overrule a pre-existing will. In a code-steered communication, expectations can be such that the will of an actor for a specific action never arises. Will is neutralised by power, not broken. Power-steered communication constitutes the will of one partner by *attributing* to his actions successes, expectations and respective motives. 'Power does not instrumentalise an already present will, it constitutes that will and can oblige it, bind it, make it absorb risks and uncertainties, can tempt it and make it fail' (Luhmann 1975: 21, my translation). 'Motives' are not an origin or cause of action. In the execution of power, the communication process itself attributes motives to systems. This allows the communicative system to socially understand action. In a nutshell: power does not cause an outcome, but communicatively regulates the attribution of causality for understanding that outcome (Luhmann 1990b: 157).

As this short discussion shows, Luhmann's concept of power cannot be accounted for within Oppenheim's conceptual frame. It is a form of power which has an agent referent, but the causality of power does not in fact derive from the agent as such but is attributed to it by the communication process. Luhmann's holistic epistemology and system theory has no place for an action-concept of power like Oppenheim's.[10] Some of our central concepts – in particular if, like power, they have an explanatory value for social theories – cannot escape a basic meta-theoretical dependence: they make sense within their respective meta-theories, which are not always compatible.

John Gray, for instance, compares individualist (voluntarist) and structuralist (determinist) frameworks of explanation and concludes that 'since judgements about power and structure are theory-dependent operations, actionists and structuralists will approach their common subject-matter – what goes on in society – using divergent paradigms in such a fashion that incompatible explanations (and descriptions) will be produced' (Gray 1983: 94). He argues that these are incommensurable views of man and society which elude a rational choice. In a similar vein, in reference to the difference between a classical Weberian and a Foucauldian understanding of power, Peter Miller (1987: 10) concludes that a 'considerable distance separates a notion of power understood as the exercise by A of power over B, contrary to

B's preferences, and a notion of power as a multiplicity of practices for the promotion and regulation of subjectivity'. Concepts of power necessarily reflect meta-theoretical divides. This calls for a position of explanatory perspectivism in conceptual analysis.[11]

Summing up, two points are worth repeating. First, it has to be noted that, although conceptual analysis is important for variable construction, variable construction is not all there is to conceptual analysis.[12] Second, taking seriously Kant's dictum that categories are the condition for the possibility of knowledge (shared also by positivists), also means that one needs to look at the way these categories are meta-theoretically embedded. Scholars need to control the assumptions upon which they make their variable construction, and this will inevitably lead them to question concepts in themselves. For, as the following sections are going to show, these concepts are a means to re-embed our knowledge into its social or political context.

A note on constructivist understandings of the meaning of power

Since constructivism is a meta-theoretical commitment, there is not one single conception of power which would be shared by all approaches. However, given its general interpretative commitments and attempts to overcome methodological individualism, constructivist theories tend to understand power as both agential and intersubjective (including non-intentional and impersonal power), and they are also more attuned to questions of open or taken-for-granted and 'naturalised' legitimation processes.[13] Indeed, some recent power approaches tend to add Foucault to Lukes's three dimensions of power (Barnett and Duvall 2005a; see outside IR, e.g., Clegg 1989).

This does not mean that the conceptual work is already accomplished. For this is just one step in unfolding the dialectical relationship between concepts and theories. Clarifying meanings of power within a constructivist understanding requires us to relate the meanings arrived at back into a coherent social theory; this is something even comprehensive taxonomies or typologies cannot do. Such comprehensive approaches risk overloading the concept, which is still too closely related to ideas of effective cause (for a discussion of this fallacy and a proposal how to coherently combine Lukes and Foucault within a wider Bourdieu-inspired power analysis, see Guzzini 1993: 468–74). Hence, just adding up facets of power is analytically insufficient and all depends upon into which kind of framework this power analysis is re-embedded; an undertaking that is far from self-evident, as Lukes's own cautious treatment of Foucault suggests (Lukes 2005).

Performative conceptual analysis: what does 'power' *do*?

The foregoing discussion has looked at conceptual analysis when used as a means for understanding. Although a necessary, if limited, tool in any analysis, it leads towards a conceptual analysis for which the better understanding of a concept arrived at is itself an aspect of that which is being explained.[14] This type of conceptual analysis is not so much about what exactly is meant by the concept, but what it achieves in communication. In a move stemming from pragmatic linguistics, it does understand the meaning of a concept by what its use *does*. This section will argue that the concept of power plays an important role in our political discourse in that it indicates realms where political action could have been different; or indeed where against apparent odds, it would have been possible in the first place. It defines the realm of political action and its justification. As such, attributing power is not innocent, but implies that things could have been done otherwise. Because they define the realm of politics, attributions of power are themselves part of politics. This performative effect illustrates a reflexive link typical for constructivism.

The effect of 'power': from essentially contested concept to the definition of political space[15]

Peter Morriss's (1987) book *Power: A Philosophical Analysis* has been rightly celebrated for including the first systematic study of the question: why do we need 'power'? Asking backwards from the purposes of power (its usage), Morriss finds three contexts of power (practical, moral and evaluative) as a way to show that we are not always interested in the same sub-category of power concepts. In the practical context we might be particularly interested in non-intentional power, since we want to guard against any adverse effects, whether intended or not. In the moral context, intention plays a more important role. Hence, according to Morriss, power debates would be less heated if only we clearly contextualised them. Yet perhaps this is not quite as easy as Morriss presents it. I will use a detour through a discussion of the concept of power as an 'essentially contested' concept to open up another way of addressing the 'purposes' of power, one which takes the role of language more seriously. The most-often-repeated reason for the essential contestability of power is the value-dependence of social theories. According to this view, if power is to play a role in social theory, its definition and interpretations will inevitably be value-laden.

> [I]ts very definition and any given use of it, once defined, are inextricably tied to a given set of (probably unacknowledged) value-assumptions which predetermine the range of the empirical application. [...] Thus, any given way of conceiving of power (that is, any given way of defining the concept of power) in relation to the understanding of social life presupposes a criterion of significance, that is, an answer to the question what makes A's affecting B significant? [...] but also [...] any way of interpreting a given concept of power is likely to involve further particular and contestable judgements.
>
> (Lukes 1974: 26; 1977: 4–5, 6)

Unfortunately, Lukes's (and Connolly's) argument was both too easily embraced and too hastily rejected. On the one hand, value-dependence quickly became synonymous with being 'ideological'. From there it was only one step to analyse Lukes's three dimensions as the three expression of our well-known Anglo-American ideological triad of conservatism, liberalism and radicalism (as, for instance in Cox *et al.* 1985). Just as in IR, questions of value dependence have been translated into well-known, yet all too facile theoretical triads (for a more detailed critique, see Guzzini 1998: Chapter 8).

Another faction of the discipline reacted with contempt upon being told that academic enterprise is politics (although nobody ever said, 'nothing but politics') and being offered this well-known menu from which to choose. Moreover, since the implication of this argument seemed to be a form of radical relativism, the argument was judged incoherent.[16] Still others argued that value dependence is nothing which distinguishes power from other concepts in the social sciences. Thus, if the determination of an evaluative character was meant to establish a particular category of concepts in the social sciences, it fails. If it aims at describing a characteristic of all social-science concepts, it is not 'enlightening' (Giddens 1979: 89–90). Although this debate therefore seemed to open up conceptual analysis to political contexts in particular, it did it in a way which is ultimately not very fruitful for conceptual research.

Yet, the attempt to limit the issue to value dependence is to underrate some other important facets of Lukes's and Connolly's argument. Connolly explicitly refers to the necessary connection between the idea of power and the idea of responsibility. This seems to fit nicely into one of Morriss's contexts, the moral one. Yet, whereas for Morriss, this closes the analysis, for Lukes and Connolly, it does not. For they are not only interested in what the concept means and where it is used, but what it does when it is used.

> When we see the conceptual connection between the idea of power and the idea of responsibility we can see more clearly why those who exercise power are not eager to acknowledge the fact, while those who take a critical perspective of existing social relationships are eager to attribute power to those in privileged positions. For to acknowledge power over others is to implicate oneself in responsibility for certain events and to put oneself in a position where *justification* for the limits placed on others is expected. To attribute power to another, then, is not simply to describe his role in some perfectly neutral sense, but is more like *accusing* him of something, which is then to be denied or justified.
>
> (Connolly 1974: 97, original emphasis).

Connolly's position here is not about why we *look* for power, as Morriss does, but why we *call* something a phenomenon of power, as Connolly and Lukes do. Put into this context, I think the latter two authors made a very important point. 'Power' implies an idea of counterfactuals; i.e., it could also have been otherwise. The act of *attributing* power redefines the borders of what can be done. In the usual way we conceive of the term, this links power inextricably to 'politics' in the sense of the 'art of the possible'. Lukes rightly noticed that Bachrach and Baratz's (1970) conceptualisation of power – which included agenda-setting, non-decision-making and the mobilisation of bias – sought to redefine what counts as a political issue. To be 'political' means to be potentially changeable; i.e., not something natural, God-given, but something which has the potential to be influenced by agency. In a similar vein, Daniel Frei (1969: 647) notes that the concept of power is fundamentally identical to the concept of the 'political'; i.e., to include something as a factor of power in one's calculus, means to 'politicise' it (for a similar point, see Hoffmann 1988: 7–8). In other words, attributing a function of power to an issue imports it into the public realm where action (or non-action) is asked to justify itself.

In return, 'depoliticisation' happens when by common acceptance no power was involved. In the conceptual analysis of power, this depoliticisation has been taking place through the concept of 'luck'. The starting point for the discussion is the so-called 'benefit fallacy' in power analysis (Barry 1988: 315). Nelson Polsby (1980: 208) explicitly mentions the case of free riders who may profit from something, but without being able to influence it. Keith Dowding (1991: 137) extended the discussion with his refusal to include 'systematic luck' under the concept of power. And since there is no power, so the argument implies, there is no politics involved and no further (public) action needed. Yet, although scepticism about the links between power and benefits are warranted, it seems reductive not to allow for a conceptual apparatus and a social theory which can account for systematic benefits in terms other than 'systematic luck'. By reducing a systematic bias to a question of luck, this approach leaves out of the picture the daily practices of agents that help to reproduce the very system and positions from which these advantages were derived. Making it conscious raises questions of responsibility, and finally also issues of political choice.[17]

Such a performative analysis of concepts is not new in IR, in particular with regard to the concept of security.[18] Jef Huysmans has worked on security as a 'thick signifier' with performative effects for ordering social relations (Huysmans 1998). Barry Buzan and Ole Wæver have proposed a performative analysis of security suggesting an approach to 'securitisation'. According to them, security is to be understood through the effects of it being voiced. It is part of a discourse which, when successfully mobilised, enables issues to be given a priority for which the use of extraordinary means is justified. In its logical conclusion, 'securitisation' ultimately tends to move decisions out of 'politics' altogether (Wæver 1995; Buzan *et al.* 1998). Curiously enough, therefore, the performative effects of these two concepts are connected: 'politicisation' is a precondition for a possible later 'securitisation', which, if successful, again puts issues beyond 'politics' (understood here as bargains within regular procedures). Whereas 'power' invokes a need for justification in terms of a debate, 'security' mobilises a pre-given justification with the effect of stopping all debate.

Reflexivity loops in IR: conceptual power analysis as part of (power) politics

A conceptual analysis which focuses on the performative character of some concepts implies a series of reflexive links. A conceptual analysis of power in terms of its meaning is part of the social construction of knowledge; moreover, the definition/assignation of power is itself an exercise of power, or 'political', and hence part of the social construction of reality. As the following two illustrations will indicate, the very definition of power is a political intervention.

This reflexive feature of power has been at the origin of some of the newer power conceptualisations in IR. It does, for instance, help to account for two components in Susan Strange's concept of structural power (Strange 1987, 1988).[19] First, Strange created this concept in the context of a perceived US decline. Thus the incapacity of the USA to keep the fixed exchange-rate system or to manage the international economy better found justification in a perceived decline in power. In other words, the US government may have been willing, but no longer able, to provide the public goods it used to provide.[20] Strange tried to argue that the declining provision had less to do with declining power than with shifting interests unconnected to power. To do this, her concept of structural power casts a wider net (her four structures) that encompasses areas in which the USA is not clearly seen to be declining. As a result, the USA has to justify its action with means other than the 'excuse' of lacking power. Second, Strange's concept of structural power also includes non-intentional effects. Whether the Federal Reserve intended to hurt anyone is less important than that it did. By making actors also aware of the unintended effects of their action, they are asked to take this into account next time. They become potentially liable to the question of why, now aware of the effects, action had not changed. Having a broader concept of power asks for more issues to be factored into political decisions and actions (exactly as in Connolly's analysis).

The link between knowledge, power and politics is also visible in the daily practices of diplomacy. Here it is less the performative aspect of language than the relationship between knowledge and conventions which directly intervenes into politics. Despite claims to the contrary, power is not especially fungible; i.e., resources effective in one area might not necessarily be so elsewhere. In more technical terms, power does not do for politics what money does for economics since it does not provide a standard measure with which a particular resource can be exchanged with another one.[21] Yet, given the special role great power status plays in international affairs, diplomats need to 'make up' indicators for overall power. Given the need to trade gains and losses so as (not) to upset the ranking of power (also achieved through politics of compensation), diplomats have to come to agree on what counts before they can start counting. Taking this link for granted, Daniel Frei (1969) had early on urged scientists to help politicians in this task.

Yet, there is still no neutral solution in sight. Indeed, the very definition of power is so contentious precisely because of its political consequences. During the Cold War, the Soviet Union resisted those definitions of power whose stress on non-military factors would imply a decline in its status. Similarly, in the recent controversy about soft and hard (coercive) power, deciding what power *really* means has obvious political implications. Focusing more on the military side and hence stressing an unprecedented preponderance of the US military made it possible to ask the USA to push its advantages further (since it is 'possible'), and at times even stress the duty of the USA to intervene given its capacities (which relates back to the performative argument above). Or, stressing US soft power and its potential decline, analysts could advocate a much more prudent and varied foreign-policy strategy sensitive to claims of legitimacy and cultural attraction (whether or not the legitimacy crisis is simply an effect of poor public diplomacy or of a more fundamental origin).[22] Or, as I have shown elsewhere (Guzzini 2006), insisting on the unipolarity of the present international system, such a power statement mobilises a justification for leadership and responsibility which, in turn, can justify the 'inescapable', and hence excusable, nature of unilateralism (and a consensus on multipolarity does the opposite).

As this section has tried to show, a constructivist conceptual analysis must, by its very assumptions, include an analysis of the possible performative effects of concepts. These are not addenda to the meaning of the concept, but an integral part of it. Hence, a constructivist analysis of power necessarily re-embeds the concept into the explanatory theory and the political discourse to which it belongs.

Conceptual analysis as conceptual history and genealogy: how has it become possible for 'power' to mean and do what it does?

The above examples show both the contribution, but also the limits, of constructivism-inspired conceptual analysis for the study of power. Indeed, as much as these reflexive loops are important, they are in themselves only understood through the political context in which they take place. Hence, although they make a conceptual analysis of power part of the definition of politics and hence a component of a wider analysis of power, it is emphatically not all that there is to a constructivist power analysis.[23] Such an analysis would look at the institutionalised systems or fields in which these performative acts are played out and which highlight the role general practices and authority positions therein play to affect the social construction of knowledge and their effect (for an application in the field of security, see Leander's [2005] study of the 'epistemic power' of private military companies). Indeed, who is authorised to speak in the first place and which authority (roles, institutions and the taken-for-granted understandings) supports the claims?

So, one could argue, here is where the reflexive loop back to actual power, hence the relevance of constructivism for a conceptual analysis of power, stops. Not yet. Since constructivism denaturalises the status quo, the performative effect of conceptual analysis must also open up to further analysis: does the effect apply to all contexts; is it always the same, over different time horizons? Precisely because constructivism shares a pragmatic approach towards concepts (i.e., it works back from their usage) and because such usage follows a certain path dependency, it seems consonant for constructivists to ask themselves how such meanings and performative effects have historically been constituted and evolved. The concept of power is not only put into a political context but is also placed in a wider historical one. If it is true that invoking power often has an effect of 'politicising' issues, when, where and how has this become possible? This leads to conceptual history, but of a kind. It is not the type of analysis that simply takes a concept and looks for its usage over time. Here, the constructivist argument runs parallel to the previous sections: meanings are derived from the pertinent contexts in which the concept has been used. If there is conceptual history, it must be one which is strongly embedded in the different historical meaning contexts of the audience its use wanted to address (this obviously points to Quentin Skinner's approach, now collected in Skinner 2002). It would include a sociology of knowledge. Moreover, it must be a conceptual history which includes the performative aspects of political language and, hence, the interplay between social history and conceptual history.[24] Finally, taking seriously the claim that 'it could have been otherwise', such a conceptual history would be akin to a Foucault-inspired genealogy.[25]

Such an analysis is obviously beyond the scope of this article. Still, I would like to use the findings of the Bielefeld approach to conceptual history to give the reader an idea of what such a historical contextualisation of 'power' in IR might look like. For this purpose, the following sketches one hypothetical lineage from eighteenth-century statecraft via German political theory to political realism as it developed in IR.[26] The starting point is that the use of 'power' as a 'politicising' act was premised on the definition of politics as the 'art of the possible' (or feasible). Yet, this naturalised understanding is of rather late origin. Volker Sellin argues that with early modernity, the Western conception of politics became dual: a neo-Aristotelian lineage stressing the common good and a Machiavellian tradition based on the reason of state (Sellin 1978). Only in the eighteenth century did an increasing reduction of the understanding of politics to *Machtkunst* (roughly the 'art/craft' of 'power/governing') appear.

To some extent, this reductionist reading was countered in liberal (and some conservative) political theories, mainly with regard to domestic constitutionalism. Yet, so Sellin, within the German context of the nineteenth and early twentieth century – the shift to positive law, and especially the idea of the reason of state and of power as the chief ingredient in *Staatskunst* (roughly 'statecraft') – had attracted an important group of followers not only interested in internal affairs. Members of this group also belonged to, or were influenced by, the German Historical School. Starting with von Ranke, and leading up to von Treitschke, von Rochau's Treatise on *Realpolitik*, Friedrich Meinecke and Max Weber – they were all strongly, at times primarily, interested in the *international* status of Germany, nascent or newly unified. At the same time when politics became defined in an increasingly narrow way, *Macht* became increasingly decoupled from the political sphere/state and diffused onto other social spheres (Faber *et al.* 1982). In other words, precisely when politics and power got conceptually coupled in the German context of the second half of the nineteenth century – in particular, but not exclusively, when applied to international affairs (which included German unification, after all) – power lost its exclusive attachment to the sphere of the state. Now moving conceptually together, with this diffusion of power, 'politics' diffused too.

Such a look at the quite recent conceptual history in Germany allows us to establish some hypotheses for answering the question of why the use of 'power' somewhat naturally 'politicises' issues and yet, why this should not be seen as a sole matter of the state. On the one hand, the 'politicisation' is but the logical consequence of a historical development of tying power so closely to politics. On the other hand, the increasing diffusion of power throughout society implies the increasing 'politicisation' of different social spheres. This tendency is well established in social history, accounting for both the increasing enfranchisement of larger portions of the society and the political struggles over the public control of previously 'private' or 'civil society' spheres like education or the economy. This, in turn, connects the political back to the state. Therefore, de Jouvenel (1972) retraces the history of *pouvoir* as one of steady state expansion. Yet the reconnection is only part of the story, and de Jouvenel therefore neglects all counter-'powers' that liberal societies have developed in the face of an ever-increasing state.

Such conceptual analysis, besides providing the historical context for studying the origins of the performative content of 'power', allows for the possibility to develop hypotheses for possible tensions in existing usages. Applying the foregoing argument to IR, it was noted that there has been a strong German tradition working with the notion of 'power politics'. Even a cursory reading of the early Morgenthau (1933, 1946) shows the importation of this actually often (German) idealist thinking (cf. Palan and Blair 1993) onto the new environments of his emigration and later also onto a particularised field, IR. Yet, Morgenthau's explicit intention was to isolate a particular 'morality' of the national interest – a reason of state, different from national morality – so as to establish the independence of the international realm in the first place. The reconceptualisations of power today – i.e., today's 'politicisations' in IR – instead undermine this specificity (Guzzini 1993). What has come under the name of 'structural power' signifies, in a certain sense, a return to the unitary vision of the political which existed in the nineteenth century and which was partly abandoned by its followers in the realist tradition in IR. Doing so, these politicisations not only expand the realm of the 'art of the feasible', inviting for more public agency, but simultaneously lay the ground for a return to notions of the common good, now thought at the international level.

Hence the return and broadening of the 'political' in IR comes at a price for more traditional power-oriented conceptions of international politics. Power and politics have a strong mutually defining link, in particular in realist theory, so much so that they are often used together as a single concept. For realists, politics is about the individual (national) pursuit of power and its collective management. Or, expressed the other way round: outcomes in international politics are decided by power differentials and their distribution. Broadening the research agenda implies a critique of this approach or, at least, exposing some of its limits. In this critique, politics is seen to be done by actors other than states. States, in turn, have international policies which in the time of 'embedded liberalism' (Ruggie 1982) encompass more than strictly military or diplomatic security. This implies new forms of collective management of international politics, from regimes in new policy areas to the new public – private arrangements in the 'global compact'. Meanwhile, the transnationalisation of politics specifically undermines the control capacities of states and other international actors, or so it seems. A first look at the power differentials no longer explains the outcomes. It seems as if 'structural' factors are increasingly shaping and moving world events.

This leads to the following hypothesis: it is this context of both an expansion of 'politics' as a potential field of action and a perceived contraction of 'politics' as real room for manoeuvre that informs and is addressed by the new power research programmes (Guzzini 1994: 14). These concentrate both on the new direct and indirect ways to control knowledge, agendas and regimes and on the increasing perception of an impersonal rule of the international scene. In today's IR, power analysis has become a critique of classical 'power politics'.

Conclusion

As I have tried to argue, a constructivist conceptual analysis of power stresses the theory-dependent meaning of concepts, the performative effects some concepts can have (and which are an important component of their meaning) and the historical and social context of the conventions which underlie this effect. Doing so, it exposes a reflexive interrelation between the concept of power, conceptual analysis and political power, which is not always that easy to disentangle. Only in the first step and claim of the conceptual analysis is there a simple link: a conceptual analysis of power is tied to the underlying social theory, such as those inspired by constructivism. The second claim includes a direct link, when the inherently performative role of power is specifically related to questions of political legitimacy. But, and this adds a reflexive twist, this performative aspect shows how the acceptance of certain usages of concepts can have an effect on social reality – an effect which as such is part of our understanding of political power, independently of the particular concept at hand. In other words, the constructivist way of understanding conceptual analysis is itself consequential for the understanding of power in the social world. For 'the theory of knowledge is a dimension of political theory because the specifically symbolic power to impose the principles of the construction of reality [...] is a major dimension of political power' (Bourdieu 1977: 165). In this context, the stress on the constitutive effects of knowledge typical for both post-Lukes power analysis and constructivists, makes power analysis and constructivism share a family resemblance.[27]

Finally, by opening up how concepts have come to mean and do what they do, this type of conceptual analysis further connects the idea of power and constructivism via their common connection to counterfactuals. Power analysis and constructivist analysis are structurally akin (Guzzini 2000a: 150, 154). By revealing how the social world is of our making, constructivism tends to question the inevitability of the status quo (Hacking 1999: 6). In an analogous way, power is usually conceived in terms of dispositions and capacities which suggest how things could have been different (Baldwin 1985: 22). Given then this particular role conceptual analysis has for and within constructivism, it was obviously not innocent to have chosen power as the concept with which to illustrate a constructivist approach. It allowed a focus on power from the very start, before this similarity between power analysis and constructivist theorising was even introduced. Yet, using 'power' to illustrate also makes the final analysis more complicated insofar as the many reflexive relations have to be thought in parallel. This chapter hopefully contributed to opening up this path.

Acknowledgments

This is a slightly revised version of Guzzini (2005). For many incisive comments and criticisms, I am indebted to Jens Bartelson, Ludvig Beckman, Andreas Behnke, Olya Gayazova, Janice Bially-Mattern, Linda Bishai, Walter Carlsnaes, Raymond Duvall, Jef Huysmans, Anna Leander, Aaron Maltais, Jörgen Odalen, Charles Parker, Heikki Patomäki, Vincent Pouliot, Gerard Toal, the editors of this volume and, not least, to Steven Lukes, on whom I first tried out some of these ideas more than a decade ago. I am only too well aware that many criticisms could not yet be satisfactorily answered. The usual disclaimers apply.

Notes

1 For a similar strategy applied to the concept of security, see Huysmans (1998).

2 A final caveat: in what follows, there will be ideas perfectly acceptable to non-constructivists. IR debates being often about turf wars, this could be seen as an unwelcome attempt to bring other schools into the constructivist fold. But that would be to misread the intention of this piece. It does not seek to establish a turf of the type: 'only if you are a constructivist can you do this type of analysis.' Rather, it wishes to impose some coherence onto constructivism itself when applied to a type of research which is crucial to it, namely conceptual analysis. Something necessary for constructivism is, however, not necessarily unique to it.

3 Crucial, but not therefore unproblematic. See Maja Zehfuss (2001).

4 Among recent constructivists, Alexander Wendt (1999) has stressed this point when discussing the possible stickiness of his cultures of anarchy.

5 For the relationship between peace research and constructivism, see Guzzini (2004a).

6 For instance, it is a crucial component of Pierre Bourdieu's social theory which is compatible with constructivism. See Bourdieu (1984, 1989).

7 In her comments, Janice Bially Mattern has suggested a more pragmatic reading of this passage: a scholar might infer such a common core knowing that it is only an interpretative exegesis. This might allow a contextualised use of concepts as variables.

8 For a more detailed analysis and critique of Luhmann's concept of power, see Guzzini (2004b).

9 This view is constant throughout Luhmann's work. See Luhmann (1990: 179).

10 Except for conceiving it as itself a construct of communication.

11 For my earlier statement on this, see Guzzini (1993). This view is more widely shared across different approaches, see for example Barnes (1988), and Merritt and Zinnes (1989: 27).

12 As it tends to be even in King *et al.* (1994).

13 For a presentation of a wider analysis of power compatible with constructivism, which stresses the need to include non-intentionality and a structural component, see Guzzini (1993).

14 For a discussion of the role of such conceptual analysis in IR theory and its teaching, see Guzzini (2001).

15 This section draws heavily on Guzzini (1994: Part II).

16 For this position, see Oppenheim (1981: 185). David Baldwin's position reads like a critique of essentially contested concepts, but seems close to the latter's precepts. See Baldwin (1989: 8).

17 For this reason perhaps, Keith Dowding (1996: 94ff.) has later rephrased his approach and now explicitly includes systematic luck into power *analysis*, although still not calling it power.

18 Some readers might wonder why I do not use the concepts of 'speech act' or 'illocutionary force' here but a more generic term. The reason has to do with the contested usages of those terms, which would warrant a longer discussion. With regard to speech acts, some might argue that the performative character of 'power' is not yet a speech act, since it is not as equally ritualised and institutionalised as 'I do' is during a marriage. On the other hand, 'power' seems to mobilise a convention in our political discourse and seems therefore akin to that which is described in Austin's or Searle's analysis. As to the type of speech act, I would see this performative effect rather as perlocutionary than illocutionary, although the concepts can slide into each other. On this last point, see, for example, the discussion in Habermas (1981: 388–97). For speech-act theory in IR, see Onuf (1989), Fierke (1998) and, most akin to the present view,

Kratochwil (1989). For an attempt to ground the performative aspect not in speech-act theory but in Derrida, see Zehfuss (2002).

19 For a more detailed discussion of Strange's 'structural power', see also Guzzini (2000b); and for its link to the purposes of power, see Guzzini (2000c).

20 The language of public goods is typical for the debate around hegemonic stability theory.

21 The best place to read about power fungibility is still the work of David Baldwin. See in particular Baldwin (1989). For a recent assessment of the fungibility debate, see Guzzini (2004c: 537–44).

22 On soft power, see also Janice Bially Mattern in this volume.

23 For such a wider power analysis in IR, see, for example, the different studies now collected in Barnett and Duvall (2005b).

24 See, for example, Koselleck (1979: in particular 107–29); Skinner (1989) and Farr (1989). Indeed, these analyses which show how rhetoric, targeting concepts, can be used to unravel historically sedimented and taken-for-granted patterns of legitimacy is congenial to the way Lukes's three dimensions have been operationalised and sequentialised in Gaventa (1980).

25 For an argument on the similarities in Skinner's and Foucault's approach, see Tully (1988). For a geneaolgical study in IR and a general discussion which has inspired this section, see Bartelson (1995).

26 For the present purposes, the following is simply meant as an illustration of how such an analysis could get started in the context of IR. It neglects many analytical difficulties, such as the variety of competing past schools of thought in different cultural contexts or the possibility of actually translating concepts from one context to another (even within Europe, now that the 'classic' and common understanding of what it is no longer exists, let alone a common language).

27 I am indebted to Vincent Pouliot for this reminder.

3   Realist conceptions of power

Brian C. Schmidt

In the field of international relations (IR), the concept of power is closely associated with the theory of realism. Realists, of course, do not monopolise the study of power, and the most recent evidence of this is the lively discussion of the concept of 'soft power'. Although all of the various schools of IR theory have something to say about the nature and role of power, it is the highly influential realist school that has been most closely identified with the study of power. Realists throughout the ages have argued that power is the decisive determinant in the relations among separate political communities and of crucial importance to understanding the dynamics of war and peace. Indeed, as witnessed by the actions of the USA in Iraq, Thucydides' ancient dictum that the strong do what they want and the weak endure the consequences is as relevant today as it was when he described Athens' behaviour towards the tiny island of Melos in 400 BCE. For all realists, John Mearsheimer writes, 'calculations about power lie at the heart of how states think about the world around them' (Mearsheimer 2001: 12).

Although realist theory remains indispensable to understanding the contemporary practice of international politics, critics continue to identify a variety of problems and inconsistencies in many of its central tenets. This is especially the case with respect to the manner in which realists define, measure and utilise the concept of power. From the birth of the modern realist school to the present, critics have commented on the ambiguity of the realists' conceptualisation of power. In fairness to the realists it must be admitted that there is a general lack of consensus on the most appropriate manner to conceptualise and measure power (Baldwin 2002; Barnett and Duvall 2005a). But since it is the realists who argue that power is the *sine qua non* of international politics, critics have targeted much of their criticism of realism at what they consider to be its inadequate understanding of power. Most recently, liberals have accused realists of failing to consider the changing nature of power in a globalised world (Nye 2004b). While such criticism has some merit, the fact that these critics often assume that all realists have the same understanding of power does not do justice to the complexity of realist thought.

Realists are the theorists of power politics; the role of power has been, and continues to be, central to any theory of realism. But while it is true that realists base their analysis of international politics on the role of power, there is a good deal of variation in how individual realists conceptualise the concept. The aim of this article is to survey the competing realist conceptions of power. Although all realists characterise international politics in terms of a continuous struggle for power, they reach this conclusion through a variety of different assumptions. Not only do realists disagree on the underlying reason why international politics can be described as a struggle for power, they also disagree on numerous other issues. These issues include: the strategies that states employ to acquire additional power, how power is utilised to attain desired ends, how power should be measured, and how – if at all – the pursuit of power can be managed within acceptable limits.

To facilitate the task of investigating the realist conception of power, I make use of the important insight that rather than being monolithic, there actually are a number of different and competing realist theories (Frankel 1996; Brooks 1997; Doyle 1997; Donnelly 2000). While there is a typical set of assumptions commonly associated with realism, key assumptions made by individual realists do vary, and sometimes conflict. Not only is there variability in the main assumptions of realism but there is also disparity in how those assumptions are utilised in the process of theory-building. Rather than viewing this lack of a consensus as an indication of a fundamental shortcoming of realist thought, recognition and acceptance of a diverse array of realist positions opens up a creative space in which to evaluate critically the realist conception of power.

The belief that there is not one realism, but many, leads logically to the task of differentiating among different types of realism. In the first section of the article, I briefly outline three different strands of realist theory: classical, structural and modified.[1] Next, I summarise some of the issues and positions that have characterised the study of power in IR. After sketching the broad outlines of the debate on power, I closely examine how classical, structural and modified realists understand and employ the concept of power. Insofar as there are different strands of realism, we should find that classical, structural and modified realists provide us with different and competing conceptions of power. My aim in this article is to determine how each version of realism comprehends the concept of power. The analysis of each of the three respective versions of realism is organised around the following questions dealing with power: (1) How is power defined? (2) Where is power located? (3) What are the effects of power and what are the prevailing patterns of behaviour that result from the struggle for power? and (4) How are capabilities and influence measured? In this manner, the article aims to bring the different realist conceptions of power into sharper focus.

Realisms

The core criticism that the early generation of realists put forward against the scholars of the inter-war period was that they had neglected the fundamental role of power in international politics. The most famous critique of the inter-war scholars' failure to recognise the centrality of power was provided by E. H. Carr in *The Twenty Years' Crisis, 1919–1939*. Carr explained that he had written the book 'with the deliberate aim of counteracting the glaring and dangerous defect of nearly all thinking, both academic and popular, about international politics in English-speaking countries from 1919 to 1939 – the almost total neglect of the factor of power' (Carr 1964: vii). In their effort to shift the analytical focus of the field away from the study of international law and international organisation and towards what they termed 'international politics', a new group of scholars, which included Frederick Sherwood Dunn, Frederick L. Schuman, Georg Schwarzenberger and Nicholas Spykman, argued that the essence of the alternative model rested on the recognition that in the absence of a higher authority, sovereign states were compelled to seek power in order to ensure their own survival and security (Dunn 1948; Schuman 1933; Schwarzenberger 1941; Spykman 1942). According to Dunn, who was one of the original members of the Yale Institute of International Studies, which was formed in 1935, 'international politics is concerned with the special kind of power relationships that exist in a community lacking an overriding authority' (Dunn 1948: 144).

The close relationship that exists between the realist school and the concept of power stems from its basic insight: conflict and competition are intrinsic to the practice of international politics. Given this unquestioned assumption by realists, which they argue is supported by history, they submit that the acquisition and management of power is the central feature of politics among nations. Thus, as Barry Buzan asserts, the 'focus on power politics provides the apparent continuity of the realist tradition' (Buzan 1996: 51). To explain the activity of international politics, according to the realists, it is necessary to focus on the concept of power. Although the realists were successful in helping to make the study of power become a central focus of the field, and did much to fuse considerations of international politics with considerations of power, the adequacy of their understanding of power continues to be challenged. There are important disagreements among realists themselves on the best way to conceptualise and measure power. Some realists define power strictly in terms of measurable material attributes, such as the size of a country's population and military forces, while others include non-material attributes that are often associated with soft power. Power is considered by some realists to be an end in itself, while others assert that it is a means to an end.

The classical realist lineage begins with Thucydides' representation of power politics as a law of human behaviour. The drive to amass power and dominate others is held by classical realists to be a fundamental aspect of human nature. The behaviour of the state as a self-seeking egoist is understood to be a reflection of the characteristics of the people that comprise the state. It is, according to classical realists, human nature that explains why international politics is necessarily power politics. This reduction of the driving force behind international politics to a condition of human nature is one of the defining characteristics of classical realism. Hans J. Morgenthau, for example, held that 'politics, like society in general, is governed by objective laws that have their roots in human nature' (Morgenthau 1954: 4). The important point for Morgenthau was, first, to recognise that these laws exist and, second, to devise policies that are consistent with the basic fact that human beings possess an inherent will to power. For both Thucydides and Morgenthau, the essential continuity of states' behaviour is their power-seeking, which is rooted in the biological drives of human beings.

Structural realism, which is most often associated with Kenneth Waltz's landmark book, *Theory of International Politics* (1979), shifts the focus away from the laws of human nature and argues that the power-seeking behaviour of states is a function of international anarchy. For structural realists, who find their progenitor in Thomas Hobbes, the condition of anarchy – that is, the fact that there is no 'higher power' to ensure the peace among sovereign states – is often viewed as synonymous to a state of war. Structural realists argue that because there is always the possibility that any particular state may resort to force, the outbreak of war is a likely scenario in an anarchical environment. According to Waltz, anarchy prevents states from entering into cooperative agreements to end the state of war. Moreover, Waltz argues that it is the structure of the system that compels states to seek power. There is, however, a recent controversy among structural realists over the question of whether states are primarily security-maximisers or power-maximisers. This debate between defensive and offensive realists is discussed below, but the important point to emphasise is that all structural realists insist that systemic forces explain why international politics is necessarily a continuous struggle for power.

The modified realist category includes those realist thinkers who have ventured to transgress Waltz's maxim to steer clear of reductionist theory. While accepting the importance of systemic forces, modified realists have sought to move beyond the limiting confines of structural realism and have endeavoured to incorporate unit-level characteristics into their account of the struggle for power among nations. Modified realists, especially neoclassical realists such as Randall Schweller, Fareed Zakaria and William Wohlforth, introduce a variety of intervening variables that stand between the state and international outcomes. By considering the role of variables operating at the domestic and individual level of analysis, neoclassical realists provide a different account of the power-seeking behaviour of states.

On power

One of the main obstacles in the endeavour to make power the central focus in IR is the difficulty of reaching a consensus on the most appropriate way to define and measure such an elusive concept. As outlined in the introduction to this volume, power, like a host of other important concepts in

IR, is an essentially contested concept – it means quite different things to different people. David Baldwin describes the two dominant traditions of power analysis in IR 'in terms of the elements of national power approach, which depicts power as resources, and the relational power approach, which depicts power as an actual or potential relationship' (Baldwin 2002: 185). Proponents of the elements-of-national-power approach equate power with the possession of specific resources. All of the important resources that a state possesses are typically combined in some fashion to determine its overall aggregate power. The resources that are most often used as an indicator of national power include the level of military expenditure, gross national product (GNP), size of the armed forces, size of territory and population. While tangible elements such as population, military expenditure and GNP are almost always included in calculations of national power, some scholars also include intangible elements such as the quality of political leadership, national morale and culture. Regardless of the particular tangible and intangible power resources that one chooses to identify, those endorsing the elements-of-national-power approach believe they can be measured and combined to provide an indicator of the aggregate power of a state. Stefano Guzzini refers to this as a 'lump concept of power which assumes that all elements of power can be combined into one general indicator' (Guzzini 2000c: 55).

One of the difficulties with the elements-of-national-power approach is the issue of power conversion; that is, 'the capacity to convert potential power, as measured by resources, to realized power, as measured by the changed behavior of others' (Nye 2003b: 59). At the end of the day, it is not the mere possession of power resources that matters but the ability to convert these into actual influence. This leads to a second problem with this approach; namely, determining the degree to which various components of national power are fungible or interchangeable. Baldwin explains that 'fungibility refers to the ease with which power resources useful in one issue-area can be used in other issue-areas' (2002: 180). Simply because a state possesses some kind of power does not necessarily mean that it can be used to attain a specific benefit. For instance, the possession of nuclear weapons, which the elements-of-national-power approach would consider to be an important source of power, does not guarantee that they can be used to gain influence in an issue-area such as trade. Because the elements-of-national-power approach adopts a 'lump concept of power', it assumes power is fungible. However, whether power actually is fungible is difficult to demonstrate, and critics of the aggregated power approach suggest it is not (Keohane 1983).

An alternative to the power-as-resources approach is the relational power approach that was championed by behavioural-oriented political scientists during the 1950s and 1960s.[2] According to Robert Dahl, who was an influential advocate of the relational conception of power, 'A has power over B to the extent that he can get B to do something that B would not otherwise do' (Dahl 1957: 202). Fundamental to the relational conception of power is the ability to demonstrate a change in outcomes. According to this view, power is a process of interaction whereby a state is able to exercise influence over the actions of another state. Power as a set of material resources is deemed to be less important than the actual ability of Actor A to change the behaviour of Actor B.

A core motivation for developing the relational approach to power was to overcome the fungibility problem associated with the lump concept of power. The relational approach rejects both the lump concept of power and the fungibility assumption and, instead, defines and specifies power in a multidimensional, causal manner. Rather than power being a 'one size fits all' category, the relational approach disaggregates power into a number of component parts in order to demonstrate how it is exercised in specific issue-areas. The dimensions of power typically include 'its scope (the objectives of an attempt to gain influence; influence over which issue), its domain (the target of the influence attempt), its weight (the quantity of resources), and its costs (opportunity costs of forgoing a relation)' (Guzzini 1993: 453). Proponents argue that the relational concept of power allows one to investigate how influence or control is achieved in a variety of specific settings. Since the relational approach equates power with outcomes, the analyst must be able to demonstrate how an actor is able to cause another to do something that they would not otherwise do. While realists are the theorists of power politics, they disagree on the best way to conceptualise and measure power. The next sections reveal that realist thinkers can subscribe to either (or even both) of the two dominant traditions of power analysis.

Classical realism and power

Forefathers of classical realists such as Thucydides and Machiavelli, as well as the members of the power-politics school that arose at the end of the inter-war period, conceptualised international politics, and politics more generally, in terms of a fundamental and never-ending struggle for power. In the beginning of *Politics among Nations*, Morgenthau proclaimed that 'international politics, like all politics, is a struggle for power'. He added that 'whatever the ultimate aims of international politics, power is always the immediate aim' (Morgenthau 1954: 25). Carr concurred with Morgenthau, claiming that 'politics are, then, in one sense always power politics' (1964: 102). And Frederick Schuman, whose popular text *International Politics* (1933) was a harbinger of the realism that Morgenthau would popularise after the Second World War, claimed that 'all politics is a struggle for power, but while power is sought in domestic politics as a means toward other ends, power is sought as an end in itself in international politics' (Schuman 1933: 491).

When it comes to providing a definition of power, Morgenthau is complex in that he appears to have endorsed both the relational and the elements-of-national-power approach. On the one hand, he clearly states that 'when we speak of power, we mean man's control over the minds and actions of other men'. Morgenthau defines political power as 'a psychological relation between those who exercise it and those over whom it is exercised. It gives the former control over certain actions of the latter through the influence which the former exert over the latter's minds' (1954: 26–7). This definition clearly places Morgenthau in the relational-approach-to-power camp. His view closely follows Max Weber's relational definition of power as 'the probability that one actor within a social relationship will be in a position to carry out his own will despite resistance, regardless of the basis on which this probability rests' (Weber 1947: 152). By endorsing a relational conception of power, Morgenthau commits himself to demonstrating how a political actor, whether it be an individual person or a state, is able to induce a change in outcome favourable to the one who is exercising power. Morgenthau does, however, make a sharp distinction between political power and physical force. He argues that there is a fundamental difference between threatening the use of violence to achieve a particular outcome and its actual use; the latter, for Morgenthau, represents an 'abdication of political power in favor of military or pseudo-military power' (1954: 27). The psychological aspect of power is lost when overt physical violence is used to influence the behaviour of another actor.

Yet, on the other hand, it is equally apparent that Morgenthau also defined power in terms of the elements-of-national-power approach. Like other classical realists, Morgenthau equated power with the possession of both material and non-material resources. Morgenthau distinguished between two types of elements that contributed to the power of a nation: those that are stable and those subject to constant change. The stable elements, which were largely of a quantitative nature, included geography, natural resources (food and raw materials), industrial capacity, military preparedness and population. Morgenthau identified four qualitative, non-material factors that have a bearing on national power: national character, national morale, the quality of government and the quality of a nation's diplomacy. Morgenthau singled out the quality of diplomacy as the most important factor contributing to the power of a nation. According to Morgenthau, 'the conduct of a nation's foreign affairs by its diplomats is for national power in peace what military strategy and tactics by its military leaders are for national power in war' (1954: 129).

Carr equated international politics with power politics, but, unlike Morgenthau, he never provided an explicit definition of power. Carr argued that power was indivisible, yet he claimed that for purposes of discussion it could be divided into three categories: military power, economic power and power over opinion. Yet because of the ever-present possibility of war breaking out, Carr argued that military power was the most important form of power in international politics. Carr explained that 'the supreme importance of the military instrument lies in the fact that the *ultima ratio* of power in international relations is war' (Carr 1964: 109). He admitted that the primary importance of economic power lay in its close association with the military instrument. Carr, in fact, concluded that military power was such an essential element in the life of the state that it served as both a means and an end in itself.

In addition to emphasising the military and economic dimensions of power, Carr, like Morgenthau, was sensitive to the role of soft power; what Nye also refers to as 'co-optive power' – 'getting others to want the outcomes you want' (Nye 2004b: 5). Carr devoted specific attention to ana-lysing propaganda as a form of power over opinion, which he considered to be a potent political force, especially when combined with military and economic power. As politics was increasingly becoming a mass phenomena, Carr recognised the power that came with the ability to shape the opinions and preferences of others. Governments also clearly recognised this as they devoted more and more resources to moulding the opinions and beliefs of the masses both at home and abroad. But while Nye basically views soft power as being essentially benign and detached from hard power, Carr did not. Carr rejected the notion that power over opinion could be dissociated from either military or economic power. Moreover, from the vantage point of Carr's peculiar form of realism, which was heavily influenced by Karl Mannheim's sociology of knowledge, opinions and beliefs which are cast as universal and mutually beneficial are, more often than not, the self-serving ideas of a dominant class or state. Just as Carr used realism to demolish the doctrine of the harmony of interests put forward by the status-quo powers of the inter-war period, the same critique could be applied to American advocates of globalisation.

Classical realists argue that the permanent struggle of states for power, in which the goal of every state is to maximise its own relative power, is ulti-mately explained by the sinful and power-seeking nature of man. They belong to what Arnold Wolfers once referred to as the 'evil school', which places emphasis on the role of forces within people and states and the overall focus is on flaws in human nature and states.[3] Thucydides and Machiavelli can both be viewed as classical realists in that their respective views of politics were largely derived from their account of the nature of human beings. Michael Doyle refers to this form of realism as fundament-alism, which 'characterizes all social interaction as fundamentally rooted in mankind's psychological and material needs that result in a drive for power' (Doyle 1997: 46). For Thucydides and Machiavelli, the passions of fear, glory and self-interest manifest themselves in a diabolical urge to dominate others. The will to power that arises from the egoistic nature of man is assumed to describe the behaviour of macroscopic political entities such as city-states and nation-states.[4]

Unlike some of his fellow realists, Morgenthau provided an explanation to account for the ubiquitous struggle for power. Although Morgenthau argued that the struggle for power took a different form in the domestic and international realm, the underlying reason why the activity of politics was reducible to the pursuit of power was the same: human nature. Like Thucydides and Machiavelli, Morgenthau located the pursuit of power to the basic human drive to dominate others. One of Morgenthau's core assumptions about human nature was that all men held an insatiable 'lust for power'. According to Morgenthau, 'man is a political animal by nature' who 'is born to seek power' (Morgenthau 1946: 168).

Morgenthau argued that while all men are born to seek power, the reality was that most people find themselves to be a 'slave to the power of others'. He held that the dynamic interaction between seeking and resisting domination contributed to the evil nature of politics. Although Morgenthau believed that the selfishness of man was a fundamental cause of political strife, he attributed the universal desire for power to two distinct human drives. The first was rooted in the drive to survive: to secure vital needs such as food, shelter and sex. The problem here is competition and scarcity: 'what the one wants for himself, the other already possesses or wants, too'. Consequently, 'struggle and competition ensue' (Morgenthau 1946: 192). The second, and more diabolical drive, is what Morgenthau termed the *animus dominandi*, the desire to dominate. Unlike the first selfish drive, the second desire for power is not associated with mere survival but with the position of one individual in relation to another. Morgenthau reasoned that while there were limits to the physical selfishness of man, the desire for power was limitless.

Morgenthau transfers the bedrock assumption of man's inherent lust for power to describe the behaviour of states. Because of the 'ubiquity of the struggle for power in all social relations on all levels of social organization', Morgenthau concluded that 'international politics is of necessity power politics' (1954: 31). Just like individuals, he claimed, the goal of every state was to maximise power. He viewed the activity of international politics 'as a continuing effort to maintain and to increase the power of one's own nation and to keep in check or reduce the power of other nations' (1954: 211). Morgenthau likened the three basic patterns of the struggle for power among states – to keep power (status quo), to increase power (imperialism) and to demonstrate power (prestige) – to man's lust for power that was manifest in the 'desire to maintain the range of one's own person with regard to others, to increase it, or to demonstrate it' (1946: 192; 1954: 36).

According to this view, international politics is a continuous struggle between the status quo and revisionist powers. But the quest for power does not take place in a vacuum. Rather, each state's attempt to act in terms of interest defined as power directly influences the actions of other states. This makes it incumbent on the statesmen to measure accurately the power and intentions of other states so as to differentiate between an imperialist and status-quo foreign policy. Yet Morgenthau maintained that one of the most complicated tasks of foreign policy was to evaluate how the individual elements of power contributed to the overall power of one's own nation as well as that of others. In reality, Morgenthau argued that while many of the elements that go into the making of power could be quantified, power itself 'is not susceptible to quantification' (Morgenthau 1967: 211). For Morgenthau and the classical realists, international politics was more of an art than a science. The power of nations could never be measured in the same way that physicists measured atmospheric pressure. To overcome this state of quandary, Morgenthau noted that many analysts chose to focus solely on the military component of power. But this, for Morgenthau, was a big mistake because national power is not equivalent to military force. A state that fails to understand this and pursues a militaristic policy will, according to Morgenthau, 'find itself confronted with the maximum effort of all its competitors to equal or surpass its power' (Morgenthau 1954: 151). This view would certainly be supported by those who have put forth the concept of 'soft balancing' to describe the actions that many states have taken towards the USA as a consequence of its post-9/11 militaristic national security strategy (Pape 2005; Paul 2005).

Morgenthau and the classical realists argued that the most basic pattern of behaviour among states was their perpetual struggle for power. One of the core manifestations of this behaviour was balance of power politics. For Morgenthau, the struggle for power leads of necessity to a balance of power and to policies aimed at preserving it (1954: 155). Yet the ability to differentiate between a status-quo and imperialist policy, and the successful pursuit of a balance of power, depends on an accurate assessment of national power, which Morgenthau admitted was fraught with difficulty. Morgenthau argued that the net result of the inability to accurately calculate the relative distribution of power, was that 'all nations must ultimately seek the maximum of power obtainable under the circumstances' (1954: 189). Thus, the universal drive to attain maximum power was not only explained by specific behavioural traits found in the nature of man but also from the fear of miscalculating the power of others. Notwithstanding their effort to focus on the key concept of power, Morgenthau and the classical realists have been sharply criticised for trying to construct a general theory of international politics on the basis of concepts as elusive as power and human nature. Stanley Hoffmann, for example, declared that 'the decision to equate politics and the effects of man's "lust for power," and the tendency to equate power and evil or violence, mutilate reality' (Hoffmann 1959: 350).

Structural realism and power

Structural realists concur with classical realists that the realm of international politics is a continuous struggle for power, but they do not accept the assumption that this is attributable to certain propensities found in the nature of man. Waltz, for example, writes, 'international politics is the realm of power, of struggle, and of accommodation' (Waltz 1979: 113). Thomas Hobbes, who is often interpreted as a structural realist, argued that in the absence of an overarching power, human beings exhibited 'a perpetual and restless desire of power after power, that ceaseth only in death'. For Hobbes, man's desire 'of power after power' was neither the result of greed nor from an intrinsic delight in dominating others, but rather 'because he cannot assure the power and means to live well, which he hath present, without the acquisition of more' (Hobbes 1985: 161). Instead of explaining the ubiquitous quest for power on the basis of human nature, structural realists, in Arnold Wolfers' terms, substitute tragedy for evil. According to the tragedy view, 'the insecurity of an anarchical system of multiple sovereignty places the actors under compulsion to seek maximum power even though it run counter to their real desires' (Wolfers 1951: 42). Structural realists shift the locus of the struggle for power from human nature to the anarchical environment that states inhabit.

Waltz explains that 'from the vantage point of neorealist theory, competition and conflict among states stem directly from the twin facts of life under conditions of anarchy: States in an anarchic order must provide for their own security, and threats or seeming threats to their security abound' (Waltz 1989: 43). In the absence of a superior authority, structural realists argue that self-help is necessarily the principle of action. Writing much earlier than Waltz, Nicholas Spykman observed that in an anarchical international society, 'each individual state has continued to depend for its very existence, as much as for the enjoyment of its rights and the protection of its interests, primarily on its own strength or that of its protectors' (Spykman 1942: 17). Because of the possibility that force may at any time be used by one state against another, all states must take appropriate measures to ensure their own survival. Structural realists argue that the most important measure that a state can take to help guarantee its own survival is to accumulate a sufficient amount of power.

Given the criticism levelled against realists that their conception of power is overly simplistic, it is somewhat odd that Waltz does not provide a sophisticated definition of power. He simply endorses the elements-of-national-power approach and equates power with the possession of material resources. However, based on the manner that Waltz has constructed his structural theory, it cannot be any other way. His commitment to parsimony necessitates that he define power in terms of resources and, furthermore, that he assume that these resources are highly fungible. Waltz is most interested in providing a rank ordering of states so that he can ascertain the number of great powers in any given international system. This, by necessity, leads him to reject the relational, multidimensional notion of power and instead endorse the lump concept of power. According to Waltz,

> The economic, military, and other capabilities of nations cannot be sectored and separately weighed. States are not placed in the top rank because they excel in one way or another. Their rank depends on how they score on *all* of the following items: size of population and territory,

resource endowment, economic capability, military strength, political stability and competence.

(1979: 131)

Conceived in this manner, the capabilities of a state represent nothing more than the sum total of a number of loosely identified national attributes. A similar degree of generality is evident in Robert Gilpin's definition of power. According to Gilpin, 'power refers simply to the military, economic, and technological capabilities of states' (Gilpin 1981: 13). Neither Waltz nor Gilpin provide a detailed discussion of state capabilities or indicate precisely how they should be measured. Although Waltz identifies a few items that allegedly determine the rank of a state, he fails to specify the criterion by which to measure them or to indicate how they can be combined into an aggregate score. While Waltz does admit that 'states have different combinations of capabilities which are difficult to measure and compare, the more so since the weight to be assigned to different items changes with time', he makes it seem that any competent student of international politics can differentiate between the capabilities of states and identify the great powers in the international system (Waltz 1979: 131).

Not only is Waltz, in fact, vague on the issue of how to appraise and rank the power of states but he also never carefully specifies what he means by capabilities. While he equates resources with capability, the question of 'capability to get whom to do what' is never addressed. In dismissing those analysts who define power in terms of getting one's way, Waltz remarks that he relies on 'the old and simple notion that an agent is powerful to the extent that he affects others more than they affect him' (Waltz 1979: 192). David Baldwin notes that, in all likelihood, a 'careful reading of Waltz generates a strong suspicion that war-winning ability is the unstated standard by which states are being ranked' (Baldwin 2002: 183). Echoing Carr, Morgenthau and Schuman, Waltz claims, 'in international politics force serves, not only the as the *ultima* ratio, but indeed as the first and constant one' (Waltz 1979: 113). It does seem that, for Waltz, power in international politics is roughly equivalent to military might.

Lack of clarity aside, Waltz and other structural realists argue that the relative distribution of capabilities in the international system is the key independent variable to explaining international outcomes such as wars, alliances and the operation of the balance of power. Although capabilities are a unit-level attribute, Waltz argues that it is a structural attribute in that he is most interested in how capabilities are distributed across the international system. Waltz explains that 'although capabilities are attributes of units, the distribution of capabilities is not' (1979: 98).

What effect does the international distribution of power have on the behaviour of states, particularly their power-seeking behaviour? Waltz argues that states, especially the great powers, have to be sensitive to the capabilities of other states. In order to ensure their own survival in a self-help environment, neo-realists such as Waltz assume that prudent states will only seek an appropriate amount of power. According to Waltz, power is a means to the end of security. In a significant passage, Waltz writes 'because power is a possibly useful means, sensible statesmen try to have an appropriate amount of it'. He adds, 'in crucial situations, however, the ultimate concern of states is not for power but for security' (Waltz 1989: 40). In other words, rather than being power-maximisers, states, according to Waltz, are security-maximisers. Contrary to Morgenthau, who 'viewed power as an end in itself', neorealism 'sees power as a possibly useful means, with states running risks if they have either too little or too much of it' (Waltz 1989: 40). The implication, for Waltz, is that states will sometimes forgo acquiring additional amounts of power if this is seen as potentially jeopardising their security. The most important factor that Waltz identifies for why a state will be disinclined to maximise its relative power is rooted in his central proposition that 'balances of power recurrently form' (Waltz 1979: 128). Aggressive and expansionist behaviour often, according to Waltz, proves to be counterproductive because it triggers a counter-balancing coalition. Waltz concludes that 'because power is a means and not an end, states prefer to join the weaker of two coalitions'. He continues, 'if states wish to maximize power, they would join the stronger side', but 'this does not happen because balancing, not bandwagoning, is the behavior induced by the system' (Waltz 1979: 126).

As a result of Waltz's belief that states are strongly inclined to balance against aggressive powers, they can be described, in Joseph Grieco's terms, as 'defensive positionalists' and 'will only seek the minimum level of power that is needed to attain and to maintain their security and survival' (Grieco 1997: 167). According to this 'defensive realist' position, the mechanism of the balance of the power is such that states will seek power only to minimise international power gaps rather than maximise such gaps to their own advantage. Randall Schweller has noted that there appears to be a status-quo bias among defensive realists such as Waltz, which begs the question: 'if states are assumed to seek nothing more than their own survival, why would they feel threatened?' (Schweller 1996: 91). Schweller, following Morgenthau and the classical realists, argues that while some status-quo states might only desire security, there are also revisionist states that seek more power. The question of whether states are security-maximising or power-maximising entities has become the basis of an important debate among structural realists. The debate is cast in terms of an opposition between defensive and offensive realists.[5]

While sharing many of the same assumptions with Waltz and defensive realists, John Mearsheimer's theory of offensive realism offers a different account of the struggle for power under anarchy. Most importantly, 'offensive realism parts company with defensive realism over the question of how much power states want' (Mearsheimer 2001: 21). According to Mearsheimer, the structure of the international system compels states to maximise their relative power position. The environment that states inhabit, Mearsheimer argues, is responsible for the ubiquitous competition for power that prompts states to search for opportunities to increase their power at the expense of rivals. He articulates five basic assumptions about the international system: it is anarchic; all great powers possess some offensive military capability; states can never be certain about the intentions of other states; survival is the primary goal of states; and states are rational actors. Mearsheimer argues that the most important pattern of behaviour that follows from these bedrock assumptions is power maximisation. Mearsheimer contends that, 'apprehensive about the ultimate intentions of other states, and aware that they operate in a self-help system, states quickly understand that the best way to ensure their survival is to be the most powerful state in the system' (2001: 33).

Contrary to Waltz, Mearsheimer argues that states understand that the best path to survival is to accumulate more power than anyone else. The ideal position – albeit one, Mearsheimer argues, that is virtually impossible to achieve – is to be the global hegemon. The impossibility of attaining global preeminence – which according to Mearsheimer is due largely to the difficulties that can be identified with projecting power across large bodies of water – does not, however, prevent states from trying to achieve hegemony. Consequently, he maintains that all great powers have revisionist aims and pursue expansionist policies.

Power is the key concept of offensive realism, and Mearsheimer admits that it is only by clearly defining power that we can understand the behaviour of the great powers. Like Waltz, Mearsheimer endorses the elements of national power approach and defines power as 'nothing more than specific assets or material resources that are available to a state' (2001: 57). Unlike Waltz, however, he devotes greater attention to discussing these elements and attempts to provide a reliable way to measure state power. Mearsheimer begins by distinguishing between two kinds of state power: military power and latent power. The essence of a state's effective power is its military power, based largely on the size and strength of the army, as it compares to the military forces of other states. Mearsheimer explains that he defines 'power largely in military terms because offensive realism emphasizes that force is the *ultima ratio* of international politics' (2001: 56). Yet, in Mearsheimer's view, there is a clear hierarchy of military power. He demonstrates how specific types of fighting forces – sea power, strategic airpower, land power, and nuclear weapons – contribute differently to the overall power of a state. Mearsheimer maintains that land power is the dominant form of military power and concludes that a state with the most formidable army is the most powerful state.

The ability of a state to build a powerful army is a function of its latent power. By latent power, Mearsheimer 'refers to the socio-economic ingredients that go into building military power; it is largely based on a state's wealth and the overall size of its population' (2001: 55). He engages in a detailed discussion of latent power and provides a way to measure it.[6] Mearsheimer repeatedly emphasises the point that latent power is not equivalent to military power. The historical record, according to Mearsheimer, indicates that states have had different levels of success in translating latent power to military power, which makes it impossible to equate wealth with military might.

There is no doubt that, compared to Waltz, Mearsheimer has devised a more reliable measure of national power. It is also clear that his account of the struggle for power is much more intense than Waltz's benign description. The question Mearsheimer takes on – do states seek to maximise power or security? – is an important one for realists. It has implications for a host of other issues such as the problem of achieving international cooperation, the degree to which states balance or bandwagon and debates about grand strategy. While utilising different assumptions about the motivations of states, defensive and offensive realism both operate from the premise that the structure of the international system explains the power-seeking behaviour of states and important international outcomes. Both theories are thus limited by their refusal to consider how factors located at the domestic and individual level of analysis impact the struggle for power. By endorsing the view that power is equivalent to the possession of material resources, both Waltz and Mearsheimer overlook the extent to which power is a matter of perception.

Modified realism

Modified realists share the view of all realists that international politics can be described as a continuous struggle for power. Modified realists also concur with structural realists that international anarchy is an important factor contributing to the relentless quest for power and security. But unlike structural realists, advocates of neoclassical realism argue, in a manner similar to classical realists, that 'anarchy is a permissive condition rather than an independent causal force' (Walt 2002: 211). Anarchy and the relative distribution of power alone cannot, according to neoclassical realists, explain the particular power-seeking behaviour that a state adopts. Contrary to defensive realists such as Waltz, neoclassical realists are primarily interested in explaining the foreign-policy behaviour and decisions of specific states. While the relative power of a state is held to be an important determinant of foreign policy, Stephen Walt explains, 'the causal logic of the theory places domestic politics as an intervening variable between the distribution of power and foreign policy behavior' (2002: 211). Rather than identifying the locus of the pursuit for power at either the individual or structural level, neoclassical realists insist that it is an amalgamation of the two levels.

Neoclassical realists refuse to 'blackbox' the state. Instead they make a number of modifications to the parsimonious tenets of structural realism and incorporate unit-level factors such as the personalities and perceptions of statesmen, state–society relationships and state interests into their explanation of international politics. These modifications contribute to a distinctive neo-classical realist conception of power. According to neoclassical realists, states are not 'like units'. Randall Schweller, a leading proponent of neoclassical realism, argues that 'complex domestic political processes act as transmission belts that channel, mediate, and (re)direct policy outputs in response to external forces (primarily changes in relative power)' (Schweller 2004: 164). Neoclassical realists do not discount the importance of the structure of the international system, in fact they argue that it is a key determinant of a state's foreign policy, but they argue that a plausible theory of international politics must also include unit-level attributes.

Neoclassical realists continue to be preoccupied with determining the concept of power. In terms of the debate between the elements-of-national-power approach and the relational-power approach, neoclassical realists endorse the former (Wohlforth 1993: 1–17; Rose 1998: 151). But while they endorse a material definition, they insist that relative power alone cannot explain the foreign-policy behaviour of states. In addition to the material capabilities emphasised by structural realists, neoclassical realists include a variety of domestic variables that help to determine the actual power that a state possesses. Compared to structural realists such as Waltz, neoclassical realists provide a more subtle definition of power that connects in impor-tant ways to the insights provided by classical realists.

Adding additional variables obviously complicates the elusive task of providing a reliable way to measure power. Of all the neoclassical realists, Schweller has made the greatest effort to specify how the capabilities of a state should be measured. He utilises data from the Correlates of War (COW) project to measure the relative capabilities of both the great powers and what he refers to as lesser great powers.[7] Schweller argues that the measures comprising the COW capability index – in which military (forces in being), industrial (war potential) and demographic (staying power and war-augmenting capability) are the three distinct measures of national power – 'provide a reasonably accurate picture of the power bases held by the major actors with respect to their relative fighting capabilities' (Schwel-ler 1998: 26–7). While Schweller's effort to provide greater precision in the measurement of capabilities is laudable, other neoclassical realists maintain that it is only the first step.

Neoclassical realists argue that one of the main obstacles to providing a reliable way to measure power stems from the fact that it is not national power per se that is of crucial importance, but rather decision-makers' per-ceptions of power that matter most. William Wohlforth writes, 'if power influences the course of international politics, it must do so largely through the perceptions of the people who make decisions on behalf of states' (1993: 2). Structural realists make it appear that the relative distribution of power in the international system has an objective existence that directly influences the behaviour of states. Neoclassical realists disagree. Not only do they argue that it is political leaders' perception of the distribution of power that is central, they do not assume that there is a direct link between systemic constraints and unit-level behaviour. Systemic pressures, they argue, must be translated through intervening variables located at the unit level.

One important intervening variable emphasised by neoclassical realists is decision-makers' perceptions of the distribution of power. Gideon Rose explains that 'foreign policy choices are made by actual political leaders and elites, and so it is their perceptions of relative power that matter, not simply relative quantities of physical resources or forces in being' (Rose 1998: 147). In highlighting the role of perception and misperception, neoclassical realists have sought to introduce a greater degree of agency into IR theory. There is no doubt that including the intervening variable of perception complicates the task of measuring power, but neoclassical realists claim that one cannot simply assume that all foreign-policy officials accurately apprehend the distribution of power or that the personalities of statesmen make no difference in the process by which the distribution of power is calculated.

A second intervening variable that neoclassical realists consider in their analysis of foreign policy is domestic state structure. For neoclassical realists, among the reasons states are not 'like units' is that they have different domestic structures. Variations in state–society relationships contribute to different forms of state, which alters the manner by which the power of a state should be measured. Neoclassical realists argue that 'power analysis must therefore also examine the strength and structure of states relative to their societies, because these affect the proportion of national resources that can be allocated to foreign policy' (Rose 1998: 147). Fareed Zakaria makes an attempt to differentiate states on the basis of their ability to extract and direct resources from the societies that they rule. When measuring power, Zakaria argues that a distinction needs to be made between national power – namely, the traditional material resources identified by classical and structural realists – and state strength, which he defines both as the ability of the government apparatus to 'extract national power for its ends', as well as the 'capacity and cohesion to carry out its wishes' (Zakaria 1998: 38–9). With respect to state strength, Zakaria argues that there is great disparity in the ability that governments have to extract resources from society to put to use in the pursuit of foreign-policy objectives. State power, which Zakaria defines as 'that portion of national power the government can extract for its purposes and [which thus] reflects the ease with which central decision-makers can achieve their ends', is the key variable of his neoclassical version of state-centered realism (1998: 9).

Finally, neoclassical realists argue that not only do states have different domestic structures, which directly impacts their relative capabilities, but they also have different interests. Schweller's work reminds us that for classical realists, such as Carr, Morgenthau and Wolfers, calculating the motivations and interests of states was of crucial importance to describing the character that the struggle for power took at any particular historical moment. He disagrees with structural realists who submit that states are all motivated by the same interests and has attempted to construct a theory that takes into account the full range of state interests. Most importantly, Schweller brings the revisionist state back in; allowing for the possibility that, in terms of power, some states do indeed 'value what they covet more than what they have' (Schweller 1998: 22).

Taken together, the modifications introduced by neoclassical realists contribute to a different explanation of the effect that the struggle for power has on states. The pursuit of power, according to neoclassical realists, is not an end in itself, but rather is one of the most important means that a state has to try and control and shape the environment that it inhabits. Rather than describing states as either power-maximising or security-maximising entities, neoclassical realists such as Zakaria prefer to describe states as 'influence-maximisers'. According to this formulation, as the power of a state increases, so does its interests. Reworking Morgenthau's classic formulation that nations define their interests in terms of power, Zakaria contends that as the capabilities of a state increase it will seek greater influence and control of the external environment, and when power resources wane, its interests and ambitions will be scaled back accordingly.

Because neoclassical realists claim that the pursuit of power is induced neither by a diabolical will to dominate nor by the structure of international anarchy, they allow for a much greater degree of flexibility in explaining how and why a particular state seeks to enhance its power. Stephen Brooks claims that 'decision makers pursue power because it is the mechanism by which to achieve the state's overriding objectives'. And because neoclassical realists view power as a mechanism rather than an end in itself, 'states are expected to pursue power subject to cost-benefit calculations' (Brooks 1997: 462). In their assessment of the impact that the struggle for power has on states, neoclassical realists are willing to trade determinacy for greater empirical accuracy in describing the policies that a state actually adopts. Just as the interests and ambitions of states vary, so do their objectives. The relative power that a state possesses continues to be a key indicator of a state's foreign policy, but neoclassical realists argue that there is no direct transmission belt linking material capabilities to foreign-policy behaviour.

Conclusion

This survey has reaffirmed that realists are the theorists of power politics. The image of states perpetually struggling for power and security provides the bedrock foundation of the realist ontology of international politics. Yet while realists share the view that states are continuously competing for power, they disagree on the factors that account for this perpetual struggle for power. Each of the three different versions of realism discussed in this article provides a different explanation for the power-seeking behaviour of states. In the case of classical realism, the power-seeking behaviour of states is attributed to the nature of man, while structural realists ascribe it to the anarchical condition of international politics and the relative distribution of power in the international system. Neoclassical realists agree with structural realists that the struggle for power between states is not a logical outcome of a biological will to power but insist that it is also influenced by intervening variables located at the level of the individual and the state. Thus, while the unifying theme of realism is that states are engaged in a competition for power, this article has shown that there is a diverse range of explanations to account for this behaviour. Moreover, the three varieties of realism each infer different patterns of behaviour arising from the struggle for power.

This finding supports the view that rather than being monolithic, there are a variety of realist positions, which each hold different assumptions about the factors that motivate state behaviour. Yet it is still appropriate to conclude by asking whether the three different versions of realism clearly offer competing conceptualisations of power. And since the focus on power provides one of the important continuities of the realist tradition, it is also suitable to ask whether any progress has been made in how realists conceptualise and understand power. In the remaining paragraphs, I briefly address these questions.

It is revealing that after reviewing the recent developments in the realist tradition, Stephen Walt concluded that 'the concept of power is central to realist theory, yet there is still little agreement on how it should be conceived and measured' (Walt 2002: 222). While I have shown that realists disagree on the factors that give rise to the struggle for power, my survey has found that there is a degree of consensus on how they define power. Although classical realists, and Morgenthau in particular, defined power both in terms of the relational and elements-of-national-power approach, the overwhelming majority of realists in all three categories endorse the latter view. Even though there is disagreement on the most important elements that contribute to the power of a state, realists have been reluctant to infer the power of a particular state based solely on its ability to influence or control the actions of another state. Instead, realists have preferred to define power in terms of the possession of material resources. This is in sharp contrast with advocates of the concept of soft power who largely define power as the ability to shape the preferences and behaviour of others (Nye 2004b). By refusing to equate power with outcomes, and by insisting that power is largely fungible across diverse issue areas, realists continue to be vulnerable to a wide range of criticisms (Baldwin 2002; Keohane 1983).

In addition to defining power in terms of the possession of material resources, there is a general tendency among realists to associate power with military might. While not taking them to be synonymous, realists do regard war-fighting ability to be the essence of state power. This is another clear difference between realists and liberals such as Nye. The concept of soft power largely gains its analytical purchase on the view that military force has lost much of its utility. Power is largely defined in military terms by realists because they believe that force is the *ultima ratio* of international politics. Waltz's statement that 'because any state may at any time use force, all states must constantly be ready either to counter force with force or to pay the cost of weakness' represents another bedrock assumption of realism that has a direct bearing on the manner in which realists conceptualise and measure power (Waltz 1959: 160). The view that a great power war continues to be a distinct possibility and that war does sometimes pay, also puts realists at odds with numerous critics.

Even if realists generally conceptualise power in terms of material resources and embrace the view that war-fighting ability is the essence of state power, they have not reached a consensus on the appropriate criteria for measuring power. Each of the three categories of realism provides a different method for calculating the power of a state. I would submit that since Waltz, who clearly devoted less attention to this issue than Morgenthau and Carr, realists have made progress in providing a more reliable way to measure power. Both Mearsheimer and Schweller devote considerable attention to the issue of how to measure power and provide their own clear criteria. Neoclassical realists have sought to improve on the manner in which structural realists measure power, but in the process they have been willing to forsake parsimony for what they believe to be greater explanatory power. Recognising the difficulty of providing an objective basis to measure the relative distribution of power, neoclassical realists have incorporated domestic variables and decision-makers' perceptions into their calculation of state power. While the burgeoning neoclassical research agenda offers many opportunities to advance our understanding of power, it does nonetheless have its share of critics who claim that it represents a 'less determinate, less coherent, and less distinctive realism' (Legro and Moravcsik 1999: 6).[8]

And yet, in the end, and notwithstanding all of the conceptual and measurement difficulties identified by the critics, the essence of the realist conception of international politics as fundamentally determined by the struggle for power seems, for many, to be intuitively correct. When Joseph S. Nye Jnr, who has been a vocal critic of realism, asked US Secretary of Defense Donald Rumsfeld about the concept of 'soft power', Rumsfeld replied 'I don't know what "soft power" is' (Traub 2005). We can, however, be fairly certain that the practitioners of international politics understand and often act on the basis of the realist conception of power. So was the case in ancient Athens and, today, in Iraq.

Notes

1 For an additional elaboration of these three categories of realism, see Dunne and Schmidt (2005).
2 The classic work is Laswell and Kaplan (1950).

3 On the 'evil' school, see Wolfers (1962) and Spirtas (1996).

4 For a fuller explanation of this move, see Tellis (1996).

5 For a general introduction to the debate between defensive and offensive realism, see Lynn-Jones (1998); Taliaferro (2000/1); and Schmidt (2004).

6 Measuring latent power in the years between 1816 and 1960, Mearsheimer uses a straightforward composite indicator that accords equal weight to a state's iron and steel production and its energy consumption; from 1960 to the present, he uses GNP to measure wealth.

7 Information about the COW Project can be found at http://www.correlates ofwar.org.

8 For a different view, see Schweller (2003).

4   Structural realism and the problem of polarity and war

Joseph M. Grieco

The demise of the Soviet Union between 1989 and 1991 and the continuing and even growing material pre-eminence of the USA throughout the 1990s and into the new millennium is thought by some to have caused a fundamental shift in the structure of the international system from bipolarity to unipolarity. This presumed shift in structure, it is also sometimes believed, means that, since bipolarity between 1945 and 1989/91 showed itself to be more conducive to peace than had multipolarity prior to 1945, unipolarity might be an even stronger force for peace among the great powers in the years ahead.[1] American foreign policy itself seems to reflect the idea that US unipolarity is a force for global peace and is something, therefore, that needs to be preserved and, indeed, enhanced.[2] In light of this presumed relationship between polarity and the likelihood of war, scholars and policy analysts have devoted themselves to three key questions: will American unipolarity produce an even more peaceful world than that achieved during the Cold War, will US unipolarity be undermined by the counteractions by individual lesser states or by balancing coalitions of such states, and can American policy itself extend US unipolarity or will it bring into being counter-balancing by other states?[3]

Given its importance to the scholarly and policy communities, it may be helpful to examine the premise that there is a systematic relationship between the power-based polarity of the international structure and the prospects for peace and war. That effort has been pursued in the past, and it is taken up again in the pages to follow. The effort below, in other words, as suggested by the introduction to this volume, is directed toward thinking seriously about the meaning of power in international relations.

The main finding that emerges from that examination is that there are very few empirical or logical grounds to believe that the polarity of the international structure influences the incidence of war or the chances for peace. Hence, while there may be interesting questions to address regarding American pre-eminence, such as whether it promotes global economic openness, it does not appear to be likely that the existence, or not, of American unipolarity matters very much in regard to the question of whether we are likely to witness greater peace or more wars in the years to come.

To develop this line of analysis, in the pages below I will concentrate on Kenneth Waltz's thinking on the relationship between polarity and the risk of war. I will do so for two reasons. First, Waltz, in developing a structural realist understanding of world politics, offers the clearest and most persuasive exposition on the subject of polarity and international politics and, in particular, on the question of how variance in polarity can lead to variance in the incidence of war. Second, most of the writers in recent years who have taken up the subject of polarity and war have more or less built their ideas on Waltz's understanding of the relationship between the former and the latter, and, therefore, it is his ideas on this subject that merit the closest attention.

The discussion below proceeds in four steps. In the first main section, I review Waltz's thinking on how polarity can influence the prospects that major states, and others, will fight or be at peace with one another. Then, in the second section, I review some of the main studies that have sought to investigate whether this relationship between polarity and war actually obtains and find there that there are weak underpinnings for the view that there is some systematic relationship between polarity and the risk of war. The third main section explores three possible reasons why there may be a mismatch between the elegance of Waltz's argument that polarity influences the incidence of war and the paucity of empirical support for that argument. Finally, while I suggest that Waltz's polarity thesis has serious limitations as a way of understanding the causes of war and the conditions for peace, there may be directions that structural realism might take to shed light on this central problem in international relations, and in the final main section I identify four such directions.

The Waltzian polarity thesis on war

Throughout all of international history, according to Waltz, the structure of the international system has had two constants: first, a unique political 'organizing principle' by which states are arranged, namely, the absence of an effective authority to which states can appeal for protection; and, second, a similar 'character' of states, namely, their tendency, as a result of their finding themselves in the same context of anarchy, to seek to fulfil similar functions, such as defence, intelligence and representation of interests towards one another (Waltz 1979: 88–97). The third element of Waltz's understanding of international structure relates to its polarity. For Waltz, polarity is defined as the distribution of capabilities among the major, structure-producing states. He argues that 'Students of international politics make distinctions between international-political systems only according to the number of their great powers', and posits later that 'The structure of a system changes with changes in the distribution of capabilities across the system's units' (Waltz 1979: 97, 99).

Waltz, then, defines polarity as the distribution of power among the great powers during a given period. He goes on to argue that the polarity of the international structure affects the level of international 'stability' that obtains during that period. In his early work on polarity, Waltz defined international stability largely in terms of (1) duration of time during which the structure of the international system, that is, the number of great powers, remains in effect; and (2) the risk of war among the great powers. In that early work, Waltz seemed to believe that the bipolar structure of the international system that had emerged in 1945 was highly stable both in terms of being more entrenched and more peaceful than the multipolar structure had been in effect between roughly 1650 and 1945 (Waltz 1964: 881–909; Waltz 1967: 215–31). By 1979, Waltz seems to have doubted that bipolarity would last longer than multipolarity, for he suggested that the bipolar system 'appears robust, but is unlikely to last as long as its predecessor' (1979: 162), and, in particular, he raised the question of whether the USSR 'can keep up' with the USA (Waltz 1979: 179–80). At the same time, Waltz in 1979 asserted that 'the barriers to entering the superpower club have never been higher and more numerous', and therefore 'The club will long remain the world's most exclusive one' (Waltz 1979: 183).

Although Waltz, by 1979, was not sure that bipolarity would endure longer than multipolarity, he retained his view that a bipolar structure of power is associated with a lower risk of war among the great powers than is true of a multipolar structure of world politics. Before looking at his views on this subject, it should be noted that there is some ambiguity in Waltz's specification of the variation in the *types* of wars that he believes have varied as a function of polarity. On the one hand, in *Theory of International Politics*, he seems to suggest that the polarity of the international structure only affects the incidence of wars between or among the *major states* that defined the structure during the two periods. For example, Waltz argues that by virtue of internal balancing, 'since 1945 the world has been stable, and the world of *major powers* remarkably peaceful'. He suggests as well that, just as small numbers of large firms makes each large firm's survival more likely, so too, 'Internationally, especially with present-day weapons, stability appears as an important end if the existing system offers the best hope for peaceful coexistence *among great powers*'. Similarly, Waltz, in his discussion of the mechanisms by which multipolarity and bipolarity might bring about serious disputes among the major states, namely, miscalculation and overreaction, respectively, suggests that the latter is the 'lesser evil' because miscalculation may 'bring the powers to war' while overreaction may produce a tendency toward 'limited wars' (Waltz 1979: 121, 136, 172, emphasis added).

Thus, in *Theory of International Politics*, Waltz seems to suggest that his views on polarity and war should be assessed in terms of whether it provides a reasonable account for the periodic outbreaks of war among the eight to twelve different great powers that constituted the multipolar structure of world politics prior to 1945 and the absence of war between the only two comparable, structure-constituting powers after 1945, the USA and the

Soviet Union.[4] However, in his 1993 essay, 'The Emerging Structure of International Politics', Waltz seems to suggest that polarity may have an effect on a relative risk of wars not just between the major structure-forming states but among states in general. That is, he puts forward the view that 'The multipolar world was highly stable, but all too war-prone', and in contrast 'The bipolar world has been highly peaceful, but unfortunately less stable than its predecessor' (Waltz 1993: 45). Here, Waltz re-emphasises his view that polarity has a big impact on the risk of war, but he does not restrict the scope of wars that may be affected by polarity to those only among the powers constituting the structure of the two eras. Instead, he seems to be suggesting that the multipolar period was *in general* more prone to wars than was the bipolar era.

Testing the Waltzian polarity thesis

From the discussion above, there would seem to be at least two ways to assess the utility of Waltz's polarity variable in regard to the question of war and peace: first, whether variation in it between Westphalia and the present helps account for variation in the frequency of wars among the 'great powers' constituting the international structure at a given time, and, second, whether its variation can help explain changes in the incidence of wars in general.

If we employ the first standard, directed to the question of war between the structure-constituting states, then it would seem that Waltz's understanding of the importance of polarity is both interesting and hard to judge and thus, ultimately, difficult to accept. On the one hand, we know the USA and the Soviet Union never fought a war against one another, and we also know that, between Westphalia and 1945, the eight to twelve great powers that constituted the multipolar structure of global politics fought all too many wars against one another. On the other hand, except for the period from roughly 1945 to 1949, there is another 800-pound variable that also perfectly correlates both with the change in the incidence of major-power war and the incidence of change in polarity, namely, nuclear weapons. As we will see below, there are good reasons to believe that it was nuclear weapons that kept the peace between the two superpowers after the Second World War, and there are grounds to doubt whether polarity contributed either to the major-power wars that occurred before 1945 or to the super-power peace that developed thereafter.

What about the possibility that bipolarity dampens the incidence of all kinds of military conflicts between states, while multipolarity is associated with a heightened risk of such confrontations? To date, studies have produced ambiguous results, but overall they seem not to favour the broader rendering of the Waltzian polarity thesis. For example, Mansfield (1992) found in a multivariate statistical analysis a discernible relationship between polarity and the incidence of war among all states between 1815 and 1964 in a manner that accords with Waltz's expectation about the impact of polarity, namely, that more wars occurred in the context of multipolarity as opposed to bipolarity. However, Mansfield cautioned that this finding was not robust across the two main data sets he employed in his analyses; his models did not control for the impact of nuclear weapons on the incidence of war after 1945 (Mansfield 1992: 3–24), and, in later work, he found no relationship between war and polarity (Mansfield 1994: 88–9). So too, Mearsheimer (2001) compiled and differentiated the number of wars during the multipolar and bipolar eras and found, as did Mansfield in 1992, that more occurred during the former than the latter. However, in his analysis, Mearsheimer did not control systematically for the influence of other possible causes of war and peace, most particularly nuclear weapons (Mearsheimer 2001: 334–59).

In seeming support of the polarity thesis, Bennett and Stam (2004) found that the risk of wars and other forms of militarised disputes was less during the post-Second World War period than the inter-war or pre-First World War eras. Bennett and Stam did include in their models of directed dyads and military conflicts a measure for joint possession of nuclear weapons. However, they point out that, because that variable is highly correlated with the polarity measure, they could not in their statistical models distinguish between the impact of polarity and nuclear weapons. Hence, they caution that, instead of bipolarity rather than multipolarity, 'it could be that nuclear weapons are contributing to the relatively low risk of war after World War II' (Bennett and Stam 2004: 147).

Huth, Bennett, and Gelpi have put forward a more definitive assessment of the polarity thesis: they suggest that structural polarity had no effect on the likelihood between 1816 and 1975 that great powers (a category which included China from 1946 onward) would initiate militarised disputes with one another (Huth *et al.* 1992: 504–6). In a subsequent essay they also found that, between 1816 and 1984, polarity had no effect on the likelihood that states would escalate such militarised disputes (Bennett *et al.* 1993: 616–17). In both instances, it should be noted, the research team controlled for a variety of alternative factors, including the possession by states of nuclear weapons (which they found had no effect on the likelihood of the initiation of conflicts between states but had a strong dampening effect on the escalation of such conflicts). Finally, even though they did not include a variable for nuclear weapons, Gortzak, Haftel and Sweeny found no discernible relationship between polarity of the international system and the onset of wars between 1816 and 1992 or of the initiation of lower-level militarised disputes between states (Gortzak *et al.* 2005: 81).

In sum, there do not appear to be solid scholarly grounds in support of the view that polarity systematically influences the likelihood of war or other forms of militarised conflicts between the structure-defining states in the international system or other states in the system. The studies that point in the direction of support for the polarity thesis do not control for a major alternative explanation, nuclear weapons. Studies that do include nuclear weapons are unable to differentiate between their impact and that of polarity, or they find that polarity does not have a clear, discernible impact on the risk of war between states. Some four decades after Waltz presented the view that peace was more likely to obtain in the context of bipolarity as opposed to multipolarity, a long line of empirical scholarship has not yet found that to be the case, raising the possibility that the relationship between polarity and war is simply not 'out there'.

Problems with the Waltzian polarity thesis on war

There are at least three serious problems with the Waltzian polarity thesis on the sources of war, and it could well be that one or some combination of these problems is at the root of the difficulty scholars have encountered in observing an impact by polarity on the risk of war. First, there may be difficulties with Waltz's characterisation of the actual polarity of the international structure during at least a part of the Cold War. Second, and more serious, there are grounds to doubt the operation of the mechanisms that, according to Waltz, are supposed to form the causal link between different forms of polarity and different risks of war. Finally, and perhaps most serious, nuclear weapons may obviate Waltz's structural-realist logic on polarity and war.

Was the Cold War bipolar?

As noted above, Waltz argues, in the first place, that the years after the Second World War were more peaceful than they had been before that war; second, the period following the Second World War was bipolar while that before it was multipolar; and third, and by consequence of the first two points, compared to multipolarity, bipolarity is associated with a reduced risk of war. Central to this line of reasoning is of course the premise that the period after the Second World War (at least until sometime after 1991) was bipolar. We all remember the Cold War, and the seeming centrality of the Soviet–American competition to world affairs, and so it is natural that we would tend to concur with Waltz's characterisation of the period as bipolar. But was the period from 1945 to the early 1990s really bipolar? Using at least one strand of Waltz's own thinking about the constitution of polarity of the international structure, doubts can be raised about that coding.

As noted above, international polarity is largely defined by Waltz in terms of the distribution of capabilities among states and, in particular, the states with the greatest capabilities. For example, in *Theory of International Politics*, Waltz posits that the international structure is defined 'by counting states', and he goes on to specify that 'In the counting, distinctions are made only according to capabilities' (Waltz 1979: 99). Waltz does not provide much detail on the procedure one might use to measure the capabilities of states and thus to identify the structure-constituting states at a given point in history (see Schmidt in this volume). It appears, however, that Waltz believes that a given state's rank, and, hence, the structure of the international system, is the product of some unspecified way of the estimating the individual and combined capabilities that states may or may not possess at a point in time. This composite-score approach seems to be what Waltz has in mind when he says that the ranking of states 'depends on how they score on *all* of the following items: size of population and territory, resource endowment, economic capability, military strength, political stability and competence' (Waltz 1979: 131).

It should be noted that it is difficult to measure the effective military strength of a given state without also taking into account the military forces of the enemies it might fight; that is, the power of a given state cannot readily be assessed when it is not related to the scope and domain of the application of that power (Baldwin 2002: 182–3). Moreover, it is extremely difficult to know what constitutes political stability, and especially governmental competence. Nevertheless, it could be argued that on the basis of the range and magnitude of their raw capabilities, and the number of issues and countries over which they held sway, Waltz reasonably saw the USA and the Soviet Union as being in a class by themselves during much of the Cold War, and thus he viewed the structure of the international system as being bipolar.

In his 'Emerging Structure' essay, however, Waltz suggests that bipolarity remained in effect militarily, and would continue to do so, because 'Russia can take care of itself' (Waltz 1993: 52). Here we have a shift away from a simple national accounting basis for polarity identification, that is, one that focuses on ranking countries on how they score across a range of types of capabilities, to one that revolves around the functionality of those capabilities, and, in particular, around the ability of a state to achieve and retain the status of being a consequential and independent actor in world politics even if others try to reduce that state's importance or independence.

If we move away from Waltz's elements-of-power basis for structural pole-counting and instead employ his view that a state constitutes a 'pole' in the international structure by virtue of being consequential and being able to 'take care' of itself even in the face of efforts by others to do it harm, then it is quite arguable that the international structure ceased to be bipolar sooner than we usually think. That is because China during the 1960s and 1970s came to be both a consequential state and one that could 'take care' of itself even when severely challenged. During that period, China not only retained a large land army (which had recently fought the USA in Korea to an utter standstill) but it also began to develop a nuclear-weapons capability. It was also locked in a contest with a major country that wished it harm: the Soviet Union. Soviet leaders were seriously worried about the rise of Chinese power throughout this period; the two states had ideological disputes that were as bitter as those between each and the USA; China and the USSR actually experienced significant direct military clashes in 1969 (something that never happened between the USA and the USSR); and the USSR apparently gave careful thought to launching a preventative war against China before it could develop a full-fledged nuclear arsenal.[5]

The Soviet Union elected not to go to war with China in part perhaps because the USA warned that this would be an unacceptable act. It is also likely that the Soviets recognised that a war with China would be long, costly and, in the end, the Chinese Communist state would never be defeated and knocked out of the international system in the way that Nazi Germany had been in 1945.

Moreover, China was not just a state that remained independent in the face of Soviet hostility, it also came to play a highly consequential role in world politics. Indeed, a good case can be made that China played at least an indirect role in the ending of the Cold War on terms favourable to the USA.[6] By the late 1970s, and in particular during 1978, we should recall that the USA and China began to deepen their relations, including the establishment of formal diplomatic relations in early 1979.[7] Especially after the Soviet invasion of Afghanistan in late 1979, the USA and China formed a strategic partnership against the Soviet Union: the USA progressively strengthened China through trade, investment, civilian technology and even limited access to US intelligence and European and US weapons and weapons-related civilian technology (Ross 1995: 120–8).

At the same time, in light of ongoing strains and moments of tension between China and the Soviet Union, the Soviets were compelled to maintain a massive military force on their eastern frontier: the allocation of Soviet combat divisions to the Soviet Far East and Siberia increased from twelve in 1961 to twenty-five in 1969 to forty-five in 1973 (Garthoff 1985: 208). The Soviets continued to maintain the bulk of their combat forces on their western borders and in the European satellite countries (especially East Germany). Still, by 1990, fully one-quarter of the USSR's total land and air forces were located along the Soviet border with China.[8]

By virtue of having to allocate such a large force to a possible second front on the East, the Soviets had a progressively less favourable chance of defeating the West in any sort of conventional war one might envision, and they were in an even less favourable position of competing with the USA in the design and acquisition of advanced weapons. Perhaps most important, by being compelled to devote a much larger percentage of economic output to the military to meet the Chinese challenge, the Soviet state was less able to invest in capital or consumer goods sectors and thus was less able to retain any semblance of social legitimacy. The USSR, in a word, became caught in a vice between a powerful America and a potent China, and the resulting pressure was in all likelihood a reason (but not the only reason) why the Soviet leadership under Mikhail Gorbachev sought reform at home and an accommodation with the West, efforts which, in combination and unintentionally, led to the fall of communism and the end of the Cold War.[9]

In light of the centrality of China to world politics during the 1970s and 1980s, arising from and consisting of its rivalry with the Soviet Union and its alignment with the USA, the world was fundamentally tripolar, not bipolar, during a good part of what we now remember as the Cold War era. If that characterisation of the international structure is correct, then studies that have coded the entire period between 1945 and the late 1980s as bipolar have been characterised by measurement error. This measurement error may explain in part such studies have not found a robust relationship between polarity and the incidence of war.

How to measure (un)certainty?

Although problems with measurement of the polarity of the international structure may be a part of the problem with Waltz's argument linking war to polarity, an even greater problem concerns the mechanisms he posits as linking the risk of war to polarity. For Waltz, it will be recalled, multipolarity breeds miscalculations among states as to their true friends and foes, and such miscalculations can end in war. In contrast, bipolarity is supposed to promote overreactions by the superpowers, and these overreactions, while they might produce 'limited wars', were less likely to end in even bigger wars.

Waltz's most extensive discussion of both of these problems is presented in *Theory of International Politics*. At the heart of his argument is the premise that the risk of war goes up in response to increases in uncertainty and miscalculation about capabilities and intentions of other states. For Waltz, states are uncertain both as to which states might be or become threats to them and which states can be relied upon to come to their aid. Thus, states have problems both in estimating the security risks they may face and the resources that might be available to them to manage those risks. Waltz then argues that both uncertainty and the consequential tendency to miscalculation are especially pronounced in multipolar systems. This is because, in the face of several powerful states, 'there are too many powers to permit any of them to draw clear and fixed lines between allies and adversaries and too few to keep the effects of defection low'. In contrast, Waltz, suggests, 'in a bipolar world uncertainty lessens and calculations are easier to make' (Waltz 1979: 172). Bipolarity still has a problem, overreaction, which for Waltz seems to occur insofar as 'Bipolarity encourages the United States and the Soviet Union to turn unwanted events into crises, while rendering them relatively inconsequential' (Waltz 1979: 172).

At the core, then, of Waltz's polarity argument is that there is greater uncertainty among the great powers during periods of multipolarity as opposed to bipolarity, thus increasing the risk of miscalculations leading to war among them. How are we supposed to identify that heightened uncertainty, or the greater tendency towards miscalculations? Here Waltz provides remarkably little discussion or guidance. Waltz refers repeatedly to the period prior to 1914 as a paradigmatic instance in which uncertainty and miscalculations about allies and enemies were engendered by multipolarity. However, he provides no coding scheme or evidentiary basis by which we can estimate whether miscalculations or uncertainty were widespread during the crisis of 1914 or the years leading up to that crisis. He does not provide a basis for determining, for example, that France was less confident of receiving aid from Britain against Germany in 1910 or 1914 or even 1938 than France was confident that it would be protected by the USA against the Soviet Union in 1950 or 1960 or 1970.

Moreover, given that French and other European leaders were progressively worried that US–Soviet nuclear parity was eroding the American nuclear deterrent guarantee made to them, a case could be made that uncertainty about the US commitment to Western Europe after the Soviets attained nuclear parity was at least as great as the uncertainty that obtained among the two main European blocs in 1914. Perhaps that it is not the case, but the point is that Waltz provides us with no basis for making that assessment. Further, Waltz provides us with no empirical basis by which we can actually ascertain whether France was less convinced that Germany was its key enemy in 1914 and 1939 (compared to Russia, for example) than Germany was convinced that the Soviet Union was its key adversary in 1950 or 1960 (compared to the USA, for example).

In sum, it could be argued that there is no observable difference in uncertainty among the main states as to friendship and enmity during the twentieth century, notwithstanding the shift in polarity at mid-century, and, thus, no reason to believe that uncertainty-based miscalculations to a greater degree occurred before as opposed to after 1945. It might even be argued that, after the Soviets developed an assured second-strike capability, France and Germany had firmer grounds to doubt US security promises than France and Britain had for such doubts in 1914 or 1939. There is another problem with Waltz's employment of the miscalculation mechanism and the underlying problem of uncertainty. That is, Waltz does not provide us with a basis for identifying those instances in which states are making miscalculations or the cases in which they are faced with uncertainty, and, therefore, we cannot readily ascertain whether the incidence of miscalculations and the persistence of uncertainty were higher before as opposed to after 1945. Similarly, Waltz does not provide us with a sufficiently clear conceptualisation of overreaction so that we can estimate whether that kind of policy error characterised great-power decision-making after 1945 more so than it did during the nineteenth century or during the period between 1900 and 1945. Hence, without knowing what precisely we are supposed to be looking for, it is not clear whether there was a relatively higher incidence of miscalculations by major states or others during multipolarity and a relatively higher incidence of overreactions during bipolarity. In other words, because we cannot make that empirical judgement, we cannot know whether the risk of war is related to either of the mechanisms that are supposed to be associated with the two types of international structure.

Perhaps even more worrying, it is not clear whether these two mechanisms really can be differentiated from one another during an actual military crisis. For example, Waltz argues that the outbreak of the First World War was due to a series of miscalculations by Austria-Hungary, Germany, Russia and France (Waltz 1979: 165–72). However, one might just as easily argue that it was the result *both* of miscalculations – for example, by Austria of how likely it was that Russia would support Serbia and by Germany of Britain's likelihood of supporting France – *and* an overreaction by Austria to the assassination of Archduke Ferdinand on June 28, by Germany to the assassination in the form of an extension to Austria of a 'blank cheque', and by Russia and Germany when they observed each other's mobilisations of forces.[10]

Similarly, it is quite possible to argue that the Second World War in the Pacific started because Japan miscalculated as to how the USA would react to the attack on Pearl Harbor. However, at the same time, it could also be suggested that the USA may have overreacted to the Japanese movement into Indo-China, or that Japan overreacted to the oil embargo that the USA imposed on that country during 1941.[11] In sum, perhaps because Waltz has not provided a clear explication about how the miscalculation and overreaction mechanisms operate, and when we see one but not the other, it is very difficult to know whether it was one or the other or both that were actually in operation during a militarised conflict.

The power of nuclear weapons

Finally, there is a good chance that it has not been polarity that has influenced the likelihood of either miscalculations or overreactions by states during much of international history. Instead, it has been the presence, or absence, of that special class of military capability, namely, nuclear weapons.[12] Many scholars have argued that nuclear weapons have fundamentally challenged world politics. However, for the present discussion, one can directly draw upon Waltz's own arguments to demonstrate not only that nuclear weapons reduce the likelihood of war but that they do so precisely by reducing the uncertainties that are supposed to be intrinsic to a multipolar structure and thus by reducing the risk that war might occur as a result of miscalculations.

Waltz, in *Theory of International Politics*, makes it clear that nuclear weapons are an alternative to bipolarity in accounting for the long peace after 1945. He notes there that 'The simplicity of relations in a bipolar world and the strong pressures that are generated make the two great powers conservative'. Yet, he also cautions that 'Structure, however, does not by any means explain everything', that other factors are important in influencing international outcomes, and in particular that 'States armed with nuclear weapons will have stronger incentives to avoid wars than states armed conventionally' (Waltz 1979: 174–5). Further, and in reply to the thesis that nuclear weapons had obviated the utility of force entirely, Waltz suggests that the USA and the Soviet Union had learned to manage the security dilemma that so often has plagued other pairs of great powers. How had they done so? Waltz again stresses that a part of the answer to this question of peacefulness between the USA and the Soviet Union is that there were only the two of them at the pinnacle of world power. However, he then suggests that 'Second-strike nuclear forces are the principal means used', and he suggests in regard to nuclear weapons that 'Great powers are best off when the weapons they use to cope with the security dilemma are ones that make the waging of war among them unlikely' (Waltz 1979: 187).

More recently, Waltz has raised his estimate of the importance of nuclear weapons in accounting for the peace that obtained between the USA and the Soviet Union during the Cold War, and, indeed, he has made nuclear weapons coequal to bipolarity in accounting for that peace. In his 1993 essay, for example, he suggests that, after the Second World War, 'The longest peace yet known rested on two pillars: bipolarity and nuclear weapons' (Waltz 1993: 44). Waltz then provides a line of reasoning that suggests that these weapons helped to bring about the long US–Soviet peace by effectively cutting the link between uncertainty and the risk of miscalculation.

Waltz prompts this line of analysis by noting that 'Because one of the foundations of the postwar peace – nuclear weapons – will remain, and one – bipolarity – will disappear, we have to compare the problems of balancing in conventional and nuclear worlds' (Waltz 1993: 73). Waltz then draws a distinction between the problem of military security with and without the presence of nuclear weapons, and in the context of bipolarity and multipolarity. He starts by suggesting that, while in bipolar-conventional circumstances, each of the main states has to estimate the sufficiency of its forces only in relation to the other, in a multipolar-conventional world, 'difficulties multiply because a state has to compare its strength with a number of others and also has to estimate the strength of actual and potential coalitions'. In addition, according to Waltz, 'no one category of weapons dominates', and therefore 'States have to weigh the effectiveness of present weapons, while wondering about the effects that technological change may bring, and they have to prepare to cope with different strategies'. By consequence, 'In a conventional world, miscalculation is hard to avoid' (Waltz 1993: 73).

Then Waltz turns to a world with nuclear weapons, but, quite revealingly, he no longer distinguishes, as he had done in his discussion of conventional forces, strictly between a bipolar and multipolar setting. There is a clear reason for this: Waltz basically argues in this section of the paper that nuclear weapons substantially efface the differences between bipolar and multipolar military dynamics.

To begin, Waltz says there is something very special about nuclear weapons, for 'In a nuclear world one category of weapons is dominant'. By consequence, he suggests, and regardless of whether we are in a bipolar or multipolar world, 'Comparing the strategic strength of nations is automatically accomplished once all of them have second-strike forces', for in these circumstances 'all would be effectively at parity'. Waltz then points out there might be two exceptions to the stability thus produced if the relevant states have second-strike forces, namely, the development of a first-strike capability or strategic missile defences. However, Waltz discounts the ability of states in a nuclear world to attain either, due to the fact that 'no one will fail to notice another state's performing either of these near-miracles' (Waltz 1993: 73).

Finally, we come to a critical moment in Waltz's logic. Because Waltz believes that states in a nuclear world can readily observe any effort by one of them to break out to either first-strike forces or effective strategic defences, he also asserts that, in a nuclear world, '*war through miscalculation is practically ruled out*' (Waltz 1993: 73, emphasis added). Why do nuclear weapons so reduce the problem of miscalculation, even in multipolar circumstances? Here Waltz offers three replies. First, he suggests that, since states have learned to employ nuclear weapons for no reason other than deterrence, and such deterrence is readily achieved with a second-strike arsenal and almost impossible to overturn with first-strike forces or strategic defence, 'nuclear weapons eliminate the thorny problems of estimating the present and future strengths of competing states'. Second, states with second-strike forces do not need allies, thus removing another source of instability and miscalculations that could otherwise lead to war. Third, nuclear weapons, Waltz suggests, 'makes balancing easy to do' (Waltz 1993: 73).

The inference that results from this line of thinking must be that, even in multipolar settings, the risk of war that might otherwise be induced by multipolarity's encouragement of miscalculations is offset by the ease and certainty of deterrence afforded by nuclear weapons. This is exactly the path that Waltz rightly takes. As he puts the point, and referring once more the present-day movement away from bipolarity, 'Multipolarity abolishes the stark symmetry and pleasing simplicity of bipolarity, *but nuclear weapons restore both of those qualities to a considerable extent*' (Waltz 1993: 74, emphasis added).

Waltz is very clear that, even as the world moves towards multipolarity, nuclear weapons may keep low the risk of miscalculations, and, thus, we may continue to enjoy major-power peace in a multipolar environment. Moreover, this peace may obtain both at the nuclear and the conventional levels, for, as he notes, 'since nuclear weapons cannot make important gains through military conquest without inviting conquest, the importance of conventional forces is reduced' (Waltz 1993: 74). Further, while an emerging multipolarity might be developing in world affairs that involves the USA as the leading state, and with Japan, China, Germany, and Russia as challengers of one sort or another, there is no heightened risk of war associated with this structural change in the international system and the presence of these challengers to America. This, Waltz suggests, is because 'even if they wished to, none could use military means for major political or economic purposes', for 'In the presence of nuclear weapons, any challenge to a leading state, and any attempt to reverse a state's decline, has to rely on political and economic means' (Waltz 1993: 74).[13]

Nuclear weapons, in sum, have the effect of throwing a great deal of sand into the mechanism by which multipolarity engenders miscalculations by states and, thus, the risk of war between them. Hence, even if we were to agree that the many wars that occurred before 1945 were due to miscalculations and, in turn, multipolarity, it may not have been bipolarity that produced the peace from 1945 to 1991, or the peace among the major states that has obtained since then, but rather nuclear weapons may be the ultimate source of peace during both of these more recent periods. Indeed, insofar as we agree with Waltz that today's multipolar peace at the conventional level is ultimately produced by nuclear weapons, then one might argue that it wasn't multipolarity that contributed to the wars that occurred before 1945 but, rather, the absence of nuclear weapons. In any event, for much of the past, and apparently for the present and foreseeable future, 'polarity' as originally defined by Waltz simply does not seem to influence very much the likelihood of war or peace.

The polarity thesis and the future of structural-realist theory

At least four possible options can be identified for the future development of structural-realist theory in light of its problems with the polarity thesis: first, continue to investigate whether there is a systematic association between polarity and war; second, undertake efforts to observe and understand the miscalculation and overreaction mechanisms that are supposed to vary with polarity; third, reconceptualise how it might be that the distribution of power is associated with increases or decreases in the risk of war; and finally, de-emphasise the distribution of power as a variable in structural-realist theory about the risk of war and, instead, redouble efforts to investigate how other realist-oriented factors, and, in particular, international anarchy, might by itself or, more likely, in conjunction with other factors, operate to influence the incidence of war.

First, it may be useful to continue to look for the impact of polarity. It is possible that polarity matters, but we just have not yet seen its effects systematically as a result of measurement error, faulty indicators or inadequate or inappropriate statistical methods. If there is a continued interest in pursuing the Waltzian coding decision regarding periods of polarity, with the one sharp break assigned to 1945, the key requirement would be to discriminate between the impact on world politics of nuclear weapons after that year from the impact of the shift to bipolarity. One possible thesis is that, since Waltz suggests that we seem to be moving toward a multipolar system once more, we should see an increase in the risk of war notwithstanding the existence and even the spread of nuclear weapons. The problem, as noted above, is that Waltz himself has come increasingly to emphasise that nuclear weapons dampen the risk of war. To the extent that the nuclear-peace thesis becomes part of the Waltzian structural-realist perspective, the possibilities for adjudication between the effects of polarity and nuclear weapons that are presented with the re-emergence of multipolarity will be severely limited. Indeed, it may be necessary to conclude that the polarity proposition in structural-realist theory is non-falsifiable – a very bad outcome for that approach.

A second way forward might be to focus greater attention on the *mechanisms* that Waltz posits as linking variance in polarity to variance to the risk of war. That is, as discussed above, multipolarity is supposed to produce miscalculations by state leaders, while bipolarity is conducive to overreactions by them, and, somehow, miscalculations are more likely to end in war than overreactions. Given the difficulties discussed above in distinguishing miscalculation and overreaction in the midst of a crisis, I personally am doubtful that pursuit of the question of the relative incidence of these two errors is likely to constitute a productive line of research. However, if it were possible to discriminate analytically and empirically between the two sources of error, such studies could yield some interesting fruits both for the field of international studies and, in particular, for structural-realist scholarship on the problem of war and peace.

A third way to press ahead on the polarity question might be to consider alternative conceptualisations of the relationship between the distribution of power and the risk of war. At least three alternatives to the Waltzian approach could be pursued. First, it may be possible that it is not the number of major states in the international system which determines the risk of war, but rather what matters is the concentration of power among those structure-defining states. This focus on the concentration of power among the major states was suggested and launched by Singer, Bremer, and Stuckey (1972: 19–48). More recently, and using different data sets and statistical techniques, Mansfield and, especially, Bennett and Stam have found that the degree to which power is concentrated within a group of major states during a given period in time seems to be related to the risk of war and other forms of military conflict during that period (Mansfield 1994: 71–116; Bennett and Stam 2004: 147–50). In a related vein, Mearsheimer has suggested that there is an especially high risk of war when the international system is characterised by a combination of multipolarity in the international structure and high concentrations of power among the structure-defining nations, as occurred, Mearsheimer suggests, between 1793 and 1815, 1903 and 1918, and 1939 and 1945 (Mearsheimer 2001: 356–8). It should be noted that Mansfield and Bennett and Stam differ on whether the relations between power concentration and war is continuous (Bennett and Stam) or curvilinear (Mansfield). Future work could build on their findings and seek to determine what functional form the relationship might in fact exhibit in light of new methods and new data.

Copeland's positing (1996, 2000) of a 'dynamic' realist understanding of power and war points in a related but different direction. He suggests that not only should we pay attention to general changes in the concentration or dispersion of capabilities in the inter-state system, but we should also look closely at which of the structure-forming states is experiencing relative decline and which is enjoying relative ascendancy in capabilities. We should do that, he suggests, because in the face of relative decline the former might be prone to be the initiator of military conflicts with the latter and, perhaps, may be especially likely to do so in bipolar as opposed to multipolar contexts.[14]

Second, it might be productive to shift our focus from the global distribution of power to the distributions of power in particular regions. This is a line of analysis that would be consistent with the discussions of contemporary world affairs that have been put forward by Joffe (1995: 94–117) and Huntington (1999: 35–49). The argument would be that regional balances of power, and changes in those balances, could influence the risk of war or peace in those regions, but not in others. Hence, the absence of a significant change in the regional balance of power after the end of the Cold War in Europe may help explain why Germany has continued to pursue European regional integration, while Japan, in the midst of more turbulence in relative capabilities in East Asia, and, in particular, in light of the rise of China, has elected not to become a leader of East Asian economic integration but instead has maintained close economic ties with the USA.[15] This approach would have to devise a reasonable coding rule by which regions are defined and for deciding which states are in which regions; surely such countries as the USA, France and, increasingly, China would need to be assigned to more than one region. If such coding and measurement challenges were met, there is a good chance that interesting work could be done on how regional power balances influences regional conflicts.

Third, it could be that the distribution of power matters greatly in determining the prospects of war and peace, but not the power of the major states either globally or regionally, but instead the balance of power between the actual states that are locked in a militarised crisis. In other words, rather than looking at the distribution of power as a contextual matter, we might want to focus on dyadic power balances between rival states as a condition that might influence conflict and war. A number of scholars have found that such balances matter greatly in determining whether country pairs that have serious political-military problems actually go to war, including Huth, Gelpi, and Bennett (1993: 618), and Bennett and Stam (2004: 124–6).

A fourth path that might be open to structural-realist theory is to put aside to some degree its interest in power balances, however they are conceived, and instead to focus on other mechanisms that arise from the anarchical character of the inter-state system and that might have an impact on the risk of war. In pursuing this alternative, we may recall that there is available to us a long line of realist-oriented thinking on the problem of war that does not rely on a characterisation of international politics in terms of the polarity of the system in which they take place. For example, such scholars as Morgenthau (1960), Aron (1966) and Waltz himself, in his seminal 1959 study, did not assign significant weight to polarity as a motor of international politics (Waltz 1959). Instead, what has been and what remains at the heart of realist theory is the insight that states coexist in a political system without a reliable third-party arbiter of their disputes; their relationships therefore unfold in the shadow of war, and sometimes the risk of war becomes a reality. In particular, keeping their eye on anarchy rather than polarity, realist-informed scholars might investigate more fully how the anarchical context of the inter-state system persistently enables or even induces the operation of such problems as private information and strategic misrepresentation in relations between states (Fearon 1995).

Moreover, realists might expand the scope of their analysis of how anarchy might influence the incidence of military conflict by considering how anarchy interacts with variables at other levels of analysis to influence the risk of such conflict. For example, it may be profitable to consider whether anarchy-induced problems such as strategic misrepresentation *interact* with variations in domestic regime type in such a way as to influence the risk of war. For example, it is possible that the problem of strategic misrepresentation in the face of conflicts of interests and the lack of a third-party adjudicator operates differently or more or less severely between pairs of democratic states than it does between pairs of non-democratic states or mixed pairs involving both democratic and non-democratic countries. This difference in the manner in which strategic misrepresentation obtains or unfolds may have differing implications for the risk of war across the three types of dyads.

Conclusion

So long as the world is divided into a multiplicity of political agents, be they empires or states or tribes, then the realist theory of Thucydides and Machiavelli and Hobbes, and that of Morgenthau and Waltz, will continue to have much to teach us about international politics and, in particular, about the problem of war and peace. It is also likely to be true that relative capabilities between and among states have played and will continue to play an important role in influencing the risk of war, and, in that sense, the structural-realist insight that capabilities matter is likely to be found correct. However, at this point, it may be reasonable to conclude that there are both empirical and theoretical grounds to doubt the veracity of Waltz's structural-realist argument that relates wars to the global distribution of power.

Waltz, through his focus on anarchy, has surely shed great light on the dynamics accounting for war and peace. But, as I have tried to show, we must continue to think more carefully about the meaning of polarity and how it influences the risk of war and the possibility for peace.

Notes

1 Krauthammer (1990–1) seems to have coined the term, 'unipolarity', and definitely launched the argument that American unipolarity would bring about a new era of global peace. Wohlforth (1999) has been the most articulate exponent of the view that American unipolarity is both peaceful and likely to be highly durable; see also Brooks and Wohlforth (2002).

2 For a superb overview of US policy efforts to maintain its pre-eminence, see Mastanduno (1997). The best critique of the strategy remains that presented by Layne (1997).

3 On the debate about balancing against American pre-eminence, see Layne (1993); also Waltz (2000); Pape (2005); Paul (2005); Brooks and Wohlforth (2005); and Lieber and Alexander (2005).

4 At one point in *Theory of International Politics*, Waltz says that 'From the Treaty of Westphalia to the present, eight major states at most have sought to coexist peacefully or have contended for mastery' (1979: 131), but later (1979: 162), he identifies twelve states that he considers to have been, at different points between 1700 and 1945, the 'great powers' of the international system.

5 See Garthoff (1985); also Kuisong (2000).

6 For a persuasive statement of this thesis, see Tucker (1995–6).

7 On the development of a deepening Chinese–American consensus throughout 1978 that the Soviets were becoming more risk-acceptant and adventuristic, see Ross (1995).

8 See *Sino-Soviet Border Clashes*, globalsecurity.org. Online. Available http://www.globalsecurity.org/military/world/war/prc-soviet.htm.

9 For a persuasive argument that Soviet relative economic decline helps account for the the end of the Cold War and, ultimately, the Soviet Union itself, see Brooks and Wohlforth (2000–1). For a number of essays putting forward an alternative view, that shifts in material capabilities were matched or surpassed in significance by domestic political or ideational developments, see, for example, Herrmann and Lebow (2004).

10 For a variety of well-argued perspectives on the origins of the First World War and an introduction to the historical controversies surrounding the outbreak of that war, see Lynn-Jones *et al.* (1991).

11 For an important discussion of the US oil embargo and the Japanese decision for war, see Sagan (1994).

12 For a superb critique of Waltz's polarity thesis that is based in part on attention to the role of nuclear weapons, see Copeland (1996).

13 It should be noted that Waltz (1993) does not just think that nuclear weapons make war between states less likely to occur but also that they make cooperation among them more easily achieved. Waltz suggests that, in a conventional- weapons world, states have to worry about the distribution of gains if they cooperate, for states that gain disproportionately from such collaboration might convert those relative gains into advantages in military capabilities. In contrast, states with nuclear forces, according to Waltz, cannot make such conversions of disparities in economic gains into meaningful differences in military capabilities. By consequence, 'an important part of the relative-absolute gains problem is negated',

thus presumably greatly increasing the opportunities for mutually beneficial cooperation among states, even in multipolar settings.

14 For Copeland's general theory on this matter, see Copeland (1996) and Copeland (2000). As has been noted many times, states that achieve nuclear-weapon status are likely to enjoy security; however, during the transition period to that status, a country seeking to acquire such weapons might invite a preventative or pre-emptive war, thus short-circuiting the stability-producing characteristics of nuclear weapons.

15 I address this further in Grieco (1999).

5 Power and the battle for hearts and minds

On the bluntness of soft power

Steven Lukes

The concept of power, according to Professor Gilpin, is 'one of the most troublesome in the field of international relations' (Gilpin 1981: 13); its proper definition, according to Professor Waltz, 'remains a matter of controversy' (Waltz 1986: 333). Quite so. I want to begin by suggesting three reasons for both the trouble and the controversy. The first is that the concept of power is *primitive* in the specific sense that its meaning cannot be elucidated by reference to other notions whose meaning is less controversial than its own. ('Truth' is another such primitive concept.) So, in particular, as I shall argue, the concept of power is intimately linked to the notion of 'interests' and how 'interests' are to be understood is certainly no less controversial than how 'power' is to be understood. The second reason is that the concept of power is *essentially contested*. By this I mean that, when some judgement is made about the presence or absence of power or the extent of some agent's power, what counts as having or exercising power, as being more or less powerful or powerless, and so on, cannot be disconnected from various controversial assumptions, among them assumptions about what is important or significant. In other words, it cannot be disconnected from what we commonly call the 'value assumptions' of the person making the judgement.

Moreover, third, the contestedness of power – the fact that what counts as power and being powerful is controversial – matters. For, as Stefano Guzzini argues, it has a *performative* role in our discourse and, more particularly, our political discourse: how we conceive of power makes a difference to how we think and act in general and, more particularly, in political contexts. As Guzzini (this volume, p. 33) puts it, 'what it does when it is used' can have significant consequences. For example, in the last US election, the evidence suggests that many voters based their choice of the president in part on the basis of their judgements about two separable questions: about which of the candidates appeared to be the 'stronger' leader and about which of them would keep American 'strong'. Obviously enough, what 'strong' means is inseparable from what 'powerful' and, thus, 'power' mean.

To see why and in what ways 'power' is essentially contested, it is helpful to recall John Locke's completely general definition of power. To have power, he wrote, is to be 'able to make, or able to receive, any change' (Locke: 111). Even that, however, is not general enough, for it excludes the power to resist change in face of a changing environment. So let us say, extending Locke's definition, that having power is being able to make or to receive any change, or to resist it. Though extremely general, this has several specific implications. It implies that power identifies a capacity: power is a potentiality, not an actuality – indeed, a potentiality that may never be actualised. As Anthony Kenny observes, failure to see this has frequently led to 'two different forms of reductionism, often combined and often confused, depending on whether the attempt was to reduce a power to its exercise or to its vehicle' (Kenny 1975: 10).

Among present-day social scientists, the 'exercise fallacy' has been committed by those for whom power can only mean the causing of an observable sequence of events. This has led behavioural political scientists to equate power with success in decision-making. To be powerful is to win, to prevail over others in conflict situations. But such victories can be very misleading as to where power really lies. Raymond Aron was rightly critical of 'the kind of sociology that prides itself on being strictly empirical and operational' and that 'questions the utility of the term "power" to the extent that it designates a potential that is never made manifest except through acts (decisions)' (Aron 1986: 256). The 'vehicle fallacy' is committed by those tempted by the idea that power must mean whatever goes into operation when power is activated. This idea has led sociologists and strategy analysts, for example, to equate power with power resources, the former with wealth and status, the latter with military forces and weaponry. But merely possessing or controlling the means of power is not the same as being powerful. As both France and the USA discovered in Vietnam, having military superiority is not the same as having power. In short, observing the exercise of power can give evidence of its possession, and counting power resources can be a clue to its distribution, but power is a capacity, and neither the exercise nor the vehicle of that capacity.

These points are elementary, though they have led many distinguished minds astray. The trouble and the controversy begin when we seek to apply the concept of power to social and political life and relations. Note, to begin with, that nothing in the extended Lockean definition requires that an exercise of power be either *intentional* or that it involve an *active* or positive intervention in the world, and yet very many thinkers have insisted that power be so conceived.

So, for instance, Bertrand Russell defined power as 'the production of intended effects'. Max Weber and C. Wright Mills connect power with the realisation of the 'will' of the powerful, and many think that power involves 'getting what one wants'. Obviously, some abilities are abilities to bring about intended consequences. If I possess such an ability, I can, given the appropriate resources, under favourable circumstances, bring it about and, if I have such an ability, you can normally count on me to bring about the desired result, if I so choose. Yet most of our actions bring in their wake innumerable chains of unintended consequences, some of them highly significant, and some of these seem obvious instances of power. Powerful people, for example, induce deferential or compliant behaviour in others but may not intend to (and are often more successful if they do not). Pollsters can unintentionally influence the outcomes of elections. Routine rule-following can have unanticipated consequences as the environment changes. And, indeed, unintended consequences of power can be unforeseen (though to count as power they must be foreseeable). The field of economic power abounds in such instances, where decisions – to raise prices, say, or to invest – foreclose or enable opportunities and choices for unknown others and where creditors have power over debtors. What actors intentionally do always generates chains of unintended consequences, and it is implausible to deny that some of these manifest their power. Of course, those which frustrate their intentions may signify a lack of power to control events, but we can, as Mills argued, properly hold responsible, or accountable, those who have the power to advance or harm others' interests but fail to realise or attend to this.

Must power be 'active' rather than 'inactive'? To exercise power is to perform actions. Indeed, the very phrase 'exercising power' suggests such activity, while the phrase 'exerting power' suggests even more strenuous activity. There are three points to be made here. First, the distinction can be merely verbal: a vote is a failure to abstain; an abstention is a failure to vote. But second, and more deeply, 'negative' actions, or failures to act, can sometimes properly be seen as actions with consequences (indeed, they can only be specified in terms of their consequences). Sometimes, therefore, abstention or non-intervention can be a form of power. Whether we count an absence of action, or inaction, as an action depends on a judgement as to whether such inaction has significant causal consequences and on whether we are disposed to regard the actor who fails to act as responsible, in one or another sense, for so failing. But this is precisely what is at issue in deciding the question of whether negative actions can instantiate power. There is no good reason for excluding failures positively to act from the scope of power on principle.

Of course, there must be some criterion for selecting the relevant non-events as actions or failures positively to 'intervene': a baseline of expectation against which, counterfactually, the putative intervention in question can be seen as both feasible and one for which the agent could be held responsible. Of course, the power exemplified by not acting thus implies the ability to act (and vice versa). But in the analysis of power, therefore, positive actions have no special significance. To act can be a sign of weakness (for instance, conforming to the demands of repressive regimes – such as voting in a Communist election in Soviet times) and the index of an actor's power can be his ability to avoid or resist performing positive actions. So the USA under the Bush Administration shows its power by not ratifying the Kyoto protocols on climate change and not participating in the International Criminal Court.

Third, the features of agents that make them powerful include those that render activity unnecessary. If I can achieve the appropriate outcomes without having to act, because of the attitudes of others towards me or because of a favourable alignment of social relations and forces facilitating such outcomes, then my power is surely all the greater. It may derive from what has been called 'anticipated reactions' where others anticipate my expected reactions to unwelcome activity (or inactivity) on their part, thereby aiming to forestall overt coercion: a clear example is the self-censorship practised by writers and journalists under authoritarian regimes. The inactive power accumulated by such regimes is, of course, often the residue of past uses of active power, often coercive and sometimes on a massive scale. But not all inactive power results from previous active power in this direct way. Sometimes, indeed, the anticipated reactions can be misanticipated reactions: that is, mistaken because deriving from misplaced fears.

Moreover, inactive power can derive from powerful agents' properties rather than from their actions, as with the power of attraction. Charismatic power, like magnetism, exemplifies this (though in reality charismatic leaders usually work hard and with skill to achieve their effects), and the inactive power that derives from status, inducing deference, relieves those who are secure in their positions from the need to focus on acting to preserve them. So James Scott suggests that 'the impact of power is most readily observed in acts of deference, subordination and ingratiation' and comments that power means 'not having to act or, more precisely, the capacity to be more negligent and casual about any single performance' (Scott, 1990: 9). The distinction between active and inactive power can be thought of in terms of the relation between power and costs. If my power declines as the costs of exercising it actively increase, and if having actively to exercise power is itself regarded as such a cost, then one can say that inactive power reduces this cost towards zero.

Power and interests

But there is a further, and intractable, source of the trouble and the controversy. Of course we can always ask and sometimes answer the question: 'How much power does this or that agent have over some given issue?' (the question typically asked by lobbyists deciding on whom to focus or businessmen deciding on whom to bribe). But typically judgements about the locus and extent of power are comparative and range across different issues. Most commonly, we are comparing the power of different agents over different issues. We are interested in comparing their overall power in cases where the scope of their respective power is non-coincident and often non-overlapping. How do we make comparative judgements of the extent of power?

I suggest that the answer is that I will have more (overall) power than you if I can bring about outcomes that are more 'significant' than those you can bring about. But how do we judge the significance of outcomes? The most natural answer is: we look at their effects upon the *interests* of the agents involved. The concept of 'interests' points us towards what is important in people's lives. This can be interpreted purely 'subjectively' so that what is in my interests is decided by what is important to me; or else it can be interpreted in a way that incorporates 'objective' judgements, concerning what benefits and harms me, where what counts as benefit and harm is not decided by my preferences or judgements. In comparing the power of agents across different scopes, or sets of issues, we unavoidably introduce judgements about the extent to which and ways in which their power furthers their own interests and affects the interests of others. Normally, we assume that the power of the powerful furthers their interests, though this power can backfire (Susan Strange [1990] has an interesting discussion of the ways in which the USA's financial power can ricochet back on its possessors to their ultimate disadvantage). Aside from that assumption, it is the impact of power on others' interests that provides the basis for judgement concerning its extent.

Thus, most would be inclined to say that a judge with the power of sentencing to life or death has greater power than a judge without that power: the second judge might have a wider range of lesser sentences, but the first would have greater power. Similarly, the Mafia, where it holds sway, has greater power than other influential groups, organisations and governmental agencies, in part by virtue of the greater harms it can inflict and the greater benefits it can bestow. The power of multimedia magnates is greater than that of, say, advertisers or rockstars. If I can affect your central or basic interests, my power (in relation to you) is greater than someone who affects you only superficially. But, of course, the question of where people's interests lie, of what is basic or central to their lives and what is superficial, is inherently controversial. Any answer to it must involve taking sides in current moral and political and, indeed, philosophical controversies. It follows that, for this reason, comparisons of power, involving such assessment of its impact on agents' interests, can never avoid value judgements.

There are alternative ways of conceiving of agents' interests. One way is the purely subjective way of straightforwardly identifying them with *preferences* (as opposed to passing wants or whims). Such preferences may, as economists say, be 'revealed', as in market behaviour, or in voting behaviour, in actual choice situations. Call such preferences *overt*. Alternatively, they may be more or less hidden from view, because unrevealed in actual choice situations: they may take the form of half-articulated or unarticulated grievances or aspirations which, because of the bias of the dominant political agenda or the prevailing culture, are not heard and may not even be voiced. Call such preferences *covert*. Behind the equation of interests with preferences, overt or covert, lies the Benthamite view that everyone is the best judge of his or her own interests: to discover where people's interests lie, either you observe their choice behaviour or else you infer, from a close observation of what they say and do, what they would choose were choices available which are currently unavailable.

An alternative way of conceiving interests is to see them as the necessary conditions of human *welfare*: what individuals generally need in order to live lives that are satisfactory by their own lights, whatever those lights may be. Here I have in mind what political philosophers variously call 'primary goods' (Rawls) or 'resources' (Dworkin) that satisfy 'basic needs' (of which there are various alternative accounts) or else endow people with 'basic human capabilities' (Sen) or 'central capabilities' (Nussbaum). These are all various ways of specifying conditions that enable people to pursue their various purposes and conceptions of what makes life valuable and without which that pursuit is frustrated or severely impeded. Among such welfare interests are such basic items as health, adequate nourishment, bodily integrity, shelter, personal security, an unpolluted environment, and so on. Some, notably John Rawls, point to 'rights and liberties, opportunities and powers, income and wealth' and, thereby, raise the question of cultural specificity. Which of these welfare interests can be treated as universal human interests and neutral between ways of life and which are internal to particular regions of culture? But, whatever the final answer to this question, welfare interests, thus conceived, are not preference-dependent, and so they can be thought of as objective. Their status as interests of persons does not derive from their being desired by them; conditions that damage your health are against your interests, in this sense, whatever your preferences, and even if you actively seek to promote them.

A third way of conceiving interests is to see them neither as preferences nor as the necessary conditions of leading any worthwhile life but, rather, as constitutive of *well-being*: that is, comprising the leading of such a life itself. Thus, your interests may be manifest in the focal aims or long-term goals in terms of which you seek to shape your life, or in the 'meta- preferences' or 'strong evaluations' in terms of which you judge which desires and preferences would make your life go better, or in the whole network of desires, preferences and meta-preferences that living such a life involves, which you may or may not endorse. Here, one's interests are given by the content of leading a worthwhile life. Of course, what counts as worthwhile or valuable and what counts as worthless or wasteful remains a deep, central and controversial ethical question – as does the question of how it is to be answered. All I mean to do here is to draw attention to the point that interests understood this way are also not straightforwardly preference-dependent, since this view of interests as well-being allows, indeed assumes, that people can in fact prefer to lead lives that are against what they may recognise to be their well-being.

So contestable judgements of significance partly determine one's assessment of the extent of an agent's overall power, and in a variety of ways. As

Morriss observes, '[p]eople are the more powerful the more important the results they can obtain are' (Morriss 2002: 89). Furthermore, if I can affect others' interests more than you can, on some view of interests, then that, other things being equal, is a ground for supposing that my power is greater than yours. But, as we have seen, there are various views of interests. And how must I affect their interests? Favourably or unfavourably? Must I further them or harm them? Many writers on power just assume the latter: that to have power is to act against others' interests.[1] This assumption may well derive from a focus on the view of power as power over others, though this can also be interest-favouring. But there is really no reason for supposing that the powerful always damage, rather than sometimes advance, the interests of others; sometimes, indeed, the use of power can benefit all, albeit usually unequally. And is my power the greater if I can *either* favour or disfavour your interests? And when seeking to assess an agent's overall power comparatively, how do we weigh the ability to favour others' interests with the ability to disfavour them? And how do numbers count? How many persons must I affect, in respect of their interests, to have more power? How do I compare affecting many persons' interests superficially and few persons' interests deeply? The truth is that the concept of power as such furnishes no decision rules for answering such questions.

(Soft) power in international relations

So far I have sought to show that the concept of power is troublesomely controversial and to explain why and how. How does all this bear upon the understanding of power within the field of international relations (IR) and, in particular, upon our approach to the present international scene? I am aware that the discipline of IR has long been characterised by overarching debates between competing 'dominant paradigms' – notably between adherents of 'realism' and then 'neo-realism' and their critics, who advocate 'liberal institutionalism' or 'neo-liberalism' (Keohane 1986; Baldwin 1993). (I leave aside world-system theories and international political economy).

Explanations, and thus explanatory approaches, are always answers to questions – to some questions rather than other questions. My suggestion is that both the realists and neo-realists and their various critics all share an identifiable explanatory approach, which addresses certain questions and not others, distinctive questions that arise out of the characteristics of the field, notably the question: given persisting conflicts of interests, what prevents and what promotes international cooperation? The contending paradigms share in common an approach that focuses on collective actors of various kinds, strategically pursuing their interests within a distinctive kind of environment. These interests are taken as given, though different scholars may differ over what they are; the point is that this approach does not focus on how those interests are determined or influenced. All are concerned with the agents of power – those who possess and exercise it – with the distinctive structures within which they interact, in pursuit of their respective interests and with the relations between those agents and structures.

Of course, within this framework, participants in these debates differ about how these various elements are to be interpreted and, thus, on a range of issues. Which are the most salient agents: states or non-state actors, such as international organisations, transnational social movements, private industry and epistemic communities? What are the interests motivating actors and, in particular, states? Under what conditions does cooperation among states occur? Is it just a temporary phenomenon, driven by states' self-interest, and what is that? Within which structures do these actors act and interact – and how are these structures to be conceived, as 'distributions of capabilities among units' (Waltz) or as also incorporating rules and norms, even ideas, or indeed as also including the relationships among the formal rules, informal customs and conventions, and the patterns of interaction among the players? Both neo-realists and neo-liberals give the (paradoxical) answer that the international structure is one of *anarchy* – but then the question arises of how it is to be understood: if anarchy is the absence of government, which features of government are taken to be absent? Neo-liberals focus on international institutions and regimes as sometimes favouring the prospects for cooperation, whereas neo-realists focus on states, in instrumentally rational pursuit of their vital interests, preoccupied with maximising their relative gains vis-à-vis other states and their own security and predisposed towards conflict and competition.

Rather than entering into these debates, I want to focus on one piece of theorising they have generated, partly for its intrinsic interest, partly because I take it to exemplify the limits of this general strategic agents-interacting-within-structures explanatory approach and partly because it seeks to extend that approach by incorporating the determining or influencing of agents' interests as a topic of explanatory concern. I also wish to discuss it because of its apparent but deceptive similarity to arguments I have made elsewhere. I refer to Joseph Nye's reflections on 'soft power' (Nye 2004b) – which, in Nye's conception, might seem to be a cousin of what I have called power's 'third dimension': the power to shape, influence or determine others' beliefs and desires, thereby securing their compliance (Lukes 2005).[2]

Soft power, for Nye, contrasts with hard power, notably economic and military, which 'can rest on inducements (carrots) or threats (sticks)'. Nye thus proposes three kinds of power: 'military, economic and soft' (Nye 2004b: 30). This suggests a threefold schema of coercion, inducement (both of them 'hard') and a third term, labelled 'soft'. Soft power 'rests on the ability to shape the preferences of others'. It is, he says, 'getting others to want the outcomes that you want'; it 'co-opts people rather than coerces them' (Nye 2004b: 5). Soft power is 'not merely the same as influence. After all, influence can also rest on the hard power of threats or payments. And soft power is more than just persuasion or the ability to move people by argument, though that is an important part of it' (Nye 2004b: 30).

Soft power, Nye writes, 'is the ability to attract, and attraction often leads to acquiescence'. Its resources are those 'that produce such attraction', such as 'an attractive culture, ideology and institutions' (Nye 2004b: 6–15). When, he writes,

> you can get others to admire your ideals and to want what you want, you do not have to spend as much on sticks and carrots to move them in your direction. Seduction is always more effective than coercion, and many values like democracy, human rights and individual opportunities are deeply seductive.
>
> (Nye 2004b: x)

Nye's central practical and political concerns, both immediate and more general, are clear. Observing that the 'sharp drop in the attractiveness of the United States' after the attack on Iraq, 'made it difficult to recruit support for the occupation and reconstruction of Iraq', he comments that '[w]inning the peace is harder than winning a war, and soft power is essential to winning the peace' (Nye 2004b: xii). In the context of the war on terror, 'the means the Bush administration chose focused too heavily on hard power and did not take enough account of soft power. And this is a mistake, because it is through soft power that terrorists gain general support as well as new recruits' (Nye 2004b: 25).

More generally, Nye argues that

> the countries that are likely to be more attractive and gain soft power in the information age are those with multiple channels of communication that help to frame issues: whose dominant culture and ideas are closer to prevailing global norms (which now emphasise liberalism, pluralism and autonomy) and whose credibility is enhanced by their domestic values and policies.
>
> (Nye 2004b: 31–2)

In short, to 'cope with a world in which the soft power of others is increasing, the United States will have to invest more in its own soft power resources, and learn to wield its own soft power more effectively' (Nye 2004b: 98). In considering the 'soft power of others', Nye turns his attention to 'the soft power of Wahhabism', which he calls a 'sorcerer's apprentice that has come back to bedevil its original creator', the Saudi Government (Nye 2004b: 96). In the context of a 'civil war between radicals and moderates within Islamic civilization', he writes, 'the soft power of the Islamists is a disturbing symptom and a warning of the need for Americans and others to find better ways of projecting soft power to strengthen the moderates' (Nye 2004b: 97). Notice that Nye makes no distinction between different ways in which soft power can co-opt, attract and entice those subject to it, between different ways in which it can induce their acquiescence. In short, he draws no distinction between modes of persuasion or ways of 'shaping preferences'. He simply says that the USA, as an agent with power, must be more strategically effective in wielding its soft power and 'projecting' its values. In order to bring the limitations of this conception into view, let us focus on this example of 'the soft power of Wahhabism' in the context of a 'civil war between radicals and moderates within Islamic civilisation'.

The soft power of the Wahhabists

In his recent book, *The War for Muslim Minds: Islam and the West* – whose original French title, oddly enough, is 'War at and for the Heart of Islam', *La Guerre au coeur de l'Islam* – Gilles Kepel (2004) focuses on that very context. The war in question is a war for what the British in Malaya christened 'hearts and minds'. In Kepel's view, the crucial battleground where this war is being fought is Western Europe, where 10 million immigrants from Muslim countries live, whose children were born in Europe and who hold citizenship in a European nation. These were 'educated in European schools, speak European languages and are accustomed to European social practices' (Kepel 2004: 295). Kepel offers us both a positive and negative vision of the future. His positive, optimistic vision of the future is to see

> the vast majority of these young people as the ideal bearers of a modernity bestowed on them as Western Europe's newest citizens. By the example they provide, they are potential purveyors of these values to the Muslim countries from which their families emigrated. They offer an alternative to increased religiosity, which has served as both ideological shield for corrupt authoritarian regimes and as an outlet for social rage of a dispossessed population. In this reading of the future, Europe's young Muslims will become the international vectors of a democratic project whose success they themselves embody – by blending innate Arab or Muslim traits with acquired European ones.
>
> (Kepel 2004: 291)

If this is to happen, Kepel writes, 'it is imperative to work towards full democratic participation for young people of Muslim background, through institutions – especially those of education and culture – that encourage upward social mobility and the emergence of new elites' (Kepel 2004: 295). The war of which Kepel writes is 'a battle over the right of self-definition' (2004: 287), in which the other side employs quite different means of shaping young Muslims' preferences or conceptions of their interests – a different way of inducing them to define themselves. His negative reading of the future focuses on the growing phenomenon of young people, living in housing projects in the outskirts of Paris and other cities, whose rigid Islamic identity leads them to reject cultural integration into the European environment and to embrace cultural separatism. Some – a minority – will pass from voluntary secession into violence, expressing social resentment through hatred that they justify on religious grounds. Others, more numerous, will be satisfied to turn inwards, or to dreams of emigrating from the land of unbelief back to the land of Islam. Both of these separatist attitudes have their roots in the salafist teachings and influence of some Saudi Arabian preachers.

(Kepel 2004: 50)

These offer 'instant legal opinions (fatwas) on the behaviour of devout Muslims wherever they may happen to be, accessible through telephone numbers and email addresses posted on salafist websites' (Kepel 2004: 251). The

intense indoctrination preached by the sheikhists reduces their flock's capacity for personal reasoning, which makes these followers easy prey for a clever jihadist preacher. Young people who were born in Europe tumble into jihad and are later jailed often follow a typical trajectory. The first stage of brainwashing occurs at the hands of a pietistic salafist imam. Later they encounter a jihadist recruiting sergeant who offers to quench their thirst for absolutes through a bracing activism.

(Kepel 2004: 256)

For salafists, Kepel writes,

all Europe is a land of unbelief, and they are obsessed by the threat of 'Christianisation' and other deviations that might affect their offspring, such as singing, dancing, co-ed schooling, sports or even biology textbooks that contradict divine revelation. The salafists see women in terms that defy any form of legal equality: this is clear from their declarations in favour of women's seclusion and their predilection for violence against women as a means of imposing correct behaviour. (Women, on the other hand, are not allowed to beat men for the same reason.)

(Kepel 2004: 283)

The freedom of conscience enshrined in European countries' laws is here

undermined by closed community identities that keep a tight rein on liberty or pit the different components of Europe's new pluralistic society against one another on ethnic, racial or religious grounds. In the early twentieth century, the Vatican brought the weight of the Index and excommunication to bear on the souls of its flocks in Catholic countries. Today, in much the same way, salafist, Hasidic Jewish communalism, and some charismatic or evangelical Christian movements – as well as various hybrid sects – endeavour to wedge their congregations into enclosures where indoctrination undermines the basic foundations of individual citizens' freedom of conscience.

(Kepel 2004: 285)

The need for distinctions

I am far from suggesting, by discussing this example, that there is a freedom-friendly 'Western' way of winning hearts and minds that contrasts with a freedom-suppressing 'Islamic' way. As this last quotation indicates, indoctrination is not unknown in the West. It is, moreover, not confined to the indicated religious contexts. There is in the West massive and continuous indoctrination, some of it strategically manipulative, much of it simply routine, that coexists with freedom of conscience, communicating racist, sexist and other stereotypes and shaping agendas, national and international, especially during times of war, including the present 'war on terror'.[3] But to explore and confirm the extent to which this is so, and the mechanisms by which it occurs, we need, as I shall now argue, distinctions that a strategic conception of power, not least in its extended 'soft' version, fails to draw.

Nor do I want to make an argument that assumes that it is ever possible in real-world social and political contexts to draw an *empirical* contrast between indoctrination and that ideal form of persuasion that consists in securing conviction through the freely exercised judgement of others, in the sense that either can exist in a pure form independently of the other. The capacity to draw this contrast is part of what enables us to distinguish democratic from undemocratic arrangements and mechanisms. Jürgen Habermas has written that 'democracies are distinguished from other systems of domination by a rational principle of legitimation' (Habermas 1979: 186). Habermas writes of democratic arrangements as those which

> can ground the presumption that the basic institutions of the society and the basic political decisions would meet with the unforced agreement of all those involved, if they could participate, as free and equal, in discursive will-formation [...]. Only the rules and communicative presuppositions that make it possible to distinguish an accord or agreement among free and equals from a contingent or forced consensus have legitimating force today.
>
> (Habermas 1979: 186, 188)

In real-life situations, of course, there are always inequalities of power, advantages and opportunities, to which people adapt their preferences, and hearts and minds are never won by pure argumentation alone without recourse to the black arts of rhetoric. Induction and deduction are invariably accompanied by seduction. Nevertheless, Kepel's examples and his discussion of them vividly illustrate the need to distinguish between different ways of securing compliance through persuasion (which is itself an ambiguous term; it can refer either to rational or to non-rational means of securing assent). We need to distinguish between different modes of cooptation, different ways in which preferences can be formed and 'self-definition' achieved. There are, indeed, two distinctions that need to be drawn here: first, between changing, by coercion or inducement, the incentive structures of agents whose (subjective) interests are taken as given, on the one hand, and influencing or 'shaping' those very interests, on the other; and, second, between the conditions under which and mechanisms by which such influencing and 'shaping' occurs, which may or may not favour 'personal reasoning' and rational judgement.

Nye's 'soft power', while relying on the first of these distinctions, blurs the second. It is distinct from coercion and inducement (both 'hard') because it involves 'the ability to shape the preferences of others', an ability that produces attraction and leads to acquiescence. On Nye's account, this ability is present not only when adherents are gained to 'liberalism, pluralism and autonomy' but also when terrorists gain general support as well as new recruits and radical Islamists gain supporters. Of course, there will be various ways in which these modes of attracting, securing and mobilising support will be interestingly similar. Doubtless, converts to 'liberalism, pluralism and autonomy' can be won by 'seduction': through propaganda and rhetoric, via compelling images and, as he suggests, the use of channels of communication to 'frame issues'.

But 'the ability to shape the preferences of others' is a troublingly obscure phrase which fails to discriminate between those causal processes which limit and sometimes undermine individuals' capacities to judge and decide for themselves and those which require, facilitate and expand such capacities. To the extent to which the latter are present, through the very practice of liberalism, pluralism and autonomy, for instance, through educational pluralism, realistic opportunities of social mobility and a favourable political context, with contending representative parties and checks and balances, then the prospects for democracy are, we may say, favoured. To that extent, those benefiting from them are empowered and enabled to resist and choose between different power relations. To label both the former and the latter causal processes, 'soft power' is to fail to make this necessary discrimination. When analysing practices and arrangements that involve the 'shaping of preferences' or subjective interests, we need, at the very least, to distinguish between those which are, in the sense indicated, disempowering and those which are empowering in their effects.

I conclude that Nye's extended version of the IR strategic conception of power is a blunt instrument. Viewing power as a set of 'resources' to be effectively 'wielded' with the aim of seduction is not a promising way of distinguishing between these importantly different ways in which people's interests can be influenced and the battle for their hearts and minds engaged.

But the (extended) strategic conception of power we have been examining is not the only way of failing to draw this distinction. There is another contrasting, and currently very popular, way of conceiving of power, one central point of which is, indeed, to put it, and its significance, into question, namely that deriving from the writings of Michel Foucault.[4] On Foucault's view, unlike the IR view, the influencing, indeed the very 'constituting' of agents' interests is the work of power. Foucault's view of power is, so to speak, subject- rather than agent-centred. Its central claim is, rather characteristically, expressed by means of a play on the very word 'subject'. The acting, choosing subject, says Foucault, is constituted through subjection (*asujetissement*) to power. Power, in Foucault's view, is productive as well as controlling. It produces, indeed 'constitutes' subjects: it forges their characters and 'normalises' them, rendering them able and willing to adhere to norms of sanity, health, sexuality, and other forms of propriety. Foucault says that these norms mould the soul and are inscribed upon the body; they are maintained by policing the boundary between the normal and the abnormal and by continuous and systematic surveillance and self-surveillance. Power, in Ian Hacking's suggestive phrase, is at work in 'making up people' (Hacking 1986).

Now, my view is that there is a valid and very fruitful idea here that is, however, clothed in extravagant Nietzschean rhetoric. The idea is that, if power is to be effective, those subject to it must be rendered susceptible to its effects. So, for instance, in contemporary societies, within interlacing networks, magistrates, teachers, social workers, psychiatrists and so on contribute to people's understandings of their various roles and interests, as active citizens, good mothers, psychiatric outpatients, and so on. The trouble is that Foucault, in his characteristic rhetorical-cum-theorising mode, says things like this: that power 'is co-extensive with the social body; there are no spaces of primal liberty between the meshes of its network' and that there are alternative 'regimes of truth' within different 'types of discourse', each with its own 'mechanisms' that 'enable one to distinguish between true and false statements' and 'the means by which each is sanctioned', determining 'the status of those who are charged with saying what counts as true' (Foucault, 1980: 142, 38). So it is not surprising that many readers of Foucault have drawn the conclusion (which some embrace and others decry) that on this view of power, there can be no liberation from power, that, as one writer has put it, 'power is ubiquitous and there can be no personalities that are formed independently of its effects' (Hindess 1986: 250) and, moreover, that rationality itself, enabling one to distinguish between what is true and what is false, is itself internal to alternative 'regimes of truth'.

I call this rhetorical version of Foucault his 'ultra-radical' view of power and observe that it has been influential in various departments of our culture, increasingly including, it seems, the study of IR. There are really profound and far-reaching insights to be gleaned from Foucault's studies of power at work, not least into the ways in which people can actively partici-pate in their own subjection to prevalent myths, seeing what is contingent as natural and failing to see the sources of what they take to be purely indivi-dual preferences. (Not that these insights are original with Foucault, though his extensive application of them is.[5]) The problem is that the rhetorical, ultra-radical view of power strips the subject of power of both freedom and reason. In short, on this view – as on Nye's – it is no longer possible to distinguish between the exercise of power as indoctrination and the pro-motion of policies, procedures and arrangements that render people more free (in Spinoza's phrase) to live according to the dictates of their nature and judgement.

Both the agent-centred, strategic view of Nye and the subject-centred, structural view of Foucault lack this distinction, the first by failing to draw it and the second by refusing to do so. I want to conclude by suggesting that it is essential to draw it and to do so in the right way. To do this, we need to focus on both agents and subjects and ask the question: exactly how do agents succeed in winning the hearts and minds of those subject to their influence – by wielding power over them or by contributing to their empowerment? How exactly do those with power 'shape the preferences' of those subject to their power? Or, better because more precisely: to what extent, in what ways and by what mechanisms do powerful agents influence others' conceptions of their own interests? And which mechanisms and which social and political contexts work to widen and which to narrow the scope for 'personal reasoning' and 'self-definition' of those subject to such power?

Notes

1 Including the present writer in the first edition of *Power: A Radical View.*
2 Confusingly, Nye also refers to soft power as power's 'third dimension'.
3 See, for example, Diego Gambetta's (2004) excellent discussion of the ways in which official post-9/11 rhetoric has made it 'hard to think straight'. On a similar theme, see Robin (2004).
4 For a fuller discussion and for references to Foucault's writings, see Lukes (2005: 88–99).
5 For example, in his study of disciplinary power in Foucault (1995) and in his account of the rise of 'bio-power' in Foucault (1988), especially the discussion of the 'care of the self' in Vol. III.

6 Why 'soft power' isn't so soft

Representational force and attraction in world politics

Janice Bially Mattern

Since 9/11, the Bush administration has consciously refashioned the American role in world politics from that of benign hegemon to that of neo-imperialist. It has abandoned the 'soft power' politics of constructive engagement and multilateralism in favour of the 'hard power' politics of the war on terrorism. But as the increasingly unpopular Iraq war runs headlong into rising expenses and American causalities it is seen as inevitable – and for many, preferable – that the US war on terrorism will eventually have to rely much more on soft-power political strategies. Understood as the ability to achieve desired outcomes through attraction rather than coercion, soft power can, advocates claim, make allies out of Islamists, repair US relationships with its disenchanted allies and even put 'third world' states on the right path toward development (Nye and Owens 1996; Lennon 2003; Fukuyama 2004; Nye 2004a, 2004d). In this way, soft power promises to be a 'means to success in world politics' (Nye 2004b). Indeed, soft power is touted not just as a tool for the USA to use in its effort to right its relations but as a tool that can be used by any country or any actor in world politics to achieve a greater degree of influence over the dynamics of world politics (Maley 2003; Smyth 2001).

At the same time, however, soft power remains rather poorly understood. For instance, soft power works by attraction: by convincing others to follow based on the appeal of one's ideas. But what exactly is it that makes an idea attractive or appealing in the first place? Attraction is a rather subjective experience, which raises the question of what makes something or someone alluring to some and not to others. How, the question is, does attraction happen? Questions that probe the character of attraction in the context of soft power arise not just from the academic impulse for theoretic clarity but also in relation to the practical uses of soft power. For actors who aim to deploy soft power, success will ultimately depend on knowing how exactly to make their ideas and themselves attractive to a target population. It is thus unfortunate for state and non-state strategists alike that international relations (IR) scholars have not engaged in explicit inquiries into attraction as it applies to world politics. Indeed, as I argue below, to date, the literature has been satisfied with accounts of attraction that rest either on unexamined assumptions about its naturalness or on a particular type of circular logic characteristic of Habermasian approaches to persuasion. In response, this essay seeks to offer an alternative framework for thinking about attraction in world politics – one upon which a more rigorous, logical and, thus, practically useful model of soft power might be built. Ultimately, such a model should be able to sustain empirical inquiry and so shape useful policy practice, but for now the goal is simply to offer a basic sketch of attraction.

My starting point, which tracks at first with the (ultimately flawed) Habermasian-inspired approach, is that attraction is constructed through communicative exchange. Thus, I abide the basic constructivist insights that 'reality' – the broadly accepted facts of the world and the socially expected behaviours that are implied by those facts – is not pre-given and objective, but socially constructed through an ongoing collective process. Actors interpret the world in unique ways, and as they communicate with one another about their interpretations, their communicative process enables them to whittle down the diversity of multiple interpretations into one or a few socially legitimated interpretations. Those then acquire the status of the 'real truth'. Since communicative processes occur most fundamentally through the medium of language, it follows that 'reality' is a *sociolinguistic construct*.[1] The same is true for the 'reality' of attractiveness. It is a sociolinguistically constructed 'truth' about the appeal of some idea, an interpretation that won out over many other possible interpretations through a communicative process.

And yet, as Jean-François Lyotard has famously noted in response to Habermas's version of constructivism and communicative exchange, if one's goal is to get some idea or thing anointed as attractive 'in fact' or in 'reality' – which is precisely why soft power is appealing to the policy community – persuasion is not likely to be the most effective strategy. This is because, as a method of communicative exchange, persuasion functions through argument, and argument, in turn, rests upon evidence-based reasoning. As Lyotard argues, though, in the context of 'reality' construction, interlocutors often don't even share understandings of what counts as evidence, and, thus, they cannot reason about it. On the contrary, in such a situation, actors often have incentives, which are rooted in the ontological (in)security of their sociolinguistically constructed subjectivity, to fix the terms of the 'reality' in question in a manner that is congenial to the perpetuation of their Self – regardless of others' views of the 'evidence'. Thus, rather than trying to persuade one another of the 'true' meaning of 'reality', they *fight over it* (verbally).[2] They sociolinguistically construct 'reality' not through evidence-based argument but through *representational force*.

Representational force is a form of power that operates through the structure of a speaker's narrative representation of 'reality'. Specifically, a narrative expresses representational force when it is organised in such a way that it threatens the audience with unthinkable harm unless it submits, in word and in deed, to the terms of the speaker's viewpoint. The unthinkable harm threatened, however, is not physical, for that would imply physical force rather than representational force. Instead the harm promised is to the victim's *own* ontological security – it is a threat that exploits the fragility of the sociolinguistic 'realities' that constitute the victim's Self.[3] When an author effectively builds such a threat into her narrative of 'reality', she can trap the victim with a 'non-choice' between compliance with the view she articulates or tacit participation in the destabilisation, and even 'death', of the victim's own subjectivity. Because it leaves the victim no viable 'out', representational force is a very effective tool for actors whose purpose is to ensure the 'reality' status of some specific viewpoint. Actors are likely to take advantage of it in world politics, where radical disagreement about the meaning of evidence is frequent and where the stakes of 'reality' construction can be quite high.

Insofar as verbal fighting via representational force does appear empirically to be a regular part of the construction of attraction in world politics, soft power is rather ironically rooted in hard power. What makes hard power 'hard' is its ability to threaten victims into compliance; that is, to coerce (Schelling 1966). Thus, where attraction rests upon coercion, the logic of a distinction between soft and hard forms of power becomes unsustainable. Certainly, the form of coercion (and 'hard' power) to which attraction (and 'soft' power) is indebted is sociolinguistic rather than physical, but it is coercive nevertheless. In this way, soft power is not so soft after all. This revelation inheres a variety of implications for those actors who wish to accumulate and wield 'soft' power.

Soft power in world politics

Few would take issue with the assertion that power is the currency of world politics. But what power *is*, exactly, remains in dispute. Military prowess and economic accumulation – both commonly recognised as hard power – are the uncontested baseline for thinking about power among IR scholars, but dissatisfaction with this simplistic conceptualisation has spurred myriad inquiries into other facets and forms of power. Among the revelations have been that power is a relationship rather than a 'hard thing'; a process rather than a 'hard condition'; and an idea or belief rather than a 'hard fact' of truth. In other words, conventional conceptions notwithstanding, it seems there is not much about power that is hard or fungible after all. And yet, when it comes to the practice of world politics (as opposed to scholarly reflection upon it) the received wisdom that guns and money are 'hard' instruments still largely holds; they are thought to speak for themselves as coercive resources and thus to work most effectively. Scholarly insight thus seems to have done little to change traditional beliefs about the nature of hard power and its practical supremacy.

But since Joseph Nye introduced the notion of soft power to the policy community (in 1990 in *Bound to Lead*) the presumption that hard power is the *only* effective means for getting what one wants in world politics has been eroding. His simple proposition is that beyond hard power there are instruments of power rooted in an actor's ideological and cultural appeal to others. This is soft power, and it promises 'a way to get what you want through attraction rather than coercion' (Nye 2004b: x). Thus, whereas hard power rests on 'carrots' and 'sticks' – inducements and threats – soft power convinces others that they should follow because of the allure of another's way of life. Of course, Nye is hardly the first to recognise that power can be expressed without making threats or promising inducements. Thinkers no less significant than Foucault (1995), Bourdieu (1993), Gramsci (1971) and others have also articulated versions of 'soft' power. Steven Lukes (2005), for instance, argues that power need not be blunt or behavioural; it can operate socially in ways that subconsciously affect the formation of preferences. Even within IR proper, scholars have been quite comfortable with 'softer' variations of power, especially the idea that it can be exercised through influence and legitimacy (Jervis 1976; Sartori 2002; Price 1998; Lebow 2005). Nonetheless, in contemporary mainstream scholarship and foreign-policy circles, it is Nye's account that has captured imaginations. Perhaps this is because Nye does more than just call attention to soft power; he also treats it as a platform for action, arguing that actors have, can and should continue to find ways to effectively develop and use this power resource. In this way, Nye conceives of soft power in much the same way as many do hard power: as a tangible tool that can be amassed and deployed through concerted effort.

So how, according to Nye, does one 'amass' soft power? As Nye argues, the sources of soft power lie in the attractiveness of political and cultural values, ideals and visions – specifically, those that are universal (as opposed to parochial) in orientation (Nye 2004b: 111). Disappointingly, Nye says nothing about why universal values are the 'right' ones or how one acquires such values. As I suggest below, this is symptomatic of the problems with Nye's account of attraction. But he does say quite a bit about how to parlay the 'right' values into soft power. He notes, for instance, that if one wants to develop soft power, consistency is key; congruity between an actor's stated values and actual action enhances an actor's appeal. Soft power also depends on others' *knowledge* of one's alluring qualities. Thus, according to Nye, regardless of how 'good' one's values and how consistent one's record at pursuing them, unless others know about it, no power can be derived. In this way, the most fundamental way to 'harvest' soft power is to spread social knowledge about one's values. Soft power, it seems, is rooted in communication.

Given that communication is so crucial, Nye draws a connection between the information age and the emergence of soft power as a practical tool in world politics (Nye and Owens 1996). Of course, Nye realises that soft power is nothing new; actors in world politics long have been engaged in activities that wield it, intentionally or not. But it is only since information technology has made it so cheap and easy to communicate with others around the world that using soft power has become feasible as part of a conscious, sustained grand strategy for all kinds of actors. This insight has become the basis for the practical suggestion that governments and other actors ought to practise public diplomacy; they ought to attempt to cultivate soft power through information and communication technologies.[4] Government agencies, academics and private think tanks have responded with vigour, devoting considerable energy and resources to developing such programmes (Zaharna 2000; Snyder 1995; Arquilla and Ronfeldt 1999; Nye 1999, 2003a, 2004b). Indeed, widespread investment in public diplomacy suggests that soft power has challenged the default dominance of hard power in world politics (Dufresne 1998; Jones 2003).

For many, this is a welcome development. To policy practitioners, for instance, the appeal of soft power is that it is relatively cheap and it does not involve sending young citizens off to war (Nye 2004b: x). Soft power may also appeal to individuals and collective non-state actors since, in contrast to hard power, which the government controls through military and economic policies, soft power is available to any actor that can render itself attractive to another (Nye 2004b: 90, 99). Third, reliance on soft power is likely to appeal to ethically concerned people. After all, hard power works via coercive force; it compels the submission of its victims through threats of unbearable harm (Schelling 1966). Thus, where hard power dominates, so do moral dilemmas. Insofar as soft power rests on attraction, it seems to promise an ethically superior method of political interaction.[5]

A final constituency that may be satisfied by the concerted incorporation of soft power into the practice of world politics are IR scholars. After all, Nye's account of soft power subtly integrates into the policy domain some of the long-standing scholarly insights about the workings of power, which have, until this point, been largely ignored as irrelevant to the bottom line of how to use power. Consider, for instance, the insight that power is a social relationship rather than some 'thing'. While this is true of hard power as well as of soft power, in the case of the latter it is much harder to ignore in practice. Unlike guns, for instance, which are presumed to endow someone with the power to coerce regardless of who they are and over whom they wish to wield their power, soft power only works on those who are attracted to the aspiring power-holder. As such, were soft power to become part of strategic doctrine, practitioners could not use it without thinking about how it works. In order to use soft power, practitioners need to know how to make their 'position attractive in the eyes of others' (Nye 1999). This is something about which IR scholars should have something to say.

The character of attraction

So far, however, the notion of attraction has been understudied in IR. On one level, this relative inattention is not surprising since hard power/coercion has been assumed to be such a more urgent and effective practice in world politics. But soft power has been a matter of discussion for at least ten years, and still there has been no sustained treatment of attraction. The result, I argue, is a confused implicit understanding that has given rise to contradictory practical implications.

Consider Nye's treatment of attraction. As the premier contemporary analyst and advocate of soft power, it would seem crucial that Nye have a sufficiently considered and articulated view of this phenomenon. But Nye is quiet on the character of attraction. In fact, in order to figure out what Nye thinks, one must read between the lines – and even his implied account yields disappointing inconsistencies. For instance, on the one hand, Nye (implicitly) theorises attraction as a *natural* objective experience when he describes the allegedly universally attractive values of cosmopolitanism, democracy and peace (Nye 2004b: 11). On the other hand, Nye implies that attraction is a *social construct*; he emphasises the utility of public diplomacy for 'converting' foreigners so that they become attracted to one's own values (Nye 2004b: 111). In short, Nye assigns two ontological statuses to attraction – one as an essential condition and one as a result of social interaction. This dual ontology is meta-theoretically problematic, which makes for bad theory; but, even worse, it sows confusion about the kinds of practical expectations one can stake on soft power. Practically speaking, the logic of natural attraction counsels a much more status-quo world than that of constructed attraction, for in the former there is no need (or ability) to cultivate attraction, while in the latter the possibilities for convincing others of the allure of one's values and culture are potentially vast. So, for a scholar trying to discern how much he can make of soft power and how much it can effect the shape of world politics, or for the practitioner trying to optimise soft power, the lack of clarity is troubling.

Certainly there exists other IR scholarship that invokes phenomena similar to attraction which could possibly offer the basis for knitting together a more theoretically and functionally consistent account of soft power. But that work too falls short. Consider, for instance, the now broad IR scholarship on the formation and maintenance of inter-state or inter-group collective identity. Although this literature is diverse – inspired variously by primordialist, social identity and 'mainstream'[6] constructivist theories – each approach nevertheless invokes something akin to attraction to do important work in its arguments (Huntington 1993; Wendt 1999; Mercer 1995). Each posits (though in different ways) that similarity is alluring to actors; that is, that attraction draws like actors together into the international group. Yet, like Nye, none of these approaches pays much attention to the logic of attraction upon which their theories depend. Each (even, ironically, the constructivists) offers a worryingly underdeveloped natural or essentialist version of that phenomenon. To begin with, consider the manner in which the various theories of identity-formation offer essentialist models of attraction. While the essentialism of the primordial view is obvious, in the case of social-identity theory, the presumed naturalness of attraction rests (without explanation) with the assumption that actors are always positively disposed toward like-characterised actors and that they are necessarily (naturally) repelled from unlike actors (outgroups) (Mercer 1995). In the case of constructivism, the curious and inconsistent alignment with a natural view of attraction surfaces in the claim that identity is formed through learning among actors. As Emanuel Adler and Michael Barnett (1998: 39) formulate it, identities emerge when members learn to share them, but learning, in turn, supposes a teacher. In this way, identity-formation actually depends on the teacher – someone, as Adler and Barnett argue, who is tacitly appointed to that status because other actors are simply *magnetically drawn*, or attracted, to him. In other words, international groups and the identities that underwrite them may be socially constructed, but the attraction necessary for that construction is magnetic; it is natural and pre-given.

Each of these 'natural' accounts of attraction are improvements over Nye's implied account of attraction, simply because they are explicit in their ontological assumptions. But each still has problems. Foremost is the conceptual problem of where and how something natural (essential, biological, permanent, irrevocable) sits or can exist within a collective social body. Crucial here is that international actors tend to be groups that are themselves made of groups – whether security communities and alliances made of states, civilisations made of ethnic populations or terrorist networks made of cells and nodes. This is important because it makes it difficult to envision where the 'essentiality' or locus of attraction exists in such an actor. There is no core, no corporate centre, no body or brain. Certainly, there is a metaphorical body in the membership, a metaphorical brain in the leadership and a metaphorical corporate centre in the bureaucracy. Certainly, a collective actor acts *as if* it were unitary. But it makes little sense to posit that natural essentiality can derive from such metaphorical imagery and *as if* ontology. As a result, the natural attraction model does not offer a very solid foundation upon which to predicate strategies designed to cultivate soft power. Anyway, if attraction were natural, one would not need to cultivate soft power in the first place. It would simply be there.

Insofar as the natural model of attraction in world politics is unsatisfying, a more constructivist-oriented model can be uncovered from the scholarship on persuasion. Drawing on the communicative theory of Jürgen Habermas, work in this vein seeks to model how actors use persuasive 'talk' to facilitate agreement, cooperation and better relations across nearly every domain of world politics – from security to economics to ethics to foreign policy (Finnemore and Sikkink 1998; Crawford 2002; Lynch 2000; Cruz 2000; Risse 2000). What is most relevant about this work is that because of its Habermasian inspiration, it treats persuasion as a practice that can be enacted only through *argument*, a specific type of communicative form in which interlocutors are motivated to achieve a consensus about the truth through reasoned exchange about evidence. On Habermas's view, then, argument is a way of 'wooing' willing interlocutors to agreement by illuminating the truth. Persuasion, that is, is a means of constructing attraction (Habermas 1990).

The model of attraction embedded in this scholarship focuses on how the process of arguing leads actors with otherwise divergent perspectives on a given matter to feel drawn into a consensus on a viewpoint that all embrace. There have been a variety of formulations of how this process occurs – from Nye's own emphasis on the persuasive effects of advertising, public diplomacy and 'narrowcasting' (engaging in directed focus-group dialogues), through which speakers seek to educate their audience,[7] to an emphasis, rather broadly embraced by various scholars, on framing. Framing is a practice in which speakers appeal to their audiences by taking a new or unfamiliar issue and making it familiar and salient by embedding it in social frames (Keck and Sikkink 1998; Payne 2001). And yet none of these alleged procedures for constructing attraction are true to the Habermasian spirit of persuasion; argument, strictly speaking, can only be said to occur where there is a reasoned exchange of evidence-based perspectives among willing, rational agents whose goal is truth. Public diplomacy, advertising and narrowcasting do not qualify because they are communicative practices that are undiscerning about whether the audience is willing to participate and about whether they are advancing the truth. Framing fails as well because it 'couches' the evidence rather than letting it speak for itself. For Habermas, such tactics imply manipulation not persuasion. Such communicative practices cultivate not attraction to truth but bias towards ideology.

So how would one model the construction of attraction in a way consistent with Habermas's framework of persuasion? Although some IR scholars have tried, so far it has proven a circular and unsatisfying endeavour (Crawford 2002; Risse 2000). The reason has to do with Habermas's theoretical edifice. In order to theorise away the need for interlocutors to resort to advertising, narrowcasting or other such 'truth-obscuring' communicative strategies, Habermas posits that any given communicative exchange only qualifies as an argument if it occurs in a strictly defined environment in which, among other criteria, the participants share a common lifeworld. Understood as a basic stock of unquestioned shared knowledge that orients actors similarly in the world, a common lifeworld can be more familiarly understood as a culture. What is important about a common lifeworld or culture is that actors – even collective ones – become embedded in it. It constitutes them such that they share values and ideas with one another.[8] This is significant, as Thomas Risse (2000) argues, because when actors from a common lifeworld engage in dialogue, they will recognise one another as *legitimate*; it enables the audience to listen to a speaker without distraction, distrust or disrespect; it makes it possible for the speaker to trust in the process enough to present evidence without prejudice. In this way, legitimacy among the interlocutors is what makes argument possible and what makes persuasion a resource for attraction rather than compulsion. Legitimacy, that is, is the core of the process by which attraction is socially constructed.

But this logic turns out to be circular. Legitimacy is taken as a necessary condition for true argument (and thus persuasion) where legitimacy is a function of a common lifeworld or culture among interlocutors. What this means is that legitimacy derives from shared sensibility among actors about the kinds of ideas and values that are appealing. In other words, *legitimacy comes from common attraction* in the first place. The model, as such, is regressive: attraction is socially constructed through argument among legitimate interlocutors, but the legitimacy of the interlocutors, in turn, depends upon attraction among them, which logically could only have been produced through argument among legitimate interlocutors, *ad infinitum*. Such reasoning offers no leverage over how, in the first instance, attraction was socially constructed. While it may not always matter for practical purposes what the origins of attraction are, where policy practitioners seek to deploy soft power over actors from different lifeworlds (and those are the actors that practitioners are usually the most eager to influence in world politics), this circular model is too thin on insight to be helpful. To really assess the promise of soft power as a 'means to success in world politics', a more complete and logical model of attraction is necessary – one that that does not assume attraction as a precondition for its own production.

The sociolinguistic construction of attraction

So what would a better model of attraction look like? The model I offer rejects the possibility of natural attraction, beginning instead with the assumption that attraction is a socially produced 'reality.' I argue specifically that 'reality' is produced through communicative exchange and that the type of communicative exchange through which a 'reality' of attractiveness is most likely to be produced in world politics is a competitive form called 'verbal fighting'. Since verbal fighting is characterised by representational force, attractiveness tends to be suffused with coercion. Soft power is not so soft.

Communicative exchange

'Realities' – whether of attractiveness, legitimacy or anything else – are simply cultures. They are intersubjectively constructed matrices of beliefs through which a population signifies things, people and ideas. In light of this, the question 'How does attraction happen?' can be reformulated as 'How is culture constructed?'. There are numerous ways to conceptualise the process through which culture/'reality' is constructed,[9] but at some implicit or explicit level, all of them depend on communicative exchange (Biernacki 2000: 304; Bukovansky 2002: 22; Neumann 2002). Understood as the process through which actors convey their interpretations and perceptions of things in the world to each other, communicative exchange is mediated through language – that is, through collective, socially shared sign systems. What makes communicative exchange crucial is that it enables actors to transform their subjective, privately held opinions about what they see in the world into public information. Only when a private thought is transformed through communication into public information does it stand the chance of becoming a social 'fact' and part of culture/'reality' (White 1987a). In this way, culture/'reality' is not just socially constructed; it is socio*linguistically* constructed.

To pin the onus of social construction on communicative exchange, however, is not to say that all publicly uttered interpretations become social 'facts' in 'reality'. On the contrary, for any given object of observation, there are quite possibly an infinite number of often-contradictory interpretations of its character and significance, and not all of them acquire the status of 'truth'. For instance, when asked the best type of political system, actors utter both that 'democracy is the best form of government' and that 'communism is more fair than democracy'. And yet, at least in the West, only the former has been anointed as 'true'. From this point, it follows that the primary burden of a sociolinguistic model must be to demonstrate how certain interpretations (in this case, of attractiveness) acquire the social status of 'truth' in a given population while others do not.

In this vein, I offer that the ultimate prevalence of one representation over another depends upon *communicative strategy*; that is, on *how* the speaker articulates his interpretation to listeners during communicative exchanges. This idea, which is informed by Lyotard, emphasises not merely what the speaker says, who the speaker is or to whom she speaks, but, even more fundamentally, *how* she speaks. It emphasises the particular manner in which a speaker links the phrases of her narrative together to form a coherent representation. This focus on micro-level linguistic structure differs from Habermasian and Foucauldian approaches (both of which have found expression in IR), for in those content trumps linguistic form as the key to 'reality' construction. An utterance's success at becoming 'fact' depends upon the positive resonance of its content with relevant and shared, extant 'realities' among the interlocutors.[10] However, since such resonance is only possible where interlocutors share a common lifeworld, those models can only explain how a social 'fact' gets selected among actors that are *already* mutually attracted. Those models, thus, could not envision how an incipient 'reality' of attraction might emerge, for instance, between Islam and the West.[11] In contrast, the model I offer does not appeal to a prior common lifeworld to explain how some utterances win out over others. Rather, it proposes that the ultimate determinant of whether something becomes 'true' is the communicative strategy that the speaker deploys.

Consider, then, communicative strategy. When a speaker (or author) wishes to convey an interpretation (content), she must craft words and sentences into a narrative (form) (White 1987b). Importantly, there are different ways to do so (genres). For instance, one might structure her narrative as an argument, a negotiable proposition, a metaphor, a direct challenge or so on. What differentiates genres is the strategy each entails for reaching the audience. When an author forms her narrative as an argument, she uses a genre that relies upon a strategy of persuasion to reach its audience. Accordingly, the words and sentences in arguments are linked together in such a way that the content is presented as a discovery of a truth realised through the accumulation of evidence. In contrast, where an author crafts her narrative as a negotiable proposition, she adopts a genre that relies upon a strategy of bargaining. In that case, words and sentences are linked together in a way intended to play on the mutual distaste among the inter-locutors for deadlock (Drezner 2000). Other genres have different strategic logics and give rise to different arrangements of words and sentences.

With so many communicative strategies, any 'reality' construction process begins with authors' choices about which genre to use. While in some cases an author's choice may be unconscious, unacknowledged or predetermined by the communicative community (and, thus, not much of a choice), in less institutionalised situations, such as world politics, authors think very care-fully before they speak. They think not just about content but about form as well. They base their choice of communicative strategy upon beliefs about which will be most effective for advancing their perspective to the status of 'reality', given the context and specific interlocutors involved. The question for an author, thus, is how to say what is on his mind in a way most likely to give it social standing.

As an important aside, this proposition that authors *choose* their com-municative strategy would seem to inhere some meta-theoretical claims that contradict the constructivist starting point of this model. Inasmuch as 'rea-lity' is a sociolinguistic construct, it follows that so must be the 'reality' of a being's Self. How then, one might wonder, can we square such a radically constructed ontology with assertions of actors that have interests and the agency and rationality to pursue them through concerted choices about communicative strategy? Upon reflection, however, it appears that there is nothing incommensurable about a sociolinguistically constituted Self and a capacity to strategise and act. A sociolinguistically constituted Self becomes 'real' as a function of the multiplicity of (often overlapping and intertwined) sociolinguistically produced 'realities' through which a being is situated in relation to others (Butler 1997). In other words, the Self emerges through the culture/'realities' in which it is embedded – so, for instance, my Self is constituted by the 'realities' that render me a scholar, mother, wife and so on; while the USA's Self is constituted by the 'realities' that render it a democracy, hegemon, global police officer, and so on. Importantly, it is precisely the embeddedness of the Self in those constitutive 'realities' that bestow beings with interests, agency and rational capacity. Just as the sociolinguistic 'reality' that constitutes me as a mother gives me the interest, agency and capacity to choose to stay home with my children as often as possible, so does the sociolinguistic 'reality' that constitutes the USA as a global hegemon give it the interest, agency and capacity to choose to try to order international politics in a way that perpetuates its dominance. There is, as Roland Bleiker (2000) puts it, an axis connecting the sociolinguistic production of culture/'reality' and the production of agency.[12]

An actor's choice of communicative strategy can be linked to the socio-linguistic ontology of her agency. Because her Self is a sociolinguistic construct, an author's interpretation of a given thing in the world – and so the representations she articulates during the course of a communicative exchange – are not just disinterested observations but also precious traces of her own subjectivity. If a sociolinguistic matrix of culture/'realities' is what gives her the capacity to act (author) in the first place, it follows that the content of her interpretations are both derivative of and reproductive of that matrix. An actor's representations of the world both issue from and reinforce her Self. Thus, I interpret the world through a sociolinguistic matrix of scholar–mother–wife and so on; the USA does so through that of hegemon–police officer–democracy and so on. The implication is that participation in communicative exchange offers actors an opportunity to reproduce the very 'realities' that author them into existence in the first place. Given that linguistic form is the ultimate arbiter of a representation's chance at becoming (or remaining) a 'reality', the author's choice of com-municative strategy during communicative exchange will bear significantly on her ontological security (Huysmans 1998; Mitzen 2006).

It bears emphasis that participation in communicative exchange is not optional for actors; it is necessary. If a particular Self is to survive, it is necessary to vigilantly protect the sociolinguistic matrix that produces it. In the absence of such protection, that matrix would be erased piecemeal by alternative contending or contradictory 'realities'. Participation, thus, has an urgent purpose; the stakes for an author of ensuring that her particular interpretation be anointed as 'real fact' may be as high as the integrity of her very subjectivity.[13] From this it follows that an author will *tend* to choose communicative strategies that are most effective at establishing or sustaining her representation as 'reality'.[14] In different contexts, different communicative strategies will be more and less effective. For instance, per-suasive arguing could be an effective strategy where interlocutors share a common lifeworld (Checkel 1999). Bargaining could be effective where interlocutors recognise each other as eager to reach a conclusion and willing to make compromises to do so (Schoppa 1999). And others – manipulation, seduction and so on – may work well in other circumstances. However, there are a variety of situations in which any of these strategies is likely to disappoint: for instance, in 'first encounters' (in which *if* actor subjectivities overlap they are not mutually aware of it); in situations in which all that the actors know about each other is that they are quite dif-ferent (in which case their subjectivities entail incommensurable, competi-tive 'realities'); or where actors are in the midst of a crisis with each other (during which their overlapping 'realities' are sociolinguistically 'erased'). In any of these cases, the interlocutors will be unable to perceive each other as legitimate, or they will lack adequate information to effectively discern each other's intentions. Yet such are precisely the necessary preconditions for bargaining, arguing, manipulation, seduction, and so on.[15]

In fact, since a communicative strategy is selected on its capacity to help an author advance her representation to 'reality', then even under perfect circumstances, persuasion, bargaining, manipulation, and seduction would be risky. None threaten to punish the audience if it fails to submit to the author's viewpoint, so the audience has room to refuse. Precisely because Self-preservation is bound up with advancing a representation to the status of 'reality', the most efficacious communicative strategy will be one that leaves the audience *no* room to refuse; it will seek to boldly defeat alternatives without hesitation, engagement, discussion or playful antics. With this in mind, the best communicative strategy is *verbal fighting*.

Representational force

Verbal fighting is a communicative form through which an author attempts to bully the audience into agreement with his interpretation. The strategy of this genre is representational force. A form of force like any other, representational force wields a blunt, non-negotiable threat intended to radically limit the options of the subjects at whom it is directed. In contrast to argument, bargaining, manipulation or other strategies that stop short of threatening the audience, representational force does just that. It aims to close off its victims' options by promising them unthinkable harm unless they comply in word and in deed with the force-wielder's demands. In this way, like physical force, representational force aspires to leave its victims no 'out'.

Of course, there are key differences between representational and physical force. By way of clarification, Thomas Schelling's observations about coercive force are useful. Schelling (1966: 3–4) argues that coercive force works by giving the victim the *appearance* of a choice about compliance. The choice, however, is actually a 'non-choice' since it is offered to the victim in the context of a credible threat – indeed, a promise – of some physical loss so horrifying (often death) that the victim must succumb to the force-wielder's wishes if she is to avoid it. Coercion thus works like a trap; either submit or risk death. Representational force works the same way: through credible threats of unbearable harm to its victims. However, the threats it poses are aimed at the victim's *subjectivity* rather than physicality and are communicated not in reference to material capabilities but through the way the author structures her narrative. This raises two questions: How can an aspiring force-wielder credibly threaten her victim's Self? and, How can she convey that threat through the organisation of the words and sentences she deploys to articulate her view of 'reality'?

In regard to devising threats, the answer returns to the sociolinguistic 'foundations' of 'reality' – this time, that of the victim's Self. I have argued that a subject is only as secure as the sociolinguistic matrix that constructs her. This suggests that the force-wielder can devise a threat by promising to narrate away some precious fundamental 'truth' in the configuration of 'realities' or cultures that constitutes her victim. One especially effective way to do this is by highlighting contradictions and inconsistencies in the narratives that produce the victim's subjectivity, especially in contexts that are intolerable for the victim. For instance, one might exploit the contradictions between professorhood and motherhood in the context of the tenure process. Exposing such inconsistencies can have serious material implications (e.g., diminishing prospects for tenure), but it can also, depending on how important each of the contradictory aspects of Self are to the subject in question, threaten the very logic of the victim's subjectivity. It can set off a 'domino effect' of instability among the narratives that make up the victim's Self, even leading to the collapse or 'death' of that particular subject. In fact, it is from this eventuality that the requirement of submission to representational force in word *and* deed follows. If the victim failed to *live* the 'reality' to which she submits, she would be subject to further coercion by the same threatening logic in the future (Cruz 2000).

So, how does an author construct a threat credible enough to be this effective on its victim? Since threats derive from inconsistencies and contradictions in the victim's Self, knowledge of the victim's subjectivity is indispensable to representational force. An author must be able to locate the contradictions and inconsistencies in her victims and exploit them meaningfully. Importantly, since any Self is constituted socially through discourse, no common lifeworld is required to acquire such information about one's victims. It is available through the public statements of Self that any actor necessarily makes. Nevertheless, and just like with physical force, there are various contingencies that may prevent the aspiring force-wielder from developing a credible threat. For instance, the contradiction between aspects of a victim's Self may have no effect at all on the target's subjectivity, particularly if the contradictory constitutive components are each instantiated by multiple, reinforcing narratives. In that case, a challenge to one such narrative can be tolerated without creating ontological insecurity. Alternatively, the force-wielder may miscalculate and threaten some aspect of his victim's subjectivity that is not at all central to the victim's Self. In that case, the victim may not care if it is destabilised or erased. Still, even though not all threats will be credible, all that is required for an author to at least attempt to devise a credible threat is that she pay attention to the sociolinguistic matrix through which her victim's Self is constituted.

Once the author has found a credible way to threaten her victim, she can construct her own preferred version of the 'truth' in such a way that entails that threat; she can deploy representational force. To do so, the author must narrate the particular representation that she wants to fix as 'real', but, in addition, she must arrange the words and sentences of that representation in a way that evokes the threat that she has devised. The content of her representation must be structured not as evidence to be argued, a demand to be considered, or so on, but as an ineluctable ultimatum. For instance, as I argue below, the manner in which the USA represented its war on terror in the early post-9/11 days contained in its very structural logic a promise of unbearable subjective harm to particular states unless they abided the American viewpoint. To construct this narrative, American authors situated particular words and phrases in particular relation to each other so that the combination conjured up the harm. They also placed words and sentences in such a way that offered the clause of exemption – the coercive non-choice in which the victims could avoid harm by committing in word and in deed to the USA's version of its post-9/11 policies. It is through just such an organisation of words and sentences that representationally forceful narratives leave their victims no room to refuse.

Where authors are concerned to preserve their Self, where they are able to learn enough about their victim's Self to develop a threat and, especially, where there is no relevant prior attraction among interlocutors, verbal fighting through a representationally forceful narrative structure will offer the most reliable (and so rational) strategy for an author to attempt to construct a 'reality'. In world politics – which is, relatively speaking, poorly institutionalised and full of actors who are either unsure about their relationships to one another or in the midst of crises – verbal fighting is bound to be the most common process through which the 'reality' of attraction is socially constructed. Of course, in that case, attraction rests on coercion, and so the soft power to which it gives rise is not so soft after all.

The 'reality' of American attractiveness

In support of the claim that soft power is not always so soft, consider how American attractiveness (and so American soft power) was sociolinguistically constructed immediately following 9/11. At the centre of that effort was the phrase 'war on terrorism'. On one level, the Bush administration had adopted this phrase to signify the 'hard power' actions it planned to undertake in response to the World Trade Center and Pentagon attacks. Yet, as Nye (2004b: 122) suggests, 'war on terrorism' was also intended to construct a 'reality' of American attractiveness and so to help cultivate soft power. This intention becomes clear in the administration's juxtaposition of the war on terror as a legal and morally righteous act of self-defence against the intractably lawless acts of the terrorists. The contrast obviously highlighted the attractive, good USA against the abjectly evil other. Perhaps more powerfully, though, the US intention to construct its own attractiveness is revealed by the very choice of the phrase 'war on terrorism', rather than, say, some phrase that conjured up a retaliation against the persons responsible for the 9/11 attacks. By choosing the former, the USA implicitly made a promise to defend the whole world from the whole phenomenon of terrorism. Rather than just redressing the threats that affected Americans, the USA committed to 'rooting out terrorism' altogether. In this way, the phrase 'war on terrorism' represented the USA as a strong, globally responsible leader – a 'fact' which supported the 'reality' of American attractiveness (Jenkins 2003; Beinhart 2004).

Of course, the narrative rendering of 'war on terrorism' as a reflection of American attractiveness was not the only one, and not everyone was naturally inclined toward it. For instance, in the direct aftermath of 9/11, one powerful alternative interpretation of 'war on terrorism' emerged among 'foreign publics' who worried that it would justify 'indefinite incarcerat[ion] of foreign prisoners' (Nye 2004b: 112). For these authors, 'war on terrorism' was not a 'fact' in evidence of American attractiveness but a caution about the ways in which the USA might expand its international control. From the perspective of the USA, such an interpretation was 'dissident'; if anointed 'reality' in the international community, this perspective would diminish American soft power. So the USA took (linguistic) action. Along with other actors who were already attracted to its policies, the USA sought to defeat the dissent through verbal fighting.[16] Using representational force to narrate its version of the meaning of 'war on terrorism', these authors cleared the field of viable alternative interpretations in a way that promoted theirs to the status of 'truth'. For at least the first six months following 9/11, representational force was effective; the American view prevailed as 'reality'.[17]

It worked like this: the USA first devised words and sentences depicting the war on terror as righteous, appropriate and the only logical response to 9/11, and then they linked those to the threat that 'you are either with us or with the terrorists' (Bush 2001).[18] In other words, US authors structured their narrative in a way that linked a representation of attraction to and approval of their policies with a representation that drew a line between good and evil. The effect of this linguistic structure was to similarly draw a line designating those against the policy and the USA as definitively evil. For members in the audience whose subjectivities depended in important part on narrative 'realities' about being on the 'good' side of the good/evil divide, this created a trap. The 'non-choice' was either to accept the US-articulated 'reality' of its own attractiveness and preserve the 'reality' of their own moral righteousness or deny it and contradict the logic and integrity of the narratives that inscribed their 'goodness'. By forging a link between the phrase 'war on terrorism' and that of 'with us or with the terrorists', the USA used the structure of their narrative to coerce.

It is important to note that the coercive threat entailed by the logic of 'with or against us' was *not* a physical threat. In fact, no US administration official ever articulated any relationship between a refusal to accept the attractiveness of the American war on terror and military repercussions. There *was* a physical threat associated with *harbouring terrorists,* but that was not the threat implied by the narrative links between 'war on terror' and 'with or against us'. The latter threat was meant for actors that dissented from the appeal of the envisioned American war on terrorism but who *did not* harbour terrorists (or acknowledge it). It was meant for those who just disagreed. For those authors, the non-choice 'offered' by the American utterance was to either reject American attractiveness, which would cast them on the side of the 'evil' terrorists in a way that contradicted their own goodness, thus making them agents of their own sociolinguistic destabilisation, or accept US attractiveness, support its post-9/11 policies and sustain the stability of their Self.

Importantly, had the American authors structured their narrative of the war on terrorism differently, the options facing the audience would have been rather different as well. They certainly would have been less restrictive. For instance, the American authors might have narrated the war on terrorism as a proposition about *the best* way to exact justice and security in the aftermath of 9/11. They might, that is, have structured their narrative as an argument based on evidence arrived at through reasoning. In that case, the audience would have had the option to contest through evidence and reasoning, without fear of punishment. Alternatively, the US authors might have structured their narrative about the war on terrorism as a bargain, inviting the audience to engage in demand exchange. By instead structuring the narrative in a way that threatened dissidents with categorisation as evil, the authors made submission unavoidable for those audience members who were unwilling to risk degradation of their status as good. Dissident narratives thus disappeared, and support for the war on terror, as almost unlimited as it was during that first half year after 9/11, became a resource for American soft power.[19]

The forceful 'war on terrorism' narrative did, of course, face limitations for shoring up American attractiveness and soft power. For instance, the threat of 'with us or against us' only compelled, trapped and effectively coerced those would-be dissidents whose subjectivities depended in part on sustaining a 'reality' of themselves as good *according to the US definition of 'good'*. In this regard, it should have been predictable that Iraq, whose subjectivity under Saddam Hussein's reign was decidedly not bound up with the same kind of goodness as that implied by the American narrative, could not be coerced into endorsing the attractiveness of American policy by this specific representationally forceful narrative. The same was true of the western European democracies (notably France and Germany), though for a rather different reason. In this case, their subjectivity as morally righteous, distinctly non-evil states was reinforced in so many ways by so many other overlapping 'realities' in the sociolinguistic matrix that made up their selves that the risk of incurring whatever contradictions might be wrought for their subjectivity as a result of resisting the US view on the war on terrorism would be minimal. Of course, in the immediate aftermath of 9/11, the western European democracies *did* support the US policies, but it is less compelling to think of that support as a function of attraction cultivated through representational force than as a pre-existing attraction, a convergence of European and US beliefs based on a pre-existing common lifeworld. Later, when the USA began planning its invasion of Iraq, the common transatlantic lifeworld about what it meant to be a morally righteous state in world politics fractured. Logically, one might thus contend that the ensuing European dissent was made possible precisely because of the imperviousness of European selves to the 'with us or with the terrorists' threat that the USA had constructed.

Not-so-soft power in world politics

Where representational force *was* effective was on those subjects whose sense of Self as morally righteous was important (unlike Iraq) but also indebted to singular or weaker sociolinguistic 'realities' (unlike many European countries). These include, for instance, Jordan, Syria, Egypt, and Turkey. These states were susceptible to the American coercive narrative (and were probably the target audience to begin with) because their status as 'good' was tenuous. The risk of association with the putatively evil terrorists would be a risk too high to bear. Consider Jordan: in exchange for fortification of the 'reality' of its moral righteousness, Jordan accepted the logic of the war on terrorism. It embraced the 'reality' of American policy as attractive. King Abdullah II of Jordan displayed the 'non-choice' logic driving his submission to the American narrative quite clearly when he stated that 'it is very obvious that there are those on the side of good and those on the side of bad and some in the middle, who haven't made up their minds, and those countries better make up their minds pretty quickly' (BBC 2002).

Beyond merely articulating agreement with the American representation, the King also abided the imperative to live the 'reality' of attraction to the USA. Even as the Jordanian people protested, their government stood by its 'attraction' by hosting US military exercises near the border with Iraq (Pelham 2002). That the Jordanian government enacted its attraction to the USA against the opposition of domestic Jordanian groups highlights that by no means did *all* Jordanians feel attracted to the US policy. But that is not required by representational force; what is required is that the government's policies forced the collectivity of Jordan to live through the effects of an attraction to the USA, even though attraction did not accurately describe the psychic state of all of the sub-actors in Jordan.[20] In fact, so effective was representational force in this case – so urgent was the Jordanian Government's desire to stave off the threats to its subjectivity by enacting its attraction to US policies – that it even took up arms against its own dissenting people. This amounted to a radical departure from one of Jordan's other cultures/'realities': its Self as peaceful (Pelham 2002; Hardy 2002). In this way, Jordan sacrificed one aspect of Self to save another that it deemed more crucial to the overall stability and security of its subjectivity. Attraction to the USA had become a matter of subjective life and death. The USA had effectively used representational force to construct a 'reality' of its own attractiveness.

What does it mean that verbal fighting and representational force can be the basis for attraction? For one, it highlights a need to reconsider what exactly is 'soft' about soft power. In Nye's formulation, the distinction between hard and soft expressions of power turns on whether power is enacted through attraction or coercion. But since representational force is a form of coercion, attraction may rest upon coercion. Where it does, the distinction Nye had in mind between 'hard' and 'soft' evaporates. While 'soft' power may still be soft in some other way, some reassessment of the conventional analyses and expectations associated with 'soft' power is in order.

Consider the way that soft power has been integrated into IR theory. It could be argued that the greatest contribution of soft power in this litera-ture has been to provide a conceptual bridge between 'ideas' and 'material' approaches to state behaviour. Soft power, after all, is a function of ideas, yet it operates in a way that recognises power as the currency of interna-tional life. The revelation that soft power is not so soft does *not* actually alter this insight – soft power rooted in attraction built on representational force is still a form of power that has its source in ideas rather than material bases. But it does great damage to a key derivative insight: that an anarchy organised through the soft power of constructive engagement avoids the relentlessly competitive world associated with materialist approaches (Nye 2002; Lynch 2000). At issue is that if soft power is the function of an attraction constructed through a coercive process of communicative exchange, it can hardly be said that soft power avoids relentless competition among actors. On the contrary, it depends precisely upon a competition among actors over the terms of the 'reality' of attractiveness. Thus, in an international relationship where soft power reigns, the anarchy among the actors would remain at base competitive. The difference is simply that the competition occurs at the level of subjectivity and 'reality' production rather than at the level of material resources.

From the preceding analytic points arise some practical suggestions that differ markedly from current suggestions about how to pursue soft power. Practitioners interested in reaping the gains of soft power have focused on 'cultivating' attraction by educating others about one's attractive qualities. As Nye (2004b: 111) argues, the best way to accomplish this is through public diplomacy – that is, through talking to broad swathes of global populations about who 'we' are, by offering information about 'our' values and culture and, importantly, by listening to who 'they' are. But when one adopts a view of soft power as rooted in representational force, all aspects of this plan for cultivating attraction change. One does not *talk* to others but verbally *fights* with them using representational force to leave them as little room as possible to refuse. Moreover, one need not address broad swathes of populations. Rather the key is to specifically trap leaders or decision-makers with threats to their subjectivities since it is they whose submission translates into policy and behaviours. They are the ones that force the entire collective to live the experience of attraction. On this view, then, cultivating attraction and producing soft power are much more intimate and intense experiences among specific people than the conventional view. Last, whereas in the conventional view, listening is crucial to the cultivation of attraction and soft power, on the view offered here, listening is dangerous. Listening offers one's adversary/interlocutor a window of opportunity in which to use representational force to coerce *you* into submission.[21]

In addition to these reconsiderations of strategies for cultivating attraction are reconsiderations of strategies for deploying soft power. For instance, Nye (2004c), among others, has been rather vocal about the importance of stockpiling soft power. Implicit in this logic is that soft power ought to be treated as if it were military power – as something that should be kept in reserve and ready to go in situations where it is appropriate. But where attractiveness and, thus, soft power are a matter of representational force, stockpiling appears impossible, or at least counterproductive. After all, where soft power is more accurately based on representational force, it exists only for as long as the coerced victims continue to feel the threat to their subjectivity. As soon as a victim ceases to feel trapped by the threat in the representational force that led him to submit in the first place, he will most likely no longer feel like he must comply. This eventuality arises from the fact that victims' subjectivities, like all sociolinguistic 'realities', change over time. Given the changeability of selves, a more efficacious approach would be to cultivate attraction and use the 'soft' power it yields on an as-needed basis.

Finally, thinking about soft power through a sociolinguistic lens has some striking normative implications. Understood through the conventional lens, soft power has appeared as an alternative to the raw-power politics that so frequently characterise world politics. It has thus been embraced by ethically minded scholars and policy-makers. But the realisation that soft power is not so soft encourages some critical rethinking about its ethical value. Where soft power is indebted to representational force, it promulgates a form of power politics that operates on the level of subjectivity. It promotes a 'power politics of identity' in which domination is played out through the representations that narrate 'reality'. In my opinion, a power politics of identity, however unappealing, is normatively more appealing than the power politics of war, empire and physical conquest. But even so, one must still question the moral logic of representational force. Given that soft power may, in the end, not be all that soft, it is worth considering the ethical dimensions and dilemmas that arise when using it as 'a means to success in world politics'.

Notes

1 Language is any sign system, whether those signs are verbal or written words, gestures, art or other forms of expression. Since it is most accessible, I focus on verbal and written language.

2 And sometimes physically, although I do not address this here since then the attempt to wield soft power slides into the use of hard power, as traditionally defined.

3 In this way, a speaker uses representational force to secure her self, but it is the (in)security of her victim's self that enables the speaker to formulate a representationally forceful threat.

4 Nye also advocates more passive approaches to cultivating soft power, for instance through entertainment. He offers no account of which – public diplomacy or passive cultural 'osmosis' – is more effective.

5 Nye apparently has a religious conviction about this point (Deakin 2005).

6 I refer at this point in my argument to the narrowly defined constructivist scholarship often associated with Alexander Wendt, Michael Barnett and Martha Finnemore, to name a few. Conceptually, this form of constructivism is 'thin' since its view of social construction does not go 'all the way down'.

7 Others have linked these practices to constructivist logic, thus emphasising the socially constructed version of Nye's approach to attraction (Arquilla and Ronfeldt 1999; Smyth 2001).

8 The various sub-actors in a collective actor become constituted by the larger cultural structures (Bukovansky 2002). Thus, unlike the natural approach to attraction, this cultural approach could theoretically offer a coherent account of where attraction 'sits' in a collective body. This conceptual improvement, however, is neutralised by the fact that this Habermasian logic of attraction is circular.

9 For instance, Bourdieu (1992) argues that culture is a product of practice; Bukovansky (2002) argues that culture is a product of rules and discourse; and, of course, even though Habermas (1990) presupposes a culture (in the form of life world), he poses argument as a way to envision the development of further culture.

10 In the case of Foucault (1972), 'truth' is produced by 'grafting' it to relevant extant discourses.

11 Which advocates of soft power believe is very possible.

12 In this formulation, I am positing that in order to participate in the construction of a culture/'reality', beings must already be actors: they must have some sociolinguistically constituted self.

13 This is even more pronounced for collective actors, whose sociolinguistic matrices are yet more intricate.

14 Actors won't always choose such strategies. There are instances in which the most appealing strategy is to *not* protect one's self (Bially Mattern 2005: 117–24).

15 On seduction and its preconditions, see Laplanche 1993; on manipulation, see Baron 2003.

16 Collective actors (in this case the USA, but also other actors in world politics who were already attracted to its policies) speak via key persons who, in a given context, are positioned so that they symbolise and embody the whole and can act on its behalf. Here this includes at least Bush, Condoleeza Rice, Donald Rumsfeld, and Tony Blair.

17 These were the months prior to the US preparations to invade Iraq. The dissent re-emerged after that period when the stakes for victim's subjectivity changed.

18 This phraseology was then adopted by other members of the US administration. See examples in Tyson 2002.

19 In this case, representational force was wielded by a materially powerful country over less powerful ones. However, it is just as easily the case that a materially

weaker state might rely on representational force to cultivate *its* attractiveness and soft power over stronger states (Bially Mattern 2005).

20 It does nothing to the logic of soft power if the attraction is just *as if* rather than real since in the end there is no difference in terms of effects. Soft power is about getting others to do what you want them to do without having to rely on hard power. It is not about cultivating the psychic experience of attraction. Moreover, there is no way to know about the kind of psychic experience the actor is *really* having and so whether they ever *really* experience attraction. Language and action are all there are.

21 Though listening in other low-stakes contexts is crucial so that one can learn where one's victim's self is vulnerable.

7 The power of persuasion

Richard Ned Lebow

This chapter discusses conceptualisations of power found in Ancient Greek philosophy, embedded in the writings of fifth- and fourth-century BCE playwrights, historians and philosophers. The insights provided by the Ancient Greeks enrich our understanding of power in several important ways. Generally speaking, they highlight the links between power and the purposes for which it is employed, as well as the means used towards these ends. More specifically, they provide a conceptual framework for distinguishing enlightened from narrow self-interest, identify strategies of influence associated with each and their implications for the survival of communities.

In the field of international relations (IR), power has been appropriated primarily by realist scholars who used it interchangeably as a property and a relational concept (Dahl 1968: 405–15; Guzzini 1993: 443–78, 2004c: 533–68). This reflects a wider failure, in particular among neo-realists, to distinguish material capabilities from influence. Classical realists – unlike many later theorists – understood that material capabilities are only one component of power, and that influence is a psychological relationship. Hans Morgenthau (1948: 270–4, 1982: 48, 52–4) insisted that influence is always relative, situation-specific and highly dependent on the skill of actors. Stefano Guzzini (2004c) observes that this political truth creates an irresolvable dilemma for realist theory. If power cannot be defined and measured independently from specific interactions, it cannot provide the foundation for deductive realist theories. Liberal conceptions also stress material capabilities but privilege economic over military power. Some liberal understandings go beyond material capabilities to include culture, ideology and the nature of a state's political-economic order; what Joseph Nye, Jnr calls 'soft power'. Liberals also tend to conflate power and influence. Many assume that economic power – hard or soft – automatically confers influence (Dahl 1968). Nye (2004a, 2004b) takes it for granted that the American way of life is so attractive, even mesmerising, and the global public goods it supposedly provides so beneficial that others are predisposed to follow Washington's lead. Like many liberals, he treats interests and identities as objective, uncontroversial and given.[1]

Recent constructivist writings differentiate power from influence and highlight the importance of process. Habermasian accounts stress the ways in which argument can be determining and describe a kind of influence that can be fully independent of material capabilities. They make surprisingly narrow claims. Thomas Risse considers argument likely to be decisive only among actors who share a common 'lifeworld' and in situations where they are uncertain about their interests, or where existing norms do not apply or clash (Risse 2000; Crawford 2002). Yet Risse and other advocates of communicative rationality fail to distinguish between good and persuasive arguments – and they are by no means the same. Nor do they tell us what makes for either kind of argument, or how we determine when an argument is persuasive without reasoning backwards from an outcome. The approach put forward here builds on the Ancient Greek understanding of rhetoric as the language of politics and considers the most persuasive arguments those that sustain or enable identities. It follows Christian Reus-Smit (2004) in arguing that political power is deeply embedded in webs of social exchange and mutual constitution and ultimately rests on legitimacy. Like thick constructivist accounts, the Greeks focus our attention on the underlying causes of persuasion not on individual instances.[2] They offer us conceptual categories for distinguishing between different kinds of arguments and a politically enlightened definition of what constitutes a good argument. The Greeks appreciated the power of emotional appeals, especially when they held out the prospect of sustaining identities. More importantly, they understood the transformative potential of emotion; how it could combine with reason to create shared identities and, with it, a general propensity to cooperate with or be persuaded by certain actors.

Before proceeding, I would like to address a stock objection that is invariably raised when Greek ideas or practices are imported into a modern setting. Because they arose in such a different context, they are sometimes described as alien, even irrelevant, to industrial mass societies. It would certainly be unrealistic to expect that some Greek practices would work the same way for us as it did in fifth-century BCE Athens. Yet while human practices vary enormously across time and cultures, human nature does not. Certain human needs appear to be universal, as do pathologies associated with human desires, information-processing and decision-making. For instance, hubris, one of the self-destructive behavioural patterns described by Greek tragedy, is a widespread phenomenon: in our age, as in antiquity, powerful actors tend to become complacent about risk and put their trust in hope rather than reason and overvalue their ability to control their environment, other people and the course of events.[3] This chapter underlines how Greek concepts, applied with finesse and suitable caveats, can shed important light on contemporary politics.

Motives

As Steven Lukes reminds us in his chapter to this volume, conceptualising and, thus, recognising power relationship between individuals requires an understanding of their 'interests' (or reasons, motives). Yet how do social scientists and, by extension, IR theorists, generally conceive of human interests and motives? Since the Enlightenment, Western philosophers and social scientists have generally emphasised the instrumental role of reason, reducing reason to a mere instrumentality, to 'the slave of the passions', in the words of David Hume (1998: Appendix I, 163; 2000: 2.3.3.4). The behavioural sciences reflect this shift in their emphasis on strategic interaction. Strategic choice, the dominant paradigm in contemporary social science, is based on an understanding of reason wherein actors rank order their preferences and act in ways best calculated to achieve them. This modern focus on reason as instrumentality encouraged a shift away from consideration of the ends we seek, or should seek, to the means of satisfying our appetites. Social scientists acknowledge the critical importance of preferences but have made no sustained effort to understand what they are, how they form or when and why they change. Their ontology is unsuited to the task. The best they can do is derive preferences from deductive theories or try to infer them on the basis of behaviour.

By making human, institutional or state preferences unidimensional, theorists oversimplify human motivation, and their theories often offer a poor fit with reality. Neo-realists greatly oversimplify reality by assuming that states seek military power, just as economists do when they assume that people seek wealth. Yet both groups have devoted surprisingly little thought to the nature and scope conditions of this most fundamental of their propositions. Assume for the sake of the argument that states have a preference for power when making political choices (Morgenthau 1960: 5). Some actors may seek power or wealth as ends in themselves. For others, perhaps most, power or wealth are instrumentalities; they are means of achieving security, comfort, reputation, honour, a good life or some other end or combination of goals. There is no way to analyse means without seriously considering ends.[4] To acknowledge multiple motives requires additional theories to stipulate which motives predominate under what conditions. Such theories would have to be rooted in sophisticated understandings of human psychology and culture.

The Ancient Greeks framed the problem of choice differently than modern social scientists. Their principal concern was human goals, and they had a rich understanding of motives. They posited three kinds of desire: appetite, spirit and reason. Appetite encompassed all physical desires, including security and wealth. The concept of spirit (*thumos*) embodies the insight that all human beings value and seek self-esteem, a desire that can come into conflict with appetite. For Plato and Aristotle, self-esteem is acquired by emulating and excelling at qualities and activities admired by one's society and, thereby, winning the respect of others. Fear becomes a motive when either the appetite or spirit breaks free of restraints normally imposed by reason and threatens the well-being, self-esteem and, perhaps, survival of other actors.

In Book One, Thucydides invokes all three motives to explain the actions of Athens and Sparta that led to war. In their speech to the Spartan Assembly, the Corinthians describe the Athenians as driven by *poly-pragmosunē*: literally, 'trespass', but widely used in the late fifth century BCE by critics of modernity to signify a kind of metaphysical restlessness, intellectual discontent that found expression in *pleonexia*, that is, envy, ambition, search of glory, monetary greed, lust for power, and conquest.[5] Thucydides is equally critical of Sparta. King Archidamus offers the Spartan Assembly an accurate account of Athenian power and urges his compatriots to reflect carefully before embarking on a war that they are likely to pass on to their sons. His argument carries less weight than the emotional plea of the ephor Sthenelaïdas, who insists that the Athenians have wronged long-standing allies and deserve to be punished. In Athens, Pericles appeals to the Athenian appetite for wealth and power, while in Sparta, Sthenelaïdas speaks to his countrymen's spirit and yearning for honour. In showing the disastrous consequences of the unrestrained pursuit of either desire, Thucydides reaffirms the importance of the traditional Greek value of the middle way (*meden agan*), something that could only be attained in practice when reason constrains both appetite and spirit.[6]

Plato articulated a similar understanding of motivation but embedded it in an explicit theory of human psychology. In his *Republic*, Socrates identifies three distinct components of the psyche: appetite, spirit and reason. Appetite (*to epithumētikon*) includes all primitive biological urges – hunger, thirst, sex, and aversion to pain – and their more sophisticated expressions. Socrates uses the example of thirst, which he describes as a desire for a drink *qua* drink, to argue that appetites are a distinct set of desires and not means to other ends. He divides appetites, as he does all desires, into those that are necessary and unnecessary. The former are appetites we are unable to deny and whose satisfaction benefits us. The latter are those we could avoid with proper training and discipline. Appetite includes the unnecessary desire for wealth, which is unique to human beings and, he insists, has become increasingly dominant. He acknowledges that we require some degree of coordination, even reflection, to satisfy our appetites, but no broader conception of the meaning of life (Plato 1996: 439b3–5, 439c2–3, 553c4–7, 558d11–e3, 559a3–6 and 580d11–581a7).

Plato's Socrates infers that there are desires beyond the appetites because someone can be thirsty but abstain from drink to satisfy other desires. The principal alternative source of desire is the spirit (*to thumoeides*), a word derived from *thumos*, the alleged internal organ that roused Homeric heroes to action. Socrates attributes all kinds of vigorous and competitive behaviour to *thumos*. It makes us admire and emulate the skills, character and positions of people considered praiseworthy by society. By equalling or surpassing their accomplishments, we gain the respect of others and buttress our own self-esteem. The spirit is honour-loving (*philotimon*) and victory-loving (*philonikon*). It responds with anger to any impediment to self-assertion in private or civic life. It desires to avenge all slights of honour or standing to ourselves and our friends.[7] The spirit requires conceptions of esteem, shame and justice, acquired through socialisation and tends to be common to a family, peer group and, perhaps, the wider society. Reason (*to logistikon*), the third part of the psyche, has the capability to distinguish good from bad, in contrast to appetite and spirit which can only engage in instrumental reasoning. Socrates avers that reason has desires of its own, the most important being discovery of the purposes of life and the means of fulfilling them. It possesses a corresponding drive to rule (*archein*) – the root from which *archē* is derived. Reason wants to discipline and train the appetite and the spirit to do what will promote happiness and well-being (Plato 1996: 441c1–2, 441e4, 442c5–6, 580d7–8 and 8505d11–e1).

In sum, Greek philosophers and playwrights draw on a rich lexicon of motives which provides insights into how power relations other than coercion can be established. As we shall see, they also use a set of binaries to describe concepts like hegemony, persuasion and power, for which we have only single words in English. These binaries generate contrasting understandings of these terms, which deepen our insights into the nature of power and provide the basis for a critique of contemporary conceptions of power.

Power as control

The Greeks generally used two words to signify power: *kratos* and *dunamis*. For Homer, *kratos* is the physical power to overcome or subdue an adversary from such action. Although fifth-century Greeks did not always make a clear distinction between these words, they tended to understand *kratos* as the basis for *dunamis*: whereas *Kratos* is something akin to our notion of material capability, *dunamis* is power exerted in action, like the concept of force in physics. As will be argued later, this conception of power must be differentiated from the Greek notion of influence through persuasion.

Thucydides' account of the Peloponnesian War encodes a profound analysis of the nature of power and influence. Central to it is the distinction he makes between *hēgemonia* and *archē*. For fifth- and fourth-century Greeks, *hēgemonia* is a form of legitimate authority associated with *timē* (honour and office), which, in this sense, also meant the 'office' to which one was accordingly entitled. Sparta and Athens earned *timē* by virtue of their contributions and sacrifices to Greece during the Persian wars. *Timē* was also conferred on Athens in recognition of her literary, artistic and intellectual, political and commercial accomplishments that had made her, in the words of Pericles, the 'school of Hellas' (Thucydides 1972: 2.4). *Hēgemonia* is an honorific status conferred by others in recognition of the benefits an actor has provided for the community as a whole. Reminiscent of Weber's charismatic *Herrschaft*, outlined in the introduction to this volume, it implies a *right* to lead.

By contrast, *archē* means 'control', and was initially applied to authority within a city-state and later to rule or influence of some city-states over others. It is always hierarchical. Control will not admit equality, and an authoritarian political structure is best suited to the downward flow of central authority and horizontal flow of resources from periphery to centre. Once established, the maintenance of hierarchy becomes an important second-order goal, for which those in authority are often prepared to use all resources at their disposal. *Archē* is founded on *kratos* (material capabilities) and, of necessity, sustains itself through *dunamis* (displays of power). Superior material capability provides the basis for conquest or coercion. Influence is subsequently maintained through rewards and threats. Such a policy makes serious demands on resources and encourages an *archē* to increase its resource base.

The years between the Battle of Salamis (480 BCE) and the outbreak of the Peloponnesian War (431 BCE) witnessed the gradual transformation of the Delian League into the Athenian Empire. Athens removed the treasury from Delos, imposed its silver coinage and weights and measures on most of its allies and made the Great Panathena an empire festival. It intervened in the domestic affairs of allies to support democratic factions and, when necessary, used force to extract tribute from restive allies. By 430 BCE, Pericles acknowledged that the Athenian Empire had many attributes of a tyranny, but could proclaim, with some justification, that it also retained important features of *hēgemonia* (Thucydides 1972: 2.63). There were few revolts in the early stages of the Peloponnesian War. They became more frequent after Sparta's successes in Chalcidice, and there was a rash of defections after Athens' defeat in Sicily.[8]

After Pericles' death from the plague in 429 BCE, Athens' military strategy changed and, with it, relations with allies. Pericles had urged his countrymen 'to wait quietly, to pay attention to their fleet, to attempt no new conquests, and to expose the city to no hazards during the war' (Thucydides 1972: 2.65.7). Cleon and Alcibiades spurned his sober advice in favour of an offensive strategy aimed at imperial expansion. As Pericles had foreseen, this offensive strategy aroused consternation throughout Greece and appeared to lend substance to Sparta's claim that it was the 'liberator of Hellas'. The new strategy required more resources and compelled Athens to demand more tribute from its allies, which provoked resentment and, occasionally, armed resistance. Rebellion elicited a harsh response, and several cities were starved into submission. Siege operations required considerable resources, making it necessary to extract more tribute, triggering a downward spiral in Athenian-allied relations that continued for the duration of the war (Meiggs 1972: 205–54).

By 416 BCE, the year the assembly voted to occupy Melos and subdue Sicily, the Athenian Empire had increasingly become an *archē* based on military might. The structure and language of the Melian Dialogue reveal how much the political culture of Athens had changed. It consists of *brachylogies*: short, blunt, alternating verbal thrusts, suggestive of the lunge and parry of a duel. The Athenian generals, Cleomedes and Tisias, dispense with all pretence. They acknowledge that their invasion cannot be justified on the basis of their right to rule or as a response to provocations. They deny the relevance of justice, which they assert only comes into play between equals. 'The strong do what they can and the weak suffer what they must', and the Melians should put their survival first and submit (Thucydides 1972: 5.89). The Melians warn the Athenians that their empire will not last forever, and if they violate the established norms of justice and decency, their fall 'would be a signal for the heaviest vengeance and an example for the world to meditate upon.' The Athenians insist that they live in the present and must do what is necessary to preserve their empire. The Melians assert that that empire is best served by a neutral and friendly Melos. The Athenians explain that their empire is held together by power (*dunamis*, power in action) and the fear (*phobos*) it inspires. Other island-states would interpret Melian neutrality as a sign of Athenian weakness, and it would therefore serve as a stimulus for rebellion. 'The fact that you are islanders and weaker than others renders it all the more important that you should not succeed in baffling the masters of the sea' (Thucydides 1972: 5.91–9).

Contemporary Greeks would have been shocked by Athens' rejection of the Melian offer of neutrality on the grounds that 'your hostility cannot so hurt us as your friendship' (Thucydides 1972: 5.95). Friendship was widely recognised as the cement that held the polis together, yet fifteen years into the war, the Athenians had inverted a core Greek value. Pericles had understood that the overriding foreign-policy interest of Athens was pre-servation of its empire and that this required naval power *and* legitimacy. To maintain *hēgemonia*, Athens had to act in accord with the principles and values that it espoused and offer positive political and economic benefits to allies. Post-Periclean leaders consistently chose power over principle and, by doing so, alienated allies and third parties, lost *hēgemonia* and weakened Athens' power base. Viewed in this light, the Melian Dialogue and the Sicilian expedition are not only radical departures from rational self-interest but also the almost inevitable result of the shift in the basis of Athenian authority and influence from *hēgemonia* to *archē*.

Thucydides' account of the Peloponnesian War is rich in irony. Athens, the tyrant, jettisoned the traditional bonds and obligations of reciprocity in expectation of greater freedom and rewards only to become trapped by a new set of more onerous obligations. The post-Periclean empire had to maintain its *archē* by constantly demonstrating its power and will to use it. Towards this end, it had to keep expanding, a requirement beyond the capabilities of any state. Athenians explicitly acknowledged that Melian independence, by challenging the hierarchy, would encourage more powerful allies to assert themselves, which could lead to the unravelling of their empire.[9] The Melian operation was part of the run-up to the invasion of Sicily – where the same Athenians who slaughtered most of the Melians and sold the remainder into slavery would meet a similar fate at the hands of the Syracuse.

The limits of *archē*

Realism assumes that influence is proportional to (the distribution of) material capabilities: the weaker the state, the less likely it is to oppose the wishes of a powerful interlocutor. Cases where weaker powers (or factions) go to war against strong ones (e.g., Athens v. Persia, Melos v. Athens), or strenuously resist them (e.g., North Vietnam v. the USA, Chechnya v. Russia) are anomalous from a realist perspective. There are three underlying causes for the failure of *archē*: a decline in material capability, overextension and inadequate resolve.

The first, a loss of *kratos*, was an underlying cause of the slow decline and shrinkage of all great colonial empires in the nineteenth and twentieth centuries. It most obviously reduces the ability to control subordinates, yet it is intrinsically linked to the other two factors. Power-transition theorists have identified a range of responses of great powers and empires to relative loss in capabilities (e.g., preventive war, retrenchment) but have been unable to explain why they chose the strategies they did (Organski 1967: 202–3; Organski and Kugler 1980; Gilpin 1981: 200–1). The distinction or, more accurately, the continuum characterised by *archē* on one end and *hēgemonia* on the other, offers some analytical purchase. The closer a system resembles an *archē*, at home or abroad, the more likely it is to resort to repression, look for opportunities to assert authority and consider preventive war. In modern times, the Ottoman, Russian and Austro- Hungarian empires adopted these strategies – all three in the case of Austria-Hungary – in response to their relative declines in *kratos*. There was fear in Constantinople, St Petersburg and Vienna, as there would be in Moscow a half-century later, that any perception of weakness or lack of resolve would invite serious challenges by domestic or foreign opponents.

Successful *archē* requires self-restraint as there are diminishing returns to territorial expansion and resource extraction. At some point, further predation encourages active resistance and makes maintenance of *archē* even more dependent on displays of resolve, suppression of adversaries and the maintenance of hierarchy. All these responses require greater resources, which, in turn, encourages more expansion and resource extraction. Yet for political, organisational and psychological reasons, self-restraint is extraordinarily difficult for an *archē*. Hierarchy without constitutional limits or other restraints makes it easier to ignore the interests and desires of domestic opinion and client states, isolates those in authority from those whom they oppress and narrows the focus of the former on efforts to maintain or enhance their authority. Over time, it can produce a ruling class – like Athenian citizens, slave-owners in the American antebellum South, the former Soviet *nomenklatura* or the present-day Chinese Communist Party – whose socialisation, life experiences and expectations make the inequality on which all *archē* is based seem natural, and for whom rapacity and suppression of dissent has become the norm.

Thucydides offers the political equivalent of what would become New-ton's Third Law of Motion: an *archē* is likely to expand until checked by an opposite and equal force (White 1984; Lebow 2003: Chapters 2, 3 and 7). Imperial overextension – *dunamis* beyond that reasonably sustained by *kratos* – constitutes a serious drain on capabilities, especially when it involves an *archē* in a war the regime can neither win nor settle for a compromise peace for fear of being perceived as weak at home and abroad. In this circum-stance, leaders become increasingly desperate and may assume even greater risks because they can more easily envisage the disastrous consequences to themselves of not doing so. Athens threw all caution to the winds and invaded Sicily, not only in the expectation of material rewards but also in the hope that a major triumph in Magna Grecia would compel Sparta to sue for peace. In our age, Austria-Hungary invaded Serbia to cope with nationalist discontent at home, Japan attacked the USA hopeful that a limited victory in the Pacific would undermine resistance in China, and Germany invaded Russia when it could not bring Britain to its knees. All of these adventures ended in disaster.

Resolve enters the picture as subordinates and third parties periodically assess an *archē*'s will to use its capabilities to sustain itself and its hierar-chical structure through rewards, threats and punishments. Resolve can be strengthened by superior capability, but there is no direct relationship between capabilities and resolve. A decline in capabilities can make it appear all the more important to demonstrate resolve, as it did for Russia and Aus-tria-Hungary in 1914, both of whom, like Athens, feared that any perceived failure of will would be the catalyst for greater internal opposition and for-eign-policy challenges. The Soviet Union under Gorbachev experienced a crisis of will. A meaningful percentage of the political elite had lost faith in Soviet-style Communism and embraced values inimical to maintaining the unchallenged authority of the Communist Party at home and of Soviet authority in Afghanistan and eastern Europe. Gorbachev's public encour-agement of reform in eastern Europe and refusal to use the Red Army to maintain pro-Soviet regimes were part of a chain of events that led to the collapse of the Soviet Union (Garthoff 1994; Brown 1996; Lévesque 1997; English 2000). The Gorbachev experience has suggested to some that an *archē* must remain firm at all costs; that repression, à la Tiananmen Square, is a more efficacious response to opposition than concession and reform. This may be true in the short term, but it is almost surely counterproductive in the longer term. Stalin's forced collectivisation and five-year plans were credited with saving the Soviet Union from Germany, but it seems likely that continuation of Lenin's New Economic Policy would almost certainly have resulted in more growth (Erlich 1967; Nove 1976: 49–62; 1982). East Germany, Cuba and, above all, North Korea, offer dramatic illustrations of the limitations of hierarchical systems built on tight state control.

The Greek lexicon of human motivation sheds an interesting light on the failure of *archē*. We tend to associate opposition by subordinate individuals and peoples experiencing resource extraction characteristic of *archē* with an unsatisfied appetite. But the Greeks would expect the spirit to inspire at least as much resentment and opposition. The spirit is angered by slights to honour, and in many societies there are few things more dishonourable than visible subordination. In particular in so-called shame cultures, honour takes precedence over appetite – even at the risk, or near-certainty, of death. Herodotus explains Athenian resistance to Persia in terms of honour, as Thucydides does with Melos. Those states, like Thebes, that made their peace with advancing Persian armies were ever after thought to have behaved dishonourably. Subordinates may be moved to accept domination by their appetite (because it will make them more secure, wealthier or more powerful vis-à-vis third parties) and to oppose it by their spirit (which insists on resistance in the name of self-esteem).

Classical realists from Thucydides to Morgenthau understood this tension – and the corollary that power must be masked to be effective. Subordinate actors need to be allowed, or at least encouraged, to believe that they are expressing their free will, not being coerced, are being treated as ends in themselves, not merely as means, and are respected as ontological equals, even in situations characterised by material power imbalance. This shifts the focus away from power through control of material resources to power exercised through persuasion.

The power of *peithō*

For the Greeks and moderns alike, power and persuasion (a principal form of influence) are closely linked in theory and practice. The strategic-interaction literature encourages us to consider influence as derivative of power, if mediated by agency. Of course, in practice, power can be used to achieve some ends (e.g., genocide) that have little or nothing to do with persuasion. However, as Clausewitz (1976: Book 1) so aptly observed, military force usually has the broader goal of persuasion; self-defence, for example, is intended to convince an aggressor that it should break off its attack because it will not succeed or it will prove too costly. Persuasion can involve the threat, as opposed to the application; deterrence and compellence only succeed when force does not have to be used. Persuasion can rest on rewards, as do strategies of reassurance. Defence, deterrence and many forms of reassurance ultimately depend on material capabilities. Yet persuasion can be based on other kinds of power, including morality, rhetoric and influence over important third parties. The degree to which persuasion is an expression of power really depends on how expansive a definition of power we adopt.

We need to distinguish the goal of persuasion from persuasion as a means. As noted above, efforts at persuasion (the goal) rely on the persuasive skills of actors (the means) to offer suitable rewards, make appropriate and credible threats or marshal telling arguments. Aeschylus, Sophocles,

Thucydides, and Plato recognise the double meaning of persuasion and devote at least as much attention to persuasion as a means as they do to it as an end. Unlike many contemporary authorities, their primary concern is not with tactics (e.g., the best means of demonstrating credibility) but with ethics.

The Greeks distinguish persuasion brought about by deceit (*dolos*), false logic, coercion and other forms of chicanery from persuasion (*peithō*) achieved by holding out the prospect of building or strengthening friendships, common identities and mutually valued norms and practices. They associate persuasion of the former kind (*dolos*) with those sophists who taught rhetoric and demagogues who sought to win the support of the assembly by false or misleading arguments for selfish ends. *Peithō*, by contrast, uses honest dialogue to help actors define who they are, and this includes the initiating party, not just the actor(s) it seeks to influence. *Peithō* constructs common identities and interests through joint understandings, commitments and deeds, through common acts of performance. As a form of influence, it is limited to behaviour others understand as supportive of their identities and interests. It begins with recognition of the ontological equality of all the parties to a dialogue and advances beyond that to build friendships and mutual respect. *Peithō* blurs the distinction between means and ends because it has positive value in its own right, independently of any specific end it is intended to serve.

Some of the Greek authors I examine – Sophocles in particular – treat *peithō* and *dolos* as diametrically opposed strategies.[10] Sophocles, Thucydides and Plato consider *peithō* a more effective strategy than *dolos* because it has the potential to foster cooperation that transcends discrete issues, builds and strengthens community and reshapes interests in ways that facilitate future cooperation. It is more efficient because it does not consume material capabilities in displays of resolve, threats or bribes. For much the same reason, *peithō* has a restricted domain; it cannot persuade honest people to act contrary to their values or identities. *Dolos* can sometimes hoodwink actors into behaving this way. In contrast to *peithō*, it treats people as means not ends – a Kantian distinction implicit in Sophocles and Plato.[11]

The contrast between the two strategies is explored in Aeschylus' *Oresteia*. In *Agamemnon*, the first play of the trilogy, Clytemnestra employs *dolos* to trick her husband, just back from the Trojan War, into walking on a red robe that she has laid out before him. She wraps him up in the robe to disable him so she can kill him with a dagger. In the next play, *Libation Bearers*, Orestes resorts to *dolos* to gain entrance to the palace and murder Clytemnestra and her consort, Aegisthus. In the final play, the *Eumendides*, Athena praises *peithō* and the beneficial ends it serves and employs it to end the Furies' pursuit of Orestes, terminate the blood feuds that have all but destroyed the house of Atreus and replace tribal with public law (Aeschylus 2003: lines 958–74).[12] *Dolos* is clearly linked to violence and injustice. Even when used to achieve justice in the form of revenge, it entails new acts of injustice that perpetuate the spiral of deceit and violence. The only escape from the vicious cycles is through *peithō* and the institutional regulation of conflict, which have the potential of transforming the actors and their relationships. This transformation is symbolised by the new identity accepted by the Furies – the *Eumenides*, or well-wishers – who, at the end of the play, are escorted to their new home in a chamber beneath the city of Athens.

Although the trilogy is ostensibly about the house of Atreus and the regulation of family and civic conflict, it is also about international relations. Many of the major characters are central figures in the Trojan War. Helen is married to Menelaus, and her seduction and abduction by Paris triggers the Trojan War. Menelaus' honour can only be redeemed by the recapture of Helen and the destruction of the city that has taken her in. Agamemnon, his brother and King of Argos, leads the Greek expedition against Troy. The *Oresteia* open with his return to Argos after a ten-year absence. In the interim, his wife Clytemnestra has taken Aegisthus, son of Thyestes, for a consort. Among her motives for murdering her husband is his earlier sacrifice at Aulis of their daughter Iphigenia in response to the prophecy that it was necessary to secure favourable winds for the departure of the Greek fleet to Troy.

The curse of the Atridae and the Trojan War are also closely connected in their origins: both are triggered by serious violations of guest friendship (*xenia*), one of the most important norms in heroic-age Greece. In Aeschylus' version, the troubles of the Atridae clan begin with Thyestes' seduction of his brother Atreus' wife. This violation of the household is followed by another more terrifying one. Atreus pretends to forgive Thyestes and allows him to return home, where he is invited to attend a feast. In the interim, Atreus has murdered two of Thyestes' three children and put them in a stew which he then serves to Thyestes. This gives Aegisthus, the surviving son, a motive for seducing Clytemnestra and assisting her in the murder of Agememnon, the son of Atreus. The curse of the Atridae and the Trojan War unfold as a series of escalating acts of revenge. If the curse of the Atridae can be resolved through *peithō* and the institutional regulation, this might be possible for the internecine conflicts among the community of Greeks, as they arise from the same causes and are governed by the same dynamics.

Peithō is also central to Sophocles' *Philoctetes*, produced in 409, five years before Athens' defeat in the Peloponnesian War. Philoctetes' father had been given Heracles' bow because he had lit that hero's funeral pyre. Philoctetes inherited the bow and trained himself to become a master archer. En route to Troy, he was bitten in the leg by a snake and left with a foul-smelling, suppurating wound. The resulting stench, and Philoctetes' repeated cries of pain, led the Greeks to abandon him on the island of Lemnos while he slept. After years of inconclusive warfare, the Greeks receive a prophecy that Troy will only be conquered when Philoctetes and his bow appear on the battlefield. They dispatch Odysseus and Achilles' son

Neoptolemus to retrieve archer and bow, and the play opens with their arrival on the island. Odysseus lives up to his reputation as a trickster; he resorts to soft words (*logoi malthakoi*) to persuade Neoptolemus to go along with his scheme to pretend friendship with Philoctetes in order to steal the bow. He does this by creating a seemingly irreconcilable conflict between two important components of his identity: the honourable man who would rather fail than resort to dishonesty and deceit and the Greek committed to the defeat of Troy. Odysseus presents his argument at the very last moment, giving Neoptolemus no time for reflection.

Philoctetes is an honourable, friendly and generous person, with whom Neoptolemus quickly establishes a friendship. When Philoctetes grows weak from his wound, he gives his bow to Neoptolemus for safekeeping and, when he awakes from his feverish sleep, is delighted to discover that Neoptolemus has kept his word and not abandoned him. In the interim, the chorus had pleaded unsuccessfully with Neoptolemus to sneak off with the bow. Neoptolemus then half-heartedly tries to persuade Philoctetes to accompany him to Troy on the spurious grounds that he will find a cure there for his wound. Philoctetes sees through this deceit and demands his bow back. Neoptolemus initially refuses, telling himself that justice, self-interest and, above all, necessity demand that he obey his orders to bring the bow back to Troy. Philoctetes is disgusted, and Neoptolemus' resolve weakens.

Odysseus returns and threatens to force Philoctetes to board their ship or to leave him on the island without his bow. Odysseus appears to have won, as he and Neoptolemus depart with the bow. However, Neoptolemus, who has finally resolved his ethical dilemma, returns to give back the bow because he recognises that what is just (*dikaios*) is preferable to that which is merely clever (*sophos*). Odysseus threatens to draw his sword, first against Neoptolemus and then against Philoctetes. Neoptolemus refuses to be intimidated, as does Philoctetes, who draws his bow and aims an arrow at Odysseus. Neoptolemus seizes his arm and tells him that violence would not reflect honour on either of them. Philoctetes then agrees to proceed voluntarily with Neoptolemus and Odysseus to Troy.

This play can be read as an important lesson on the power of persuasion, specifically that the principal human capital is not material but social and cultural, an insight Odysseus fails to grasp. It consists of the relationships of trust we build with neighbours and friends through honest dialogue and the communities which this sustains. Odysseus is willing to use any means to accomplish his ends because he lacks any definition of self beyond the ends he can accomplish. He is incapable of interrogating those ends or the means by which they might be obtained. His attempts to exercise power through deceit and threats fail, leaving him something of an outcast (Knox 1982: Chapter 5; White 1985: 3–27; MacIntyre 1984: 134). Odysseus comes close to imposing his will on both his protagonists and fails only because Neoptolemus and Philoctetes have established a friendship based on mutual trust and respect. His emotional attachment puts Neoptolemus back in touch with his true self and the values that make him who he is and give him the resolve and the courage to return to Philoctetes with his bow, apologise for having obtained it dishonourably and face down an enraged Odysseus. The emotional bond Neoptolemus and Philoctetes establish also leads Philoctetes to imagine an encounter between himself and Heracles, who tells him that it is his fate to go to Troy with Neoptolemus and there win glory. He agrees to proceed because he too has been restored as a full person through his relationship with Neoptolemus.

The language of persuasion

The power of persuasion is fundamental for *hēgemonia*. It is only possible within a community whose members share core values and is limited to activities that are understood to support common identities. *Peithō* can also help to bring such a community into being. The spirit can strengthen *hēgemonia* if it is managed in way to confer honour on those who are subordinate.

The Athenian Empire grew out of the Delian League, an alliance to liberate those Greek communities still under the Persian yoke. Members willingly accepted Athenian leadership because it was considered essential to their common goal, one from which all would gain honour (*timē*). Even in the early days of empire, many Greeks apparently felt a sense of pride in being part of such a powerful and glorious enterprise. Pericles almost certainly encouraged this sentiment by using a sizeable portion of the allied tribute to construct the Parthenon, the Athena Parthenos and Propylaea, all of which bespoke the wealth and grandeur of Athens and its empire. While *peithō* operates largely independent of material capabilities, it can help to sustain those capabilities because it does not require the constant exercise of *dunamis*. Material capabilities come into the picture in so far as they provide the raw materials that facilitate the attainment of excellence and honour. Athens was greatly inferior to Persia in its material capabilities, but its willingness to take on that empire at the risk of annihilation made it all the more praiseworthy and honourable. As Pericles recognised (to a point), but his successors did not, self-restraint and generosity were the most effective way to enhance Athenian reputation and influence.[13]

The founding fathers of the post-Second World War order – some of whom, like George C. Marshall, regularly cited Thucydides in their writings and speeches – recognised this political truth. They created economic, political, military, and juridical institutions that, at least in part, tended to restrain powerful actors and reward weaker ones, providing the latter with strong incentives to retain close relations with the dominant power. American hegemony during the Cold War was based on the sophisticated recognition that the most stable orders are those 'in which the returns to power are relatively low and the returns to institutions are relatively high' (Ikenberry

2001: 248, 257–73). Influence depended as much on self-restraint as it did on power.

Of course, *peithō* can function independently of *hēgemonia*. Actors at any level of social interaction who earn the respect of their interlocutors by making claims supported by arguments that appeal to their interlocutors' feelings, opinions and interests – and offer them the possibility of reaffirming their identities – are likely to have some influence. A recent example is the success of a diverse coalition of non-governmental organisations (NGOs), who coordinated their efforts to persuade a majority of the world's states to negotiate and ratify the International Criminal Court (Benedetti and Washburn 1999; Glasius 2003). Osama Bin Laden wields influence for much the same reason, albeit within a very different community. This is a useful reminder that the power of rhetoric is not necessarily a force for the good, or that honest dialogue is the most persuasive one. Gorgias (circa 430 BCE), described language (*logos*) as a 'great potentate, who with the tiniest and least visible body achieves the most divine works'. When employed in tandem with persuasion (*peithō*) it 'shapes the soul as it wishes' (Gorgias 1956: frg. 82, BII, 8, 13–14). Words are the ultimate convention, and they too succumb to *stasis* in the sense that civilised conversation is replaced by a fragmented discourse in which people disagree about the meaning of words and the concepts they support and struggle to impose their meanings on others – as Odysseus did with Philoctetes. Altered meanings changed the way people thought about each other, their society and obligations to it and encouraged barbarism and violence by undermining long-standing conventions and the constraints they enforced.

Thucydides exalts the power of rhetoric and its ability to create and sustain community but recognises how easily it can destroy that community when employed by clever people seeking selfish ends. I have argued elsewhere that one of the key themes of his text is the relationship between words (*logoi*) and deeds (*erga*) (Lebow 2003: Chapter 4). Speech shapes action, but action transforms speech. It prompts new words and meanings and can subvert existing words by giving them meanings diametrically opposed to their original ones. The positive feedback loop between *logoi* and *erga* – the theme of Thucydides' 'Archaeology' – created the *nomoi* (conventions, customs, rules, norms, and laws) that made Greek civilisation possible. His subsequent account of the Peloponnesian War shows how the meaning of words were twisted and transformed to encourage and justify deeds that defied *nomos* and how this process was responsible for the most destructive forms of civil strife (*stasis*) that consumed Hellas (Lebow 2001; 2003: Chapter 4). For Thucydides, *dolos* was an important cause of war (Lebow 2003: 154–9). Although to this point I have stressed the beneficial consequences of *peithō*, Greek narratives also speak of circumstances in which *dolos* may be necessary or beneficial to achieve an end. As readers of Homer know, Odysseus devised the scheme of the 'Trojan horse' to gain the Greeks entry into Troy. Thucydides' Mytilenian debate is sometimes cited as another example of the benefits of *dolos*. In this episode, Diodotus convinces the Athenian assembly not to execute all Mytilenian adult males but only a limited number of aristocrats who can be held responsible for the rebellion. He openly acknowledges that it is no longer possible to defend a policy in the name of justice; Athenians will only act on the basis of self-interest. He carries the day by using his considerable rhetorical skill to mask an appeal based on justice in the language of self-interest.[14]

Modern examples abound. Franklin D. Roosevelt has been almost uniformly praised by historians for the rhetorically dishonest but strategically effective way he committed American naval forces to engage German submarines in the Atlantic before America entered the war. Modelling himself on Roosevelt, Lyndon Johnson campaigned as the peace candidate and promptly exploited an alleged attack on American naval vessels in the Gulf of Tonkin to intervene militarily in Vietnam. As that war ended in disaster, historians condemn Johnson's deception. George W. Bush and his advisers made multiple false claims to gain public and congressional approval for an invasion of Iraq. It is too early to offer a definitive judgement, but it seems highly likely that history will judge Bush's *dolos* at least as critically as it has Johnson's. More generally, leaders genuinely believe that they know better than public opinion what is good for their countries and feel justified to use *dolos* to achieve their policy goals. More often than not, *dolos* is simply a political convenience; leaders use it because it is the only way, or at least the easiest way, of gaining popular support. Yet they risk exacerbating the political problem by making the public less responsive to honest, and inevitably more complicated, arguments in the future. Thucydides uses the sequence of Pericles' funeral oration, the Mytilenian and Sicilian debates, to track this decline. The Bush Administration's knowingly false claims about Saddam's possession of weapons of mass destruction or the link between the Iraqi regime and Al Qaida offer a striking contemporary example. In the short term, it helped to gain congressional and public support for the invasion of Iraq, but, once exposed as the false claim it was, it helped to erode support for the war and the administration more generally.

Plato's opposition to *dolos* was unyielding for these reasons. He understood that rhetoric was at the heart of politics and sought to develop dialogue as an alternative to speeches that so easily slipped into reliance on *dolos*. Quite apart from dialogue's ability to produce consensual outcomes through reason, the free exchange of ideas among friends and the give and take of discussion had the potential to strengthen the bonds of friendship and respect that were the foundation of community. Plato portrays Socrates' life as a dialogue with his polis, and his acceptance of its death sentence as his final commitment to maintain the coherence and principle of that dialogue. Plato structures his dialogues to suggest that Socrates' positions do not represent any kind of final truth. His interlocutors often make arguments that Socrates cannot fully refute, or chooses not to, which encourages readers to develop a holistic contemplation of dialogue that recognises that unresolved tensions can lead to deeper understandings and form the basis for collaborative behaviour (Cooper 1999: 28–75).

The Greek emphasis on dialogue has been revived in the twentieth century and is central to the thought and writings of figures as diverse as Mikhail Bakhtin, Hans-Georg Gadamer and Jürgen Habermas. Bakhtin suggests that even solitary reflection derives from dialogues with others against whom or with whom we struggle to establish ourselves and our ideas (Bakhtin 1984; Holquist and Clark 1984; Wertsch 1991). Habermas's (1984–7: Vol. II; 1990) 'critique of ideology' led him to propose a coercion-free discourse in which participants justify their claims before an extended audience and assume the existence of an 'ideal speech situation', in which participants are willing to be convinced by the best arguments. Greek understandings of *peithō* have much in common with, but are not entirely the same as, Habermas' conception of communicative rationality. Habermas puts great emphasis on reasoned argument among equals, and its ability to persuade – an outcome so essential to democracy. *Peithō* values reason, but less for its ability to convince than for its ability to communicate openness and honesty. These values help to build the trust and friendship on which the underlying propensity to cooperate and be persuaded ultimately depend.

Gadamer's conception of dialogue is closer to the Greeks. For Gadamer, dialogue 'is the art of having a conversation, and that includes the art of having a conversation with oneself and fervently seeking an understanding of oneself' (Gadamer 1997: 3–63, 33; Fabian 1994: 81–108). It is not so much a method, as a philosophical enterprise that puts people in touch with themselves and others and reveals to them the prior determinations, anticipations and imprints that reside in their concepts. Experiencing the other through dialogue can lead to *exstasis*, or the experience of being outside of oneself. By this means, dialogue helps people who start with different understandings to reach a binding philosophical or political consensus. Critical hermeneutics in its broadest sense is an attempt to transgress culture and power structures through a radical break with subjective self-understanding (Gadamer 1980: 39–72; 1989; 1997: 17, 27).

Of course, dialogue does not operate in a vacuum. Material capabilities may influence acceptance or rejection of subordinate status, but not for the reasons commonly assumed. Small powers may offer less resistance because it is not as severe a blow to their self-esteem to give way to an actor many times more militarily powerful. The hierarchical relationship is least likely to generate resistance when initiated by an actor whose right to lead – which the Greeks associated with *hēgemonia* – is widely accepted. It helps to explain why lesser powers often fail to form alliances to balance against a power that is dominant or on its way to becoming so. The general acceptance of Chinese regional hegemony by most of the countries of the Pacific rim could be seen as a contemporary example (Kang 2003). It may also explain why the initial Iraqi euphoria at the overthrow of Saddam Hussein quickly turned into opposition to the USA as an occupier. This transition was facilitated by American occupation policy, which aimed – but never really succeeded – in addressing Iraqi appetites (by providing security, food, electricity, etc.) to the exclusion, and often the detriment, of satisfying Iraqi needs for self-esteem.

Conclusion: power and ethics

My discussion so far points to a complex relationship between power and ethics. While recognising that might often makes for right, it reveals that right can also make might. Of equal importance, it provides a discourse that encourages the formulation of longer-term, enlightened self-interests predicated on recognition that membership and high-standing in a community is usually the most efficient way to achieve and maintain influence. Such commitments also serve as a powerful source of self-restraint. For all of these reasons, ethical behaviour is conducive – perhaps even essential – to national security. At a minimum, ethical behaviour requires us to distinguish between good and persuasive arguments. The former are based on the facts – as we understand them – rooted in commonly shared values and intended to advance common interests. Good arguments are not always persuasive and may lose out to bad arguments (based on falsehoods or distortions and intended primarily to advance the interests of those making them) because the intended audience is ignorant and emotionally aroused. We need to refrain from making bad arguments even when they might be expected to be persuasive.

In modern discourses, ethics and behaviour are generally considered distinct subjects of inquiry because they are understood to derive from different principles. Many modern realists consider these principles antagonistic; not all the time to be sure, but frequently enough to warrant the establishment of a clear hierarchy with interest-based considerations at the apex. For the Greek tragedians – and I number Thucydides among them – there was no dramatic separation between ethics and interest. Their writings show how individuals or states that sever identity-defining relationships enter a liminal world where reason, freed from affection, leads them to behave in self-destructive ways. The chorus in *Antigone* proclaims in the first *stasimon*: 'When he obeys the laws and honours justice, the city stands proud [...] But when man swerves from side to side, and when the laws are broken, and set at naught, he is like a person without a city, beyond human boundary, a horror, a pollution to be avoided' (Sophocles 1999: 267–9).

Behaviour at odds with the accepted morality of the age undermines the standing, influence and even the hegemony of great powers. The Anglo-American invasion of Iraq is the latest example of this age-old phenomenon. The national security elite of the USA still considers its country 'the indispensable nation' to whom others look for leadership. Public-opinion polls of its closest allies – countries like Canada, Japan and the countries of western

Europe – indicate that the USA has lost any *hēgemonia* it may once have had and is overwhelmingly perceived as an *archē*, and one that many people believe is the greatest threat to the peace of the world (Lebow 2003: 314–15). In the run-up to the invasion of Iraq, it surely behaved as an *archē*; the Bush Administration's duplicitous claims about weapons of mass destruction and false claims that the purpose of an invasion was to remove these weapons and introduce democracy to Iraq were a quintessential exercise in deceit (*dolos*). Its subsequent occupation began with efforts to protect only those assets of strategic or economic value to the Bush regime (e.g., the oil ministry and refineries) and was followed by the installation of an American proconsul, unwillingness to share authority with any international organisation and the denial of contracts for the rebuilding of Iraqi infrastructure to companies from countries that had not supported the war. Such behaviour is typical of an *archē* who can no longer persuade but must coerce and bribe; and, Blair's Britain aside, this is the basis of the so-called coalition of the willing.

At least as far back as Homer, Greeks believed that people only assumed identities – that is, became people – through membership and participation in a community. The practices and rituals of community gave individuals their values, created bonds with other people and, at the deepest level, gave meaning and purpose to peoples' lives. Community also performed an essential cognitive function. To take on an identity, people not only had to distinguish themselves from others but also 'identify' with them. Without membership in a community, they could do neither, for they lacked an appropriate reference point to help determine what made them different from and similar to others. This was Oedipus' problem; because of his unknown provenance, he did not know who he was or where he was heading. His attempt to create and sustain a separate identity through reason and aggression was doomed to failure.

For the Greeks, this pathology extended beyond individuals to cities. There is reason to believe that Sophocles intended Oedipus as a parable for Periclean Athens. Like Oedipus, Athens' intellectual prowess became impulsiveness, its decisiveness thoughtlessness and its sense of mastery, intolerance to opposition. Oedipus' fall presages that of Athens, and for much the same reasons (Knox 1970: 99; Euben 1990: 40–1). The USA would do well to consider the extent to which the foreign policies that it has pursued since the end of the Cold War are taking it down the same path as Oedipus and Athens. Its unilateral foreign policies, often accompanied by 'in your face' rhetoric, have opened a gulf between itself and the community of democratic nations that has previously allowed it to translate its material capabilities into influence in efficient ways. Once outside this community, and shorn of the identity it sustained, Washington must increasingly use threats and bribes to get its way, and, like Athens and Oedipus, the goals it seeks are likely to become increasingly short-sighted.

Acknowledgement

This is a revised version of Lebow (2005). I am indebted to the participants of the 2004 annual *Millennium* Conference at LSE, panelists and participants at the 'archeopolitics' panel at BISA in the University of Warwick, the PIPES seminar of the University of Chicago and the comparative politics seminar at Dartmouth College for their thoughtful comments and criticisms. Special thanks to Stefano Guzzini, Nick Rengger, Chris Reus-Smit, Lucas Swaine, Felix Berenskoetter, and the other editors of *Millennium*.

Notes

1 See Reus-Smit (2004: 64–5) for a critique of Nye.
2 Martha Finnemore and Stephen J. Troope (2001) make this argument in the context of compliance with international law.
3 For an elaboration of this theme see Lebow (2003).
4 Harold Lasswell (1958: Postscript, 202–3) is one of the few social scientists who addressed this problem. He posited a plurality of motives, each of which could serve as an end in itself or a means towards achieving other ends.
5 Thucydides uses *polypragmosyne* only once in his text, to characterise Athenians as 'hyperactive' (1972: 6.87.3), but it is widely used by other authors to describe Athens. See Ehrenberg (1947), Finley (1938) and Allison (1979).
6 See Thucydides (1972: 1.80–5, 1.86–8) for the two speeches. The war developed as Archidamus predicted, and Sparta was forced to sue for peace after a sizeable number of its hoplites were taken prisoner on the island of Sphacteria in 426. Athens subsequently broke the truce and was defeated in 404, but Sparta's victory left it weak and unable to maintain its primacy in Greece.
7 Plato's conceptions of the *thumos* are developed in Books V, VIII and IX of the *Republic*.
8 On the Samian revolt see Meiggs (1972: 188–92).
9 The Soviet Union, another classic *archē*, periodically intervened in eastern Europe for the same reason.
10 This reflects the tendency of Greek tragedy to pit characters with extreme and unyielding commitments to particular beliefs or practices against each other in order to illustrate their beneficial and baneful consequences. I do the same, while recognising, as did the Greeks, that pure representations of any strategy of influence are stereotypes. *Peithō* and *dolos*, like other binaries I describe, have something of the character of ideal types. Actual strategies or political relationships approach them only to certain degree and, in practice, can be mixed.
11 *Gorgias*, Plato's Socrates maintains that rhetoric, as practised by sophists, treats others as means to an end, but dialogue treats them as ends in themselves and appeals to what is best for them. See also Plato (1996: 509d–11d, 531d–4c).
12 Aeschylus' *Prometheus* also explores different kinds of persuasion and shows how they can fail.
13 Thucydides' account of Pericles' funeral oration turns a solemn recognition of the sacrifices of the fallen into an uplifting commemoration of Athens and its values and how they are maintained by the love, sacrifice and the self-restraint of its citizens. Pericles acknowledges that the Athenian Empire has come in some ways to resemble a tyranny yet still retains its *hēgemonia* and achieves

excellence by demonstrating generosity (*charis*) to its allies. 'In generosity', he tells the assembly, 'we are equally singular, acquiring our friends by conferring not by receiving favours.' See Thucydides (1972: 2.34.5) and Hooker (1974).

14 Thucydides (1972: 3.36–49); See Orwin (1994: 161).

8 Contested credibility

The use of symbolic power in British exchange-rate politics

Wolf Hassdorf

'Black Wednesday', 16 September 1992, the day when sterling was humiliatingly ejected from the European Exchange Rate Mechanism (ERM), remains a key date in the economic history not just of Britain and the European Monetary System (EMS), but of the post-war international monetary order. The collapse of the British exchange-rate peg was part of the wider currency crisis of the ERM in 1992/3; the type of financial crisis that would become a feature of the liberalised intentional financial system of the 1990s. At first glance, the crisis seems to confirm that with the liberalisation of international capital flows a qualitative shift of power from the nation-state to globalising financial markets had taken place. After all, the policy of the British Government to peg sterling to the Deutschmark, the anchor currency of the ERM, without backing up this policy by strictly following disinflationary German interest rates, was ultimately overpowered by speculative global finance. The outcome of the crisis confirmed that under conditions of full international capital mobility, an exchange-rate peg would, de facto, result in the surrender of monetary policy autonomy to the key currency country.[1]

Intuitively attractive as such an interpretation of the disastrous outcome of Britain's ERM membership may be, it overlooks the significance of the process that led to this outcome. The economic and political fragility of the sterling peg was evident from the moment sterling entered the ERM in 1990. However, it took financial markets until late August 1992 – less than four weeks before Black Wednesday – to fully realise that the peg lacked substance.[2] The authorities impressed markets up to this point by tough rhetoric about the strength of the pound and by persistently voicing the commitment to do whatever it would take to defend parity. An internal document by the UK Treasury describes this as the Government hoping to maintain the exchange rate by 'words'. As the treasury official put it, the authorities 'duped' or 'tricked' the market into believing that there was only a small risk that sterling would be devalued.[3] It is this policy to compel belief in a strategy ultimately to be recognised as lacking substance which evokes images of the 'emperor without clothes' tale. Helen Thompson describes the hard currency rhetoric of Prime Minister John Major and

Norman Lamont, his Chancellor of the Exchequer, as 'bravura in the face of the foreign exchange market' (Thompson 1996: 191). Given that it was bravura without substance, I prefer to call it 'currency machismo'.[4]

The success of British currency machismo, although limited, challenges the cliché of a shift of power from the nation-state to unbound and efficient global financial markets. If, following Guzzini (2000a: 171), power is an indicator of politics as 'the art of the possible', the relative success of currency machismo by the UK suggests that it is possible for national governments to exert power over international finance by directing market sentiment through symbolically charged signalling. This paper investigates how this kind of power operated in practice. From which issue area did the trust of markets in the British Government's utterances originate? What does the ability to exert power in an area where the Government's policy lacked substance tell us about the fungibility of the power resources across issue areas?[5]

This work takes a social-constructivist approach to understand the effectiveness of currency machismo. It draws on Pierre Bourdieu's concept of 'symbolic power', the power to impose socially accepted meanings (Bourdieu and Passeron 1977: 4). The British Government's symbolic power, its capacity for manipulation, operated through the social construction of mutual understandings between policy-makers and financial market agents. The thesis is that symbolic manipulation succeeded temporarily because the resource of symbolic power, symbolic capital, is fungible. The Major Administration could sustain the ERM peg by leveraging and consequently depleting the trust which the previous Thatcher governments had accumulated in a different setting in financial markets. In making this argument, the chapter is organised as follows: the next section gives a brief review of the politics of Britain in the ERM and criticises monetary economics and the power analysis of international relations (IR) theory as inadequate to explain the hold the UK Government exercised over market sentiment through symbolically laden language. The third section suggests a constructivist understanding of the fungibility of symbolic capital, centred on Pierre Bourdieu's concept of symbolic power. The fourth section applies this approach to reconstruct the working of British currency machismo in the ERM in 1992. The fifth section concludes.

The politics of sterling in the ERM

British membership in the ERM lasted from 8 October 1990 until 16 September 1992 ('Black Wednesday'), when sterling was forced out of the system by overwhelming speculative pressure from the foreign-exchange markets. The sterling crisis was part of the wider ERM crisis of 1992/3.[6] Although triggered by the rejection of the Maastricht Treaty and its designs for the European Monetary Union (EMU) in the Danish referendum of 2 June 1992, the crisis had its roots in the excessively disinflationary monetary-policy stance imposed by Germany, the anchor currency country of the ERM, on the rest of the system. In British domestic politics, the ERM episode represented the beginning of the end of a long period of majority government by the Conservative Party, which had lasted since 1979. Britain had entered the ERM with Margaret Thatcher as Prime Minister. After her resignation in November 1990, John Major, who had taken sterling into the ERM as Chancellor of the Exchequer, took over as Prime Minister and managed to return the Tories to power for a fourth term on 9 April 1992 with a slim majority.

From the outset, British ERM membership lacked longer-term strategic consistency. In contrast to the long-term European monetary strategies of Germany and France, Britain had, since the collapse of the Bretton Woods System, never consistently prioritised exchange-rate stability over domestic monetary-policy objectives.[7] The episode of sterling in the ERM is typical in this respect: Britain's decisions to join and to leave the ERM were to some extent opportunistic moves, motivated by domestic-policy considerations.[8] To join was a tactical decision, made after alternative monetary-policy frameworks had failed. It was seen as the clever option left to bring inflation under control without having to maintain an excessively tight monetary-policy stance. All of this followed the disintegration of the monetarist strategy of targeting domestic money supply, which lay at the heart of the Tory economic-policy project but which had been left discredited by the inflationary 'Lawson boom' of the late 1980s.[9] Fixing the sterling exchange rate within the ERM would allow the Government to combine interest-rate cuts with bringing down inflation before the General Election of April 1992. Politicians hoped that this would be achieved by borrowing anti-inflationary credibility from Germany through the anchoring of British monetary policy to the stability stance of the German Bundesbank.[10] Thus, the ERM peg was little more than an international means to a domestic end: to beat inflation after the domestic monetarist framework of the Thatcher era had failed. Consequently, Norman Lamont, in his defining speech asserting that there was no alternative to the Government's ERM strategy, emphasised that the objective of the ERM was to break the cycle of inflation.[11] Other objectives which would have pointed at longer-term commitment to the ERM parity, such as becoming a full political player in the project of European monetary integration, were only of secondary importance.[12] As Walsh (2000: 139) asserts, once the domestic objective had been achieved and the election was won, 'the political logic for this strategy was finished', and in the summer of 1992, the Major Government had little incentive to back up the ERM parity as forcefully as other ERM member countries.

Politically, the idea to make external stability the key objective of monetary policy-making had no coherent socio-political backing. Britain's key economic interest groups, the manufacturing sector and the financial industries, were split over the need for exchange-rate stability (see Henning 1994: 337). Furthermore, the attempt to stabilise sterling by participating in

European monetary integration was viewed with great suspicion within the ruling Conservative Party (split between Eurosceptics and Europhiles), by the English political establishment, and by the Whitehall ministerial bureaucracy.[13] As Nigel Wicks, Head of the Treasury's international division during the ERM period, pointed out, 'The political consensus in favour of the ERM was fairly superficial. [...] There are no doubt many explanations for the difference between French and UK attitudes here, including the French belief in EMU, a more cohesive political class, a less hostile media.'[14]

Adding to the lack of social embeddedness, sterling's ERM peg suffered from clear-cut economic and political sustainability problems. By entering the ERM, the Government had committed itself to maintain and defend a central rate of 2.95 Deutschmark, with a fluctuation band of +/-6 per cent, the wider of the two fluctuation bands of the ERM.[15] At this rate, sterling was overvalued, as indicated by a growing current-account deficit.[16] Furthermore, to maintain exchange-rate stability, British monetary policy was constrained to shadow the monetary policy of Germany.[17] In the 1991/2 period, this meant that the high levels of interest rates imposed on the ERM by the German central bank, the Bundesbank, translated into severe disinflation for Britain. The administration was constrained to maintain official interest rates above German rates, despite a deepening recession and unemployment rising above the 10 per cent mark in 1992,[18] since undercutting German interest rates would have triggered capital outflows which would have destabilised sterling's ERM parity.

ERM-imposed disinflation resulted in immense social and economic stresses. Britain's overextended banking and credit structure was particularly vulnerable to high interest rates. High levels of corporate debt, overexposed bank balance sheets and a housing market which relied on the massive accumulation of mortgage debt at floating interest rates made wide sections of the British economy and society highly sensitive to continuously high official interest rates, not to mention possible increases in line with Bundesbank policy. The economic distress of homeowners translated into political sustainability problems of the ERM peg for the ruling Conservative Party, not least since the spread of homeownership was central to its project of socio-economic reform.[19]

Consequently, and contrary to the practice of other ERM countries, Britain did not shadow Bundesbank monetary policy consistently but opted for a semi-autonomous path of gradually cutting official interest rates from 14 per cent in October 1990 to 10 per cent in May 1992, against the trend of Bundesbank rate increases. Even after the rejection of the Maastricht Treaty in the Danish referendum on 2 June 1992, the Government held rates steady – despite further rate increases by the Bundesbank. Although the crisis of European monetary integration weakened the glue of confidence and triggered mounting speculative tensions within the wider ERM, the UK relied on intervention only to defend sterling. Bank rate increases of up to 15 per cent were only announced on 'Black Wednesday' in a futile attempt to stem the speculative avalanche once it had broken loose. Once sterling had been forced out of the ERM, interest rates were cut rapidly – they were at just 6 per cent by January 1993.[20] As one treasury official succinctly put it:

> [T]he position that 'unemployment is a price well worth paying' is one Ministers find difficult to defend. Thus, in practice, once it was clear that the UK was in recession – and that was soon after the UK joined the ERM – the policy objective of Ministers was to cut interest rates as fast as the need to maintain confidence in sterling's ERM commitment permitted.[21]

Thus, the UK Government presented itself to financial markets as having constrained its monetary policy-making autonomy within the tight ERM straightjacket, hoping that in practice this impression would allow it to get away with a policy of further autonomous loosening of the monetary stance. Critical for the success of this confidence-building trick was an escalating use of tough rhetoric purporting commitment to defend parity to cover up active domestic monetary policy de-escalation. The puzzle is why markets fell for this rhetoric. After all, markets had good reason to discount the rhetoric as bluff: why did they, until mid-September 1992, trust a hawkish monetary-policy rhetoric which was contrary to the dovish action on the interest-rates front, presented by a government which was economically and socially plagued by mounting sustainability problems of the peg? Furthermore, the Government had no track record of prioritising exchange-rate stability. It lacked consistent political backing for its strategy and had little economic-policy incentive to maintain the peg once domestic inflation had been brought under control. Both economics and IR theory have problems explaining the efficacy of the Government's currency machismo given these shortcomings.

The two standard economic theories of financial-market behaviour, rational expectations analysis and behavioural finance, are inadequate to solve the puzzle. Rational-expectations analysis in mainstream monetary economics offers little when it comes to explaining why markets could be bluffed.[22] Behavioural finance is more useful in explaining this denial by looking into the cognitive reality of decision-making in global finance.[23] According to this approach, market participants operating in a speculative, highly competitive and result-oriented environment look for explanations that 'satisfice': that are good enough to provide short-term practical direction to handle a momentary situation quickly and decisively.[24] Rather than making optimising choices using all available information, satisficing behaviour relies on 'psychological anchors' to make decisions (Shiller 2000: 135–47).

Psychological anchoring suggests that speculative financial markets are inclined to rely on 'storytelling' by authoritative figures, on narratives constructed by influential actors (Shiller 2000: 139). Once authoritative narratives are routinely accepted by market participants, herding behaviour –

that is, actual investment behaviour following conventional wisdom – leads to 'looping effects', which can turn the predictions of the authorities into self-fulfilling prophesies (Shiller 2000: 144). The pattern of authority dependence structuring market behaviour has been confirmed by econometric studies on the power of signalling by respected central-bank authorities. As Amato *et al.* (2002) demonstrate, authoritative public figures lay down a marker with their public pronouncements around which financial-market opinion coalesces, providing a rallying point for conventional wisdom in financial markets. As they put it, for the signalling power of central banks: 'The more authority that the central bank commands among the economic agents, the greater the danger that the aggregate outcome is tinged by the central bank's own prior beliefs' (Amato *et al.* 2002: 4).

Although this analysis brings in the dimension of inter-subjective 'symbolic' power in the shape of authority, it fails to explain why UK policy-makers were commanding such authority in markets. As previously noted, when it came to exchange-rate stability, the policy-making track record of all post-war British administrations was dismal, leaving the Government with no *Vertrauenskapital* or 'trust' in this issue area.[25] The possibility exists, however, that *Vertrauenskapital* 'earned' by government in another issue area could have been borrowed for use as a resource for exerting authority in the issue area of exchange-rate policy, in analogy to the borrowing and lending of monetary capital among different economic agents and across different economic activities.

It is here that IR power analysis and the issue of fungibility comes into play. The possibility that trust earned in a different context can be borrowed to wield authority in another context suggests that the power resources on which authority is based are fungible. Whether this is the case is highly contested in IR theory. Neo-realists such as Waltz and Art support the idea of fungibility (see Waltz 1986 and Art 1999). Baldwin, however, is sceptical, arguing that power capabilities do not make sense in general abstract terms but only within the scope and domain of a specific power relationship. Consequently, for Baldwin, the effectiveness of power resources are issue-area specific and thus of limited fungibility (Baldwin 1999; 2002: 180). This line of thought is, from a constructivist angle, supported by Guzzini (2004c: 539–42). Both Baldwin's and Guzzini's argument rests on their critique of the power–money analogy made by realism. In their view, money as a general standard of value is distinguished by universal liquidity or ultimate fungibility. It is thus seen as conceptually opposite to the domain-dependent effectiveness of political power resources (Baldwin 1989: Chapter 2).

Constructivism frequently draws on the example of money, however, to demonstrate the inter-subjective construction of social reality, which, of course, includes power relations (Searle 1995). Paper money is fungible as a mere symbol, whose unconditional acceptance is based on the inter-subjective agreement that it represents purchasing power.[26] Value is created in a specific social realm, and purchasing power is realised in another specific issue area.

The fungibility of value though rests solely with its symbolic appearance as money, which is the inter-subjective attribution of purchasing power to government-issued pieces of paper. Only by detaching value from specific origins and attributing it to abstract symbols can it become fungible. The question is whether it is possible to identify a similar process in the language of currency machismo by the British Government in 1992/3. Was it possible for the UK Government to exert authority over markets in the ERM issue area through the use of symbolic language which mobilised a hawkish reputation earned in a different issue area? If reputation as a power resource could be mobilised across issue areas because of its attribution to symbolically significant language, it would point at a considerable degree of fungibility.[27]

Currency manipulation as socially constructed by 'symbolic power'

A critical social-constructivist approach to the investigation of the international political economy of money and finance is by now well established.[28] Bourdieu's sociology, and especially his concept of symbolic power, is particularly suited to investigate what kind of power resources policy-makers can command to exert authoritative influence over financial markets.[29] First of all, Bourdieu pays unique attention to power. Second, he locates power in the interaction between symbolic rhetoric and social reality, with the possibility of socially constructed meaning becoming detached from social reality, addressing the structure–agency problem at the heart of any social constructive explanation of financial crises. Finally, he emphasises reflexivity: the reflexive interaction between actors' symbolic discourses and the shape of social constructed reality ('the field of practice' to use Bourdieu's terminology), which allows for a precise location of international financial crises in the objective–subjective dichotomy.[30]

As Brubaker elaborates, Bourdieu interprets social life as materially grounded and conditioned but as existing only through symbolically mediated experience.[31] Social structures thus shape symbolic behaviour, which in turn reproduces social structures. Or, in Bourdieu's words, 'Objective relations do not exist and do not really realize themselves except and through the *system of dispositions* of the agents, produced by the internalization of objective conditions' (Bourdieu 1968: 705). Symbolic power is, then, the power over the symbolic mediation of social experiences. It imposes *how* objective conditions are internalised by individual agents. Bourdieu defines symbolic power as 'worldmaking power': 'The power to constitute the given by stating it, to act upon the world by acting upon the representation of the world [...] it operates only inasmuch as those who undergo it recognizes [*sic*] those who wield it' (Bourdieu and Wacquant 1992: 148).

This 'worldmaking' capacity of powerful ideas is what distinguishes symbolic power from other forms of power. It represents, in Stephen Lukes's terms, the third dimension of power, the power of 'securing the consent to domination of willing subjects' (Lukes 2005: 109). According to Bourdieu, symbolic power results from 'symbolic capital': the accumulated capital of honour, respect, prestige, and renown attributed to an actor. It originates from an actor's past strategies expending other forms of capital (such as political or economic capital) to cultivate his or her social reputation. Not only are symbolic capital and economic capital mutually convertible, but, once obtained, symbolic capital can substitute for economic capital by functioning as *Vertrauenskapital*, as 'credit', 'capital of trust', 'a sort of advance' the dominated credits to the dominant (Bourdieu 1977: 178–83). The analogy to the monetary sphere is important. Like money capital, *Vertrauenskapital* can be leveraged as a power resource in different issue areas by policy-makers who want to signal commitment. By doing so, they, de facto, transfer their reputation from one issue area to another, putting it up as collateral to garner trust in a field of practice in which they have no track record. Symbolic capital becomes fungible in this process.

Symbolic power operates in practice by acceptance and consent: dominant actors can impose their understanding as the field's 'authoritative' vision because they are acknowledged for their competence in other fields. Symbolic language referring to these field practices triggers this acknowledgement in the addressee. Thus, social recognition of competence is a precondition for successful symbolic manipulation. It allows the acknowledged agent to impose 'misrecognition' and 'denial' of the social reality of a new field of practice (see Swartz 1997: 88–91). In the words of Bourdieu, effective political action presupposes the '*competence* (in the sense of a *capacity socially recognised in a public authority*) required in order to manipulate the collective definition of the situation and thereby win the means of mobilizing the largest possible group' (Bourdieu 1977: 40). A means of symbolic manipulation is to evoke analogies to symbolically significant past experiences, to facilitate the misrecognition of present experiences. As Swartz puts it, Bourdieu's actors' choices are, 'tacit, practical and dispositional, reflecting the encounter between the accumulated capital and corresponding dispositions from past experience and the present opportunities and constraints of the field where they act' (Swartz 1997: 78).

Critical for the transfer of symbolic capital accumulated in the past to new and different issue areas is Bourdieu's concept of *habitus*, defined as,

> a system of lasting, transposable dispositions which, integrating past experiences, functions at every moment as a *matrix of perceptions, appreciations, and actions* and makes possible the achievement of infinitely diversified tasks, thanks to analogical transfers of schemes permitting the solution of similarly shaped problems.
>
> (Bourdieu 1977: 82–3).

That dispositions are transposable, as long as a certain analogical relationship can be drawn between the problems posed in different issue areas, confirms the unique quality of symbolic capital: its transferability, rooted in its attachment to symbolically significant actor behaviour rather than specific situations. Symbolic capital, although accumulated in specific situations, is negotiated across issue areas as inter-subjective meaning, through the attribution of dispositional features to actors who are able to symbolically associate themselves with the past experiences in which it was originally obtained. By transposing symbolic capital from past issue areas, agents do not have to accumulate it again in the present new issue area through politically costly sacrifices; rather, they can thrive for the time being on past glory. What is needed for this to occur is to present new problems in the shape of successfully overcome old problems. If such historical association succeeds, symbolic capital can be used across various domains, allowing the actor to wield symbolic power in issue areas where they lack a track record of competent behaviour. What matters for the effective mobilisation of symbolic capital is not *what* an agent does, but *how* this behaviour is presented: whether the *habitus* of the agent is in keeping with the acknowledged *habitus* attributed to them in the domain where the trust accumulated from past experience. This unique transferability of symbolic power is even more significant, considering that other less fungible forms of power, such as military power, only become fully effective if they are given symbolic meaning.

Critical for the relative fungibility of symbolic capital is that it is symbolically represented in both the *habitus* of the dominant actor, who is imposing his or her worldview on reality, and that of the dominated actor, who accepts this worldview as social truth. Only if the symbolic signals and actions of the dominant actor elicit almost instinctive acceptance as being 'authoritative' by the dominated actors – are thus ingrained in their *habitus* – can the dominant actor regulate the 'reasonable' practical responses of the dominated to her or his activity and, thus, succeed with manipulation in different issue areas. Thus: 'Collective mobilization cannot succeed without a minimum of concordance between the habitus of the mobilizing agents (e.g. prophet, party leader, etc.) and the dispositions of those whose aspirations and world-views they express' (Bourdieu 1977: 81).[32]

It is in this concordance where symbolic power is realised regardless of its area-specific origins. To put it in the words of Robert J. Art (1999: 185), the fungibility of power is constituted by the domain unspecific mutually shared perception of a 'hierarchy of clout'. The efficacy of symbolic power, but also its limitations, is situated in the double hermeneutics of constructivism, the interaction between socially constructed meaning and constructed social reality. First, once symbolically charged rhetoric has succeeded in mobilising fungible symbolic power to impose meaning on social reality, symbolic power is self-fulfilling through 'the dialectic of mutually self-reproducing objective changes and subjective aspirations' (Bourdieu and Passeron 1979: 97). As a discourse of practice, symbolic rhetoric instructs not just social understanding but also social action. Those actions will, in practice, reaffirm the vision of the trusted authority. Symbolic power is, thus, 'capable of producing real effects without any apparent expenditure of energy' – constructing a social reality which matches the social expectations it conjures up.[33]

Second, the efficacy, as well as the limitations of symbolic power, are situated in the fact that it constitutes 'collectively concerted make believe' (Bourdieu 1977: 173). This leads to the misrecognition of the underlying socio-economic reality through orchestrated social repression of cognitive dissonance. A discrepancy between habitual behaviour grounded in past experiences and the present field of practice is thus possible in the form of cracks in the social construction of meaning. Bourdieu uses the term 'hysteresis' to describe the 'specific inertia' of habitus in the face of 'objective changes': 'Agents whose mental structures have been moulded by [...] prior structures [...] act inopportunely (*à contre-temps*); [...] they are "out of sync"' (Bourdieu and Wacquant 1992: 130). The extent to which the prevailing social representations and routine behaviour can be 'locked in' in the face of objective change through hysteresis depends on the effective employment of symbolic power by those interested in the status quo. However, it is also within this disjuncture that the limits of symbolic power are rooted. Change does become possible if the contradiction between objective changes and relatively permanent habitus escalate to the point of general and profound uncertainty. As Bourdieu put it, 'Practices [constituted by habitus] are always liable to incur negative sanctions when the environment with which they are actually confronted is too distant from that to which they are objectively fitted' (Bourdieu 1977: 78).[34]

In such situations, 'collective disillusionment' (Bourdieu, quoted in Brubaker 1985: 759) with the symbolically imposed dominant representations can be exploited by reputable agents who see it in their interest to challenge accepted social meanings in an attempt to impose their own version on the world as social truth. In such moments, the economic field will turn from a set of practices of conformity into an arena of struggle for legitimation (See Leander 2002: 11). Competing actors will draw on their respective stock of symbolic capital in a struggle of 'symbolic violence' to define the field in accordance with their vision (Swartz 1997: 123). Such struggle represents a moment of severe crisis in the field, since not only is the system of representations which give social meaning to the field at stake, but also the field-stabilising practices. The outcome of the struggle depends on whether the established authorities retain enough symbolic power to sustain social acceptance for their vision of the field or whether the collective rallies behind the rhetoric of a challenger who can draw on more *Vertrauenskapital*. If the vision of the challenger prevails, a paradigm shift in field-specific hegemonic interpretations and a revolution in the field's socio-political structure results. Authoritative symbolic power dominating a field thus finds its limits in the symbolic power of other actors offering contesting visions of the field.[35] It is in this contest for symbolic domination between an established and an alternative worldview, that symbolic power, which in 'normal' times appears as the 'third dimension' of power, reveals its 'first dimension' in the form of symbolic violence.[36]

Finally, the practice of symbolic power – symbolically charged rhetoric – has a tendency towards 'symbolic overreach', contributing to its own undoing.[37]

Paradoxically, this tendency is intrinsic to its operational efficiency. To maintain the symbolic power of the manipulative rhetoric, fungible symbolic capital resources attached to significant language have to be continuously mobilised through the use of this language. Sustained construction of meaning and social reality based on misperception, denial and bluff requires the persistent actualisation of the 'authenticity' of the manipulator. The manipulative discourse is 'a structure of meaning in-use', persistently actualised by the regular use of modes of signification (see Milliken 1999: 231). The manipulator thus faces a 'symbolic dilemma'. In a situation of mounting anomaly, the only way to stabilise the hegemonic discourse is to escalate rhetoric signalling. By doing so, manipulating agents end up over-extending their symbolic capital in a desperate attempt to reinforce their increasingly fragile symbolic hold over the present social domain.

In this way, the manipulator unwittingly entraps him- or herself in an 'emperor without clothes' situation, a situation in which the decoupling of social understanding and social reality is suppressed only by the collective illusions maintained by escalating symbolic overreach. Like the emperor in the tale, it leaves the manipulator highly vulnerable to exposure by those who dare to state the naked truth. A truth which is there for everyone to see but requires the veil of collective illusion to be lifted. It is precisely when the collective illusion is challenged by a dissident actor that the field of conformity is turned into a field of struggles between competing visions of the situation. Symbolic over-reach, if successfully challenged, results in a breakdown of socially constructed credibility. It leaves the symbolically dominant actor in a state of symbolic bankruptcy, with his or her symbolic capital accumulated in past collective experiences depleted by the collective realisation of his or her bluff.[38] Thus, the field of British monetary policy in Europe in 1992/3 demonstrates how the fungibility of symbolic power operated in practice, allowing UK policy-makers to impress financial markets through the rhetoric of currency machismo.

UK currency machismo as practice of symbolic power

The reconstruction of the success and ultimate failure of British currency machismo reveals the astounding, albeit temporary, degree of mutual understanding between the Government's symbolic proclamations and financial-market sentiment. Representative of the Government's strong currency rhetoric are three key statements by the Prime Minister and the Chancellor of the Exchequer. First is the keynote speech 'Britain and the Exchange Rate Mechanism' by Norman Lamont, the Chancellor, made to the European Policy Forum in London on 11 July 1992. Second is John Major's ultimate and uncompromising public defence of his sterling policy in a speech to the Scottish Confederation of British Industry (CBI) in Glasgow on 8 September 1992. And third is Major's informal, but highly publicised, remarks on the future of sterling at the end of July 1992.[39] In essence, all three statements signalled to markets that ministers had nailed 'their reputation to the mast of the ERM. As Major put it, regarding his CBI speech, 'I went for broke' (Major 1999: 326).

Both Lamont's and Major's speech framed the exchange-rate commitment in a classic bipolar discourse structure full of symbolic references, projecting a black-and-white world of strength against weakness, triumph against utter defeat and sacrifice against easy options of false escape. Only by sticking to sterling's ERM parity, the 2.95 Deutschmark central rate, would Britain claim victory over the nation's economic nemesis, domestic inflation. There was no alternative: realignment or leaving the ERM was out of the question; it would destroy the Government's anti-inflation strategy and herald economic disaster. According to Lamont's memoirs, in response to pressure by Major to be more 'convincing' and 'forceful' about the commitment to the ERM, Lamont pointed out that cutting interest rates and leaving the ERM would 'be the cut and run option: cut interest rates and a run on the pound' (Lamont 1999: 212). Proponents of alternatives to the Government's strategy of sacrificing growth, jobs and the housing market for the sake of exchange-rate stability were dismissed as irresponsible wimps, pleading for a free lunch: 'Sadly, there is no such thing [as a free lunch]. As the Russians say, only mousetraps have free cheese.'[40] John Major's CBI speech gives an even more drastic representation of the Manichaean worldview of currency machismo:

> All my adult life I have seen British governments driven off their virtuous pursuit of low inflation by market problems or political pressure. I was under no illusions when I took sterling into the ERM. I said at the time that membership was not the soft option. The soft option, the devaluer's option, the inflationary option, would be a betrayal of our future; and that is not the government's policy. [...] We must bite the anti-inflationary bullet or accept that we will be forever second-rate in Europe. [...] There is no subtler, no surer means of overturning the existing basis of society than to debauch the currency.[41]

Finally, the strongest and almost sensational representations of official currency machismo are John Major's excessive claims about the future of sterling in summer 1992. At a Downing Street party on 16 July, he trailed his thinking to journalists that he wanted to make sterling the strongest currency in the ERM, stronger perhaps than the Deutschmark. On 29 July he went even further, speculating to Andrew Neil of the *Sunday Times* that the pound might become one of the strongest currencies in the world (Stephens 1997: 218–19). These comments produced a headline in the *Sunday Times* on 2 August: 'Major aims to make sterling best in Europe' (Seldon 1998: 298).

The resonance of this symbolic rhetoric with financial markets is astounding. Until summer 1992, they accepted official currency machismo as the authoritative interpretation of the situation. Traders rallied behind sterling, despite the official policy to reduce interest rates against the trend of rising German rates. Just as outlined by Bourdieu, symbolic power operated in inter-subjective practice. Market acknowledgement granted the strong currency rhetoric a self-fulfilling quality by empowering the Government to constitute social reality by stating it in a language of macho symbolism. The efficacy of the Government's symbolic rhetoric is best described in an internal treasury assessment of the ERM strategy, written fifteen months after sterling's exit from the system:

> Ministers were able to move the exchange market by what they said as well as what they did. [... W]hat mattered was not whether there [*sic*] claims were true, nor even whether the authorities persuaded the markets that the claims were true. What mattered was that the authorities persuaded the markets that they (i.e. the authorities) believed these claims.
>
> ('ERM Project, Part Two', paragraphs 52 and 59)

Duping markets into believing, the authorities managed to narrow the gap between official German and British interest rates from 8 per cent in October 1990 to only 1.25 per cent in July 1992.[42] Markets responded to each of these cuts positively by demanding an ever-lower risk premium for holding sterling rather than Deutschmarks, with British short-term borrowing costs falling in summer 1992 to only 0.25 percent above their German equivalent. Officials started to ponder the possibility of cutting rates unilaterally below German rates (see Lamont 1999: 197). The self-reinforcing dynamics of disinflation, official interest-rate cuts and market enthusiasm which underpinned confidence in sterling is reflected in a comment by Salomon Brothers which, as late as 31 July 1992, suggested that 'falling UK inflation should still allow UK short-term interest rates to fall to or even below German levels.'[43] Buoyed by market optimism, the Government reinforced the machismo attitude in its rhetoric, first, by presenting severe disinflation – which, de facto, strangled the British economy – as evidence for the success of its exchange-rate stance. Second, it signalled firm determination to fix sterling in the core of the ERM by stating the 'absolutely clear commitment' to shift to the restrictive narrow fluctuation bands of +/−2.25 per cent at the existing rate as soon as possible ('ERM Project, Part Two', paragraph 52). Again, markets responded enthusiastically. Salomon Brothers asserted that Britain was 'within reach of the low-inflation heart of the ERM' and Goldman Sachs pointed out that markets believed that the UK Government's commitment to narrow bands was credible.[44] When market confidence in sterling weakened in the wake of the Danish referendum on 2 June 1992, the Government raised the stakes by categorically ruling out the devaluation of sterling except as part of a general ERM alignment including the French franc. This commitment linked sterling to the 'franc fort', the strongest ERM currency next to the Deutschmark. Again markets bought this rhetoric, dismissing the possibility of a unilateral devaluation by the UK as unrealistic.[45]

Clearly, symbolic power was at work in maintaining concordance between the Government's commitment to the exchange rate and market confidence in this commitment. The *habitus* of financial markets to look for authoritative guidance is not a sufficient explanation for why markets granted authority to a government without a track record in maintaining exchange-rate stability. Therefore, one has to ask where the symbolic power over market sentiment originated from. For the Major Government's exchange-rate commitment to be trusted by markets, it adopted a *habitus* in line with previous encounters of Conservative governments with financial markets. These previous encounters accrued considerable symbolic capital. By adopting such a *habitus*, the Conservative administration of John Major managed to activate the symbolic capital accumulated over eleven and a half years by successive Conservative administrations led by Margaret Thatcher. As Thatcher reminded her successor in April 1992:

> I don't accept the idea that all of a sudden Major is his own man. He has been prime minister for seventeen months and he has inherited these great achievements of the past 11½ years which have fundamentally changed Britain, ridding it of the debilitating, negative aspects of socialism. [...] There isn't such a thing as Majorism [...] Thatcherism will live. It will live long after Thatcher has died, because we had the courage to restore the great principles and put them into practice.[46]

Obviously, Major's strategy of pursuing external monetary stability through European exchange-rate cooperation was the antithesis of Thatcher's pursuit of domestic monetary stability through nationalist monetarism. But it was possible to transpose the symbolic capital accumulated by Thatcher in the field of past monetarism to the field of present exchange-rate cooperation, thereby transferring symbolic power from Thatcher to Major. Both strategies shared the objective of bringing inflation under control, and both strategies required a similar commitment to tolerating the sacrifices required by the rigid pursuit of a monetary target. Thus, in Bourdieu's terms, the similarity of the problems posed in the two diverse fields allowed for an analogical transfer of symbolic schemes permitting their solution. In practical terms, the Major Administration could mobilise the symbolic capital accumulated by Thatcher to wield symbolic power over financial markets, as long as its *habitus* in managing the exchange rate was in keeping with the *habitus* of Thatcher's monetarism. This suggests that symbolic capital is fungible, not only between political issue areas, but also between policymakers, as long as some similarity of the political options available and of political identities concerned is perceived.

Thatcher's *habitus*, adopted by Major for the practical purpose of lending credibility to his *turning away* from her monetarism towards the ERM, was distinguished by a macho attitude to monetary policy management. The 'Iron Lady' had built a reputation for monetary competence because she had pursued monetarist radicalism through strong, determined and inflexible leadership in the face of adversity. The underlying machismo in Thatcher's political *habitus* is well expressed in her legendary Conservative Party conference speech of 1980. After proclaiming that the 'prime objective' of her Conservative government was the 'defeat of inflation', she continued with a rhetorical question:

> 'Has Britain the courage and resolve to sustain the discipline for long enough to break through to success?' Yes, Mr Chairman, we have, and we shall. This Government are determined to stay with the policy and see it through to its conclusion. That is what marks this administration as one of the truly radical ministries of post-war Britain. [...] If our people feel we are a great nation, and they are prepared to will the means to keep it great, a great nation we shall be. [... W]e shall not be diverted from our course. To those waiting with bated breath for that favourite media catchphrase, the 'U turn', I have only one thing to say: 'You turn if you want to. The lady's not for turning.'
>
> (Thatcher 1997)

To wield symbolic power over financial-market participants, John Major chose to signal in his language that he was the legitimate heir of the trust and authority Thatcher accumulated in the markets during her premiership. This required adopting the same macho *habitus* which was so significant to Thatcher. Consequently, his administration framed the exchange-rate commitment in nationalistic, narrow anti-inflationary and inflexible rhetoric, turning the defence of sterling's ERM parity into a 'badge of national pride' and dismissing any thought of devaluation as national humiliation (see Stephens 1997: 219). It was by presenting the new policy in the dispositional characteristics that symbolised the strength of the past government that the administration could capture the imagination of financial markets, as suggested by one financial analyst:

> I think the markets [then] were Thatcherite and pro-European. So, in a sense they reflected the contradictions of the entire Conservative party. They said, 'we want to move on with these Europe things because this is the brave new world, these are the modern boys, Major and these people.' But markets are reflective of British characteristics: you have the hang-over from Thatcherism which is that radical measures are positive and that determination, if you will, is a virtue in itself; that policy flexibility is a sign of weakness and not strength. If you understand that devaluation is a humiliation, then you equate that with power and therefore they [the markets] knew the government would be deeply committed to parity.[47]

The contradiction in the Conservative Party was a necessity, since the specific symbolic conditionality of fungibility of the *Vertrauenskapital* accumulated by Thatcher required that the 'modern boys' presented themselves in the old habit. Constructing the ERM strategy around a commitment to the existing parity as a matter of national pride and anti-inflationary credibility, rather than around a spirit of European monetary cooperation and a stable but adjustable exchange rate, brought short-term credibility gains but came at the price of losing touch with reality. It meant forgoing political and economic flexibility in times when such flexibility was urgently needed. Symbolic power transposed from another issue area came at the price of symbolic dilemma and ultimately of symbolic overreach. Nailing its political and economic reputation to defending an exchange rate that was objectively increasingly indefensible left the administration in a symbolic trap. As John Gray, a senior treasury official put it:

> For the most part this process of nailing ourselves ever more firmly to the DM2.95 parity was unplanned. But once in the mechanism as it proved to be we were trapped; to have done other than pledge our loyalty to DM2.95 would probably have led to a lower exchange rate and higher interest rates.[48]

The more the administration found itself in an 'emperor without clothes' position – unable to raise interest rates in defence of parity or to devalue – the more dogmatic currency machismo became. With the politicians themselves 'mesmerised' by the shift to a fixed exchange rate,[49] thinking about alternatives in the civil service became virtually impossible. The Treasury's own analysis describes this symbolic dilemma well:

> There is a general problem with fixed exchange rate regimes that Ministers get into positions where regime changes can take place only at enormous political cost. It becomes very difficult for civil servants to recommend (or even think of) measures that they know may well cost their political masters their careers. There is no obvious solution to this problem.[50]

Being caught in this symbolic dilemma, the Major Administration decided to opt for a strategy of symbolic overreach. Unable to bring relief to the domestic malaise by lowering British interest rates unilaterally, the Government decided to challenge the German Bundesbank's monetary leadership of the ERM. At a critical and notoriously ill-tempered meeting of European monetary officials in Bath on 4 September 1992, Norman Lamont tried to browbeat the President of the Bundesbank Helmut Schlesinger to cut official German rates so that Britain and other ERM follower countries could lower their interest rates without risking exchange-rate instability. The aggressive handling of Schlesinger by Lamont was sanctioned by Major, who before the meeting had advised his Chancellor of the Exchequer to 'have the row now', rather than 'a slow death later'.[51] The strategy seemed to offer a way out of the Government's dilemma: to attack the German central bank, the hegemon of the system, was in keeping with Thatcher's nationalist machismo, and it promised relief from the increasing unease in financial markets about the absence of British rate increases in defence of parity.

However, by confronting the Bundesbank, the British Government man-oeuvred itself into a highly exposed position. First, it made clear the survival of its hard currency strategy depended on European cooperation, after having neglected European coalition-building through fifteen months of nationalistic currency machismo. Second, it challenged the authority of the Bundesbank, whose reputation for effective and independent anti-inflationary monetary leadership of the ERM was already under strain from the inflationary consequences of German unification. The symbolic power of British currency machismo reached its limits when the Bundesbank, rather than cooperating, decided to set its own vision of the position of sterling in the ERM against the vision of the British Government. On 15 September 1992, in a highly publicised interview with the German financial newspaper *Handelsblatt*, Schlesinger indicated that the Bundesbank thought that sterling should be devalued to resolve ERM tensions.[52] By, de facto, stating that the 'emperor has no clothes', Schlesinger's remarks turned the ERM from a field of conformity into a field of struggles. Markets now had the choice between two competing versions to make sense of the situation: the version of the ERM's key currency monetary authority that sterling was a weak and overvalued currency against the British view that the problem lay not with a strong sterling, but German leadership itself. The shallow and increasingly fragile credibility of British currency machismo found itself in conflict with what markets understood as the 'Bundesbank's intrinsic credibility'.[53] Symbolic power relying on transposed symbolic capital was outgunned by the symbolic power resources of the Bundesbank, resources not borrowed from another issue area but genuinely accumulated in the issue area concerned through years of authoritative leadership of the ERM.

The Bundesbank's superior symbolic power resources allowed it to commit an act of symbolic violence which 'finished sterling off', as the Treasury put it.[54] It's signalling shattered the remaining market illusions about the sustainability of sterling. On 16 September, Black Wednesday, the Government was forced by a massive and unprecedented wave of speculative selling to withdraw sterling from the ERM and to float the currency, leaving the authorities in a state of shock and their reputation for monetary and wider economic competence in ruins.

Conclusion

Fungibility of symbolic power resources was essential to both the temporary success and ultimate failure of British currency machismo. The UK

Government under the leadership of Major only succeeded in bluffing the market because the symbolic capital accumulated in financial markets by Thatcher's domestic monetarism could be transposed to a new policy commitment to international exchange-rate stability. The trust elicited in financial markets through rhetorically signifying association with Thatcher's symbolic capital, however, was wasted to prop up an unsustainable policy. When the Major Administration tried to make up for the depletion of domestically borrowed symbolic capital by borrowing credibility internationally from the Bundesbank, the Germans' refusal to put their stock of *Vertrauenskapital* at risk to bail out Britain was correctly understood by markets as symbolic default. Like financial capital, symbolic capital can, through symbolic association via rhetoric signalling, be put to use in issue areas different from the area of origin. But the symbolic borrower lives, like the economic debtor, on borrowed time. If the transposed trust is not productively put to work to engender fresh reputation for political competence in the new issue area, but exploited to cover up policy failure, it will be wasted. The limits of symbolic power fungibility become apparent in symbolic bankruptcy. For symbolic power as world-making power to last, it needs the valorisation of transposed symbolic capital in the new issue area. Otherwise, exploiting fungibility of accumulated symbolic capital in different issue areas will only run down the overall stock of *Vertrauenskapital* held by financial markets.

The fungibility of symbolic capital in the form of borrowed credibility is akin to the fungibility of financial capital in the form of credit. This suggests that the critics of the fungibility-of-power notion should reconsider the specific nature of the symbolic dimension of power: first, their critique of the fungibility proponents, centred on the dismissal of the money–power analogy, overlooks analogies between the symbolic nature of money and powerful language. At the heart of the fungibility of money lies its quality of being an inter-subjectively acknowledged symbol representing capital beyond the specific issue area of its accumulation. This quality is analogue to the quality of inter-subjectively acknowledged imposing language representing symbolic capital beyond the specific issue area of its origin. A possible reason that even constructivists neglect this analogy might be a simplistic understanding of money, looked at primarily as means of exchange, overlooking its dimension of representing credit. The findings of this chapter ask for a renewed investigation of the power-fungibility problem, focusing on symbolic capital as the resource of symbolic power. This would contribute to the ongoing debate about the role of power in the social constructivist worldview.

Acknowledgement

The author thanks Felix Berenskoetter, Michael J. Williams and two anonymous reviewers for their valuable comments on an earlier versions of this essay. The usual disclaimers apply.

Notes

1 The argument draws on the Mundell–Fleming model in international economics. See Cohen (1993).
2 See the econometric analysis of realignment expectations by Rose and Svensson (1995).
3 'ERM Project: The UK's Membership of the ERM, Part Two', study conducted by Stephen Davis, 21 December 1993, paragraphs 68, 47 and 105, in *Sterling Withdrawal from ERM*. HM Treasury, Freedom of Information Disclosures, 9 February 2005. Available online. HTTP: www.hm-treasury.gov.uk/about/infor mation/foi_disclosures/foi_erm_090205.cfm. Accessed 10 March 2005. The author's identity is given in an internal treasury e-mail, mistakenly sent to the BBC on 9 February 2005. See 'Leaked e-mail', 7. Available online. HTTP: news.bbc.co.uk/1/shared/bsp/hi/pdfs/09_05_foi_template280105.pdf. Accessed 10 March 2005.
4 The Oxford English Dictionary Online (Oxford University Press, 2005), defines *machismo* as 'the quality of being macho', and *macho* as 'assertively masculine or tough; producing the impression of manliness and toughness' (Accessed 20 February 2005).
5 According to Baldwin, 'fungibility' refers to the ease with which power resources useful in one issue area can be used in other issue areas. See Baldwin (2002: 180). Baldwin (especially 1989 and 1999) still is the key source when it comes to the discussion of the fungibility issue in power analysis.
6 For a brief account of the 1992/3 ERM crisis, see Kenen (1995: 150–64). For a good summary of the British ERM experience in 1992, see Blair (2002: 160–78).
7 See C. Randall Henning (1994: 336–9). The Conservative neglect of the exchange rate is demonstrated by the fact that, since Margaret Thatcher came into office in 1979, sterling had gone through successive cycles of severe appreciation and depreciation against the US dollar. The sterling–Deutschemark rate displayed great volatility, within a long-run trend of depreciation (Source: Datastream; Deutsche Bundesbank).
8 See Grahl 1997: 96.
9 See study conducted by Stephen Davis, 21 December 1993, 'ERM Project: The UK's Membership of the ERM, Part One', in *Sterling Withdrawal*. Paragraphs 34 and 35 of the paper point out that by 1990 joining the ERM was seen to be an 'institutional alternative' in face of the 'collapse in credibility' of the Government's monetarist policy framework.
10 See minute from Paul Gray to Sir Terry Burns, 'Reflections on the UK's Membership in the ERM, 5 January 1995', 2, in *Sterling Withdrawal*. The author's identity is given in 'Leaked e-mail', 8.
11 The speech was given to the European Policy Forum, Queen Elizabeth Centre, 11 July 1992. See Lamont (1999: 212). For an assessment of the speech as a decisive statement of the Government's argument that fighting domestic inflationary was at the core of the ERM strategy, see 'Britain and the Exchange Rate Mechanism: Chancellor's Speech to the European Policy Forum', 29 July 1993, 2, in *Sterling Withdrawal*. As Stephens (1997: 212) points out, the speech reflected the consensus at the top of the Treasury.
12 Britain had negotiated an opt-out from the EMU project at the Maastricht conference in December 1991.
13 This split was particularly severe between 1990 and 1993. See Forster (2002: Chapter 6). The lack of 'Europeanisation' in the Whitehall culture has been identified by Dyson (2000) as a major obstacle for a constructive engagement of Britain with European monetary cooperation.

14 Note written by Sir Nigel Wicks, 'Reflections on the UK's Membership of the ERM, 10 January 1994', 1–2, in *Sterling Withdrawal*. The names are given in 'Leaked e-mail', 9.

15 The narrow band being +/-2.5 per cent.

16 Although the question of whether the entry rate was overvalued is still a matter of some dispute, the recently released internal treasury documents by and large conclude that, as one paper puts it, 'sterling's ERM entry rate was much too high.' 'ERM Project, Part One', paragraph 42. See also note from Chris Riley to Allan Budd, 'The Exchange Rate, 17 September 1992', in *Sterling Withdrawal*. The names are given in 'Leaked e-mail', 6.

17 This need stems from the nature of the ERM as an asymmetric key currency system. See De Grauwe (1997).

18 Sources: Datastream; OECD Economic Outlook 66, December 1999, Statistical Annex.

19 The Treasury clearly recognises that the state of the housing market and its potential implications for the financial position of major building societies constituted a major cause for the political unsustainability of the British ERM commitment. See 'ERM Project, Part Two', paragraphs 21–7.

20 Clearings Bank Base Rate. Source: Bank of England.

21 'ERM Project, Part Two', paragraph 10.

22 In the rational-expectation model of market behaviour, markets, realising the 'time inconsistency' of the ERM peg, should not have granted temporary credibility to the UK Government's policy statements. On the time-consistency problem, see De Grauwe (1996).

23 Behavioural finance builds on the common heuristics and biases identified by cognitive psychology. For a good summary, see Barberis and Thaler (2002).

24 See Shefrin (2000) and Shiller (2000). The concept of satisficing has been developed within Simon's theory of 'bounded rationality' (Simon 1997).

25 The German word *Vertrauenskapital* translates directly as 'capital of trust'.

26 Baldwin (1989: 21–3) points out the symbolic aspect of money, but does not recognise the potential of the symbolic nature of money's fungibility for political power analysis.

27 Language is central to the constructivist project, not only in regard to the construction of social reality as a system of inter-subjective meanings, but also regarding the inter-subjective dimension of power and hegemony. See Adler (2002: 103).

28 For a ground-breaking application of constructivism to European monetary affairs, see McNamara (1998); for a representative application of constructivism directly to British monetary policy-making in Europe, see Dyson (2000); for a constructivist theory of financial crises, see Wildmaier (2003); for a critical investigation of the behaviour of financial markets from a neo-Gramscian/Polanyian approach, see Harmes (1998), and Harmes (2001) for an application of this approach to explain the ERM crisis; for contructivist/Polanyian approaches to the politics of financial governance, see Best (2003) and Blyth (2002); and, finally, for an example of the post-structuralist work highlighting the importance of discourse practices in financial markets, see De Goede (2001).

29 For original statements of Bourdieu's theory of practice, see Bourdieu (1977; 1992), and Bourdieu and Wacquant (1992). Good discussions of Bourdieu's sociology are Brubaker (1985) and Swartz (1997).

30 I draw here on Anna Leander's (2002) argument for an IPE inspired by the thought of Bourdieu. Leander has previously pointed out the importance of Bourdieu for an open interpretative IPE. See Leander (2000). Stephano Guzzini (2000a) has introduced Bourdieu's theory as a way to locate the power at the centre of the double hermeneutics of constructivism.

31 See Brubaker (1985: 750). Brubaker offers an excellent discussion of how Bourdieu 'transcends' the objective/subjective divide (1985: 749–53).
32 See Brubaker's (1985: 758–60) elaboration of Bourdieu's notion of habitus.
33 Bourdieu (1991: 170). The tendency in financial markets towards self-fulfilling behaviour is widely accepted in monetary economics. See for example Willett (2000: 53–6).
34 See also Swartz (1997: 111–12).
35 This model of change has clear similarities to Kuhn's model of scientific paradigm shifts. See Kuhn (1996), especially Chapters 7 and 8.
36 For the three-dimensional view of power, see Lukes (2005) and the introduction to this volume.
37 'Symbolic overreach' defined as failing by trying to achieve more than is possible through the exclusive and excessive use of symbolic power.
38 Wendt (1992: 422) describes the social disrecognition of agents whose symbolic strategies fail as 'sucker' payoff.
39 All three sources are widely acknowledged as key representative statements of the Government's attitude to sterling. As Seldon (1998: 298) notes, Lamont's speech 'became the government's point of reference in the stormy waters of the next two months.' Its importance is acknowledged by the Treasury's internal documents. See 'Britain and the Exchange Rate Mechanism: Chancellor's Speech to the European Policy Forum, 29 July 1993', *Sterling Withdrawal*. Major's CBI speech was deliberately directed at financial markets as an unequivocal reassurance of the Government's commitment to robustly defend the pound. See Major (1999: 326).
40 Norman Lamont, 'Speech to the European Policy Forum, 10 July 1992', quoted in Stephens (1997: 213).
41 John Major, Prime Minister's Speech at a dinner of the Scottish Confederation of British Industry, Glasgow, 8 September 1992 (Press Office, 10 Downing Street, 10 September 1992), quoted in Stephens (1997: 237).
42 Source: Deutsche Bundesbank (Discount Rate) and Bank of England (Clearing Banks Base Rate).
43 Salomon Brothers, 'International Market Roundup', 31 July 1992, 5. This and the following quotes of financial market participants are from a reconstruction of market sentiment in the ERM crisis based on the systematic analysis of a sample of representative market reports during the crisis. For details, see Hassdorf (2003).
44 Salomon Brothers, 'International Market Roundup', 14 September 1992, 5; and Goldman Sachs, 'International Economics Analyst', May 1992, 7/5, section 1.14.
45 See Goldman Sachs, 'International Economics Analyst', May 1992, 7/5, section S. 10.
46 Margaret Thatcher, interview with *Newsweek*, 27 April 1992, quoted in Seldon (1998: 290).
47 Adam Cleary, Director, EMEA Corporate Debt Research, ING Bank NV, interviewed by author on 18 August 2004.
48 'Reflections on the UK's Membership in the ERM, 5 January 1995', 3.
49 In the description of Leigh-Pemberton, Governor of the Bank of England in 1992. Robert Leigh-Pemberton, Evidence to the House of Commons Treasury and Civil Service Committee, *The Autumn Statement and the Conduct of Economic Policy* (HMSO, 13 January 1993).
50 'ERM Project, Part Two.' The passage was deleted from the released version of the paper, but published in 'Leaked e-mail', 15.
51 Major (1999: 322). For a colourful description of Lamont's confrontation with the Bundesbank President, see Connolly (1995: 144–7).
52 Although the interview was only first published on 16 September 1992, the essence of it was distributed by the news wires already in the evening of 15 September.
53 Goldman Sachs, May 1993, 8/5, section S.02.
54 'ERM Project, Part Two', paragraph 92.

9 Notes for a soft-power research agenda

Joseph S. Nye, Jnr

When I coined the term 'soft power' in 1990, I envisioned it as a positive rather than a normative concept. I was trying to explain why I disagreed with the then prevalent view of the decline of American power (Kennedy 1987). After examining American economic and military power, I thought that something was still missing – the ability of the USA to attract others and thus increase the probability of obtaining the outcomes it wanted. It has been interesting to see an academic concept migrate to the front pages of newspapers and to see it used by leaders in China, Europe and elsewhere over the past decade and a half. But wide usage has sometimes meant misuse of the concept as a synonym for culture, economics or anything other than military force. For example, a Heritage Foundation paper refers to 'soft power options such as economic sanctions', and one observer argues that China thinks that 'soft power implies all elements outside of the security realm' (Brookes 2006: 1; Kurlantick 2006: 1) The rock group Ladytron even used soft power as the title of a song in a recent album. In contrast, the contributions in this volume suggest thoughtful criticisms that point the way for further research on soft power. These notes are my response.

Though the concept is recent, the behaviour it denotes is not new. Mencius said 'win the people if you will win the empire' (Lau 1970: 120). In 1762, when Frederick the Great was on the brink of defeat, he was saved when 'the Prusso-phobic Czarina Elizabeth died and was succeeded by her son Peter, who idolized the soldier-king [...] and ordered home the Russian armies' (Byman and Pollack 2001: 107). Similarly, when the USA wrestled with the choice between Germany and Britain in the First World War, the soft power of Britain in the USA was a significant factor. 'Germany's primary disadvantage in 1914 was not its record in American opinion, but the absence of a record. So little existed to counteract the natural pull toward Britain [...] which dominated the channels of transatlantic communication' (Wiebe 1967: 264). And although I introduced the concept in the field of international relations (IR) which tends to focus on states in an anarchic international structure, soft power is not restricted to IR. Politicians in democratic polities are constantly relying on their soft power of attraction, and university presidents often find that their soft power is far greater than their hard power.

Steven Lukes correctly points out that power is a primitive and contested term (Lukes, this volume, p. 83). Which interests the analyst chooses to consider as important inevitably involves value judgements. Different social-science disciplines also focus on different aspects of behaviour. Lukes's adapted Lockean definition of power as the ability to make, receive or resist change is a useful general definition. For my purposes, I chose an agent-focused definition of power that was quite close to the common usage implied by the dictionary – the ability to affect others to obtain the outcomes one wants. Of the three main ways to affect others' behaviour – coercion, inducement or attraction – I used the term 'soft power' for the third. Lukes is correct that one can also take a subject- rather than agent-focused approach and ask what are the different ways that soft power can co-opt, attract and entice. What makes people susceptible to attraction? To what extent are perceptions of interests shaped by myths and indoctrination and to what extent by free reasoning? How do agents win the hearts and minds of subjects? I argued that the spectrum of behaviours between command and co-optation runs through coercion to inducement to agenda-setting and attraction (Nye 2004b: 8). Soft power is attraction, but agents can control agendas and structure subjects' preferences so that some things appear attractive that might otherwise not be so.

Many of the contributions in this volume, including an interesting essay by Janice Bially Mattern, make the point that much more work needs to be done on the concept of attraction. I agree. Bially Mattern argues that I treat attraction both as 'natural', assuming such broad values as freedom and human rights are naturally attractive, and as socially constructed through reasoned persuasion. But I am not convinced by her argument that this is an ontological contradiction. In the short term, attraction to the prevalent ideas in any given era can be treated as a given, but these ideas are not necessarily universal or immutable. 'Democracy' is a prevalent idea in the current era, but it was not in some past eras. Nor is it the goal of the current violent *jihadi* terrorists who are struggling to construct alternative ideas that can become viewed as a 'natural' part of Islamic identity. The outcomes of such struggles are partly through narratives of reasoned persuasion and partly through what Bially Mattern calls coercive verbal wars over non-physical representational force (which I discuss further below).

However, it is simply not true, as Ned Lebow asserts, that 'Nye takes it for granted that the American way of life is so attractive, even mesmerising, and the global public goods it supposedly provides so beneficial, that others are predisposed to follow Washington's lead. Like many liberals, he treats interests and identities as objective, uncontroversial and given' (Lebow, this volume, p. 120; 2005: 552). On the contrary, much of my writing has been to warn American policy-makers that they cannot take American attraction as given and that they are in danger of squandering soft power. I point out that there are areas and groups that are repelled rather than attracted by American culture, values and policies and that polls show their numbers to be increasing. I also point out that opponents like Osama Bin Laden have impressive soft power among their followers and are struggling by word and deed to increase it and diminish the soft power of the USA (and the rest of the West). Where I do agree with my critics is that the concept of attraction is ripe for further research. I list below some areas that deserve further exploration in future work on soft power.

Culture and attraction

Some analysts treat soft power as a synonym for culture, and then go on to downgrade its importance. For example, Niall Ferguson described soft power as 'non-traditional forces such as cultural and commercial goods', and then dismissed it on the grounds that, 'it's, well, soft' (Ferguson 2003). Of course drinking Coca-Cola or wearing a Michael Jackson shirt does not necessarily convey power. But this view confuses the resources that may produce behaviour with the behaviour itself – what Lukes (following Anthony Kenny) calls the 'vehicle fallacy' (Lukes 2005: 70). Whether the possession of power resources actually produces favourable outcomes depends upon the context and the skills of the agent in converting the resources into behavioural outcomes. This is not unique to soft-power resources. Having a larger tank army may produce victory if a battle is fought in the desert but not if it is fought in a swamp. As David Baldwin has pointed out, whether power resources produce power behaviour depends on the context (Baldwin 1979).

I have argued that the soft power of a country rests primarily on three resources: its culture (in places where it is attractive to others), its political values (when it lives up to them at home and abroad), and its foreign policies (when they are seen as legitimate and having moral authority) (Nye 2004b). The parenthetical conditions are the key in determining whether soft-power resources translate into the behaviour of attraction that can influence others towards favourable outcomes. But more research needs to be done on the connection between culture and power behaviour. For example, during the Cold War, the popularity of Western culture in eastern Europe gradually eroded Communist control, but there was already an historical affinity between eastern and western Europe. Can cultural attraction play a similar role in warding off violent *jihadi* appeals in Muslim cultures? Some see an unbridgeable cultural divide. But consider the Islamic state of Iran. Western music and videos are anathema to the ruling mullahs but attractive to many of the younger generation. We should be careful not to use stereotypes of civilisations to construct artificial cultural monoliths.

In East Asia, for example, many Western cultural ideas are proving more attractive in China when they arrive via South Korea. As a university student put it in discussing television shows,

American dramas also show the same kind of lifestyle. We know that South Korea and America have similar political systems and economies. But it is easier to accept the lifestyle from South Koreans because they are culturally closer to us. We feel we can live like them in a few years.

(Onishi 2006: A1)

This is an interesting example of the indirect effect of culture in attraction, as well as a situation where soft-power relations are not zero sum. If a long-term American foreign-policy objective is democratisation in China, it may have a better prospect of success if the cultural soft power is mediated by South Korea rather than coming directly from the USA.

At the same time, China itself is trying to use culture to soften its image as a rising power and avoid the prospect that other nations will perceive threatening intentions and react to balance Chinese power. It has tripled the number of foreign students in its universities, increased its international broadcasting and is creating 100 Confucius Institutes (not Mao Institutes!) to promote Chinese culture and language overseas. 'Beijing has succeeded in pushing Taiwan out of regional politics and increasingly marginalizing Japan' (Kurlantick 2006). Ironically, Japanese pop culture is attractive to younger generations in China and Korea, but it provides little soft power because Prime Minister Koizumi's visits to the Yasukuni Shrine (which includes the burial place of several war criminals) undercut the pop-cultural message and diverted attention to historical conflicts. Policies can negate the effect of cultural resources in producing net attraction or soft power.

Similarly, American policies in the Iraq war have undercut the soft power produced by American high and low culture. When broad cultural goals are involved, indirect means may be more effective. If the USA wants to encourage democracy in the Middle East, it may benefit from the efforts of the European Union. If the soft power of Europe increases in the process, it benefits but so does the USA, and so may the residents of the countries involved. Soft power arising out of cultural attraction can be positive sum, but where objectives differ, that soft power can become a zero-sum relationship. In any event, Lukes's suggestion of a more subject-oriented approach could provide a fruitful avenue for exploring the direct and indirect relations between cultures and soft power.

Economic resources: inducement and attraction

Economic resources can produce both hard- and soft-power behaviour. They can be used to coerce as well as attract. As Walter Russell Mead has argued, 'economic power is sticky power; it seduces as much as it compels [...] A set of economic institutions and policies [...] attracts others into our system and makes it hard for them to leave' (Mead 2004: 25). A successful economy is an important source of attraction. At the same time, it can provide resources that can be used as hard-power inducements in the form of payments as well as coercive sanctions. Richard Cooper argues that there is little economic power (in Dahl's one-dimensional behavioural definition of power as the ability to get others to do what they would not otherwise do) where there are consensual market conditions (Cooper 2005). Buyers and sellers consent to a price that clears a market.

But as Robert Keohane and I argued some years ago, where there is an asymmetry between buyers' and sellers' dependence upon a consensual market relationship, the more dependent party is more vulnerable to the disruption of the market relationship, and that can be used as a source of coercive power by the less dependent party (Keohane and Nye 1977). But the power depends upon the asymmetry. For example, some Americans worry that China's holding of large dollar reserves gives them power over the USA. But there is symmetry in the interdependence. If China were to rapidly dispose of those reserves, it would hinder its exports to American markets and greatly damage the Chinese economy. When Russia first subsidised the export of gas to the Ukraine and then, after a change of government in Ukraine, insisted that prices quadruple to a pure market price, economic resources were being used more for coercion rather than attraction. Yet the power relationship in a game with a single play is different from that in a continuing game. As Robert Axelrod has pointed out, the optimal strategy depends on the 'shadow of the future' (Axelrod 1984). Russia quickly discovered that the costs of its threats to Ukraine in 2006 hurt its reputation as a reliable supplier and its soft power in Europe. When considered in this wider context, there was more symmetry in the Russia–Ukraine energy relationship than the simple numbers on energy dependence implied at first glance. In real world cases, hard and soft power are often mixed.

Sometimes in real-world situations, it is difficult to distinguish what part of an economic relationship is comprised of hard and soft power. European leaders describe the desire by other countries to accede to the European Union as a sign of Europe's attraction or soft power (Wolf 2005: 17). It is impressive, for example, that former Communist countries oriented their expectations and revised their laws to comply with Brussels' framework. Turkey today is making changes in its human-rights policies and laws on the same grounds. But how much are the changes the result of the economic inducement of market access and how much is the result of attraction to the Europe's successful economic and political system? The situation is one of mixed motives, and different actors in a country may see the mix in different ways. When Europe links market access to changes in Turkey's human-rights legislation, many Turks are replying to the hard power of inducement, but some liberals may also be attracted to the European model of human rights. One may similarly ask whether Mexican immigrants are induced (hard power) or attracted (soft power) by economic conditions that lead them to emigrate to the USA. Many cases will involve both motives, but some Mexicans (and others) who hate the USA may nonetheless be induced to emigrate.

A number of observers see China's soft power increasing in parts of the developing world (Gill and Huang 2005). The so-called 'Beijing Consensus' on authoritarian government plus a successful market economy has become more popular than the previously dominant 'Washington Consensus' of liberal market economics with democratic government. But to what extent are Venezuelans and Zimbabweans attracted to the Beijing consensus, or admire China's tripling of its gross domestic product over three decades, or are induced by the prospect of access to a large and growing market? And the same growth model that produces attraction in some authoritarian countries may hurt Chinese soft power in democratic countries. In 2005, the prospect of greater market access nearly induced Europe to remove a punitive (coercive) arms embargo that it had imposed after Tiananmen Square, but the prospect changed after China passed anti-secession legislation against Taiwan that undercut China's soft power in Europe and reinforced American pleas to leave the embargo in place.

Indeed, the case of Taiwan had been an exception to China's growing skill at using soft power in its Asian diplomacy. When China threatened Taiwan with missiles and paid poor countries to withdraw recognition of Taiwan, it employed hard power. China is now gradually beginning to use the considerable power assets of economic ties and culture. A large number of Taiwanese companies are investing on the mainland because of the hard-power inducement of lower labour costs. But this is reinforced by the attraction of shared Chinese culture, so there is a soft-power dimension as well. Investigating the complex manner in which economic resources produce a mix of hard- and soft-power behaviour in such cases is another promising avenue for future research.

Military resources and soft power

Military force appears to be a defining resource for hard power, but the same resource can sometimes contribute to soft power. Dictators like Hitler and Stalin cultivated myths of invincibility and inevitability to structure expectations and attract others to join their bandwagon. The term 'Stockholm syndrome' was developed to describe hostages who were initially coerced by their captors but in the constrained circumstances of stress and fear came to identify with their captors. And some people are generally attracted to strength. As Osama bin Laden has said, people are attracted to a strong horse rather than a weak horse. A well-run military campaign can be a source of attraction. The effectiveness of the Desert Storm campaign in 1991 (and the legitimacy of its broad coalition) enhanced American soft power and helped propel the Oslo Peace Process. In another dimension, military-to-military cooperation and training programmes can establish transnational networks that enhance a country's soft power. Or to take another example, the rapid and effective use of the American military to provide supplies to tsunami victims in Indonesia helped to reverse the precipitous decline of American soft power in that country. Like economic resources, military resources can produce soft as well as hard power, depending the context of how they are used.

Of course, military resources can also undercut soft power. Brutality and indifference to just war principles of discrimination and proportionality can destroy legitimacy. The efficiency of the initial American military invasion of Iraq in 2003 may have created admiration in the eyes of some Iraqis and others, but that soft power was undercut by the subsequent inefficiency of the occupation and the scenes of mistreatment of prisoners at Abu Ghraib. Reports of the Pentagon paying to place stories in the Iraqi press at the same time that the State Department was training Iraqis to develop an independent press also undercut credibility and soft power. The American military refers to the 'kinetic' and 'non-kinetic' aspects of its campaign to pacify Iraq. Ironically, it might have done better if more troops had been deployed in April 2003 and prevented the looting, violence and insurgency from metastasising. With more kinetic hard power, the military might have created conditions where its units and contractors could have built schools, clinics and other things that create non-kinetic soft power. The effort to repair this mistake by increased use of propaganda was a misunderstanding of how attraction and soft power are created. We need more serious research on the relationship of military resources and soft power.

Coercion and attraction

Janice Bially Mattern argues that 'soft power is rather ironically rooted in hard power' (see this volume, p. 100). The sources of attraction can be posited as natural, socially constructed through persuasive argument or constructed through verbal fighting and representational force – a non-physical but nevertheless coercive form of power that is exercised through language. The powerful 'socio-linguistically construct "reality" not through evidence-based argument but through representational force', a form of narrative that 'threatens the audience with unthinkable harm unless it submits, in word and deed, to the terms of the speaker's viewpoint.' 'Like physical force, representational force aspires to leave its victims no "out"' (Bially Mattern, this volume: p. 110; 2005: 583, 586). The American construction of the 'war on terrorism' in the aftermath of 9/11 is a case in point.

Bially Mattern argues that 'since representational force is a form of coercion, attraction may rest upon coercion. Where it does, the distinction Nye had in mind between "hard" and "soft" evaporates' (Mattern, this volume: p. 116; 2005: 609). This strikes me as an overly broad use of the term 'coercion', but even if we grant such usage and include verbal bullying and indoctrination, I would respond that not all situations of attraction in the world today are based upon representational force, and not all subjects are equally susceptible to representational force – witness the resistance in Europe and elsewhere (including the USA) to many aspects of the 'war on terrorism'. I agree with Bially Mattern when she says that 'if soft power is the function of an attraction constructed through a coercive process of communicative exchange, it can hardly be said that soft power avoids relentless competition among actors' (Bially Mattern, this volume, p. 116). But that is not the same as concluding that soft power is rooted in hard power. Some is and some is not – witness the soft power of the papacy. Some of the attraction of a dominant state like the USA may be rooted in verbal fighting and a Gramscian-style hegemony of controlled discourse, but not all is. Given the political diversity and institutional fragmentation of world politics, it is difficult for the powerful to maintain a Gramscian-type hegemony over discourse. Otherwise there would be far more uniformity of views than now exists. Lukes properly observes that 'both the agent-centred, strategic view of Nye and the subject-centred, structural view of Foucault lack this distinction' between indoctrination and the exercise of power that leaves those subject to it free to live according to the dictates of their nature and judgement (Lukes, this volume, p. 97). What would be interesting would be more empirical research that investigates the extent of Bially Mattern's and Lukes's different sources of attraction or indoctrination in specific cases.

Normative implications

Bially Mattern argues that 'understood through the conventional lens, soft power has appeared as an alternative to the raw power politics that so frequently characterise world politics. It has thus been embraced by ethically minded scholars and policy-makers' (Bially Mattern, this volume, p. 117; 2005: 611). Perhaps so, but that is not my view. I have treated soft power as a descriptive rather than a normative concept. Like any form of power, it can be wielded for good or bad purposes. Hitler, Stalin and Mao all possessed a great deal of soft power in their heydays, but that did not make it good. It is not necessarily better to twist minds than to twist arms. If I want to steal your money, I can threaten you with a gun, or I can swindle you with a get-rich scheme in which you invest. I can also persuade you that I am a guru to whom you should hand over your estate and that I will save the world. The third means depends upon attraction or soft power, but the result remains fraud and theft.

We often judge ethics in the three dimensions of motives, means and consequences. While soft power can be used with bad intentions and wreak horrible consequences, it does differ in terms of means. Power defined in behavioural terms is a relationship, and soft power depends more upon the subject's role in that relationship than does hard power. Attraction depends upon what is happening in the mind of the subject. While there may be instances of coercive verbal manipulation, there are often more degrees of freedom for the subject when the means involve soft power. I may have few degrees of freedom if the person with the gun demands my money or my life. I have even fewer degrees of freedom if she kills me and simply takes my wallet from my pocket. But to persuade me that she is a guru to whom I should leave my estate leaves open a number of degrees of freedom as well as the possibility of other outside influences arising and influencing the power relationship. After all, minds can change over time while the dead cannot be revived.

It is in the dimension of means, that one might construct a normative preference for greater use of soft power, even if international dialogues are not based solely on reasoned persuasion. And this could be coupled by research on the consequences of historical choices to use soft power. Contrast the consequences of Gandhi or Martin Luther King's choosing to emphasise soft power with Yassir Arafat's choice of the gun. Gandhi and King were able to attract moderate majorities over time, and the consequences were impressive both in effectiveness and in ethical terms. Arafat's strategy of hard power, particularly in the second intifada, drove Israeli moderates into the arms of the hard right. One might investigate a counterfactual of what might have happened if Arafat had chosen King's or Gandhi's soft-power strategy. Perhaps he might have achieved his goal of a Palestinian state by now. Even positive concepts can have normative implications, and research can illuminate them.

Realism, strategy and soft power

Some authors cast the difference between hard and soft power in the tradition of realism vs. idealism, but the shoe does not fit. Traditional realists like Hans Morgenthau objected to what they saw as the naiveté of idealists, but they were not indifferent to the importance of ideas (Schmidt, this volume). In fact, in 1939 E. H. Carr described international power in three categories: military, economic and power over opinion. Much of this subtlety was lost by the neo-realists in their desire to make power measurable for their structural judgements. They committed what might be called 'the concrete fallacy'. Power was reduced to hard, measurable, tangible resources. It was something that could be dropped on your foot or on cities, rather than something that might change your mind about wanting to drop anything in the first place.

More recently, those whom Schmidt terms 'modified realists' have restored the importance of perceptions and the role of ideas. They have rediscovered something that Machiavelli already described five centuries ago. It may be better for a prince to be feared than loved, but the prince is in greatest danger when he is hated. There is no contradiction between realism and soft power. Soft power is not a form of idealism or liberalism. It is a simply a form of power, one way of getting desired outcomes. As Inis Claude pointed out, legitimacy is a power reality (Claude 1966). Competitive struggles over legitimacy are part of enhancing or depriving actors of power. Countries can develop a variety of strategies to undercut or deprive others of soft power or to balance their soft power (Walt 2005).

There is some controversy among realists about the new concept of soft balancing. It is not the same as soft power. The soft balancing that Robert Pape or T. V. Paul (2005) describe is not simply an attempt to balance against soft power or to use only soft power to balance against another country. It is balancing by less than military means. They argue that other states did not balance against the USA until recently because American objectives and means were seen as legitimate and non-threatening. But when the Bush Administration adopted a doctrine of unilateral preventive war, it lost legitimacy and soft power. In the absence of an ability to create a hard military balance, other states then turned to soft balancing by a variety of means as a response to that loss of American soft power. Critics like Stephen Brooks and William Wohlforth (2005) argue that soft balancing is a misnomer because there is little empirical evidence (other than some loose rhetoric) to support the idea that other states have been willing to invest much in checking the USA systemically rather than in merely resisting and bargaining on particular disputes. Even in the absence of systemic objectives, however, the ability to deprive a superpower of its soft power proved costly to American hard power in the case of Iraq (Pape 2005; Paul 2005; Brooks and Wohlforth 2005; Lieber and Alexander 2005).[1]

Brian Schmidt describes me as 'a vocal critic of realism', and observes that practitioners of international politics understand and often act on the basis of the realist conception of power (Schmidt, this volume, p. 62). But I am critical only of structural realists who succumb to the 'concrete fallacy' and also ignore other dimensions of international politics such as the roles of non-state actors like corporations, institutions, non-governmental organisations and transnational terrorist networks, many of which have soft power of their own. When I was practising international politics, I often turned to realism as a first approximation of reality, but I did not stop there (Nye 2004b). And that is why I believe there is a fruitful research path for post-structural realists to explore past and future means of combining hard and soft power in larger grand strategies.

Incorporating soft power into strategy is more difficult than may first appear. For one thing, in some governments, such as the American one, the resources that can produce soft power – educational exchanges, broadcasting, development assistance, disaster relief and so forth – are dispersed among a number of departments and agencies. Even more important, as mentioned above, whether these resources produce success in terms of outcomes is more in the control of the subject than is often the case with hard power. A third problem is that the results often take a long time, and most politicians and publics are impatient to see a prompt return on their investments. Fourth, the instruments of soft power are not fully under the control of governments. While governments control policy, culture and values are embedded in civil societies. Moreover, soft power depends upon credibility, and when governments are seen as manipulative and information is perceived as propaganda and indoctrination, credibility is destroyed.

Finally, there are some situations where soft power provides very little leverage. It is difficult, for example, to see how soft power would solve the dispute over North Korea's nuclear weapons. On the other hand, when a government is concerned about what Arnold Wolfers described as milieu goals, or general-value objectives, such as promotion of democracy, human rights and freedom, it may often be the case that soft power turns out to be superior to hard power (Wolfer 1962).

It is time for academic research to go beyond sterile debates over structural realism and structural liberalism, or realism vs. idealism, and to look carefully at particular cases that can illuminate how to integrate hard and soft power into successful strategies which I have called 'smart power.' And in evaluating such strategies, it is important to remember that success can be judged in terms of ethical values as well as effectiveness.

Note

1 I am indebted to the editor of *International Security*, Sean Lynn-Jones, for help on this point.

10 Reflecting on normative power Europe

Thomas Diez and Ian Manners

There is a widespread belief that the European Union (EU) is a novel kind of power not only in its own institutional set-up but also in its external relations. It is said to rely on civilian rather than military means and to pursue the spread of particular norms rather than self-interested geographical expansion or military superiority. In the 1970s, François Duchêne called it a 'civilian power' (1972: 43); in the early 2000s it was argued that the label 'normative power' would be better suited (Manners 2000, 2002). Just as Duchêne's civilian power reflected the Cold War milieu of the 1970s, the normative-power approach signified a crystallisation of the EU in the post-Cold War era.

That the EU is a different type of international actor and represents a new kind of power in international politics is not much disputed. More controversial is why and in what way the EU is a 'normative power'. Robert Cooper (2003), for instance, has argued that the post-modern EU must engage in 'liberal imperialism' in dealing with what he identifies as the pre-modern world. In contrast, Robert Kagan (2003) argues that the difference between the foreign-policy values predominant in Europe and those in a more traditional power like the USA largely reflect different power capabilities. There is also some dispute about the consistency of EU behaviour: are there double standards in the application of norms in EU policies towards other parties? Do different EU actors (e.g., the European Commission, Parliament and Council, as well as different actors within these institutions) pursue different norms and interests? And is there an increasing militarisation of EU external relations? To address these questions, the normative-power approach has been recently used in studies of EU environmental policy by Simon Lightfoot and Jon Burchell (2004a, 2004b, 2005); the EU and global governance by Zaki Laïdi (2005a, 2005b); EU actorness by Charlotte Bretherton and John Vogler (2006); EU foreign policy by Helene Sjursen (2006); Euro-Mediterranean relations (Adler *et al.* 2006); Europe and its others (Diez 2004, 2005); or EU values and principles (Lucarelli and Manners 2006).

While these questions and studies are important, this chapter is primarily interested in the discursive representation of the EU as a normative power.

Not only is the success of this representation a precondition for other actors to agree to the norms set out by the EU; it also constructs an identity of the EU against an image of others in the 'outside world'. This has important implications for the way EU policies treat those others and for the degree to which its adherence to its own norms is scrutinised within the EU. In that sense, the discourse of the EU as a normative power constructs a particular self of the EU (and it is perhaps the only form of identity the diverse set of actors within the EU can agree on), while it attempts to change others through the spread of particular norms. Pursuing this line of argument here will lead to the observation that the EU's normative power may not be a unique phenomenon, if it prioritises itself over others. The USA, for instance, has exemplified the concept of a normative power during parts of its history, but its historical fate also calls for a closer examination of different kinds of normative power. In this context, we argue that academic discussions about normative power, and political representations of the EU as a normative power, which are both part of the same discourse, need to adopt a greater degree of reflection and reflexivity. Rather than the propagation of particular 'European' norms, it is such reflection and reflexivity that constitute the EU as a normative power that is different from pure self-interested hegemony.

This chapter is the outcome of an ongoing discussion between the two authors over the past few years on the merits and problems of a normative power approach. The discussion emerges out of and evolves around two positions: One (Ian Manners), coming from a critical social-theory perspective that seeks to understand and change politics, advocates the normative power approach (Manners and Whitman 2003; Manners 2007). The other (Thomas Diez), coming from a post-structural perspective that seeks to use discourse analysis in order to gain a greater understanding of politics, is critical of the normative-power approach (Diez 1999/2001; Diez 2005). Accordingly, the first has acted as a participant in constructing a normative power discourse that seeks to push the EU towards a certain identity, whereas the second has taken the role of an analyst of the success of this construction who wants any such exercise to be self-critical. The chapter follows the development of this discussion around three major points of disagreement – civilian and normative power; the USA as a normative power; and the power of normative power discourse (see Diez 2005). On the first two points (civilian power and the USA as a normative power), Thomas Diez came to agree that civilian power is not the same as normative power and that the USA is no longer a normative power in the same way as the EU. On the third point (the power of normative power discourse), Ian Manners came to agree that discursive representations of the EU as a normative power are important and should be analysed critically. Both authors are in agreement when concluding that reflection and reflexivity are crucial in a sustainable normative-power 'Europe'.

In the next section of the chapter, we review the literature on the concept of normative power and relate it to the earlier literature on civilian power.

We argue that civilian power can be read as one specific kind of normative power, but that while many elements of François Duchêne's original 1970s '*idée force*' remain, in the post-Cold War era, the EU has moved from civilian to normative power. In this section we will also briefly set out the differences between normative power and Nye's notion of 'soft power'. Next, a brief comparison with the United States of America allows us to reflect on the similarities and differences between historical instances of US normative power and more contemporary EU normative power. We then suggest that discourses of 'normative power Europe' are themselves a form of representational power that contributes towards particular EU identity constructions. This leads us to our concluding call for reflection and reflexivity.

What is normative power?

The introduction of the concept of normative power into the discussion of the EU's foreign policy involved a definition of EU power as neither military nor purely economic, but one that works through ideas, opinions and conscience. 'Normative power', in this reading, is a power that is able 'to shape conceptions of the "normal"' (Manners 2000: 32; 2002: 239). We can therefore identify such a normative power by the impact it has on what is considered appropriate behaviour by other actors. Three aspects of this definition need further elaboration.

First, the 'power' originally discussed by Manners (2002) is a particular kind of entity characterised by change rather than conserving the status quo, unlike 'great powers' or 'superpowers' (see Manners 2006a: 182–3). The notion of 'normative power' was introduced in part to get away from the question of whether the EU is an actor in international politics or not, which misses the point that the EU *is* influential, independent of its standing as an 'actor' in the realist sense. This discussion need not concern us for present purposes, yet it should be clear that 'normative power' denotes not only a specific kind of entity in international politics but also a specific aim, namely, the setting of standards. Thus, normative power, based on ideas and conscience, differs from relational power or structural power (see Lukes, this volume; Strange 1996: 25–30). Moreover, normative power refers to particular means – it is not a power that primarily relies on military force but one in which influence is exerted by norms themselves rather than military arsenals or economic incentives.

Second, the normative power argument has a critical social-theory ring to it in that it is interested in the political consequences of the social construction of the EU in world politics. It focuses on the power of norms to influence actors' identity and behaviour. To the extent that normative power is used as an analytical category to distinguish a particular kind of actor (such as the EU), it relies on the possibility of tracing empirically the impact of norms in contrast to other possible factors. However, as we will see, a lot of the discussion about 'normative power Europe' does not really examine the de-facto impact of EU policy (and therefore whether it *has* normative power) but focuses on whether it employs particular means (and therefore whether it *acts* as a normative power).

Third, this does not mean that normative power cannot go alongside other forms of power in international relations, notably military and economic forms of power. Although normative power must be analytically irreducible to other forms of power if it is to make sense as a separate category, economic incentives or military capabilities may underpin normative power. For instance, research has shown that the EU is most likely to 'shape conceptions of the normal' (and therefore have greater normative power) in the context of EU membership candidacies, when perceived economic benefits of joining the EU can be assumed to be important factors for compliance with EU norms (Oguzlu 2002, 2003; Diez *et al.* 2006).

The original normative-power Europe argument used empirical evidence relying largely on one case study, leading some to wrongly suggest that the claim to normativity rests solely on human rights. It was pointed out that since the 1980s the EU has fought to abolish the death penalty worldwide and notes that within that context it was willing 'to impinge on state sovereignty', to intervene 'in support for individuals' and to pursue this course of action in 'the absence of obvious material gain' (Manners 2002: 252–3). Other examples of the normative power of the EU in this policy sector include the large budget now available within EU member states for the promotion of human rights (Youngs 2004: 422; K. Smith 2001: 186–8). It is also stressed that the EU is committed 'to placing *universal* norms and principles at the centre of its relations with its Member States [...] and the world' (Manners 2002: 241, emphasis added). Much is made in this respect of the explicit references to the European Convention of Human Rights and the United Nations Charter in the Treaty on European Union (TEU) (Manners 2002: 241). This normative engagement can be attributed to the founding principles of the Union (set out in Art. 6 TEU), including 'liberty', 'democracy', 'respect for human rights and fundamental freedoms', 'rule of law', as well as to the unique political set-up of the EU (which includes the idea of the 'pooling of sovereignty', the principle of subsidiarity and the transnational representation in the European Parliament) (Manners 2002: 243, 252–3). It was concluded that

> because of its particular historical evolution, its hybrid polity, and its constitutional configuration, the EU has a normatively different basis for its relations with the world. [... N]ot only is the EU constructed on a normative basis, but importantly [...] this predisposes it to act in a normative way in world politics.
>
> (Manners 2002: 252; also Wæver 1998)

Maybe most importantly, the concept of normative power contains an 'ontological', 'positivist' and 'normative' element and, thus, was found to be quite attractive for the study of European foreign policy. All three elements fit into a larger, still ongoing debate in which the EU is conceptualised as a different type of actor in world politics, specific EU policies were shown to be different from those of great powers, and in which it has been argued that the EU *should* indeed be a different kind of power (Whitman 1998; Padoa-Schioppa 2004).

Differences between normative power and civilian power

The EU had been regarded as a 'civilian power' long before its labelling as a 'normative power'. The idea that Europe could become a different kind of entity that does not rely primarily on military but on civilian means was first explicitly formulated in the early 1970s by François Duchêne. He argued that, given that the people of Europe had largely formed 'amilitary' values, the stalemate of the Cold War had 'devalued purely military power', and Europe was far from a consensus on its own development as a military superpower between the two poles, the then European Community 'would have a chance to demonstrate the influence which can be wielded by a large political co-operative formed to exert essentially civilian forms of power' (Duchêne 1973: 19).

In more recent works on civilian power, Knut Kirste and Hanns Maull define a civilian power as a state 'whose conception of its foreign policy role and behaviour is bound to particular aims, values, principles, as well as forms of influence and instruments of power in the name of a civilisation of international relations' (Kirste and Maull 1996: 300). Similar to the concept of normative power, the notion of civilian power describes a particular kind of actor, relationships and means. The two concepts of normative and civilian power may thus seem to be very close to each other. Indeed, because a civilian power advocates and practises particular kinds of norms, above all the use of civilian means to achieve one's policy goals, civilian power can be read as one specific form of normative power.

However, over the past thirty-five years, a rich smorgasbord of varieties of civilian power conceptualisations have been on offer, and all these readings are located within particular historical contexts. The first phase of civilian power writing was set within the period of détente and oil crisis where the structural context of the Cold War determined the EC's civilian power: 'the natural expectation is a shift away from the quasi-military confrontation of the cold war to civilian and political processes gradually increasing the interdependence of industrial societies with potentially complementary interests' (Duchêne 1971: 69). During this first phase Duchêne, Shonfield, Twitchett, and Sjöstedt all made important, although quite different, contributions to this Cold War-bound notion of civilian power (Shonfield 1973; Twitchett 1976; Sjöstedt 1977).

The second phase of civilian-power writing was set within the period of glasnost and the single market, when the structural context of the ending of the Cold War redetermined the EC's civilian power. What is interesting about this second phase is that its authors were less certain about the value of civilian power and about what the concept actually stood for (Pijpers 1988; Tsakaloyannis 1989; Hill 1990; Laursen 1991; Lodge 1993). The third phase of civilian-power writing is set in the post-Cold War debates of the acquisition of military capabilities by the EU. What these writers share is both a concern and scepticism for the concept of civilian power (M. A. Smith 1998; Whitman 1998; Zielonka 1998; K. Smith 2000; Freres 2000; Stavridis 2001; Treacher 2004; Telò 2005). They are concerned that the movement away from civilian to military forms of power marks a lost opportunity for the EU to make distinctive contribution to the civilising of international politics. They are also sceptical of the extent to which the EC ever was civilian and the EU ever will be military.

Some of the distinctions between normative power and civilian power are to be found in the discussion of the international identity of the EU (including civilian, military and normative power) from the late 1990s and early 2000s (Manners and Whitman 1998, 2003). The manifold and moving interpretations of civilian power converge around three central characteristics – 'diplomatic cooperation to solve international problems' (multilateralism); 'centrality of economic power' (non-military); and 'legally-binding supranational institutions' (international law) (Manners 2000: 26; 2002: 236–7). From Duchêne to Twitchett to Sjöstadt to Maull, these three characteristics have been constitutive of civilian-power resources, objectives and strategies.

Clearly, Duchêne and his contemporaries were trying to capture a transmutation of military confrontation and war towards civilised politics and essentially civilian forms of influence (Duchêne 1971: 69; 1972: 43 and 47). No matter how much academic acrobatics is practised, the emphasis on civilian ends and means is not satisfied by the civilian control of military strategy, as some more recent commentators have suggested (K. Smith 2005). Thus, the normative power approach encourages us to differentiate between the civilian nature of the EU prior to circa 1999 and the normative justification for use of military power when appropriate, for example, in humanitarian intervention. Similarly, most civilian power formulations place an emphasis on the importance of being 'long on economic power' or 'the concentration on nonmilitary, primarily economic, means' (Duchêne 1973: 19; Maull 1990: 92). Civilian power writings tend to place much importance on non-military or economic resources, objectives and strategies. It is clearly no accident that the objects of most civilian power writing have been some of the wealthiest places in the world, namely, 1970s western Europe and 1990s Japan and Germany. As has been previously pointed out, the emphasis on material assets and physical power in civilian power approaches contrasts with the emphasis on the normative power of non-material exemplification found in the contagion of norms through imitation (*mimétisme*) and attraction (Manners 2000: 35; 2002: 238 and 244; Manners and Whitman 2003: 385 and 399).

In addition, civilian power writings emphasise the communitarian nature of civilian resources, objectives and strategies, exercised primarily for the benefit of the owners. The communitarian aspect is compounded by the turn taken by Maull and others to apply civilian power to Germany and Japan (let alone the USA) in the service of 'national goals', 'national interest', and 'national values'. As discussed elsewhere, this has led the civilian-power concept to become far too related to the ontology of states, rather than to a 'style of action' or 'domestication' (Manners 2006a: 184). In contrast, the normative power approach emphasises the cosmopolitan nature of EU normative power, in particular through reference to norms and principles considered more universal because they are embedded in UN treaties and organs (Manners 2002: 241). Finally, civilian-power writings have come to accept a Westphalian cultural emphasis on international society as the form and means of world politics. Even Duchêne (in contrast to Shonfield), whilst talking about the transformation of world politics, was actually reinforcing the status quo of international politics with references to 'international twentieth-century society', 'a powerful co-operative' and 'international open society' (Duchêne 1971: 82; 1972: 47; 1973: 20). This acceptance of Westphalian culturation, including the status quo of an international society between states, contrasts with the emphasis of the normative power approach on transcending the 'normality' of world politics towards world society (Manners 2000: 32; 2002: 236 and 253).

It is also worth briefly setting out the differences between normative power and Joseph Nye's 'soft power', as these are sometimes mistakenly confused. As Nye acknowledges in his contribution to this volume, he envisioned soft power as an empirical ('positive'/'descriptive') rather than theoretical concept. Clearly, his advocacy of the concept must be located in the US debate over the relative merits of Democratic Party soft power vs. Republican Party hard power in the pursuit of US national interests and foreign policy (Manners 2006c). Nye generally discusses the 'soft power of a country' primarily in reference to the USA, sometimes in comparison with China. From this perspective, soft power is a resource or tool of national foreign policy to be chosen and wielded alongside hard power. He also acknowledges that as a foreign-policy tool, soft power 'can be wielded for both good and bad purposes' (p. 169). In contrast, normative power is an explicitly theoretical concept requiring an understanding of social diffusion and normative practices. Similarly, normative power is not a foreign policy tool to be wielded for national interests. As we shall discuss in the third section of this chapter, normative power is part of discursive practices that are both constitutive and always present. Finally, as Janice Bially Mattern discusses in her contribution to this volume, there is absolutely nothing soft about 'soft power' – the ability of capitalist cultural practices to disadvantage and shorten the lives of the poor across the world cannot be considered merely soft or attractive.

Differences between the EU and other powers

The concept of normative power in IR has largely been developed in relation to the EU, yet a historical perspective suggests that the notion of normative power may not be novel and unique to the EU. Throughout history, different actors can be seen as exercising normative power, ranging from the Vatican to the USA. Yet these actors differ from the EU in the extent to which the spread of universal norms plays a role as an aim as well as the means, and to what extent it is combined with or is dominated by military or other forms of power.

It is important to note that, in contrast to civilian power, normative power is *not* the opposite of military power. It is entirely conceivable that military force is used to back up the spread of normative values, partly because their successful diffusion implies the corresponding institutionalisation of normative values in order to be sustainable (Sjursen 2004: 122; Jünemann 2003: 40). Yet the more normative power builds on military force, the less it becomes distinguishable from traditional forms of power, because it no longer relies on the power of norms itself. Indeed, the imposition of norms through military force cannot be equated with changing the behaviour of other actors, which relies primarily on socialisation processes. Thus, in contrast to Nye's arguments about combining soft and hard power, normative power invariably diminishes in the presence of military force.

The USA is a particularly interesting case in this context, not least because some of the writing on normative power develops the concept *in contrast* to the USA. Yet is the USA not also a normative power? Confirming evidence would be the long-established assessment of US foreign policy as strongly influenced by the frontier myth and the notion of manifest destiny, resulting in the 'God-given duty to spread the dream and promise of America beyond its own shores' – a predisposition that, as Michael Cox notes, 'inevitably infused American foreign policy with a particularly moralistic and idealistic tone' (Cox 2003: 8–9). Leaving aside its rather more openly ruthless engagement in the Americas in accordance with the Monroe Doctrine, most of the USA's international engagement has had strong normative under- if not over-tones. At no point has the USA's normative power been more visible than it was in the first part of the twentieth century, an era which had Woodrow Wilson's Fourteen Points as a cornerstone. And of course after the Second World War, when one could already see the dominance of military power and American hegemony in play (in the Western world at least), the USA helped create a series of international institutions that would civilise international politics (Menon *et al.* 2004: 7).

Even the invasion of Iraq, driven by a neo-conservative ideology, cannot easily be dismissed as mere power politics – it is driven by a particular worldview with strong ideas of how democracy should work within a particular liberal governmental frame. And in the 2002 National Security Strategy, the invocation of norms and the commitment to spreading those norms, which are held to be universal, plays a central role (Berenskoetter, 2005: 75–6, 86; Rhodes 2003). Yet interests and norms cannot easily be separated (Cox 2003: 9). Building up institutions after the Second World War was a projection of American norms, but it also, intentionally or not, safeguarded US interests because those norms would spread a conception of life that would match that of the USA and build a 'community of ideals, interests and purposes' (Secretary of State Charles Hughes cited in Link 1988: 68). Undoubtedly, the impact of Eleanor and Franklin D. Roosevelt between 1941 ('The Four Freedoms') and 1948 (Universal Declaration of Human Rights) instilled the USA with a strong normative international presence. However, the series of international institutions created tended to reinforce, not transform, IR, in particular by sustaining the hegemony of the imperial powers in the UN Security Council and ensuring other UN organs reflected US power (for example, the IMF, IBRD and GATT).

Here the concept of American 'exceptionalism' is helpful in assessing its normative power. The concept of exceptionalism encourages us to judge whether a claim to normative power is based on cosmopolitan normative theory ('we are all equal') or not. Thus, a claim of exceptionalism located in communitarian self-understanding would seem to be one which cannot be shared with the rest of the world on an equal and just basis. But what if universal norms are being propagated in a normative project based not on exceptionalism but on ordinariness, as in the case of the EU? Undoubtedly, there are claims of 'normative power Europe' that have been used by EU politicians in a communitarian attempt to legitimise the EU project to member states and citizens. Similarly, references to certain constitutive norms, such as social solidarity, sustainable development and good governance, may be desirable for the many, but not for those who profit from inequality, pollution and corruption. From a relativist perspective, it could be argued that all 'particularist' claims to normative power are relatively similar – from the American and French Revolutions to those of the Russian Revolution. It is the lack of exceptionalism, rather than the claim to being special, which characterises most of the normative claims in the EU – particularly those located in past European failures and crimes (such as colonialism, nationalism, world wars, the holocaust, and inequality). Generally implicit in any EU claims to being '*sui generis*' are built on humility for historical failures such as injustice, intolerance and inhumanity (see Fossum 2006). As we discuss in the next section, this historical context of reflexive humility and attempts to build non-hierarchical relationships contribute to normative power. The stark contrast between the EU and US claims to exceptionalism could not be clearer in discussions of the 'God-given duty' of the American dream, where the USA is '*the* land of the free and *the* home of the brave' (see Lipset 1996).

Another difference between the EU and the USA, however, is that the USA has sought to project, and often impose, its own norms while (unlike the EU) refusing to bind itself to international treaties. Although it could be argued that the EU has been doing something similar in imposing its own norms on candidate states, they are acceding to membership of the Union, with all the eventual equality this implies (see Jileva 2004; Juncos 2005; Balfour 2006). Yet while the EU's formal commitment to international law should be highlighted (Manners 2002: 251), this can only be the characteristic of a *particular* kind of normative power, namely, one favouring multilateralism.

One could furthermore point to the fact that the EU or, rather, EU member states consider the use of force a last resort and, exceptions aside, are reluctant to militarily intervene on a global scale. However, during the first part of the twentieth century, the USA, like today's EU, was not at all eager to intervene in conflicts outside its own hemisphere. Like the EU, Wilson's aim was to spread peace throughout the world so that interventions would no longer be necessary. And, just like the EU, the idea was to do so not with military means but with binding normative commitments. Yet over time, the military back-up of this normative power came to be of ever-increasing importance. And even though US reluctance to entertain imperial ambitions should not be overestimated, the supplementation of norms with force was partly a response to calls for engagement that were coming from outside the USA (as the EU is facing calls for more military power now).

There is, however, one further aspect for judging between EU and US claims to normative power, which is expressed in Etienne Balibar's notion of Europe as a 'vanishing mediator'. Balibar takes Fredric Jameson's 'vanishing mediator' a step further by giving it the meaning of an EUtopia or myth, where the EU becomes the anti-systemic mediator – 'a *transitory* institution, force, community [...] that creates the conditions for a new society by rearranging the elements inherited from the very institution that has to be overcome' (Balibar 2003: 334). In contradistinction to the concept of exceptionalism as expressing a hierarchical power relationship, the extent to which the EU becomes a 'vanishing mediator' helps to judge the claim to normative power. If the successful exercise of normative power with reference to external points of international reference (such as the UN) leads to a wider acceptance of those norms, then the expectation would be that the EU would become less, not more, powerful. It would, in effect, increasingly vanish through its mediation. This is not to say that the EU, nor its member states, regions and localities, would vanish as institutions but that they would become less powerful as forces of change as they would become, quite simply, normal in the multilayered processes of post-national politics. As Kalypso Nicolaïdis puts it, the EU 'would preferably not refer to itself in terms of power at all, but as an intervener, a global partner, a "vanishing mediator"' (Nicolaïdis 2004: 117).

In contrast, in the case of the USA, the entanglement of normative and military power is underpinned, most evidently in the Bush Administration, by a secure belief in the universal validity of its own norms and a missionary zeal to spread these norms to places marked as 'evil'. It is such a stance that legitimises the use of military force: were there doubts about the underlying norms, military force would not be considered legitimate. This indicates another dimension along which normative powers can be differentiated, and it is one that we will further explore below: the degree to which norms are subject to reflection both inside the EU and (in the way that the EU binds itself to international norms) in the context of the international society.

The power of the 'normative power Europe' discourse

The two previous discussions of differences in the normative-power debate illustrate that 'normative power', as it has emerged in its application to the EU, is not an objective category. Instead, it is a practice of a specific discursive representation. >From a discourse-analytical point of view, the most interesting question about normative power, therefore, is not whether Europe is a normative power or not but how it is constructed as one, paraphrasing Stefano Guzzini, what the use of the term 'normative power' does (see Guzzini, this volume, p. 24). This shifts the focus of the analysis from a discussion of normative power as an empirical phenomenon to a second-order analysis of the power inherent in the representation of 'normative-power Europe'.

Kalypso Nicolaïdis and Robert Howse offer one road into this problematisation of the EU as a normative power. They consider the narrative of the EU as a civilian power, trying to export its model to other regions and even globally. To them, this involves the values of 'inclusion, participation, transparency, attentiveness to distributive effects, tolerance of diversity and of other levels of legitimate governance' (Nicolaïdis and Howse 2002: 782). In particular, they consider the EU's role as a model for the World Trade Organization (WTO), which they contrast with 'the negative external spillover of many of the EU's internal policies, from agriculture to standardization, competition or the movement of people' (Nicolaïdis and Howse 2002: 773). They conclude that

> the EU that serves as the basis for such extrapolations to the world level is part analysis of existing realities, part prediction about their development, but also part utopia. [...] Ultimately, the EU would need to model itself on the utopia that it seeks to project on to the rest of the world.

> (Nicolaïdis and Howse 2002: 783, 788)

However, Nicoloaïdis and Howse do not address the point that the EU's projection of a 'utopia' is the construction of the EU as a better 'self' that is likely to prevent it from succeeding in 'modelling itself on this utopia'. In other words, the narrative of 'normative power Europe' constructs the EU's identity as well as the identity of the EU's others. Unless a degree of self-reflexivity is introduced into such debates and/or policies, EU actors will tend to disregard their own shortcomings (see Tonra 2003: 743–6). The lack of such reflexivity often stands out as a major weakness of normative power in the US case, as we shall now discuss.

Such a reading of the concept of 'normative power Europe' takes its inspiration from post-structuralist work on self/other constructions in international politics. From this point of view, identities are seen always to require an other against which they are constructed; an other which they thus construct at the same time (see, for example Connolly 1991a; Neumann 1999; Walker 1993). A common strand in international politics, for instance, is the representation of the 'sovereign domestic' as peaceful and secure and the 'world outside' as anarchic and dangerous, a threat to the cosiness of the nation (Ashley 1988). Within this argument, the characteristics of the domestic sphere are presented as existing prior to the external threat, but, in fact, they are constructed in this very statement – there is no homogeneous and clearly delineated 'inside' to be defended against the 'outside', apart from a historically contextual representation of social relations infused with power and distinctions between 'self' and 'other'. Foreign policy, from such an angle, is not the representation of the nation to others as a pre-given object but a construction of the nation in the very moment of representation (Campbell 1998).

The projection of American ideals, for instance, is at the same time the construction of these particular ideals and a particular American identity. Indeed, although David Campbell's seminal study of US foreign policy and identity focuses on the construction of danger and identity, it also repeatedly refers to the notion of 'civilising' others through the projection of norms, a practice that at the same time 'serve[s] to enframe, limit and domesticate a particular identity' commensurate with the norms espoused – an identity which 'incorporates, for example, the form of domestic order, the social relations of production, and the various subjectivities to which they give rise' (Campbell 1998: 158). It is helpful to summarise some of the strategies of constructing 'self' and 'other' in international politics in order to trace them in articulations of normative power Europe:

- Representation of the other as an *existential threat* ('securitisation'). This practice has been highlighted and analysed by the Copenhagen School of security studies (Buzan *et al.* 1998). In their work, issues are turned into a security threat through a speech act of securitisation, i.e., the representation of that issue as an existential threat, legitimising extraordinary measures (classically: war), but also constructing a particular subject as the threatened 'referent object' at the same time.
- Representation of the other as *inferior*. In this weaker version of 'othering', the self is simply constructed as superior to the other. In practices of Orientalism, for instance, the other becomes the exotic; as such the other is feted but, at the same time, looked down upon (Said 1979). To

the extent that the other is seen as undermining the standards of the self, this strategy approximates the first one.

- Representation of the other as *violating universal principles*. This is a stronger variation of the second strategy. Here, however, the standards of the self are not simply seen as superior but of universal validity, with the consequence that the other should be convinced or otherwise brought to accept the principles of the self (Ashley 1989).

- Representation of the other as *different*. This fourth strategy of othering differs from the previous three in that it does not place an obvious value-judgement on the other: the other is represented neither as inferior nor as a threat but merely as different. While this is not an innocent practice (it still imposes identities on others), it is preferable to the other three in that it reduces the possibility to legitimise harmful interference with the other (Linklater 2005a; Rumelili 2004).

- Representation of the other as *abject*. Julia Kristeva's Lacanian psychoanalytically based work has illustrated over the past three decades that the other is always part of the self – an abject foreigner which is part of our conscious and unconscious selves (Kristeva 1982: 4; 1991: 191–2; Kinnvall 2004: 753). Kristeva advocates recognising that 'the foreigner is within us' and 'by recognising *our* uncanny strangeness we shall neither suffer from it nor enjoy it from the outside' (Kristeva 1991: 191–2).

It is the latter two forms of othering that a normative power Europe, as a more 'humble' power attempting to construct non-hierarchical relationships, would have to strive for. The recognition of the 'other within' demands from such a Europe that it recognises its own multiplicity and the failures within. The discourse of the historical other of Europe's past was a discourse that instilled such reflexivity within the self-representation of Europe (see Wæver 1996), but it is a discourse in decline (Diez 2004). There are, of course, tensions between the articulation of a normative power Europe and the promotion of norms, on the one hand, and reflexivity, on the other. But these tensions do not constitute two poles that are impossible to bridge. Instead, they instil an ethos that strives towards the spreading of norms more through example than preaching; the acceptance and addressing of failure also within rather than its demonising; a dialogical orientation towards the other instead of simply trying to change it; and binding oneself to norms set by others. This ethos is in contrast to securitisation strategies advocated by Robert Cooper, who invokes the threats that the modern (and pre-modern) world present to the post-modern world of the EU (Cooper 2000). It is here that a core norm of 'sustainable peace' becomes clearer at the heart of normative-power Europe's ethos (see Manners 2006a; 2006b).

Furthermore, to say that the articulation of normative power is a discursive practice that constructs the EU's identity does not mean that this is in itself a bad thing (for examples, see Lamy and Laïdi 2002; Ioakimidis 2003; Garton Ash 2004; Linklater 2005b). Any articulation of identity is infused with power. Discursive practice enables us to speak and make sense of the world, but we should always be reflective of the context in which we are engaging. Whether or not a particular identity construction is regarded as problematic depends on the context in which it is viewed – this is ultimately what politics is about. In the case of 'normative power Europe', we suggest four political implications. First, the content of the norms is to be welcomed as they envision a world of more peaceful and just relations. Second, if those norms, however, are projected without self-reflection, the identity construction that they entail allows the continued violation of the norms within the EU. Third, such an unreflexive projection of norms and construction of European identity risks being undermined by military power. Fourth, we need to be critical of the way in which assumptions of a single EU 'self' are structured – it is too common to approach the EU as if it was *a* self which was capable of a strategy.

> Thus, from the viewpoint of conventional work on identity, the notion of a difference engine reflects the attempts within the EU to engineer a single, essential, categorical identity which acts as a multiplier of differences between the EU and the world. However, critical social theory encourages us to analyse the international identity of the EU as far more fluid, consisting of ongoing contestations of complex, multiple, relational identities. From this critical viewpoint the notion of a 'difference engine' is a means to analyse these ongoing contestations as part of the international identity of the EU which does not add up to a single, integrating whole.
>
> (Manners and Whitman 2003: 397)

As the above quote from work on the 'international identity' of the EU illustrates, there is no *one* EU identity – the EU cannot be considered a 'difference engine' in the multiplication of a separate, single, essential, categorical, supranational EU self. It is the fluid, complex, multiple, and relational aspects of the self–other contestations which define the EU as a normative power, rather than the other way round. This self-pluralism makes it very difficult to consistently crystallise either self or other. In our discussions of self–othering practices, we need to constantly reflect on the way in which these practices are *always* present as part of human social existence. These practices are always for someone and for some purpose – our task, as political scientists, is to ensure we are critical (in the sense of challenging the prevailing order of the world) of othering practices (see Cox 1981). If we accept that such practices are always present, then we need to reflect on how these may best escape essentialist interpretations.

Conclusion: reflection and reflexivity in a sustainable normative-power Europe

With the rise of social constructivism in IR, the role of norms in international politics has become a widely studied subject. European integration is often seen as a 'best case' for the application of social constructivism (Christiansen *et al.* 2001). This is largely because of the characteristics of the EU polity, such as 'the goal or finality of European integration, the competing ideas and discourses about European governance, and the normative implications of particular EU policies' (Diez and Wiener 2004: 10). Yet the nature of the EU's external relations also plays a crucial part in the Union's 'postmodern' features, insofar as it is seen as a new kind of 'normative power' (Ruggie 1993: 172). Thus, social constructivists, like other scholars, would focus their analysis of 'normative power Europe' on the exact role that norms play in the formulation of a European foreign and external policy. We have argued in this chapter that this focus neglects an important aspect of the discourse on 'normative power Europe': its contribution to the construction of a European identity.

To summarise, we have put forward three specific claims: first, that the concept of 'normative power' is distinct from 'civilian power', although 'civilian power' can be read as a particular kind of 'normative power'. Second, the EU is not the first normative power, and the 'self'/'other' practices constituting the 'normative-power Europe' discourse can be observed in other historical periods, notably in the practices of the USA in the inter-war and immediate post-war periods. Finally, the discourse on 'normative power Europe' is an important practice of European identity construction, but one that needs to be seen as complex, multiple and relational.

The example of the USA is also where the lessons start. We have argued that normative and military power are not necessarily incompatible. The history of the USA illustrates this, but it also shows how military power can 'take over'. The development of the European Security and Defence Policy (ESDP) needs to be set against the US example and assert the civilian features of European integration against an unreflective drive to increase military power (such as one driven by the demands of the European aerospace and armaments industry), even if this is linked to the spread of norms (Manners 2006a, 2006b). As we have tried to show, one of the differences between the USA–American and the EU–European discourses is that the latter still maintains a higher degree of reflexivity, although the attempts to project norms held to be universally valid beyond the EU runs a similar risk of articulating a much less reflexive position. The European Security Strategy offers perhaps a bit of relief in this respect. While it does locate the most challenging threats mainly outside Europe and engages in the reproduction of the image of Europe as a Europe of peace (European Union 2003: 7), it is also characterised by more regional and less global aspirations, by an emphasis on different and not only military means of influence and a lack of 'missionary spirit' in comparison with the US National Security Strategy (Berenskoetter 2005: 76).

Nonetheless, for the study of 'normative power Europe', the discussion of the power of the 'normative power Europe' discourse (in the previous section) with respect to the example of the USA, has at least two implications. First, the difference between the EU as a civilian power and as a normative power should be analysed more carefully. Second, the discourse constructing 'normative power Europe' should be analysed more systematically, particularly regarding forms of othering and the degree of reflexivity it entails. The original conceptualisation of normative power already provides a lead on this with reference to the EU's self-binding to international law. As we have discussed here, the characteristic of reflexivity would be another distinguishing feature of a more normative power Europe.

Reflexivity has a dual meaning in social science, involving both an understanding of the monitored character of social life and the need for reflexive research characterised by interpretation and reflection (Giddens 1984: 3; Alvesson and Sköldberg 2000: 5). This dual reading of reflexivity should be taken seriously when arguing that the normative-power argument has 'a normative quality to it – that the EU should act to extent its norms into the international system' (Manners 2002: 252). We understand that our social life has a monitored character to it involving social reflection and readjustment. In this respect, anyone arguing that the EU does 'good' in the world causes us to engage in socially contextual consideration and contestation of this argument. Yet we also understand that our research should constantly be interpreting the practices of others and reflecting on the impact of our work, as we have tried to do through our conversation presented here.

Acknowledgements

We are very grateful to a large number of people, including Felix Berenskoetter, Giovanna Bono, David Chandler, Geoffrey Edwards, Simon Lightfoot, Kerry Longhurst, Anand Menon, Kalypso Nicolaïdis, Michelle Pace, Bahar Rumelili, Helene Sjursen, Ben Tonra, and Jevgenia Viktorova for their helpful comments on earlier versions of the papers that make up this chapter.

11 Empowerment among nations

A sociological perspective

Erik Ringmar

The position of the USA in world politics is today quite ambiguous. The only superpower and arbiter of matters of war and peace around the globe, the country commands a position sometimes compared to that of the Romans at the height of their pre-eminence. On the other hand, American troops have been quite unable to stabilise Iraq – evoking memories of Vietnam where a peasant army defeated a nuclear power – and they have had little success on North Korea, Iran, or in catching Osama Bin Laden. For all its power, the USA seems oddly impotent. Something close to the opposite could be said about the European Union. The EU is invariably derided for its 'weakness' and for the 'endless squabbles' of its members. A political entity without a foreign policy and an army, it has, time and again, shown itself inept at dealing with the crises that land on its own doorsteps. And yet it is in many ways remarkable how much the Europeans have achieved. From being a continent constantly torn by wars, Europe has become a zone of peace. These are economically successful, decent societies, and, despite their interminable quarrels, they have reached agreement on difficult-to-agree-on issues such as a common currency and an ever-expanding body of Europe-wide legislation. Cross-national civil-society groups have often been misjudged in a similar way. Anti-globalisation protesters may be angry, vocal and, in some cases, armed, but they are also few in numbers, socially marginalised and their messages are far from coherent. Showing up at meetings of world leaders, they seem to make more enemies than friends and are subsequently quickly dismissed as utterly powerless. Yet they clearly do have a measure of influence. Their mere existence points to the possibility of there being alternative solutions to world problems and, as such, they are guaranteed a place both on the evening news and in academic discussions (see, however, Lipschutz, in this volume).

What these examples illustrate is a confusion regarding the meaning and nature of power in world politics – what it is, what it does and who has it. Clearly the powerful are often not as powerful as they appear to be and the powerless are not as powerless (cf. Havel 1986: 36–122). Yet this is surely a perverse conclusion. By any reasonable definition, surely the powerful should have power and the powerless should not. As long as this is not the case, there must be something seriously wrong with the way the concept is defined. If the difficulties only were conceptual, little damage would ensue. The real problem is rather that the analytical confusion is reproduced among policy-makers, with far-reaching and often disastrous results. Believing themselves to be more powerful than they are, the Americans have overextended themselves and sought to dominate situations they clearly cannot control. Meanwhile, believing all the talk about powerlessness, many Europeans have said their respective *nons* to further and deeper collaboration. Something similar has happened to the ragtag band of anti-globalisation protesters. Concluding that their efforts are in vain, they have often abandoned their protests for other political, or utterly non-political, activities (cf. Hirschman 1985).

The aim of this chapter is to rethink the concept of power as it currently is used in international relations (IR). The basic strategy is to invoke the help of scholars writing in an adjacent field of social enquiry – sociology. Sociologists, on the whole, may not be smarter than IR scholars, but their definitions of power are certainly far richer. Studying power within societies rather than between them, they are, for example, less likely to be impressed with the sheer force of military hardware. Their definitions are also likely to be less politically pernicious. Anticipating the conclusion, what sociology can teach scholars of IR is that, more than anything, power is a matter of capabilities – what really matters is the 'power to' rather than the 'power over'. How much power we have is not determined by the extent to which we can dominate others as much by what it is that we can get done. Instead of understanding power as a zero-sum game of control and counter-control, what we should study are the processes through which states and other international actors are empowered or disempowered.

IR scholars on power

IR scholars have a poor understanding of the concept of power. This is surprising given the centrality of the concept in studies of international affairs (Baldwin 2002; Barnett and Duvall 2005a; Guzzini 1993). As the Athenians already pointed out to the Melians in Thucydides' *History of the Peloponnesian War*, 'the strong do what they have the power to do and the weak accept what they have to accept' (Thucydides 1972: 402). Providing their respective versions of this basic insight, statesmen, diplomats, generals, and scholars have endlessly repeated that 'calculations about power lie at the heart of how states think about the world around them' – and that we forget this basic truth only at our peril (Mearsheimer 2001: 12; cf. Carr 1964: vii). Yet this leaves the question open as to what exactly power is. At this juncture, students of world politics seem to rely mainly on their intuition; somehow or another, 'we know what power is when we see it'. This is most obviously the case, we are told, at times of war – from the Peloponnesian War onwards – when strong states are able to force weak states to concede to their demands. Power, that is, is known above all through its successful exercise; 'A has power over B to the extent that A can get B to do something that B would not otherwise do' (Dahl 1957: 202). Conversely, if the exercise fails, it turns out that A was not as powerful as he/she/it initially had thought.

The shortcomings of this definition are obvious (Lukes 2005: 38–48; Nye 2004b: 2). One problem is how to demonstrate causation. Somehow we need a way to establish that an actor is able to make another actor do something that the latter would not otherwise have done. For this purpose, we need access to the intentions both of the person exercising power and of the person over whom power is exercised. In addition, we need to establish that the failure to carry out the intended action indeed was a result of the exercise of power and not due to some other extraneous event. In most real-life cases, gathering all this information is, of course, difficult if not outright impossible. Besides, it is surely too restrictive to look only at cases where the exercise of power is explicit. Clearly much power can be wielded in other ways, for example, through the control of an agenda (Bachrach and Baratz 1963: 641–51; Lukes 2005: 20–5). Through such control, by making sure that certain issues never are raised in the first place, overt conflicts can be avoided. As a result, no arms need to be twisted, and consensus and social peace can appear to prevail. Meanwhile, beneath the surface social life, the exercise of power may only be too obvious. How to study these hidden non-cases is, however, far less clear.

Faced with such seemingly insurmountable obstacles, the time-honoured cop-out is to look not at actual exercises of power but instead at the kinds of resources which all exercises of power are thought to require. That is, instead of trying to solve the problems of intentionality and agenda-setting, the assumption is that there are resources that matter regardless of where and how the exercise of power takes place (Morgenthau 1948: 27; Waltz 1979: 131; Mearsheimer 2001: 55; Schmidt, this volume). Foremost among such resources – at least as far as IR are concerned – is military hardware, but indirectly also all resources that go into the production and use of military hardware. Thus, a country's level of economic development matters together with its natural-resource endowment, its industrial base, its territory, the size of its population and so on. Less directly, it is possible to include factors such as a country's leadership and its command and control structures, the morale of its people and the overall legitimacy of its regime. No one can be powerful in world politics, the argument goes, who lacks access to resources such as these.

The obvious problem here is the rate at which resources can be converted into actual political outcomes. There is, for example, hardly any doubt that weapons matter for warfare, but as the Soviet *débâcle* in Afghanistan and the American *débâcle* in Iraq have shown, military hardware does not always translate neatly into displays of power. This is, a fortiori, the case in situations that fall short of war, and, in an increasingly interdependent world, such situations are arguably more common than ever previously (Nye 2004b: 18–21). The power of the USA is today largely disconnected from its nuclear arsenal; Russia and the UK have nuclear arsenals too, but it is far from clear what kind of power, if any, emanates from them.

The problems of the resource view has led some scholars to emphasise instead what has come to be known as 'soft power' (Nye 2004b; Nye, this volume). Soft power is exercised, above all, through persuasion and leadership; it is the power to convince rather than to coerce and to make others follow us through the attractiveness of our ideals and the example set by our actions. In today's post-belligerent world, it is argued, this is a vastly more important kind of power than the old sabre-rattling. As long as we can seduce our opponents, we need neither sticks nor carrots. The real super-power is the country which people find the most attractive (Nye 2004b: 10–11). The idea of soft power is surely an important addition to the traditional accounts. There is indeed such a thing as the power of persuasion (Lebow in this volume). Yet the emphasis on soft power is best understood as an extension of the traditional model and not as a break with it. What matters are still resources, although the relevant resources are ideational – 'culture', 'institutions', 'ideals' (Bially Mattern in this volume). Moreover, soft resources also have to be converted into successful exercises of power, and no such conversion is likely to be straightforward (Lukes in this volume). Making oneself popular is hard work; it is easy to overdo it, and one's best efforts are often counter-productive. Seeing power in terms of attractiveness turns world politics into a beauty contest in which real power rests not with the prospective beauty queens as much as with the people judging them. A state that derives its position from its attractiveness is effectively handing power over to the ever-shifting verdicts of a global public opinion.

The fundamental problem of all traditional accounts – be they hard or soft – is that far too much attention is paid to the power that individual actors exercise over other individual actors. What is ignored is, above all, what we could refer to as 'structural factors'. After all, power can be exercised anonymously, and we can be manipulated by processes and institutions just as much as by individuals or by states. Often, in fact, such structural power is the most pervasive form of power, and it clearly operates also in relation between states. So far, however, scholars of international relations have paid structural factors only scant attention (Guzzini 1993). For a proper discussion we need help from sociologists.[1]

Structural power

Sociologists have a richer understanding of power since their descriptions of domestic society are richer than the descriptions most scholars have of international society (cf. Wendt and Duvall 1989). Sociologists pay proper attention to the relationships of power obtaining between social groups, movements and classes and to the power exercised by the economic system, by institutions, the media, religion, and the family. This allows them to talk about forms of power which are anonymous, impersonal and unintended and to talk about power which is structural in nature.

Take a basic social mechanism such as the division of labour (cf. Lindblom 1976; Ringmar 2005). As a result of the expansion of markets, people are forced to specialise on their comparative advantages and to live and work under conditions which are not of their own choosing. In this way, the traditional fabric of social life is undermined, together with traditional social positions and identities; people can no longer be who they were and live the way they used to live. This is an exercise of power to be sure, yet it is not the kind of power one individual exercises over another. Instead, it is best described as the power of a structure – as structural power. The same mechanism operates also in relations between states, distributing and redistributing power between them. The division of labour forces countries to focus on the production of particular goods and services and, in the process, it rearranges patterns of income and wealth as well as trade patterns and alliances. Ultimately, the division of labour may undermine the position of the state itself and its ability to defend itself against enemies. Again, this is power exercised by a structure rather than by individuals, groups or states.

As a sociologist might go on to argue, structural power shapes not only what we do but also what we want (Lukes 2005: 38–48). Growing up in a certain society, we are socialised into accepting its basic norms and prejudices. This process of socialisation is empowering since it provides us with the means of asserting ourselves as social beings, but it is also constraining in that it compels us to think in certain ways rather than in others. For example, in many societies, women have been socialised into accepting roles that are inferior to those of men, and, in many societies, religion is used to justify social inequalities (cf. Bordo 2003: 99–138, 245–75). As a result, people ask for less than what could be considered their fair and proper share. Similar processes of socialisation operate in relations between states. Compare, for example, the notion of a 'national interest' (Hirschman 1977). When first learning about world politics, we learn that the world is divided into discreet entities with borders between them and that each entity has a set of interests which it is the duty of decision-makers as well as ordinary citizens to defend. In the pursuit of a national interest, a state will undertake certain actions while disregarding others; typically, states will arm themselves and prepare for war. Yet there is nothing inevitable about such a conclusion, and the reason why people reach it is that they have been socialised into accepting certain international norms (Wendt 1992: 391–425). That is, structural power has been exercised over them.

Although the existence of such thought-moulding power hardly is in doubt, it is a kind of power which is devilishly difficult to study. It is next to impossible, after all, to identify the preconditions of our thoughts – like our eyes, our presumptions are themselves not directly available for inspection. Exercises of structural power are, for that reason, not necessarily recognised as such. Often, people who ostensibly are 'oppressed' – women in patriarchal societies and so on – profess themselves to be quite content with their lot. From the point of view of an outside observer, people like this seem not to be the best judges of their own predicament (Connolly 1974). The international relations equivalent readily suggests itself: traditional definitions of a national interest constitute a form of oppression which we perpetuate by denying the existence of it. Yet such conclusions are problematic. Who are we, as outside observers, to say that people misunderstand themselves and that we know their interests better than they do? And how can we say that a state's official interests are different from its true interests? The only way to defend such conclusions is to have some alternative standard that tells us what a human being, or a state, is and might be. Yet such a standard may, of course, never be more than an expression of the particular prejudices of the outside observers themselves and of the structural power exercised *on them*. Outsiders may indeed have a privileged perspective but they may also be far too removed to see what is going on. Twentieth-century history was replete with examples of such 'experts' who mistook their ignorance for superior wisdom (Scott 1998: 103–306; Siniavski 1988: 47–76).

A way around this problem is to look not at the content of the decisions but rather at the character of the process through which the decisions was reached (Lukes 2005: 48–58). Thus, one could, for example, demand that the individual concerned has thought long and hard about which actions are in his or her best interest to pursue. If such deliberation has taken place, we would have to argue that the conclusions reached indeed are genuine. And, conversely, in the absence of evidence of such deliberation, we could conclude that the person has been manipulated. That is, that power has been exercised over him or her. A woman who carefully considers her options before she subjects herself to the rules of a patriarchal society is free in a sense that the eventual choice itself does not reveal (Connolly 1974).[2] She is also in a better position to silence critical outside observers.

It would be wrong to think of this only as an intellectual process. Often it is, instead, some unexpected empirical event that suddenly forces us to reconsider our options. The definition of a national interest provides a good illustration. A state may go into a war with one definition of its national interest but come out of the war with a very different definition (cf. Skocpol 1979). No longer able to defend our collective self-conceptions, we are forced to reformulate them. The aim of such reformulations is typically to bring about a closer match between what we are and what we can be or between what we have and what we can have. As such, they are effectively empowering. Thus, the UK became more powerful, not less, when it decided to withdraw its troops east of Suez in 1968. Similarly, it could be argued that the USA is less powerful as today's single world hegemon than it was during the Cold War as one of two ferociously competing super powers.

Power and potentiality

These sociological insights are helpful, but they need to be further developed. A proper understanding of power, we said, requires knowledge of counterfactuals, of how life would be if only the relevant social structures were differently configured. What needs to be investigated here are the potentialities inherent in social life; not how things *are* but how they *could be*. In order to pursue such an investigation, we need some way of reflecting on ourselves and the options open to us. We will understand the power exercised by existing social structures only once we have learnt to imagine alternatives to them. Reflection thus understood is empowering. Yet the kind of power that empowers is quite different from the kind of power we discussed above. What matters here is not 'power over' but instead 'power to' (Mann 1986: 6; Giddens 1987: 7; Morriss 2002). 'Power over' is what historical sociologists have discussed as *Herrschaft*, domination, or what in the Middle Ages was known as *potestas* (Lukes 2005: 74–85; cf. Bendix 1960: 290–300). The contrasting term – 'power to' – is instead referred to as *Macht* or *potentia*. As the seventeenth-century philosopher Baruch Spinoza explained, *potentia* signifies 'the power of things in nature, including persons, to exist and act', whereas *potestas* is used 'when speaking of being in the power of another' (Spinoza, quoted in Lukes 2005: 73).

Power defined as *potentia* is best understood as a capability or a faculty. It is the kind of power we exercise when we rely on our 'power of speech', 'power of reason' or the 'power of flight'. Differently put, power defined as *potentia* is the ability to transform something potential into something actual (von Wright 1971: 44–9). What matters here is not how we allocate the stuff which makes up the existing world but rather how we allocate the stuff which makes up the possible world; power is exercised over what could be rather than over what is. Power understood as *potentia* is a sort of gate-keeper that regulates the relationship between the actually existing and the potentially existing. *Potentia* guards this gate, letting some things slip through into actuality while keeping other things waiting *in spe*. While *potestas* is the power through which the world is governed, *potentia* is the power through which the world is made.

This world-making power has its origins in magic and religion (Caillois 1939/2001: 87–96). It is the *potentia* of the religious doctrine which commands our allegiance and the *potentia* of its messengers which proves their official, authorised status. A magus waves his wand and things appear out of thin air, a shaman is transported from one place to another, the sick are healed and the dead are awoken. In monotheistic religions, such powers can always be traced back to an almighty god who is the final arbiter between that which exists and that which does not exist (Kantorowitz 1957: 42–86). The *potentiæ* of all human beings – including the power of secular rulers – are ultimately derived from this supreme source. Or, to be more precise, power is never permanently received but only temporarily borrowed. The debt has constantly to be remembered, the source of one's abilities acknowledged, and, in the end, all one's powers have to be returned to one's maker. As gatekeepers and arbiters, monotheistic gods are characterised by two exceptional qualities: their omniscience and their omnipotence. There is nothing they do not know and nothing they cannot do. The *potentiæ* which humans borrow never give them anything like the same powers, yet the more godlike they become, the more powerful they are. The more human beings know, the better they understand the potentialities inherent in their lives and their societies; the more they can do, the better they are at actualising these potentialities. Expressed in more secular language, *potentia*, the 'power to', entails both to the ability to reflect and the ability to act. It is through reflection that new potentialities come to be discovered, and it is through action that they are actualised.

To develop one's powers of reflection and one's powers of action is to become empowered. Reflection, we said above, is empowering, and so is the ability to act. Understood in this fashion, the exercise of power is not necessarily a zero-sum game. You can have a faculty without ever using it, and several social actors can simultaneously reflect or act without one's increase in power necessarily detracting from another's. For the same reason, empowerment does not necessarily mean that one is able to achieve one's goals. You can develop a faculty, you can exercise it and yet fail to get your way. To what extent you are successful depends on how hard you try, on the situation you are in, on how other social actors act and react. Thus 'power to' is best understood as a precondition for 'power over' – *potestas* requires *potentia* – no one can be powerful who is not first empowered. Yet the opposite is not the case: *potentia* does not require *potestas*. You can have the power to do something without necessarily having power over others.

Structural empowerment

All definitions of power require a social ontology of some kind, a basic model which tells us what the components of society are and how they are put together (Ringmar 2007a). Power defined as *potestas*, the 'power over', requires an ontology made up of actors – individuals, groups and states – whose relationships are determined by the power they have over each other. Here powerful actors do what they like and powerless actors suffer what they must. This is most obviously the case in hierarchical social systems such as feudal societies or totalitarian regimes, but it is true also of systems – such as economic markets – where actors formally are both equal and independent of each other. Markets are self-equilibrating devices where order is assured through the interrelationship of supply and demand, that is, through the relative market power of each actor.

By contrast, power understood as *potentia* implies a constructivist ontology of society (Ringmar 2007a). This metaphor takes society to be a building which human beings construct and reconstruct according to whatever plans they draw up (Scott 1998; cf. Lakoff and Johnson 2003: 46). Constructivism is a reformist faith, a belief that human beings can understand the world since they have made it and make it since they understand it (Vico 1986: § 331, p. 96; Tully 1980: 22–3). The most important relationships here are not those obtaining between social actors but instead between social actors and the projects they share. You need *potentia* in order to get things done; above all, you need the power to draw up the best possible plans and the power to actualise them. The more social actors are empowered, the more successfully they can achieve their goals.

In the study of international politics, these two ontologies correspond reasonably well to the time-honoured distinction between realism and idealism.[3] Realists define power as *potestas*, and their world is made up of actors whose relationships are determined by the power each has over the other. Just as in an economic market, world politics is regarded as a self-equilibrating system where a change in the balance of power triggers countervailing forces which restore order (Hirschman 1977; Mayr 1986: 148–54; Waltz 1979: 115–29). Idealists, for their part, define power as *potentia* and see world politics in terms of challenges that must be overcome and projects that much be achieved – peace, prosperity, democracy, and development. The way to reach these goals, idealists insist, is to empower individuals, groups and states.

During the past couple of decades, there has been a general move away from constructivist ontologies towards self-organising ones (Hayek 1988: 83–8; Scott 1998: 316–19; cf. Ringmar 2007a). The most ambitious constructivist projects – the great revolutions, the leaps forward, the modernisation schemes – all failed, in some cases spectacularly so. At its best, constructivism equalled liberal do-goodery, but at its worst, it equalled totalitarian dictatorship. By contrast, self-organisation seems less fraught with danger: no common plans have to be made and no common decisions taken; decentralised decisions leave freedom to individuals to work out their differences between themselves. This is, of course, the same lesson which scholars of international politics have taught for years: it is so much safer to organise social interaction on the basis on *potestas* than on the basis of *potentia*.

But let us not give up on empowerment too quickly. Common problems cannot always be solved through decentralised decisions and 'power over' cannot substitute for 'power to'. Broadly speaking, empowerment is surely a good idea. The problem with the constructivist ontology is rather its simplistic faith in plans, central directives and in goal-oriented rationality (Scott 1998: 339–41). Society is clearly not a building which we can construct and reconstruct according to our fancy. Somehow or another, we need to rescue the idea of *potentia* from the clutches of the constructivist metaphor. Let us instead think of empowerment as a structural feature of society. Some societies seem to be far more empowering than others. In some societies, it is much easier to imagine alternatives to the present social order and easier to act on these alternatives – people are better at reflecting on potentialities and better at actualising them. Clearly this has little to do with the personal qualities of the individuals concerned, and, instead, everything to do with the presence or absence of certain kinds of institutions. It is institutions in the end that determine the degree to which social actors are empowered (Ringmar 2007b).

Consider, for example, the many institutions that help us reflect on ourselves and on the societies in which we live – including media and the press, universities, scientific academies, even religious institutions and the arts. Or consider the many institutions that facilitate action – including banks and stock markets that provide funding, property rights and commercial laws that protect investments, or the political framework of the state that guarantees the peace and security which all ventures require. Once institutions like these are in place – and many others could be mentioned – it is a lot easier for individuals both to reflect creatively and to act decisively. Empowerment is a consequence of institutions such as these. Conversely, disempowerment is a consequence of the lack of such institutions.

Taken together, institutions that enable both reflection and action constitute an empowering structure. No matter who we are and what we want, the institutions are there to support us. A society where such institutions are strong is more creative, dynamic, and its inhabitants are more likely to fully develop their various skills and faculties. An empowering structure thus understood could perhaps be compared to a 'field' such as the electromagnetic or gravitational fields discussed by physicists. Social potentialities placed within this field become charged, as it were, and, as a result, they are able to make the transition into actuality; they flip, much as bundles of energy flip from a status as light to a status as matter. This is not a causal process to be sure and no outcomes are inevitable. Rather, the empowering structure is a condition of possibility of many alternative realities becoming actualised, none of them determined by the structure itself but by the human ability to imagine and make things happen one way or another.

To be sure, being structurally empowered does not necessarily mean that you are able to achieve your goals. The reason is that social actors interact with other social actors who also want to achieve their goals. Reflection and action are both bound to produce conflict among actors. Reflection is a critical activity and, as such, often subversive, and since resources always are limited, not all plans can simultaneously be actualised. As a result, there will always be competition over who gets what and on what terms. For this reason, empowering structures must be combined with institutions that are able to resolve conflicts peacefully. Nothing accomplished by reflection or entrepreneurship will last unless a way is found of allowing for the coexistence of different, perhaps contradictory, projects, entities, beliefs, and ways of life. There are various examples of such institutions, but, in contemporary society, the economic, the political and the judicial systems play this conflict-resolving role.

This is, thus, how individuals and societies come to avail themselves of *potentia*, the Spinozian power 'of things in nature, including persons, to exist and act'. We reflect in order to discover the potential which exists in the actual; we act in order to put these discoveries into practice; we eventually find ways of integrating our ideas and our project with those of others. Yet none of this is down to individuals and all of it is down to institutions. By moving the boundary between the potential and the actual, institutions are empowering.

The empowerment of nations

This argument has implications for how we understand power in international affairs. As an illustration, consider the historical evolution of the sovereign state as a process of empowerment. The modern international order – the 'Westphalian system' – is usually described as decentralised and anarchic. Lacking a central authority which can keep peace among its constituent units, wars are a perennial threat (Morgenthau 1948; Waltz 1979). Not surprisingly, power is here equated with 'power over' – it is power over others which guarantees security and peace. Yet this is an exceedingly poor and partial picture. What is ignored is, above all, 'power to' and the fact that the Westphalian system, since its very inception, has operated to empower and disempower social actors (Ringmar 2007b). While 'power over' determines how the world is governed, 'power to' determines how the world is made.

The most obvious flip from potentiality into actuality happened through the creation of the state in the Renaissance (Skinner 1989: 90–131). There were no states, properly speaking, in the European Middle Ages, and the state had to be imagined before it could come to exist. There were many institutions which facilitated such reflection. The feudal system, with its decentralised authority structure, provided one source of imagination, but so did reflections on *dominatio* and *imperium* inspired by canon law and investigated by scholars working under the auspices of the church (Pagden 1987). Such reflections were also greatly enhanced by the rediscovery of the political writings of classical antiquity (Hale 1977: 304–6). In addition, the institutional structures of medieval society – in particular, the division between secular and religious authorities – helped facilitate political action. The best examples of political entrepreneurs are perhaps the *condottieri*, the mercenary soldiers who found themselves thrust into positions of power in various cities in northern Italy from the thirteenth century onward (Bozeman 1960). In this part of Europe, the authority of the pope overlapped with the authority of the emperor, but, often enough, the *condottieri* were able to play the one against the other and make themselves independent of both (Mattingly 1955: 78–86). From the end of the fifteenth century, these new rulers began to claim 'sovereignty' over the territories they controlled.

The transformation from a feudal to a state-based international order was surprisingly smooth. Again, the reason was institutional. Medieval society had multiple sources of authority – the whole feudal network of overlapping loyalties and obligations – yet they were all incorporated into one pan-European and Church-led authority structure. Medieval Europe was at the same time one and infinitely many (Ringmar 2007b). When the states declared themselves sovereign they became parts of a similar set-up. The Westphalian order was held together through the interaction of its constituent units, and sovereignty coexisted with participation in an international system of states. Medieval Europe and Westphalian Europe were both extremely violent to be sure, yet the transition between them was not particularly traumatic. The pan-European institutions of the Middle Ages were reformulated rather than replaced.

The state, once firmly established, can be described as a network of empowering institutions that facilitated reflection and action and also helped solve conflicts. Reflection took institutional form in state-sponsored universities and scientific academies but, above all, by means of the newspapers, journals and books which the newly invented printing press made possible (Eisenstein 1983: 148–86). Soon a 'public opinion' came to be formed, constituting a collective reflective faculty which took the state as one of its main subjects (Baker 1990: 167–79; Koselleck 1988: 62–75). The state also empowered new actors. The existence of parliaments and parties made a great difference to political entrepreneurs, and economic action was facilitated by state-supplied institutions which organised and regulated markets (Polanyi 1944). Religious entrepreneurs typically found sovereign princes a more receptive audience than the feudal princes of the pre-state era.

The result of this outburst of reflective and entrepreneurial activity was conflict, and soon the newly independent states were riven by civil wars (Toulmin 1990: 46–62). The initial reaction on the part of state officials was to restrict the range of allowed opinions and to crack down on dissent. Peace was restored à la Thomas Hobbes and Jean Bodin, through the *diktats* of absolutist rulers. Gradually, however, more sophisticated means of resolving conflicts were developed. In the course of the eighteenth century, civil society reasserted itself, and self-regulatory devices such as Adam Smith's 'hidden hand' became more prominent (Mayr 1986: 102–14; Hofstadter 1969: 40–73). Conflicts, it was discovered, could often be avoided through political debate and by allowing economic agents and political parties to compete with each other for the favours of the public at large (Ringmar 2007b).

Yet the state was not only an empowering structure but also a subject in its own right. As such, it acted and interacted with other states in an international system which empowered and disempowered its constituent units. On the international level, too, there were institutional structures that facilitated reflection, action and helped solve conflict. These institutions were typically European in origin, dominated by European concerns, and European statesmen, corporations, scientists, and preachers were their main beneficiaries. Although many non-Europeans benefited too, the losers were more than anything the traditional authorities, ways of knowing and ways of living of non-European societies. Consider, for example, the gradual universalisation of European ideas regarding science, economic rationality and human rights during the course of the nineteenth century. Once a scientific attitude came to be adopted, the Europeans had a powerful new way of making sense of overseas discoveries; and once economic rationality came to dominate their outlook, the Europeans knew what to do with the things they discovered. Ideas regarding human rights set limits to the way they could treat their new subjects, or at least they were forced to come up with arguments why human rights had to be set aside. For the colonised peoples, the spread of these European notions provided powerful new ways of reflecting both on their own traditional societies and on the actions of the Europeans. The outcome was simultaneously both empowering and disempowering.

In addition, the international system of the nineteenth century provided institutions that facilitated action. Ideas regarding economic rationality were complemented with institutions that encouraged international trade, investments and the use of foreign natural resources. An international capital market was created together with an international currency, and agreements were signed – in many cases far from voluntarily – regarding open markets and free trade (Ferguson 2001). The European-dominated world system facilitated other forms of action as well – the work of states-men, soldiers, scientists, missionaries, adventurers, and thieves. As for conflict resolution, the colonial wars abated once the Europeans were firmly in control, and in Europe itself the nineteenth century was unusually peaceful. As the twentieth century was to show, however, conflicts were not really solved, only postponed.

Today's world is characterised by the same empowering and disempowering structures. The universalisation of European ideas has continued; reflection discovers new opportunities; old authorities are undermined and new ones supported. Today, reflection is, more than anything, sponsored by commercial enterprises, by development agencies, the World Trade Organization, the World Bank and by great European and North American universities. In an increasingly globalised world, where sovereignty means less and less, economic action is easier than ever and political action is increasingly in the hands of a few dominant actors. There are new twenty-first-century versions of the nineteenth-century missionaries, adventurers and thieves. Conflicts between states are not resolved through wars as much as through the imposition of norms regarding democracy, human rights and economic rationality. New actors dominate a world which continuously is being reconfigured.

Conclusion

Accepting these sociological insights, we can briefly summarise the conclusions as far as the study of international politics is concerned. The main conclusion is surely that power needs to be more broadly defined than traditionally has been the case. If the study of international politics is the study of how actors define and achieve their aims, what matters is *potentia* rather than *potestas*. While *potestas* is the power through which the world is governed, *potentia* is the power through which the world is made. We need to study the ways in which actors are empowered and disempowered and, thus, which institutions enable or disable reflection, action and compromise. A second conclusion is that the concept of 'the political' itself is far too narrowly defined. Politics, in Harold Lasswell's classical formulation, has usually been understood as a matter of 'who gets what, when, how' (Lasswell 1936). The image here is that of politics as an antagonistic struggle between actors who meet each other head-on as though on a metaphorical battlefield (Jullien 2000: 35–53). And while there is no denying that such clashes do take place – indeed actual battlefields have not yet disappeared – a sociological understanding of power reminds us that this is a very partial view of what politics is all about. Before overt clashes can be staged, power has been exercised in forming the actors, their identities, outlooks on life, and the definition of their interests.

It is perhaps worth reminding ourselves that the stakes in these definitional debates are not scholarly reputations as much as real-life outcomes. Mistakes about power get people killed. Consider again the three examples briefly discussed in the introduction. The USA is generally considered the most powerful country in the world, an empire even, yet it seems strangely powerless when dealing with a number of contemporary challenges including Iraqi insurgents, fugitive terrorists and North Korean bombs. The reason is that the USA, in its foreign policy in recent years, has prioritised the pursuit of *potestas* at the expense of *potentia*; what the USA can do to others has mattered far more than what it can get done together with others. Above all, it has neglected to sustain systematically the kinds of international institutions which empower its friends and disempower its enemies. Ironically, this has made the USA far less powerful than it could have been.

As for the EU, it has, largely despite itself, pursued the opposite policy. From the time of the Coal and Steel Union in the 1950s, the EU's emphasis has consistently been on the administrative and managerial aspects of European integration – on 'peace by pieces' and the profoundly unglamorous job of building pan-European institutional structures (cf. Mitrany 1943). As a result, the EU has next to no 'power over' anything at all – not even, in fact, proper power over its own constituent units – yet it evidently has a considerable amount of 'power to'. This is why the Union has achieved some remarkable feats of social engineering while getting next to no credit for it with European electorates. Clearly, the exercise of *potentia* is less attention-grabbing than the exercise of *potestas*.

As far as the ragtag bands of anti-globalisation protesters are concerned, they are surely by all accounts next to completely powerless. What they do have, however, is the ability to present the rest of us with alternative images of who we are and what our future is likely to be. Above, this was referred to as the power of reflection, and it is through reflection that we come to discover the potentialities that exist in our societies and in our lives. The point is not that the anti-globalisation protesters necessarily are correct, or that we have to listen to them, but instead that the future of our societies requires the constant consideration of alternatives to the existing order of things. The self-confident hubris of the most ardent globalisers is, in the end, undermining their own power. The day dissenting groups become convinced of their own powerlessness and abandon their quixotic quests, we will all be worse off.

Notes

1 When Joseph S. Nye asked Donald Rumsfeld about the concept of 'soft power', Rumsfeld replied 'I don't know what "soft power" is.' (Nye 2004b: ix). When Joseph S. Nye was asked what he thought of Steven Lukes's concept of power, he replied, 'I was not aware of it when I conceived of soft power in 1989', Joseph S. Nye, email to Tim Mackey, 5 May 2005.
2 Although the logic of this argument is not in doubt, one may wonder how important such outcomes are as an empirical category. The deliberative process is rarely independent from the substantive choices one reaches. It seems unlikely that one would make a fully considered choice to subject oneself to a superstitious faith, yet cases of this kind are not unknown.
3 Or realism and 'liberalism' or 'reformism' or some similar distinction. Note that 'constructivism' here denotes a social ontology and not, as in recent IR literature, a position in a debate regarding theories of knowledge.

12 Levels, spaces and forms of power

Analysing opportunities for change

John Gaventa[1]

The chapters in this volume seek to broaden the understanding of power amongst scholars of world politics, in part by drawing upon perspectives on power from other fields and disciplines. While accepting that the field of international politics may have much to learn from other perspectives, in this chapter I shall also argue the converse: contemporary trends in globalisation and governance that preoccupy many scholars of international politics today also challenge some of the earlier approaches to the study of power in political science, which had their roots in attempts to understand local and national patterns of power some forty years ago. By linking current thinking on the nature of power in an era of globalisation – and with it, multilayered, diffuse approaches to governance – to these earlier approaches, we gain a more multidimensional view of the levels, spaces and forms of power, and how they interrelate than through any singular approach.

In 1961, Robert Dahl famously asked about New Haven, Connecticut, 'Who Governs?'. His book was one of the best known in a genre of work on community power in the USA at the time, launching a large debate on who had power, and indeed, how one understood power in American democracy, especially at the local level. Earlier Dahl (1957: 202) had written, 'my intuitive idea of power, then, is something like this: A has power over B to the extent that he can get B to do something that B would not otherwise do.' Power in this approach could be found very simply by examining 'who participates, who gains and who loses, and who prevails in decision-making' (Polsby 1963: 55), especially at the community level, where power might be most observable.

As the introduction to this volume recounts, this view of power was challenged in 1974 by Steven Lukes, in his perhaps even more well-known book, *Power: A Radical View* (and in his expanded version in 2004). Critiquing the argument that power could be studied by observing who prevailed in decision-making arenas, Lukes argued that power must be understood not only in terms of who participates but also in terms of who does not. Power he argued, had three faces: the public face which Dahl, Polsby and others had studied; a hidden face, which served to keep issues off the agenda of decision-making arenas (Bachrach and Baratz 1962); and an even more 'insidious' third face, through which the relatively powerlessness came to internalise and accept their own condition and, thus, might not be aware of nor act upon their interests in any observable way. Lukes's analysis of what he called the three 'dimensions of power'[2] has spawned a series of debates and studies about how power affects not only who participates in decision-making processes, but also who does not, and why (see further elaboration in the introduction and in Ringmar, this volume, p. 189–203).

As a student of Steven Lukes at Oxford, I was influenced by the debates between himself and Peter Bachrach on the faces of power. I later applied the Lukes approach to an understanding of power and participation in a small coal-mining valley in the heart of the Appalachian Region in the USA (Gaventa 1980). However, in this essay, I extend the approach, arguing that while the three views or 'dimensions' of power elaborated by Lukes continue to be important, in the contemporary era they must also be understood in relationship to other aspects of power, which were not considered clearly in earlier work. First, I argue that while many of the earlier debates on power focused at the community level, changing patterns of globalisation have changed the territorial or spatial relations of power, meaning that power increasingly must be understood not only at the local, the national or the global level but also in their interrelationships. A focus on decision-making arenas in locality alone – be it New Haven or rural Appalachia – will rarely help us understand who really governs, though nor, of course, will only a focus on the national or supra-national.

Second, while many of the earlier debates focused on who participated in decision-making arenas of government, either at the local level or vis-à-vis the nation state, increasingly political-science discussions of public authority have moved from *government* to *governance*, which consists of multiple intersecting actors, arenas and networks and in which the decision-making arenas in which power may be found become more varied and porous. Political power may be understood not only in the state arenas, be they city halls, parliaments or the World Trade Organization (WTO), but also through a variety of other quasi-state and non-state spaces for decision-making (or in the hidden faces of power, for non-decision-making). For students of power, this broadens considerably where we study power, and for activists seeking to challenge power relations, it challenges received wisdom of where and how they should focus their attentions on changing the status quo. As Beck writes in his book on *Power in a Global Age*, globalisation

> has introduced a new space and framework for acting: politics is no longer to the same boundaries as before, and is no longer tied solely to state actors and institutions, the result being that additional players, new roles, new resources, unfamiliar rules and new contradictions and conflicts appear on the scene. In the old game, each playing piece made one move only. This is no longer true of the new nameless game for power and domination.

> (2005: 3–4)

For those familiar with recent writings on international relations (IR), the discussion of how power and authority are being reshaped by the twin forces of globalisation and changes in governance will not be new. However, I suggest that when these trends are considered in relationship to the earlier understandings of power that derived from the community power debates, we gain a far more complex and nuanced understanding of the location and dynamics of power. Power, I shall argue, must now be understood not only in relationship to the three dimensions outlined by Lukes but also in relationship to the *levels* of power, from local to global, as well as the *spaces* of power, from closed to claimed, and their interaction. With this more complex approach, the three dimensions or faces of power earlier elaborated by Lukes may be seen as three *forms* of power along a single dimension or continuum. By thinking of the levels of power and the spaces of power also as dimensions, or continua, each of which interacts with the other, we can visually understand power as a sort of Rubik's cube, which, for purposes of illustration, I have called 'the power cube' (See Figure 12.1).[3] In turn, the power cube may help us analyse and make more legible 'the new nameless game played for power and domination' outlined by Beck above.

In this task, at least two caveats are important. First, while the study of power is a very broad field, both within and beyond the field of IR, the focus of this chapter is primarily on how power interacts and shapes citizen action, especially from the grass-roots perspective, (though I recognise that this does not cover the full terrain of discussions about power in IR or more broadly). Also, my concern in this chapter is not only with the analysis of power for its own sake but also, from an actor-oriented perspective, to understand where and how those seeking to change power relations intervene to do so, especially from a normative stance of seeking to make power more just, democratic and accountable in favour of the interests of the relatively powerless. For those concerned with how power affects citizen participation and with how and where citizens individually and collectively

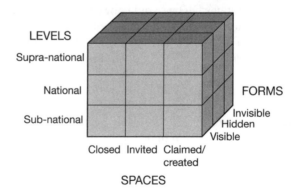

Figure 12.1

act for change *as social actors,*[4] the need for such an analytical lens for 'seeing' and understanding power is becoming increasingly more important. Put simply, if we want to challenge and change power relationships and their uses, we must understand more about where and how to engage. For that, we need new analytical tools.

Reflecting on the analysis of power and participation

The meanings of power – and how to analyse it – are diverse and often contentious, as the introduction and essays in this volume illustrate. Some see power as held by actors, some of whom are powerful while others are relatively more powerless. Others see it as more pervasive, embodied in a web of relationships and discourses which affect everyone, rather than something that is possessed by some and not others. Some see power as a 'zero-sum' concept – to gain power for one set of actors means that others must give up some power. Since rarely do the powerful give up their power easily, this often involves conflict and 'power struggle'. Others see power as more fluid, accumulative or productive. Power is not a finite resource; it can be used, shared or created by actors and their networks in many multiple ways. Some see power as a 'negative' trait – to hold power is to exercise control over others. Others see power as about capacity and agency to be wielded for positive action.

Understandings of power, I would argue, are shaped not only by conceptual debate but also by how it is experienced. Certainly, my view of power was shaped by my own history of engaging with power relations in a particular context. As a young graduate in political science, I began working with grass-roots citizens in a remote mining valley of one of the poorest parts of the USA in their efforts to claim political, economic and social rights vis-à-vis government and a London-based corporate mine-owner. The conventional views of democracy and power in America, which I had been exposed to in my studies, failed to explain the reality I encountered. Though violations of democratic rights, enormous inequalities in wealth and appalling environmental living conditions were to be found everywhere, there was little visible conflict or action for change.

There was something about power that had led not only to defeat where voices had been raised, but also, somehow, over time the voices had been silenced altogether (Gaventa 1980). Much of my work then shifted to how citizens recovered a sense of their capacity to act and how they mobilised to get their issues heard and responded to in the public agenda. After joining the Institute for Development Studies (IDS) at the University of Sussex in the mid-1990s, I continued to work on processes of citizen participation and engagement in other parts of the world. In the international development field, I discovered a host of approaches for participation, be they in development projects, local governance, national policy-making or engagements with global development institutions. At the same time, with their increasing acceptance in mainstream development discourse, many of these approaches risked becoming techniques that did not pay sufficient attention to the power relations within and surrounding their use. Increasingly, the work of the participation group at IDS and many of our associates began to look for approaches that put an understanding of power back in the centre of our understanding of the concepts and practices of participation (Eyben *et al.* 2006).

It was in this context that I and others began to search for approaches that could make the implicit power perspective more explicit and that would help to examine the interrelationships of the forms of power that we were encountering in different political spaces and settings. Building on my previous work based on the 'three faces' of power developed by Lukes (1974), I began to argue that Lukes's three faces of power must also be understood in relation to how spaces for engagement are created and the levels of power (from local to global) in which they occur. Understanding each of these – the spaces, levels and forms of power – as themselves separate but interrelated dimensions, each of which had at least three components within them, these dimensions could be visually linked together into a 'power cube'. By using this framework, I argued, we could begin to assess the possibilities of transformative participatory action in various political spaces. Moreover, the approach could be a tool for reflection by activists and practitioners to map the types of power which we sought to challenge and to look at the strategies and entry points for doing so. While some thought the 'cube' image risked being a bit too static in its portrayal of power, for many practitioners the approach seemed to have some resonance.

Understanding the levels, spaces and forms of power

As mentioned above, the power cube is a framework for analysing the levels, spaces and forms of power and their interrelationship. Though visually presented as a cube, it is important to think about each side of the cube as a dimension or set of relationships, not as a fixed or static set of categories. Like a Rubik's cube,[5] the blocks within the cube can be rotated – any of the blocks or sides may be used as the first point of analysis – but each dimension is linked to the other. In this presentation, we begin with a discussion of the *levels of power* (vertical axis), drawing heavily on writing in the IR field. We then move to consider the *spaces of power*, here referring to the relative openness and boundaries of arenas and opportunities for citizen engagement (horizontal axis), in which we draw from discussions of power in other fields as well. We then return to a discussion of the three 'faces' or 'dimensions' of power earlier developed by Lukes, which are here elaborated and developed as the visible, hidden and invisible *forms of power*. Finally, we examine the interrelationships of the levels, spaces and forms, concluding with an example of the application of the framework.

The levels[6] of power

While in 1961 Robert Dahl asked 'Who Governs?' in relationship to New Haven, some forty years later Held and McGrew (2003b: 8) asked a similar set of questions: 'who rules, in whose interests, by what mechanisms and for what purposes?' Though the inquiry is similar, the level at which it is addressed is entirely different. Dahl's work sought to analyse how power and participation interacted at the local (city) level, reflecting a pre-dominant focus of 'community power' studies at the time. Held and McGrew, on the other hand, ask their questions in relationship to global governance in an age of globalisation. Globalisation, they argue, is taken to express the expanding scale on which power is organised and exercised. In this respect, Held and McGrew say that

> at the core of the globalist account lies a concern with power: its instrumentalities, configuration, distribution and impacts [...] It involves a reordering of power relations between and across the world's major regions such that key sites of power and those who are subject to them are literally oceans apart.
>
> (Held and McGrew 2003a: 8)

At the heart of their question, as well as those posed by others in an increasingly growing literature on power and globalisation, is this: where does power reside? For Held and McGrew as well as others, the study of power can no longer be focused only on a particular place: 'the exclusive link between territory and political power has been broken. The con-temporary era has witnessed layers of governance spreading within and across boundaries' (2003a: 11). Theirs is part of a growing literature on global governance which warns us of the dangers of focusing only on the 'local', or the 'national' in a globalising world. Governance has become 'multi-layered', ranging from the subnational, to the national to the supra-national (Keohane and Nye 2000), encompassing a range of sites from the very local, to the regional, to the global.

To Robert Dahl's question of 'Who governs?' in New Haven, the globalist response might be, 'Don't just look in New Haven', a retort which raises serious methodological challenges for how and where power is to be found. Yet, to some extent, the debate on the levels and sites of power is not new. For many years, those concerned with power have argued about where it is located. Feminist scholars have challenged the focus by political science on the search for power in the public sphere, arguing for the primacy of the relations of power at the intimate or household sphere as well (e.g., Kabeer 1994).[7] For those who focus on public spaces for participation, there are some who argue that participatory practice must begin locally, as it is in the arenas of everyday life in which people are able to resist power and to con-struct their own voice. Others argue for the importance of the nation-state and how it mediates power, suggesting that the possibilities of local spaces often depend on the extent to which power is legitimated nationally but shared with the locality. Others, such as Beck (2005: 81), challenge this view, arguing that

> there is a new dialectic of global and local issues that do not fit into the scheme of national politics. As these kinds of global problems increasingly impact on people's everyday lives and yet are dealt with either inadequately or not at all at the national level, the crisis of legitimation in nation-state politics deepens.

As the globalisation debate challenges our understanding of where power resides, it also challenges traditional assumptions of how and where citizens mobilise to hold states and non-state actors to account (Tarrow 2005; Della Porta and Tarrow 2005). For scholars and activists concerned with change, this reconfiguration of political power also has enormous consequences. On the one hand, the globalisation of power has created a vast array of political opportunities at the international level in which civil society actors seeking change may engage, demanding greater transparency and accountability, participation in policy formulation and monitoring, or formal mechanisms for redress (Scholte 2002) or, increasingly, at the regional level, such as the African Union or the New Partnership for Africa's Development. A number of writers have outlined the growing influence of transnational civil society in these spaces (Florini 2000; Edwards and Gaventa 2001; Batliwala and Brown 2006). Others, such as Lipschutz, argue that the engagement of civil society in such arenas risks re-enforcing dominant power, as to be effective civil society must become a part of the project of governmentality in the neo-liberal order (see this volume pp. 89–90, and Lipschutz 2004). Others, however, challenge us to go further, arguing that not only are the sites of power multilayered, but they are also interrelated. The study of power is not only about who participates or who does not at one decision-making level but also how power or its absence at one level shapes mobilisation and action in another, linked together by highly interconnected networks and rapid diffusion of information and knowledge (Della Porta and Tarrow 2005).

Thus, just as globalisation contributes to a separation of power from territory, while also creating new territories, so does it open up broader possibilities for action by relatively powerless groups not only at the supranational level but also through the interaction of these various levels. Those seeking to act on a local injustice may choose not to confront those perceived to be responsible at the local level but may go to other levels of power in order to exercise their voice and express their demands. Work by Keck and Sikkink, for instance, demonstrates how advocacy networks may employ a 'boomerang pattern', in which 'State A blocks redress to organizations within it; they activate networks, whose members pressure their own state and (if relevant) a third-party organization, which in turn pressure State A' (1998: 13). Similarly, Callaghy and Kassimir (2001) argue in an African context that the interrelationship of the local and the global may mean that citizens will attempt to influence external actors – e.g., bi-laterals and donors – in order to bring about change on their own, often relatively weak or undemocratic states. In another example, in her work on globalisation and cities, Sassen demonstrates how migrants and asylum-seekers who lack substantive forms of citizenship within their place of residence are able to mobilise diasporic networks to strengthen their voice. Indeed, she argues, the 'cracking' of 'the national as container of social process and power [...] facilitates the ascendancy of sub and transnational spaces and actors in politico-civic processes' (2002: 217).

For students of power and participation, the implications of this analysis are important. Just as globalisation delinks power from traditionally understood territories, it also delinks participation from locality, potentially opening up new strategies for by-passing local power-holders. Local actors may use extra-local forums as arenas for action just as effectively – or more effectively – than they can appeal to institutions of local governance. To use the language of community power: while A may exercise power over B, B may in fact respond by influencing actors C, D or E, who in turn challenge A's dominance.

The above discussion then suggests that contemporary students of power, especially those concerned with how power shapes the capacities for action, must look at the vertical interrelationships of power, from the subnational, to the national, to the supranational (as seen in Figure 12.1) in searching for the strategic opportunities for change. While appearing fixed in this diagram, this vertical dimension of power should also be seen not as a fixed set of categories but as a flexible, adaptable continuum, in which each layer interacts with the other, sometimes opening and other times closing opportunities for action. The relevance and importance of these levels of potential engagement varies according to the context and to the purpose of the intervention.[8] Many of these are shaped by the relevant legal frameworks of governmental administration and may differ across rural and urban communities, yet increasingly extra-local arenas seem to grow as centres of power and decision-making. As Darby (2004: 10) insists, 'in attempting to develop a politics of change', there cannot be 'any spatial either/or about targeting the global and the local. It is not as if the one can be put on the side of domination and the other on the side of resistance.'

While the multiple levels of decision-making, and their interaction, create new opportunities for citizens and civil society actors, the changing local, national and regional levels of power also pose new challenges. Most civil society organisations or actors tend to focus on only one level and lack the capacities and networks to link across levels. Indeed, there is a growing critique about the lack of such meaningful links between those organisations doing advocacy at an international level, often led or supported by international NGOs, with those working to build social movements or alternative strategies for change at the more local levels (see for example, Batliwala 2002) and about the representation and accountability of those who seek to speak for others across the levels (van Rooy 2004). Yet, the interrelationships of these levels of power with one another suggest that the challenge for action is not only how to build participatory action at differing levels but also how to promote the democratic and accountable vertical links across actors at each level. As Pieterse puts it, 'this involves a double movement, from local reform upward and from global reform downward – each level of governance, from the local to the global, plays a contributing part' (quoted in Mohan and Stokke 2000: 263). How to create such vertical links across the interrelating levels of power becomes a key challenge for those seeking change.

The spaces of power

Not only have concepts of globalisation changed our understanding of the vertical relations of power but so too changing ideas of governance influence our notions of where decision-making (and non-decision-making) might be found. When Dahl wrote his book on 'Who Governs?' in New Haven, it was assumed that the answer might be found in looking at decision-making arenas within formal arenas of government. Since that time, the rise of the idea of governance – in which authority cuts across state and non-state actors alike – means that we must also broaden our understanding of the spaces or arenas in which decisions are made and power contested (as illustrated along the horizontal dimension of the power cube).

For many of those who write about globalisation in IR, there is a connection between the changing levels and proliferation of spaces in which power may be found. Held and McGrew point out that not only is governance in a global world multilayered but it consists of a dense web of interconnected policy fora, such that there is no single locus of authority (2003b: 9). Similarly, in his discussion of global governance, Rosenau argues that the 'steering mechanisms' of global governance exist through several channels: 'through the sponsorship of states, through the networks of actors other than states at the transnational or subnational levels, or through states and other types of actors jointly sponsoring the formation of rules systems' (2002: 51). Making a similar point, Scholte argues that not only is contemporary governance 'multilayered', but it 'has in recent years worked through private as well as public instruments. In this situation, regulatory authority has become considerably more decentralised and diffuse' (2002: 328). Such ideas chime with others who also write about the shift from government to governance and, with it, the ways in which policy is shaped through networks of state and non-state actors in multiple spaces and arenas of deliberation (e.g., Hajer and Wagenaar 2003). Still other literatures have focused on the rise of participatory forms of governance, in which we see the emergence of an array of new institutional spaces and opportunities for democratic participation, which, in turn, are challenging existing assumptions of state–society relations (Gaventa 2004). Some observers have written about the new forms of authority as representing a model of 'co-governance' in which state and society share decision-making power (Ackerman 2004) while others talk about the rise of 'empowered participatory governance' (Fung and Wright 2003) or the rise of a new 'participatory sphere' (Cornwall and Coelho 2006).

The explanations of the forces contributing to the expansion of these new arenas and spaces of governance are many and often contradictory, ranging from arguments that they are neo-liberal efforts to weaken the state, efforts to re-establish state legitimacy or have emerged from demands for greater 'voice' from below (see Gaventa 2006). Whatever the reason, new spaces for engagement in governance processes from the local to the global abound. For some analysts, this leads to the potential of new spaces for change, while, for others, the pluralisation of governance arenas simply leads to diffusion of lines of accountability, making it all the more difficult for activists to make governance processes more legible.

Discussions of power in relationship to space have occurred across a wide range of literatures. As Berenskoetter observes in the introduction to this volume, the very definition of power 'determines where political spaces are located, and which actors and relations are being looked at' (p. 1). Other writers refer to 'political spaces' as those institutional channels, political discourses and social and political practices through which the poor and those organisations working with them can pursue poverty reduction (Webster and Engberg-Pedersen 2002). Other work focuses on 'policy spaces' to examine the moments and opportunities where citizens and policy-makers come together, as well as 'actual observable opportunities, behaviours, actions and interactions [...] sometimes signifying transformative potential' (McGee 2004: 16). Other work examines 'democratic spaces' in which citizens can engage to claim citizenship and affect governance processes (Cornwall and Coelho 2006). In this paper, which takes citizen action and participation as its starting point, 'spaces' are seen as opportunities, moments and channels where citizens as social actors can potentially challenge and change policies, discourses, decisions, and relationships which affect their lives and interests.

One thing is clear: the creation of the new spaces for participation does not automatically change power relationships. Rather, power still surrounds and fills each potential space for engagement, making the link between power and space more important to understand, as Cornwall (2002) reminds us. Among others, she draws upon French social theorists (Lefebvre, Foucault and Bourdieu) for whom the concept of power and the concept of space are deeply linked. Quoting Lefebvre: 'Space is a social product [...] it is not simply "there," a neutral container waiting to be filled, but is a dynamic, humanly constructed means of control, and hence of domination, of power' (Lefebvre 1991: 24).

Inherent also in the idea of spaces is also the imagery of 'boundary'. Power relations help to shape the boundaries of participatory spaces, what is possible within them and who may enter, with which identities, discourses and interests. Using the idea of boundary from Foucault and others, Hayward suggests that we might understand power 'as the network of social boundaries that delimit fields of possible action.' Freedom, on the other hand, 'is the capacity to participate effectively in shaping the social limits that define what is possible' (Hayward 1998: 9, 21). In this sense, participation as freedom is not only the right to participate effectively in a given space but also the right to define and to shape that space, i.e., 'to act upon the boundaries that constrain and enable social action' (Hayward 1998: 12). Hayward's view of power echoes the introductory chapter of this volume in which power is defined 'as the ability to shape the future'. In that shaping, power is linked not only to participation and contestation in a particular space, but also to the capacity to define and shape the space itself, the rules within it and the boundaries which surround it.

For students of power, in order to understand where power is located, as well as to explore the opportunities for participation which can challenge unequal power relations, we must not only examine formal government or decision-making spaces but other spaces for potential influence as well. In examining the spaces for participation, we must also ask how they were created, with whose interests and what terms of engagement? While there is much debate on the appropriate terminology for these spaces, previous work seems to suggest a continuum of spaces, which vary according to their potential openness for citizen engagement. This includes:[9]

- *Closed spaces.* Though we want to focus on levels and spaces as they open up possibilities for participation, we must realise that still many, many decision-making spaces are closed, with little democratic opportunities for participation. Decisions are made by a set of actors behind closed doors, without any pretence of broadening the boundaries for inclusion. Within the state, another way of conceiving these spaces is as 'provided' spaces in the sense that elites (be they bureaucrats, experts or elected representatives) make decisions and provide services to 'the people', without the need for broader consultation or involvement. In these settings, actors may seek to challenge power by demanding greater public involvement, transparency or accountability or through lobbying, protest and campaigning activities which attempt to change the outcomes of decision-making, but in such spaces, the boundaries between those with the formal power to make the rules and decide the outcomes, and those who are the subjects of these rules, are clearly defined.
- *Invited spaces.* As efforts are made to widen participation – e.g., to move from closed spaces to more 'open' ones, new spaces are created which

may be referred to as 'invited' spaces, i.e., 'those into which people (as users, citizens or beneficiaries) are invited to participate by various kinds of authorities, be they government, supranational agencies or non-governmental organisations' (Cornwall 2002: 17). Invited spaces may be regularised, that is, they are institutionalised, ongoing or more transient, through one-off forms of consultation. Increasingly, with the rise of approaches to participatory governance, these spaces are seen at every level, from local government to national policy, and even in global-policy forums. In such spaces, formal power may be more diffusely shared between states and non-state actors.

- *Claimed/created spaces.* Finally there are the spaces which are claimed by less powerful actors from or against the power-holders, or created more autonomously by them. Cornwall refers to these as 'spaces as which arise more organically out of sets of common concerns or identifications' and 'may come into being as a result of popular mobilisation, such as around identity or issue-based concerns, or may consist of spaces in which like-minded people join together in common pursuits' (2002: 17). Other work talks of these spaces as 'third spaces' where social actors reject the hegemony of dominant spaces and create spaces for themselves (Soja 1996). These spaces range from ones created by social movements and community associations, to those simply involving natural places where people gather to debate, discuss and resist, outside of the institutiona-lised policy arenas.

While this approach has been developed and used more in relationship to participation at the local level (Gaventa 2004; Cornwall and Coelho 2006), one can easily think of parallels at the international level, especially invol-ving the relationship of civil society in global governance. For instance, one can think of the power in the WTO, or indeed the World Bank, as often involving closed decision-making spaces, in which direct citizen engagement is not invited. At the same time, one can see numerous 'invited spaces' or fora, such as the UN summits, or the former NGO Working Group on the World Bank, in which global policy-makers and civil society organisations have come together to discuss key global policies. And there are a multitude of spaces in which civil society groups have created their own spaces for engagement – the World Social Forum, with its theme 'Another world is possible', being only one.

Whatever the terminology, who creates the space is critical – those who create it are more likely to have power within it, and those who have power in one space may not have so much in another. In some settings, the 'claimed or created' spaces may indeed have more influence and control over decisions that affect peoples' lives than the closed or invited state spaces, especially in settings of weak or illegitimate states. In other settings, such as we have seen in the rise of participatory budgeting in Porto Alegre, Brazil, shared forms of authority between state and society may, in fact, have more influence than those that are legally ascribed. So, for the student of power, to ask 'who governs?', also necessitates asking, 'in which space?'

As with the levels of power, the spaces exist in dynamic relationship to one another and are constantly opening and closing through struggles for legitimacy and resistance, co-optation and transformation. Those who pre-dominate within closed spaces may seek to restore their legitimacy by creating invited spaces, which may sometimes create opportunities for change, and other times simply shore up the status quo. Similarly, invited spaces may be created from the other direction, as more autonomous people's movements attempt to use their own fora for engagement with the state. Power gained in one space, through new skills, capacity and experiences, can be used to enter and affect other spaces. From this perspective, the transformative potential of spaces for participation must always be assessed in relationship to the other spaces which surround them.

The interrelationship of the spaces also creates challenges for civil society strategies of engagement. To challenge 'closed' spaces, civil society organisa-tions may serve the role of advocates, arguing for greater transparency, more democratic structures or greater forms of public accountability. As new 'invited' spaces emerge, civil society organisations may need other strategies of how to negotiate and collaborate 'at the table', which may require shifting from more confrontational advocacy methods. At the same time, research shows that 'invited spaces' must be held open by ongoing demands of social movements and that more autonomous spaces of participation are important for new demands to develop and to grow. Spanning these spaces – each of which involves different skills, strategies and resources – is a challenge. In reality, civil society organisations must have the 'staying power' to move in and out of them over time or the capacity to build effective horizontal alli-ances that link strategies across the various spaces for change.

In this sense, then, those seeking to challenge and change the status quo have to deal not only with the vertical axis of decision-making, which span the subnational, the national, regional, and global, but they also have to examine the horizontal interaction of spaces for engagement at each level. While this is itself complex terrain, we now return to where we started. The levels and spaces for change are also laced with different forms of power, as originally outlined in the Lukes model, adding a third dimension to our analysis.

The forms of power

As we examine the relationships of place and space, we must also examine the dynamics of power that shape the inclusiveness of participation within each. Here much of the literature of power is concerned with the degree to which conflict over key issues, and the voices of key actors, are visible in public arenas. In his earlier work Lukes (1974), followed by others (e.g., Gaventa 1980; VeneKlasen and Miller 2002),[10] explored the differences between:

- a public 'face' of power, in which contests over interests are assumed to be visible in public spaces, which in turn are presumed to be relatively open, and where the focus is 'winning conflicts' (Introduction, this volume);
- a second face of power, in which the entry of certain interests and actors into public spaces is privileged over others through a prevailing 'mobilisation of bias' or rules of the game, and where the focus is on 'limiting alternatives' (Introduction, this volume, p. 7) through more hidden forms of power;
- a third face of power, in which conflict is more invisible and the focus is on 'shaping normality' (Introduction, this volume, p. 9) through internalisation of powerlessness, or through dominating ideologies, values and forms of behaviour, which keep issues and contests from emerging, in what may be called the invisible forms of power.

The importance of these forms of power for how we analyse the dynamics of participation in differing levels and spaces is relatively obvious. Historically, many pluralist studies of power have mainly examined power in its visible manifestations. One looked at who participated, who benefited and who lost in order to see who had power. But as we have seen, power in relationship to place and space also works to put boundaries on participation and to exclude certain actors or views from entering the arenas for participation in the first place. Or power, in its more insidious forms, may be internalised in terms of one's values, self-esteem and identities, such that voices in visible arenas are but echoes of dominant discourses. Such power analysis points again to the importance of establishing the preconditions of participation in order for new institutional spaces to lead to change in the status quo. Without prior awareness-building so that citizens possess a sense of their own right to claim rights or express voice, and without strong capacities for exercising countervailing power against the 'rules of the game' that favour entrenched interests, new mechanisms for participation in the more public arenas of power may simply be captured by prevailing interests.

As in the other dimensions of the power cube, the multiple forms of power also pose challenges for civil society actors trying to change power relations, at all levels. At the international level, for instance, some groups may focus on advocacy approaches, challenging the visible forms of power in public arenas through informed research and campaigning to influence what goes on *inside* public decision-making bodies, e.g., the WTO. Others may focus on mobilising and collective action strategies, which work to challenge barriers that prevent certain actors and forms of knowledge from entering public arenas in the first place, e.g., what goes on *outside* WTO gatherings. Yet others may focus more on changing the invisible, internalised forms of power, through awareness and consciousness-raising efforts, e.g., through helping disenfranchised farmers affected by global trade decisions understand how these distant forms of power affect their interests. While often these are different strategies, involving different organisations and interventions to change power, in fact strategies are also needed which link across them. For instance, a policy victory in the visible arena of power may be important but may not be sustained if those outside the arena are not aware that it has occurred and how it relates to their interests, or if they are not mobilised to make sure that other hidden forms of power do not preclude its implementation. Or those seeking to raise the awareness of rights may find their approach limited if there is not a formal political arena or functioning legal institutions in which these rights may be claimed.

The interrelationships of levels, spaces and forms

Each of the dimensions of the power cube – the levels, spaces and forms of power – may be seen as a continuum or a scale whose components are constantly interrelating with one another, constantly changing the synergies of power. Those who study the Rubik's cube argue that there are literally billions of different positions[11] that the blocks of the cube may have, illustrating the complexity and permutations in which power can take across level, space and form in any given context.

The ability of each dimension of power to re-enforce the other can allow those who dominate in an unequal and unjust order to maintain their domination in any number of ways. Conversely, the interrelationships of the levels, spaces and forms of power, while potentially opening new opportunities and entry points for change, also poses enormous barriers for those seeking to challenge the status quo, due to the sheer complexity and permutations of the interactions of each dimension. A sustained and effective change strategy must concern itself with how to work across the scale, from the subnational to the supranational, the closed to the claimed or the visible to the invisible. While linking the elements *within* any one of these dimensions can be critical and indeed empowering for those involved, the most transformative, fundamental change happens, I suggest, in those rare moments when social movements or social actors are able to work effectively both *within and across* each of the dimensions simultaneously, i.e., when they are able to link the demands for opening previously closed spaces with people's action in their own spaces, to span across local and global action and to challenge visible, hidden and invisible power simultaneously. Just like the Rubik's cube, successful change is about getting each of the pieces on each dimension of the cube to align with the other.

'Alignment' of strategies for change within each of the dimensions of the cube is a huge challenge. For instance, along the spaces dimension, while many groups seeking action work *either* on opening closed spaces through demanding more transparency or supporting internal reform, *or* on building social movements and mobilisation in claimed spaces, much research suggests that it is when horizontal alliances are built across these spaces that real change occurs (see, for instance, Coelho 2006). Similarly, advocacy and change strategies must often build vertical alliances across local, national and global levels to make sure that changes are meaningful at each level. And those seeking not only to influence policies in the public arena but also to change power relations more fundamentally must simultaneously think about winning the issue, mobilising to broaden the political space and building awareness of those who are excluded. Rather than any single strategy, an ensemble of strategies, which work together and not against each other, are required to fully challenge these sets of power relationships.

For any given issue or action, there is no single strategy or entry point. Much depends on navigating the intersection of the relationships, which, in turn, can either contribute to new misalignments and distortions of power or can simultaneously create new boundaries of possibility for strategic action. For instance, linking local-national-global campaigns to open up previously closed spaces may be important, but in so doing, they may re-enforce forms of hidden and invisible power, if they simultaneously exclude certain potential actors or forms of knowledge. On the other hand, the opening of previously closed local spaces can contribute to new mobilisations and conscientisation, which may have the potential to open other spaces more widely and to create momentum for change at national or global levels. Sometimes the dimensions may appear chaotic, random and confused; at other times they may appear as if alignments will be possible. In fact, those who study the Rubik's cube also tell us that any cube can be realigned in a maximum of twenty-nine moves, taken in the right sequence. While not wanting to reduce social change to a formulaic solution, this does suggest that those seeking to challenge power in all of its spaces, levels and forms should not search only for one solution but should build multiple, linked strategies and in different sequences, depending on the starting point in any given context. The challenge is to understand what these strategies might be, and how they can be linked, to realign all of the dimensions of power. That's when transformative change might really occur.

The power cube approach doesn't give us the formula for how to do this. It is not a checklist – e.g., the idea isn't to tick off each box, as the significance, dynamics and interrelationships of the dimensions are constantly changing and vary enormously from one context to another. Nor is it prescriptive, valorising local, claimed spaces over the distant global, closed spaces, for it suggests that each has forms of visible, hidden and invisible power within them. Rather, the power cube is meant to be more of an analytical device, which can be used – along with other approaches – to reflect on power and to analyse how strategies for change in turn challenge power relations.

Applying the power cube lens: an example

An illustration of the use of the power cube may be found in applying it to an analysis of the issue of debt and its relationships to poverty. From a power perspective, the issue demonstrates how global policies can affect and usurp local participation. Global policies on debt, like most macro-economic policies, have traditionally been decided in 'closed' spaces, with little invited public consultation with or participation by those poor people directly affected and few alternative spaces for debate to occur. And this form of power in the policy-making process is surrounded by forms of hidden and invisible power: the prevailing mobilisation of bias re-enforces the idea that policy is the province of expert economists. Poor people – whose schools may be closed as result of such policies – are often socialised to accept the legitimacy of such expertise, even when it apparently contradicts their own interests. While participation might be invited on issues of poverty, issues of how macro-economic policies contribute to the underlying causes of poverty are often systematically kept off the agenda (for a very good analysis of this see Rowden and Irama 2004).

Yet, against this usual backdrop of power, we witnessed in less than a decade the emergence of a global movement to put the impact of debt on poor nations on the public agenda and to challenge the power relationships that linked debt and poverty. Led by a broad coalition known as Jubilee 2000, which in turn built on previous efforts and coalitions, the movement at its peak had mobilised millions of people in both north and south. It is widely credited not only with putting the issue of debt on the international agenda but also for contributing to debt cancellation for dozens of countries, with consequent tangible effects in some places on education, housing and health care (Mayo 2005). While there were tensions within the movement, and while the issues of debt, aid and service delivery still remain, of course, an enormous public issue, more than many such transnational movements, Jubilee 2000 has been held up as an example of success that not only succeeded in winning relevant gains on a concrete issue but also, in the process, began to challenge the prevailing 'mobilisation of bias' which surrounded who should be involved in making macro-economic policy. Though some would argue that the 'mobilisation of bias' was later re-strengthened by new aid conditionalities and mechanisms, such as the Poverty Reduction Strategy Paper (PRSP) process (Rowden and Irama 2004), for a period at least, the Jubilee 2000 appeared to offer the potential for positive change for those living in poverty. How do we explain this relative success?

The analysis in this chapter would suggest that in part its success is found in the ways that the movement was able to align itself across all the dimensions of power outlined in the power cube. Along the vertical dimension, not only did it mobilise at global meetings of the G7, International Monetary Fund (IMF), World Bank, Paris Club and others, but it also built links with national organisations and campaigns in over sixty countries, which lobbied, campaigned, protested and educated in their own countries as well.[12] In many places, the campaign linked with local groups, such as in Uganda where the Ugandan Debt Network mobilised and educated debt-awareness groups at the village and district level, who could articulate the connection between the global movement and budget priorities of local governments (Collins *et al.* 2001).

Along the horizontal dimension, the campaign spanned mobilisation in multiple spaces. While much attention was focused on challenging and making more transparent the deliberations of relatively closed decision-making spaces, at the same time it took advantage of new opportunities for consultation, e.g., invited spaces, where campaigners could also negotiate and make their case, such as those related to discussions around the Heavily Indebted Poor Country (HIPC) programme, led by the World Bank, IMF and other bilaterals. At the same time, it carried out mass mobilisation outside of both the closed and invited spaces, often simultaneously, symbolised most powerfully in July 1998 in Birmingham when a 70,000 person human chain surrounded the G7 meetings and demanded to be heard.

And finally, and perhaps most importantly, the style of the campaign was not only to win the issue but also to do so in a way that changed the rules of the game about the transparency of global economic decisions and that changed the awareness of those directly affected, as well as broader publics, about how debt affected poverty. Economic literacy and public education which enable local people to speak for themselves were just as important as technical research, professional advocacy (for further examples of this approach, see Just Associates *et al.* 2006). As one analyst of the movement has written, Jubilee 2000 'enhanced participants' critical consciousness, facilitating collective action as the basis for social empowerment and social transformation' (Mayo 2005: 189).

Throughout all of this, there were, of course, difficult tensions and conflicts, e.g., about who spoke for whom across the local, national and global spaces, about working on the inside to reform global institutions vs. creating spaces and challenges from the outside, about technical advocacy for winning an issue vs. building popular awareness and self-empowerment that would sustain a long-term movement. All of these were contestations about power within the movement itself, yet, despite the internal conflict, the coalitions, collaborations and commitment to address these issues internally meant that the movement was somewhat aligned across all of the dimensions of the power cube. Other perhaps less successful global movements either fail to embrace such diversity, remain relatively localised or specialised though addressing only one aspect of power, or self-destruct from internal tensions when they try and fail to align with others using different strategies.

The relative success of the Jubilee 2000 Campaign compared to many transnational campaigns and movements does not of course mean that the problems it sought to challenge have gone away – quite the contrary. The issues continue but are contested on a slightly new terrain. Now, several years after the campaign, we could perhaps also use the frame of the power cube to analyse how power was able to re-accommodate and re-establish itself – while once decisions about aid might have been made behind closed doors, the new 'invited spaces' for participation, created through the PRSP mechanisms, also created new rules of the game that shored up the status quo; while aid flows might have increased from richer to poorer countries, the battlegrounds for action simply then shifted to national and subnational arenas. The point is that just as movements to challenge the status quo need to 'align' their own strategies for change along each dimension of the power cube, so power also constantly realigns itself to accommodate and respond to new pressures, creating new spaces for action and closing others, requiring reassessment of strategies and new forms of contestation.

From a point of view of how to strengthen actor-oriented approaches which challenge the status quo, other approaches to power analysis, which focus on only one dimension of the power cube, I would argue, fail to give us the full complexity of the workings of power in a globalised world. Even if the power-cube approach does not provide a formula or checklist for challenging power, it can be used to analyse the power field affecting any given issue or set of issues in different contexts. And, it can be used by actors seeking to change to reflect on where and how they do so, how they work across boundaries with others who are also working for change to align their efforts and how power constantly shifts in response to their efforts. In this sense, finding new ways to analyse and reflect on power in all of its dimensions is perhaps the first step in making more visible its most hidden and invisible forms. It is when we link the forms of power outlined many years ago by Steven Lukes, with the analysis of the new levels and spaces in which these forms are found, that we gain a more complete understanding of power in world affairs.

Notes

1 This chapter builds upon earlier work, including 'Finding the Spaces for Change: A Power Approach,' in Eyben, Harris and Pettit (2006) and 'The Uses of Power in Framing and Shaping the Spaces, Places and Dynamics of Participation' (Gaventa 2006) prepared for *Assessing Civil Society Participation as Supported In-Country by Cordaid, Hivos, Novib and Plan Netherlands*, co-ordinated by Irene Guijt of Learning by Design (2006). My thanks to the many colleagues from the 'Civil Society Participation' evaluation, the Participation Group, Just Associates, and others from whom I have learned in using and discussing the power-cube approach. Special thanks for assistance to Tamara Levine and Nicholas Benequista for help in reviewing IR literature which contributed to this article and to Felix Berenskoetter, Andrea Cornwall, Peter Newell and Jan Aart Scholte for their helpful comments on earlier versions.

2 While Lukes refer to these faces of power as 'dimensions', in this essay I shall refer to them as 'forms' of power, arguing that in the power-cube approach outlined here, they represent three aspects of one dimension.

3 In other work, I have described the evolution and use of this power–cube approach in my own thinking and with others (e.g., Gaventa 2005; 2006).

4 The term 'citizen' throughout is based on actor-oriented approaches to citizenship, which put more emphasis on agency rather than legal identity ascribed through the nation-state. For further work on this approach, see the work of the Development Research Centre on Citizenship, Participation and Accountability (http://www.drc-citizenship.org), and Kabeer (2002).

5 Rubik's cube refers to a mechanical cube invented in 1974 by the Hungarian sculptor and professor of architecture Ernö Rubik and marketed widely as a puzzle. The sides of the cube can rotate, though the whole remains intact.

6 I recognise that the word 'level' may be limiting, as these may in fact be overlapping and not distinct levels. The literature uses a variety of words, such as 'layers', 'sites' or 'scales' to capture this dimensions, any of which is inadequate. I have chosen the terms 'supranational' and 'subnational' rather than global or local, because each may also have various layers or sites of power within it.

7 In this paper, the 'power cube' focuses primarily on power in the 'public sphere', while recognising that this approach fails to capture the full range of power relations.

8 In applications of the power-cube approach in Colombia, for instance, civil society organisations identified eight different relevant levels for civil society engagement each of which has its own types of spaces, including the international, national, departmental, regional/provincial, municipal, communal, and neighbourhood levels (Pearce and Vela 2005).

9 These ideas have developed from Cornwall (2002); Brock *et al.* (2001); Brock *et al.* (2004) and in earlier applications of the cube. Some have suggested that it would be better to depict these spaces as governmental, joint, and social or social movement spaces, reflecting a state–society continuum. However, this approach focuses more on the porousness of power and can be applied to other non-state settings, such as corporate power, as well. The critical kinds of spaces for engagement will vary across context and historical setting. In various applications and uses, many other relevant terminologies have been added to this continuum, such as 'conquered', 'instigated' or 'initiated' spaces. In work with civil society actors in Colombia, Pearce and Vela (2005) identified a continuum of spaces which included: formal by invitation (participation is officially offered in some way), formal by right (participation is mandated or legislated), created by non-state institutions (e.g., by church, parties, donors), created by civil society organisations (e.g., by non-governmental organisations or grass-roots organisations), collective transitory action (such as protests or land occupations).

10 In Gaventa (1980), I examined the ways in which these forms of power worked to instil a sense of quiescence and inaction amongst impoverished residents of an Appalachian mining valley and later explored how an understanding of each form of power had implications for different strategies for citizen action (Gaventa 1999). In more recent work which in turn builds upon this approach, VeneKlasen and Miller (2002) argue more simply for distinguishing between the visible, hidden and invisible (or internalised) forms of power, as outlined above and in the power cube. I am grateful to them for this language.

11 More specifically, about 43 quintillion, or 43,252,003,274,489,856,000, according to Wikipedia!

12 In her work on transnational civil society campaigns, Florini also argues for the importance of links between transnational and domestic actors:

The efforts of human rights international NGOS to change the behaviour of repressive governments had little effect unless the domestic civil societies in those countries were able to act, as least to provide the credible information on which the transnational campaigns depended. If a significant, organized domestic constituency is lacking, external actors usually can accomplish little.

(Florini 2000: 218)

13 On the transformational potential of global civil society[1]

Ronnie D. Lipschutz

My objective in this chapter is not to argue for the existence of global civil society (GCS) but rather to ask what it is and what has produced it. Is GCS a space or locus of sovereign agents or merely a structural effect? Does it wield direct power over states, or it is a mere epiphenomenon, a reflection of the state system? Is GCS an institutional phenomenon – the result of the exercise of power by other agents and actors acting within and through institutions – or is it a product of that power through which society is produced, constituted by the social roles and relations growing out of contemporary states and markets? In surveying the growing literature on GCS, one can find advocates of each of these, as well as other perspectives. This is not wholly surprising, since there is hardly a consensus to be found about the origins of domestic civil societies or their relationship to state and market (Cohen and Arato 1992; Colas 2002; Lipschutz 2006).

In this chapter, I propose that GCS is best understood in terms of a dialectical relationship between developing modes of public global governance and a global market system that is only weakly regulated by states and international institutions (Holzscheiter 2005). In particular, I problematise much of GCS as a central and vital element in an expanding global neo-liberal regime of governmentality. GCS is constituted out of social relations within that regime and, with and through the capillaries of productive power (Foucault 2004a), helps to legitimise, reproduce and sometimes transform *internally* that regime, its operation and its objectives. In this respect, GCS is generated by agents who seek to resist or moderate the expansion of the market into various realms of social life but who may, nonetheless, act in ways that, perhaps unwittingly, support the logics of the market and its further expansion. Paradoxically, the same relations of power that give rise to this form of social action also engender movements that pursue major structural change in the global political economy, this in a quest to alter the social ethics that enable or constrain individual and corporate autonomy within politics and markets. I argue, in other words, that GCS manifests in two forms: one moral, the other ethical, acting alternatively through markets *or* politics. In making this claim, I draw on Hegel's distinction between moral and ethical behaviour, the former having to do with individual conscience, the latter with the foundations of political community (in his terms, the state; Hegel 1942; Colas 2002).

There is no global state, of course, but, to a growing degree, the global political economy constitutes a singular transnational capitalist social formation that resembles, more and more, a state in formation. Inasmuch as its regulatory elements largely reflect the post-Second World War preferences and practices of an increasingly imperial USA, this state in formation remains quite underdeveloped by comparison with its market elements. In light of the growing global role of US military and market discipline in keeping order, we might even call it an emerging 'watchman' state (Gill 1995, 2003: Chapter 7). To put the point another way, following Hardt and Negri's (2000) notion of *Empire*, this entity is bound together through an integrated global network of accumulation and exchange, but the governmentality through which it is managed emanates from the centre and is struggling to establish full domination through military means (Lipschutz 2002). This emerging global unit is, moreover, a *single capitalist formation*, in which new property rights and rules of the political economy are being created through a system of national and international institutions dominated by the American executive and legislative branches and through which 'imperial' law comes to trump international law (Mattei 2003).[2]

Within this arrangement, GCS is generated through productive power – in a sense, it is *willed* into existence – as particular agents in command of certain discursive resources seek to impose limits on the autonomy of market-based actors in the face of a very weak global ethical and normative regulatory structure. As explained later in this chapter, the majority of these agents pursue their goals through institutions – that is, through the rules and authority of national and transnational agencies and association – and attempt to induce change in the *moral* behaviour of state- and market-based actors. Some agents – especially those commonly described as 'social movements' – work through productive power in an effort to transform the *ethical* bases of political action and thereby to reconstruct the structural principles governing both domestic and global political economy.

The empirical grounding for the arguments presented here is found, first, in the welfare activities of many GCS organisations. Here, I discuss activities by private relief organisations following the Indian Ocean tsunami of December 2004, as well as social struggles to regulate the negative effects – what I call 'externalities' – of global capitalist accumulation.[3] In contrast to such welfare-oriented activities, those who are active in the more inchoate 'global justice movement' appear intent on changing the structural framework of political action through the state and its domestic and transnational agencies rather than reforming capitalism or making it 'friendlier' (Notes from Nowhere 2003). In this sense, the global *Salafist jihadi* movement, of which Al Qaida is the most prominent element, must also be understood as an ethically oriented agent, even if its ethics and tactics are not to our liking. For its empirical data, however, this chapter draws specifically on work on social movement activism in the Clayoquot Sound of British Columbia (Magnusson and Shaw 2003).

I begin by offering a typology of four types of power and outlining the particular understanding of power employed here, which rests on Foucault's notion of governmentality. I then turn to a discussion of GCS: what it is, why it has emerged in its present form over the past few decades, and its role in the reproduction of liberalism with its peculiar public–private divide. In the third part of the chapter, I examine the problem of 'politics via markets', which involves the use of market-based tools and techniques to achieve political goals. This, I argue, represents the bulk of GCS's social activism and does little to alter the structure of either national or global political economies. I then examine how 'productive' power can operate to alter the structural context of politics and create 'zones of sovereignty'. I conclude the chapter with a few thoughts on the difficulty of practising politics under conditions of neo-liberal globalisation. To understand GCS and its politics, in short, requires us to consider how 'global' actors are produced in a realm characterised by diffuse forms of power and why GCS must be recognised as a product of neo-liberal globalisation rather than something distinct from or necessarily in opposition to it.

Power reconsidered

As a general rule, scholars of political science have focused on two forms of power: direct and institutional. In classic political theory, direct power is seen as the ability of A to make B do something that B does not want to do; in international relations (IR), direct power commonly underlies realist theorising (Dahl 1957; Lukes, this volume). Institutional power, by contrast, resides in the capacity and authority of established collective groups (agencies, organisations, etc.) to manage and manipulate situations in their interest through agenda-setting or mobilisation bias (Bachrach and Baratz 1962). This is the focus of what is known as 'regime theory' in IR and the 'new institutionalism' in comparative politics, both of which focus on the 'principles, norms, rules and decision-making procedures' that lead to convergence of actor expectations and constraints on actor autonomy (Krasner 1983: 2). These two forms of power, direct and institutional, are generally directed toward *distributive* matters: 'who gets what, when, and how' in Harold Lasswell's (1936) classical formation. They do not, however, exhaust the types of power important in politics.

Drawing on Foucault (2004a, 2004b), as well as a typology recently offered by Barnett and Duvall (2005b: Chapter 1), we can discern and define two other forms of power, which are not distributive, involving the division of resources (the famous liberal 'pie'), but rather *constitutive*, having to do with the structures and organisation of society, state and market. These two are structural and productive power. 'Structural' power resides in the sovereign's authority to establish and alter the overarching regulatory conditions through which institutions are created and by which they are able to function – it is a part of sovereign authority (Schmitt 1988). The state, for example, is in a position to specify what constitutes a market, to formulate the regulations governing markets and to determine the circumstances under which they apply. The 'sovereign' is able to determine the rules that constitute a particular game and how the agents that play it can score points. Being in a position to determine the rules of the game (structure) is much more advantageous than simply being able to dominate a market (distribution). 'Productive' power, by contrast, resides in political subjects and, if we accept Foucault's arguments (2004a, 2004b) about the 'capillaries of power' (see below), such power also constitutes subjects as the seemingly autonomous individuals of modern liberalism. To put this another way, our subjectivity is generated through the social and structural conditions – the cultural and material relations – that constitute individuals and collective identities within liberal society. Such power is exercised – if it can be said to be exercised at all – through discursive means; at the level of language, cognition, social construction and so on.

Table 13.1 offers a typology of these four forms of power along two axes: the type of authority (either constitutive or distributive) and the type of agent (sovereign or social). Note that none of these categories says anything about the specific nature of the agent imbricated within a particular form power – it may be an individual, a corporation, a group or a state. What matters here is the *arena* in which power is exercised (the household, the group, the company or society) and the *purpose* of power (constitutive or distributive; Lipschutz 2005: Chapter 3). 'Social subjects', for the most part,

Table 13.1

	Sovereign agency	*Social agency*
Authority to define, decree, decide ('rules of the game')	Structural power: The 'sovereign' can structure conditions through rules governing political economy (e.g., creation of property rights to pollute)	Productive power: Social subjects can affect ethical basis of action through language, habitus, structuration (e.g., generating a broad ethical sense that there should be no 'right to pollute')
Authority to divide, distribute, expropriate ('scoring points')	Direct power: 'Sovereign' can use force, coercion, manipulation, influence to protect or pursue its interests (e.g., imposing fines and punishments on polluters in order to cause them to cease)	Institutional power: Social subjects can engage in agenda-setting, law-making, role-setting to distribute resources to favoured interests (e.g., trading in pollution rights in order to reduce it, as opposed to requiring reductions)

Adapted from Michael Barnett and Raymond Duvall (eds.) (2005) *Power in Global Governance*, Cambridge: Cambridge University Press, p. 12.

engage in distributive point-scoring, although they may fight over the interpretation or legality of a particular move or play in a game. But by drawing on productive power, through collective political action social subjects can also produce change in the forms and exercise of structural power by the sovereign.[4] How these different forms of power are exercised can be seen in the respective examples concerned with 'rights to pollute' given in Table 13.1.

At the same time, however, these distinct categories do not quite capture the nuances of Foucault's conception of power, especially as instantiated in and through *governmentality*. This is of particular importance in thinking about power in contemporary global politics, in that it can be understood as bridging structural and productive power. Foucault argued that power is 'productive' and not something that can be accumulated for purposes of compulsion. As he (2004b: 307) famously wrote,

> If power were never anything but repressive, if it never did anything but say no, do you really think one would be brought to obey it ...? It needs to be considered as a productive network that runs through the whole social body, much more than as a negative instance whose function is repression.

Governmentality is related to this conception of power. As Foucault (2004a: 241) put it, governmentality 'has as its purpose not the action of government itself, but the welfare of the population, the improvement of its condition, the increase of its wealth, longevity, health, etc.' As Mitchell Dean (1991: 172) points out, governmentality is the name for those roles, rules and relationships that shape behaviour in this 'whole social body' and which do so in the service of a self-regulating order.

In the management of populations and the conditions of their existence by the organisations of governmentality, the diffusion of power serves to construct the identity of subjects whose agency is, in turn, constrained by that very identity and what is regarded as the 'normal'.[5] Governmentality can thus be regarded as a regime in which the coercive power associated commonly with government – the monopoly of violence – is subsumed into a dialectic between structural and productive power, which 'produces' populations that behave 'normally'. Individuals comport themselves according to the standards of 'normality' of their specific population. The right disposition of things is then maintained through the standardisation of populations within certain defined parameters, the self-disciplining of their own behaviour by individuals conforming to these parameters and the disciplining function of surveillance, force and law that seeks to prevent any straying outside of those parameters.[6] Taken together, these constrain individuals' practices to a 'zone of stability', or 'security'. Power is, therefore, embedded within the discursive formations that naturalise normality and that motivate the reproduction of normal populations through associated practices. This is one of the senses in which, as Foucault (1980: 109–33) puts it, we are the products of power circulating through society in capillary fashion.

The concept of governmentality becomes important especially in understanding the relationship of the state and 'international' institutions and practices. The state has not ceased to exist as a distinct territorial unit, but it has become structurally intertwined as an integral element in a global system of diffuse and diffused power.[7] In terms of the political economy, which I define here as the organisation of relations between production and reproduction, the state (notionally) possesses the sovereign authority to structure social life and make constitutional decisions that organise and legitimate institutions and their productive and reproductive remits.[8] In theory, only the state is permitted to create or change those structures – that is, only the state possesses the sovereign authority to determine 'exceptions', in Carl Schmitt's words (1985: 5). In practice, of course, the state is the site of struggles among all manner of social forces (Halperin 2004), some of whom gain leverage or control over various parts of the state and influence or change these structures.[9] Under liberalism, institutions are the arenas in which 'games' of distributive production and reproduction are played. Agents are constituted through the particular contractual relationships that define their assigned role, which may involve overseeing the rules and play (e.g., referees), or playing the game (e.g., workers and staff). In other words, the organisation of social life is structured by the state, institutions and practices are reproduced by repeated play according to distributive rules, and the players' identities arise in the playing of the game. The state has the authority to ensure that the rules of subordinate institutions are obeyed and to punish those who violate those rules. But inasmuch as the state is itself made up of institutions that are themselves open to influence by other institutions and social forces that might well be located outside the borders of that state,[10] the exercise of structural authority in a liberal system is never an easy or straightforward proposition. Social struggle among contending interests and forces is the order of the day.

'Productive' power is thus more difficult to identify and locate in this liberal scheme, but it is that power rooted in the language and practices that construct and organise social life, individual and collective identities and membership in political community. That is, productive power is that which is exercised through both collective discourse *and* action by groups engaged in social struggles and determined to affect both institutions and structures (Halperin 2004: Chapter 1). This could mean changing the distributional rules of social institutions through lobbying legislatures or campaigning to influence public opinion. But it could also involve attempts to change the constitutive structures that frame and shape the environments within which institutions operate, altering a collectively held sense of what is 'right' and appropriate, and using a variety of tactics that, ultimately, result in state action and discipline.

What is this 'civil society?'

Civil society cannot therefore simply be taken as a given, as something that emerges 'naturally' to fulfil functional needs and demands or to 'protect society' (Polanyi 2001). Rather, it must be regarded as an integral and constitutive element of market society. My argument in this chapter is that *global* civil society is a foundational element of an emergent, globalised, neo-liberal system organised around individualism, private property and exchange. The USA has taken on the dominant role in structuring this political economy under which capitalism can maximise its global accumulation possibilities. While a great deal of contemporary research on the activities of GCS focuses on its human-rights advocacy against an overweening state, we must not ignore the comparably predatory nature of an unregulated market, in which the agents of capital are only too eager to commodify the body and human labour in search of profits (Polanyi 2001; Stanley 1998). Civil society becomes an arena of social struggle over this tendency as well, as certain fractions of the bourgeoisie seek to avoid impoverishment by market forces via action through both state and market (Polanyi 2001; Agathangelou 2004). What we see here, however, is a dialectic rather than causality: while civil society cannot exist absent a liberal system, a liberal system also cannot exist if civil society is absent. They are mutually constitutive, having come into existence through an historical materialist process that, today, continues to generate states, markets and civil societies.

It is possible through historical analysis to see how struggles between bourgeois social forces and the absolutist state during the eighteenth century gave rise to a 'liberal' formation composed of representative state, deregulated market and what we now call civil society (Halperin 2004; Koselleck 1988). Under the principle of 'divine right', the sovereign possessed the authority to expropriate, at will and whim, possessions and bodies of landlords as well as the urban bourgeoisie. Quite understandably, neither group favoured this principle, since it opened them and their property to arbitrary expropriation. But, unable or unwilling to invoke such divine authority themselves for the protection of property and person, these groups began to call on the Enlightenment concept of natural law as an alternative source of authority that infused them with rights to autonomy from royal property relations. Thus was civil society born. Individualism, representation, human rights and naturalisation of the market all emerged from this doctrine through the exercise of constitutive power. In different forms, and with different trajectories, this pattern emerged in England, France, the USA and other liberal societies. More recently, a similar process has taken place in eastern Europe, Latin America and other parts of the world too, even in decidedly non-liberal societies.[11]

There are two rather broad conceptualisations of civil society in tradition and in the literature that illuminate its existence, if not its origins. The first is associated with the market and the private sphere (Ferguson, Smith and

Marx), the second with politics and the public sphere (Hegel, Gramsci and Alejandro Colas). Although we tend to view Ferguson (1995) and Smith (1982) as the intellectual antagonists of Marx and Engels (1970), all four worked within the framework of classical political economy and understood civil society in terms of (a) a separation between state (public) and market (private); and (b) as a realm of civil association beyond the reach or authority of the state. As propagated by de Tocqueville in *Democracy in America* (1966), the liberal version of civil society extant in the USA provided both public goods that the state was unable to supply *and* private goods and affiliations that could only be obtained through the market and outside the state. Marx understood civil society in much the same terms, but regarded it as the cat's paw of a bourgeoisie concerned to mark a very visible border between state and market in order to fence off its private property from the grasp of both the poor and the state. In Marx's teleology, consequently, when the proletarian revolution finally arrived, not only would the state wither away but so would civil society. And with them would go private property as well as the market.

The contrasting version of civil society's origins is associated with philosophers such as G. W. F. Hegel (1942) and Antonio Gramsci (1971; Adamson 1980, 1987–8) and has more recently been explored by Alejandro Colas (2002) among others (e.g., Keane 2003). This one is, in many ways, a less prosaic and more romantic explanation, perhaps in keeping with its strong German influences. All the same, it is not any less correct than the classical and Marxist political economists' version. As Shlomo Avineri (1972: 137) explains, Hegel distinguishes between *Moralität,* which is individual, subjective morality and *Sittlichkeit*, the 'wider totality of ethical life'. *Moralität* regulates relations among individuals; *Sittlichkeit* involves ethical relations among people as members of a wider community. Expanding on this, Colas (2002: 41) points out that 'for Hegel, morality can only become meaningful if it operates within a community, if it is given content through the individual's involvement in public life'. Through association in civil society, individuals are integrated into the community, its ethics, and its virtues. And as Hegel (1942: 'Remark' 3.3, §258) wrote:

> [i]f the state is confused with civil society, and if its specific end is laid down as the security and protection of property and personal freedom, then the interest of the individuals as such becomes the ultimate end of their association, and it follows that membership of the state is something optional. But the state's relation to the individual is quite different from this. Since the state is mind objectified, it is only as one of its members that the individual himself has objectivity, genuine individuality, and an ethical life.

Hegel seems not to have been much interested in the sources of this ethical life – whether it originated in the family, civil society or elsewhere – only that it must be lived through the political community. But Hegel's distinction between the *private* life of the individual and the *public* life of the members of the political community underlines a critical point: that constitutive politics must be something apart from distributive politics and that civil society plays a central role in marking this divide. I shall return to this point, below.

Gramsci placed civil society between state and market and outside of the private sphere of family and friendship. In his framework, the 'corporate-bureaucratic state order with its linked capitalist economic order' stood as a more-or-less unitary arrangement through which the hegemony of the capitalist class was both exercised and naturalised (Nielsen 1995: 58). Civil society then became 'primarily a sphere of "ethical-political" contestation among rival social groups' struggling for ideological hegemony (Adamson 1987–8: 325). As Kai Nielsen puts it, civil society is found not in groups and organisations that fulfil roles of administration or social welfare – i.e., those associated with governmentality or the 'social' (Arendt 1958) – but, rather, in those collectivities that 'seek not only to influence wider opinion and policies within existing structures and rules, but *also sometimes to alter the structures and rules themselves*' (emphasis added). Under these circumstances, evidently, civil-society groups can become a threat to the established order, especially if they have political objectives or 'seek to alter the structures and rules' regulating the political economy.

Colas (2002: 43) draws on Gramsci to argue that civil society is the setting from which social movements and political activism originate 'within the context of capitalist modernity'. In order to reconcile the two apparently conflicting views offered by the political economists and the political philosophers, Colas (2002: 47) further asserts that 'civil society has historically found expression in two predominant forms – one linked to the private sphere of the capitalist market, the other to the struggles against the all-encroaching power of the state.' The former is populated by those organisations and actors who pursue their self-interest through the mechanisms of the market; the latter by those who seek to challenge and change the ethical structures and politics of the state. These are, of course, idealised forms; operating within the structures and strictures of economic liberalism, in which reproduction necessitates activities within the market; even the most dedicated social movement cannot survive on air alone. But note: activism through the market presumes that individuals' morality can be relied upon to effect social change; activism directed toward the state seeks to change the ethics binding state society and the market (Lipschutz 2005: Chapter 7; Chandler 2004).

Civil society thus plays a dual role in liberalism and its maintenance: on the one hand, contesting distributive policies and outcomes through the market, on the other, struggling to instantiate constitutionally the social ethics that underpin the specific form of and limits on both market and state. Not all elements of civil society are therefore political in this 'constitutive' or constitutional sense; indeed, by the conventional definition (one shared by Locke *and* Marx, although to differing conclusions) civil society exists in some twilight zone between state and markets, engaging in activities that constitute and reproduce the fabric of everyday social life. By this definition, civil society is not considered to include the purely private realm, such as the family or the body, even though the norms of civil society as well as the laws of the state and the practices of the market all thoroughly permeate and colonise the household, family and body.

But this conventional definition is almost surely incorrect, inasmuch as the 'private' is integral to the organisation of this state–market–society structure. Where, then, can we locate civil society? In a liberal system, civil society is concerned not only with social reproduction but also with ensuring that neither state nor market take complete control of the bourgeoisie and its 'life, liberty and property.' And it is civil society that, ultimately, is the location of contestation over the public–private divide. The particular organisation of market societies, with public and private constituted as distinct realms of activity and rule, is hardly 'natural' as so often claimed (Rosenberg 1994; Wood 2002; Lipschutz 2005). From the classical perspective, the public–private divide is essential to protect private property from expropriation by the state or the masses. From a Marxist perspective, however, the division between public and private, and the structural reasons for that distinction, are foundational to capitalism, the liberal state and the activities of capital. Justin Rosenberg (1994) and Ellen Meiksins Wood (1995, 2002) both argue that capitalism represents a separation of the political and the economic, the public and the private, that is historically unique. Political authority over segments of the public realm is hived off into the private sphere, where property rights are guaranteed by, but insulated from, the state's direct and structural power.

From an analytical perspective, however, the boundary between the public and private is a puzzling one: how is it created, naturalised and maintained? It is one thing to argue, as did Locke (1988), that private property is the product of one's labour and investment. It is quite another thing, however, to privatise that which is arguably, or customarily, public goods or common property (Drahos and Braithwaite 2003; Barkin 2004). In particular, the 'privateness' as such of even private property can be contested. Property is best understood as a *relation* among people, rather than a thing possessed by an individual (Macpherson 1962). That is, for individually held property to exist, others in a society must acknowledge, either through title or custom, that an 'owner' holds some essential relationship to the thing that is 'owned' (Veblen 1898). Consequently, property exists only by virtue of the willingness of society to accept both the relationship between owner and owned *and* the relation between owner and society. Property is, in other words, a social construct whose privateness is subject to social intervention (and this is, as well, central to the concept of the 'social contract'; Stanley 1998).

In putting such a fine point on the line between constitutive and distributive authority, and between public and private spheres, the liberal state is subject to social forces engaged in constant struggle over the maintenance and reproduction of that boundary, as well as resistance to it. To wit, the expansion of the private realm can take place only under the authority of the state and at the expense of a contraction of the 'public', as seen, for example, in the privatisation of formerly state-provided services and protections.[12] This particular and peculiar organisation of liberal societies, with public and private constituted as distinct realms of authority and activity, relies heavily on civil society to maintain and reproduce the boundary and the distinction. Because of competition between capitals and capitalist organisations, as well as the uneven distributive outcomes of capitalist accumulation, the threat of an unravelling of the social contract and destabilising of society is always present, as Polanyi (2001) argued. Under conditions of globalised neo-liberalism, however, the mechanisms through which such struggles occur are very underdeveloped, and the 'state' is engaged primarily in providing attractive and stable conditions for capital accumulation and is less interested in addressing externalities or market failures (Cerny 2001; Hurt 2007). Under these circumstances, it falls to civil society to become more politicised and, through its own regulatory activities, to reinforce or reinscribe the separation between the public (politics) and the private (markets).[13]

To what, then, does all of this add up? Structural power exercised by and through the state reflects not only the conventional 'balance of social forces' within a society – both directly and institutionally, as discussed above – but also a *discursive* sense of how things should be ('common sense' in Gramscian terms). Growing contradictions in the social and material organisation of a society tend to affect this discursive sense, which can ultimately inspire the formation of social organisations and movements seeking to resolve the contradictions through social and class struggles. However, for the most part, civil society organisations (i.e., non-governmental organisations [NGOs]) focus on institutions and the practices associated with social and material functions, trying to exert direct influence (e.g., through consumer boycotts of offending companies) to induce capital to protect human rights. But these particular struggles serve only to reform the practices of concern. That is, they do not articulate or instantiate those *ethical* limits that movements demand, society expects and states have agreed to (e.g., labour and other rights, environmental protection, etc.). It is only through changes in the *structural* rules that do articulate such limits that these struggles and demands can be transformed into social ethics, to which agents must adhere and which structurally constrain them. Thus, much of what is regarded as political activity by GCS is the exercise of institutional power taking place within the context of the market, the so-called private realm.

Politics via markets

Keeping in mind the bifurcation of GCS into distributive and constitutive fractions, the relative lack of constitutional political mechanisms in the emerging arrangements of global rule leaves distributive politics through markets as the most accessible mode of action open to social activists. The process and consequences that result can be seen in two examples I present here: first, the upsurge in NGO activities and solicitations in the wake of the tsunami in the Indian Ocean on 26 December 2004 and, second, 'corporate social responsibility' (CSR) projects in which NGOs and companies compete to protect workers' labour rights. Although in the first case the private provision of donations and relief services to the victims of the disaster were dwarfed by public commitments, the global response to the tsunami showed how 'international emergencies' have become one of the mainstays of financial support for aid organisations. In the second instance, CSR campaigns seek to influence producer and consumer behaviour as a means of pressuring corporations to do well by doing good. In both instances, the state's responsibility to treat people in an ethical fashion *as a public good* has been displaced by private provision of services and protection.

In the ten countries hit by the tsunami, as many as 250,000 people died, while millions were made homeless, in desperate need of food, water and medical care. For the most part, the affected states had only very limited capacity to respond to the disaster, lacking the personnel, resources and equipment needed to provide both short- and medium-term relief. We need not explore here the reasons for this chronic lacuna in underdeveloped states – it is worth noting that only India refused, at first, to accept outside assistance – except to point out that, to a growing degree, an extensive network of private international relief and aid agencies have become mainstays of global responses to such 'complex emergencies' (Dillon and Reid 2000; Etzioni 2004; Powers 2005). Within days of the tsunami, growing numbers of groups around the world were soliciting private donations from concerned individuals, while others were consulting and contracting with donor and recipient governments to provide both immediate and longer-term relief services. Radio and television stations, schools, corporations and others were holding fund-raising campaigns as well, with the intention of supporting international aid groups.

Undoubtedly, these NGOs, which are indisputably part of GCS, do serve important international and institutional functions, providing a range of goods that states are either unable or unwilling to offer. Yet, it is also the case that many of them rely on state permission, and often protection, to enter a disaster zone and work there. While many non-profit international relief organisations rely heavily on volunteers willing to work in these disaster zones, they nonetheless are 'businesses' that require a steady income in order to continue their operations. Staffs must be paid, offices maintained, travel and transport costs paid. They are part and parcel of the global capitalist economy and, to generate revenues, rely on the full panoply of techniques used by corporations seeking to increase profits. Whether donors are called members, associates, customers or consumers, the goal is to grow and reproduce the organisation. Thus, relief activities are not only charitable, they are also fundamental to production by and the reproduction of these organisations.

This is not to deny that NGOs play an important role in disaster relief and assistance. Without them, many millions of people would go without basic needs and essential services. In this respect, they may, indeed, be part of and integral to what John G. Ruggie (2004: 500, 517–18) calls 'a fundamental reconstitution of the global public domain' in which states, NGOs and corporations 'seek to take advantage of the scope of the transnational private sector in the attempt to create global public value.' Nonetheless, these NGOs are for the most part dedicated to complementing the distribution of such social services as are available (or not), and not working to restructure the political economy that leaves people impoverished and at risk in the first place.[14] In that respect, they are expanding the realm of private action at the expense of the public or, more precisely, fusing public with private.

The nature of politics via markets can be seen more clearly in CSR campaigns. The refusal of many states to regulate the activities of capital and force it to internalise or eliminate various social costs has led to the generation of a vast number of national and transnational campaigns that utilise lobbying, public pressure, influence and expertise to impose regulation on capital (DeWinter 2001; Esbenshade 2004; Cashore *et al.* 2004). The majority of these campaigns seek regulation through markets, trying to convince individuals to engage in 'socially conscious consumption' and businesses to adopt 'corporate social responsibility' (Lipschutz 2005: Chapter 3; Keck and Sikkink 1998). In other words, through an elucidation of 'real' interests within market settings, civil-society organisations seek to use institutional (market-based) power to influence consumer and corporate behaviour as a means of improving labour conditions in factories, reducing environmental effects from industry and managing international trade in various kinds of goods, such as clothing and coffee (Kolk 2005). Consumers come to believe their selective purchasing can induce fear of loss of market share and profits in corporations, who will then internalise social costs in order to protect their bottom lines.

Many of these campaigns have been successful in terms of these instrumental goals, but they suffer from serious *political* limitations (see Lipschutz 2005: Chapters 4 and 5). The most significant of these arises from the ways in which those whose rights are being violated by externalities are treated as objects rather than subjects, of the campaigns, and are thereby deprived of both structural and productive power. Moreover, although individual corporations may change their behaviour, those individual changes have little or no effect outside of the factory walls. Under neo-liberal conditions, in other words, the only obvious and acceptable means of *regulating* markets – in effect, moving the public–private boundary – are based on the *methods* of the market, that is, action articulated through institutional power. Consequently, what appear to be acts by the autonomous agents of civil society to promote workers' rights become, instead, programmes to privatise these rights within a corporation's commodity chain.

Thus, the crucial question: what have been the *constitutive* (as opposed to distributive) effects of such campaigns? How have they altered either corporations or capitalism in *structural* terms? For example, are workers in the Nike commodity chain now able to exercise their productive power, that is, to unionise and bargain collectively? Has the public–private boundary actually been moved? Nike offers improved conditions and higher wages to the workers in its subcontractors' factories, but workers as well as consumers remain fully integrated into the regime of consumption that constitutes contemporary globalisation and subjectifies those workers and consumers. Workers are still unable to influence or change constitutional arrangements on the factory floor or in society at large. They remain the object of corporate authority. To put this another way, in host societies as a whole, there has been little in the way of political reform, of stronger state regulation, or greater exercise of labour's right to unionise. Capital continues to exercise institutional power, which is structurally authorised by the state. At the end of the day, the result is little social change. Structures receive a paint job, so to speak, but underneath, they are still the same.

What is lacking in these regulatory campaigns is any sense of the political inherent in the very notion of social policy or a recognition of the ways in which *power constitutes not only that which activists seek to change but the activists themselves*. Decisions must be made by those who are subjectified about what is necessary for the good and just life; that is, they must become autonomous subjects themselves rather than objects dependent on corporate munificence. What we find instead are versions of what Sheldon Wolin (1996) attacks as 'fugitive democracy', that is, non-political decision-making or 'subpolitics' through markets and expertise (Beck 2000), or what Chantal Mouffe (2000) calls the 'democratic paradox', in which liberalism seriously constrains the political in the name of order and profit.

Productive power and political change

Foucault's conception of governmentality helps to illuminate and clarify the problem of 'politics via markets' discussed above. In developing this concept, Foucault (2004a: 236, 244) also proposed that it replaced *sovereignty*, that is, the autonomy of the sovereign (Schmitt 1985). Today, the residue of such autonomy is to be found in the concept of 'consumer sovereignty', the freedom to choose in the market (Friedman and Friedman 1980).[15] Foucault did not argue that autonomy is impossible but thought that, at best, it is highly constrained within contemporary liberal systems. Moreover, 'opposition' to governmentality may reinforce the very conditions that generate that opposition, for two reasons. First, if an action is deemed threatening enough to society, authorities (including a broad range of state and economic actors) are likely to attempt to manage the agents involved, through institutions – making the activities illegal – and force – using the monopoly of violence to suppress the now-illegal activities. Second, actions whose goals are the regulation or modification of socially damaging practices tend to be absorbed into the governing mechanisms of society, through institutional means. That means is, increasingly, the market. Ultimately, many forms of global social activism are dependent on producer behaviour and consumer choice for their political effects and can be seen as one more manifestation of this very limited autonomy within the market.

On the one hand, consequently, power 'produces' the subject, but the subject that is produced is not always as standardised as the parameters of governmentality might suggest. We are not mere social automatons. On the other hand, agency seems to be highly constrained. Is there no way to break out? In a discussion of 'The Subject and Power', Foucault (2004c: 129) suggested that 'in order to understand what power relations are about, perhaps we should investigate the forms of resistance and attempts made to dissociate these relations.' He described a set of 'transversal struggles [...] that are not limited to one country', in which people 'look not for the "chief enemy" but for the immediate enemy.' In this, they do not seek to realise their long-term, perhaps utopian dreams – 'liberations, revolutions, end of class struggle' – but, rather, those that are closer to home. As Foucault (2004c: 129) put it, 'In comparison with a theoretical scale of explanations or a revolutionary order that polarizes the historian, they are anarchistic struggles.'

In the course of these struggles, people attack those things that, in effect, lead to alienation of the individual from others, from the community, indeed, from the self: they are struggles against the 'government of individualisation' (Foucault 2004c: 129). And, argued Foucault (2004c: 142), if we recognise that power generates its own resistance, insubordination and 'a certain essential obstinacy on the part of the principles of freedom, then there is no relationship of power without the means of escape or possible flight.' But flight is not a simple matter; there is no abrupt or global escape 'by a sort of radical rupture or by a flight without return' (cited in Chaloupka 2003: 73). What is required is strategy (Foucault 2004c: 142–4). Strategy is not merely about oppositional tactics within an existing regime of governmentality, or resistance without reason. Rather, it involves careful mapping of power relations and those points or nodes where language and action can be applied strategically towards transformation of that regime. This is what politics is about.

In a recently published volume on activist struggles to defend forests in and around Clayoquot Sound, in British Columbia, Canada, William Chaloupka (2003: 68) addresses the question of strategy. He writes that 'ethics alone does not a strategy make', and that 'when we strategize, we bring the normative into contact with the pragmatic.' Pragmatism, in turn, brings in agency. According to Chaloupka (2003: 69), '[e]very movement based on civil disobedience (or other forms of ethical protest) must confront the gap between the moralism of protest's justifications and the strategies such protest must usually deploy when it interacts with the political world, which is contingent and multileveled.' Strategy is exercised by all actors as they seek to achieve their ends; it involves the exercise of power, but not simply the power to influence or coerce. Instead, it is the power that emerges through doing those things that are naturalised discursively and normally. In the case of timber companies, writes Chaloupka (2003: 77), '[t]hey are engaged in (more or less effective and thus challengeable) strategies of maintaining their power to continue their operations as they see fit. They wish to appear inevitable, and the notion that their prerogative is a question of property rights abets this wish.' And, he continues (Chaloupka 2003: 77), 'the moral power associated with protests against logging is not "possessed" or owned on the basis of righteous analysis. *That authority has to be created in action*' (emphasis added).

Those who participated in and those who later analysed the activism at Clayoquot Sound seem to agree that such authority (or 'authorisation') was created there. Over the course of more than two decades, First Nations, in coalition with a broad range of local, national, and transnational NGOs, were able to create a political space from which to upset and restructure the authority of both province and the Canadian state. From that space, activists interrupted the predominant pattern of development in the region – one of timber extraction – and forced an alternative developmental path. The regional political economy that has emerged – one that emphasises tourist attraction more than resource extraction – is not without its problems (Luke 2003; Sandilands 2003), but is interesting insofar as it safeguards environmental sustainability without completely denying resource extraction and productive relationships with the land. This newly constituted economy did not emerge until after considerable struggle among activists, and between activists, state and capital, and its continued existence is never guaranteed. Yet, what made it possible was the productive power inherent in that social activism (Rowe 2006; for a more recent example, see Kraus 2006).

The exercise of productive power evident at Clayoquot and other comparable sites of social-movement politics seem to allow for what might be thought of as ruptures or discontinuities in the web of governmentality, the creation of small zones of 'sovereign action'. These ruptures are small and are hardly noticeable, at best, but they represent zones of agency, autonomy, resistance and contestation within which forms of sovereign politics can take place. Such zones might involve 'unauthorised' actions focused on the environment, the mobilisation of political movements or mass demonstrations that drive presidents from office. Whether peaceful or violent, political action in such zones of agency serve to expose the contradictions inherent in the increasingly dense web of global governmentality and make it possible for people to act in spite of those webs. Whether political resistance and contestation can change or overcome governmentality is much less clear. Perhaps new webs can be spun within these ruptures, webs that begin to restructure the state through the weaving of ethical strands, as it were (for a critique, see Chandler 2004).

The image of a 'web' of governmentality is only a very crude metaphor, but it begins to suggest something about power: it must be exercised within the microspaces and capillaries of contemporary life, in the 'spaces of appearance' (Arendt 1958), and it must be a politics in which not only Habermasian discussion but also group action are possible. Politics, in the sense I mean it here, has to grow out of some form of face-to-face praxis, not because place is central, as many environmentalists have argued (Lipschutz 1996: Chapters 7 and 8), but because a democratic politics is subsumed into governmentality when it comes to depend wholly on representative forms. And politics must involve *action*, for it is only then that power becomes productive and the political can be practised (Mouffe 2000). This suggests a rather different conception of democracy than that commonly held, one that is based in practice rather than platitudes, one whose apotheosis is not the vote but debate and action, as it were (Lipschutz 2005: Chapter 8).

Conclusions

The 'problem' of accounting for GCS in its many variants and alternatives, as well as explaining its relationship to global governance, arises for several reasons. First, many scholars are more interested in analysing and fostering the efficiency and transparency of non-governmental participation and process. Second, they seek to elucidate and develop mechanisms through which the desires, needs and interests of those blocked by powerful actors can be fulfilled (see Keck and Sikkink 1998). They are less interested in the normative implications and consequences of how power is exercised and the results of that exercise. These are forms of theorising aptly suited to a liberal worldview, which eschews foundational questions of politics and power and deals with distribution rather than constitution. Such a focus accepts the deployment of power as a given and begs for dispensations from the powerful.

From this view, GCS is less a 'problem' for power than a product of power. It is deeply enmeshed with forms and practices of governmentality. It accepts the naturalisation of the market as 'efficient' and 'effective'. GCS is a means whereby those matters that cannot or will not be addressed by the agents of the state or interstate institutions will, nonetheless, be dealt with by someone. In this, most of the organisations of GCS accept the order of governmentality as a given (Etzioni 2004). A concern with distributive governmentality not only leaves the offending discourses and structures intact but also leads to collaboration with those who exercise domination and institutional power. Mixing the metaphors of neoliberalism, it is not sufficient to focus on the size of the pie's slices, it is necessary to act to change the filling, the crust and, indeed, the pudding.[16]

My account of GCS does not undermine its potential so much as it forces us to recognise how particular forms of society and governmentality are constituted and reconstituted, sometimes through the very agency that, at first glance, appears to be a means of opposition and resistance, if not liberation. It also motivates us to ask whether it is possible to (re)create forms of political sovereignty that can function, perhaps, to challenge the discourses and structures of neo-liberal governmentality. What is important, in my view, is finding strategic ways of generating productive political engagement and authority directed towards social transformation through the structural capacities of the state. Here, we must see the 'state' not as the self-governing or autonomous territorial or juridical unit of international relations, or an institution of order and welfare of neoclassical economics but, rather, as a political collective that can authorise itself to act ethically in pursuit of specific political ethics and goals. This is not what GCS is about. The agencies and organisations of GCS, as they are constituted today, cannot and will not become 'political', engaged as they are in simply reproducing neo-liberal governmentality through 'global governance' or 'cosmopolitan democracy' (Lipschutz 2005: Chapters 7 and 8).

Notes

1 This chapter is drawn from my book (with James K. Rowe), *Globalization, Governmentality, and Global Politics: Regulation for the Rest of Us?* (Lipschutz and Rowe 2005).

2 I should note that the form and substance of this 'entity in the making' is quite unclear. Recent work by Shelley Hurt (2007), a Ph.D. candidate at the New School, suggests that the integration of state and capital through the global political economy – and the general exclusion of labour – are increasingly erasing any useful distinction between state and market.

3 I use the economic term 'externality' for both analytical and ironic reasons. First, when 'normal' production and economic exchange generate social costs that are not absorbed by the beneficiaries of those activities, a classical externality results. Second, many economists are quick to point out that such social costs are more appropriately subsumed under the category of comparative advantage and market equilibrium. Consequently, the low wages received by workers in 'Third World' factories represent the normal functioning of international supply and demand, rather than a subsidy – or positive externality – to 'First World' consumers (Lipschutz 2005: Chapter 2).

4 I elide here what, precisely is meant by the 'sovereign'.

5 If power constructs the subject, as Foucault suggests, and governmentality functions as something that manages and regulates populations and their welfare, agency is constrained by what is considered to be normal and acceptable. That does not mean that one cannot resist such limits; indeed, it is such resistance that represents much, if not all, of what I think of as politics (see below).

6 Much like 'Newspeak' in George Orwell's *1984* (1949: Appendix), these are meant to make even the notion of dissent impossible.

7 This does not mean that direct power disappears – far from it. But, as the USA's recent experience in Iraq seems to illustrate, direct power hardly serves to 'produce' the either a managed population or to benefit its welfare.

8 To be sure, the extent of the contemporary state's 'sovereign' authority in both regards is fiercely debated. As these are ideal categories, the issue of sovereignty can be put aside for the moment.

9 In other words, the state is not simply an autonomous institution but reflects a balance of social forces within the polity (Halperin 2004).

10 *Where* such social forces are 'located' – that is, in what political space – is not easy to specify. This is tangled up in the emergence of the imperial 'entity-in-the making,' whose political shape and structure remains vague.

11 This is an admittedly very brief summary of a much more complex and contested project, but it offers the essential elements for our purposes (Halperin 2004; Koselleck 1988).

12 Indeed, such 'enclosures' might even be seen as forms of primitive accumulation.

13 For a discussion of the growing role of business in global politics, see Fuchs 2005; Levy and Newell 2005.

14 Although no one could have foreseen this particular tsunami, the vast majority of the people who perished or were left homeless were already quite impoverished. Few organisations and agencies paid any attention to these conditions during the decades prior to the disaster.

15 It is interesting to consider the subject of sovereignty as addressed by Michael Ignatieff (2003: 4): 'Regime change is an imperial task par excellence, since it assumes that the empire's interest has a right to trump the sovereignty of a state.'

16 'Pudding', of course, being the British term for 'dessert'.

14 Discourses of power

Traversing the realist–postmodern divide

Jennifer Sterling-Folker and Rosemary E. Shinko

Power is a fundamental concept within both the realist and postmodern perspectives, and both characterise power in essentially negative terms, with realists describing it as coercive and postmodernists describing it as disciplinary.[1] Yet beyond this, there is little common ground. For realists, power is something that is accumulated and possessed, usually by nation-states. It may be measured with comparative indicators, such as military hardware and gross national product (GNP), and it is used to force others, typically other nation-states and international entities, to do something they would otherwise not do. Power is seen by realists to work on the surface. For postmodernists, however, power operates beneath the surface. It is a web that permeates all relationships, institutions and bodies of knowledge. It manifests itself in hegemonic discourses that impose particular meanings as truth and marginalise alternatives. It cannot be measured in a positivist sense, but it can be revealed by examining the marginalised silences on the borders of the hegemonic (Westphalian) discourse.

Because these differences are relatively sharp, there has been little dialogue between realists and postmodernists. This is disappointing as the realist–postmodernism divide represents one of the more important philosophical debates of our discipline, if not of modern social and political theory in general (Walker 1987). Namely, the debate over the extent to which either transhistorical structure or contingent history has the last word in shaping global politics. In other words, is the constitutive structure of the international system universal and timeless; or is it merely the particular consequence of contingent, historical conditions?[2] The first position suggests that change within the international system occurs within margins so narrow as to be hardly worth discussion; the second position suggests that such change is always possible and should be central to our deliberations. Given the arguments of leading realists such as Waltz, Mearsheimer and Gilpin, it is not surprising that realism has typically been consigned to the transhistorical, universal structure end of the theoretical spectrum (Waltz 1979; Mearsheimer 2001; Gilpin 1981). Similarly, the arguments of leading postmodernists such as Ashley, Der Derian and Walker have resulted in postmodernism's consignment to the opposite end, that of historical contingency, ambiguity and the proliferation of difference (Ashley 1986, 1989; Der Derian 1997; Walker 1993, 2003).

Yet structure and history are not mutually exclusive, and there are philosophical strands within each perspective that reveal a common desire to explore structure and history as a relationship rather than opposite, irreconcilable ends. Thus, to relegate realism and postmodernism to opposite ends of such a spectrum is to frustrate any inclination realists and postmodernists might have to explore together how and why this is the case. As Walker has noted in his examination of the multiple traditions of realism, 'the problematic of change, time, and becoming is in fact constitutive of the realist position itself', and this may be particularly true of classical or neoclassical realist variants (Walker 1987: 72). And while the critique of structure is the point of postmodernism, postmodern scholars also recognise that change is not easily effected; as Walker puts it, they 'readily affirm that much of human existence, international and otherwise, is constrained in highly deterministic structures of one kind or another' (Walker 1987: 82).

Thus, there is common ground for realists and postmodernists to explore the relationship between structure and history, even as irreconcilable tensions between these two theoretical perspectives remain. Teasing out those tensions is precisely the point of this article, which follows Walker's lead in seeking to reconstitute the 'tensions and contradictions' in the realist and postmodern positions on structure and history 'in a more critical and creative manner' (Walker 1987: 65). The article is a collaborative effort by a realist (Sterling-Folker) and a postmodernist (Shinko) with the intention to traverse the divide between them by discussing how each perspective conceptualises power. We do this within the context of an empirical case study which evokes central themes for each perspective, such as relative power, national security, the deconstruction of discursive structures and the problematisation of identity: the China–Taiwan relationship.

This case allows us to theorise power from both a realist and postmodern perspective in order to reveal what each perspective takes for granted and what each prioritises. It also reveals how each perspective is forced to grapple with the possibility of the simultaneity of stasis and change, even as each prefers to preserve analytically a preference for one over the other. Thus, realism and postmodernism are forced to confront the relationship of structure and history in their own representations of the world. In this way, our examination of these alternative discourses of power confirms that the standard realist–postmodern divide obscures philosophical avenues that are worth traversing if our goal is to understand power and the discursive frames we choose to describe it. Before traversing them, however, it is necessary to review how each perspective conceptualises power, its link to the tension between structure and history and the relevance of ethics to our discussion.

Power, structure, history and ethics

For realism and postmodernism, power is pervasive and functions as both a capability and an effect. Beyond these generic similarities, however, lie vast analytical differences. Realism locates power in things – such as bombs, money, people, and institutions – but these things must have an effect on others.[3] That is, a gun in a closet of which no human being is aware is not power. Instead, realists know that power exists when it is exercised by an actor (whether it a state or individual) that utilises things regarded as powerful in order to impose their preferences on others who would, in turn, prefer not to have such imposition. Alternative preferences lead to resistance, the disruption of the balance of power and, thus, the use of power in order to re-establish such balance. Resources that signal power are used to get one's preferences or to resist letting others have their way. It is in its effects that power is made known, thus, as Guzzini notes, realist 'power implies potential change, which in turn implies a counterfactual situation of potential continuity' (1993: 446, 449).

Control and struggle are also relevant to postmodern conceptualisations of power.[4] According to postmodernists, these two facets of power manifest themselves in two distinct yet interrelated ways. First, there are the physical and intellectual structures that impose certain ways of knowing and doing things. Physical structures include the institutions of governmentality, such as bureaucracies, while the intellectual structures are those which determine how we frame things and our knowledge of the world. Such structures are reflective of the productive and deterministic aspects of power in that they produce fixed identities, territorial grounding, origins of meaning and presence. But the second sense in which power is analysed emerges within Foucault's understanding of the relationality of power and the possibilities for resisting structural domination. Since power is conceptualised as fluid, reversible and non-linear (i.e., as a network or web), it carries within it productive possibilities that can serve as resources not only to resist structural constraints, but to (re)configure them.

Within both perspectives, then, resistance to the power imposed by structure is a key point of analysis, but realists are more interested in how alternative preferences, which are embedded in and produced by alternative and competing structures, utilise power in order to resist one another. Postmodernists, on the other hand, are interested in how resistance to *all* structure is an act of power in itself and has the potential to reconfigure existing physical and intellectual structures. Hence, while both perspectives concur that power is pervasive and simultaneously a structural *and* individual phenomenon, their analytical focus is very different. Neo-realists and neo-classical realists focus on state structures, with the former concentrating on inter-state competition while the latter concentrates on intra-state competition.[5] Alternatively, postmodernism is interested in acts of resistance to what is structurally fixed and disciplinary. Resistance is a power resource that insists upon being ad hoc and fluid, thereby preventing structures from solidifying. In other words, while realism examines the competition of structures which want to stay *in* being, postmodernism examines resistance to structural ways *of* being.

In both instances, power is seen as a resource that is capable of simultaneously maintaining structures and inducing historical change, but what wields power and why it does so are seen to be very different. For realists, historical change occurs within a timeless context of competing structures which wield power against one another either to change the status quo or to maintain it. For postmodernists, historical change occurs when structural fixity is displaced by acts of resistance, which are a form of power. Because realists take as given the very structures that postmodernists see as disciplinary and oppressive, postmodernists regard realist analysis as part of the problem. Epistemologically, realists separate the analysis of power from its practice, but postmodernists argue that analysis *is* practice, and therefore taking structures as analytical givens only reifies them. Because structure and domination are intertwined, there is an openly ethical dimension to all postmodern international relations (IR) analysis, and heeding those voices that contest the disciplinary power of ostensibly given structures is central to postmodernism's analytical practice. Such voices are found at the margins of inter- and intra-state relations.

Realism, on the other hand, ignores these voices because it is sceptical of the ability to displace existing structures, and it assumes that structural reconstitution in one form or another is a fact of human existence. What happens *after* the power of resistance has been unleashed and existing structures are displaced is a particular worry of realists, since the opposite of structure is anarchy and newly constituted structures may be relatively worse than what was displaced (see Brooks 1997; Spirtas 1996; Freyberg-Inan 2004). This may explain why realists analyse power as outcome, and the limitations on power identified by realists involve the relative inability to exercise power effectively and obtain one's preferences. Realism focuses on the aftermath of power's exercise, because it is sceptical and fearful of structural disruption.

The similarities and differences between realist and postmodern conceptions of power, structure, history, and ethics are reflected in our discussion of the China–Taiwan relationship that follows. The realist analysis conceives of the China–Taiwan relationship as a power struggle between three states, which each have contradictory preferences: the United States (USA), the People's Republic of China (PRC) and Taiwan. Taiwan's intra-state political structures are particularly important to this trilateral power struggle because Taiwanese and Chinese preferences are zero-sum, and Taiwan's electoral politics (and the role of identity formation in these politics) impacts its relationship with China. State structures on both sides of the Taiwan straits reinforce the desire for settled identities that are ultimately zero-sum, as does the inter-state relationship between all three states. Thus, the possibility of violence among these three states remains relatively high.

The postmodern analysis, conversely, conceives of the China–Taiwan relationship as representing both structural closure and an opportunity for structural change. State leaders and policy-makers on both sides of the straits are seen as seeking to impose a closure of identity and thus to fore-close more ethically acceptable change. Postmodernists thus focus on the voices of resistance to such closures, particularly in Taiwan (and in contra-distinction to realism's focus on its intra-state structures). These voices must be recognised and thereby encouraged, since it is in the act of resistance that the possibility of radical reconfiguration of existing structures may be found. In this way, the belief that identity relationships are zero-sum and violence is inevitable may be subverted from within the relationship itself. We now turn to a dialogue between realism and postmodernism in order to problematise these conceptualisations of power.

Realist power struggle: USA–China–Taiwan

What does it mean to say 'the China–Taiwan relationship'? For a structural realist there is an obvious reality with respect to Taiwan, but it begins with the USA and the PRC, which are both concerned with the potential damage that the other could do to their national security and economies (Christensen 2001; Mearsheimer 2001: Chapter 10). These concerns result from each nation-state's desire to dominate the politics and economics of the region, and both possess substantial resources in this regard, including large numbers and types of military weapons, large portions of their citizenry engaged in their militaries, sizeable economies, vast networks of trading partners and linkages and considerable financial resources and influence. Given the military resources each possesses, combined with the trade lin-kages they have developed with one another, both nation-states seek to avoid direct military confrontations with one another. Yet they also simul-taneously seek to balance one another's military and economic power in order to avoid any advantage the other might accrue in their competition for regional domination.

From a structural realist perspective, Taiwan represents a third and rela-tively weaker entity in the mix. For the PRC, Taiwan represents unfinished business (Copper 1999; Zhao 1999; Christensen 2002; Russell 2000). Ori-ginally a province of China, Taiwan is an island 100 miles off the coast of China's Fukien province, and the body of water that separates them, the Taiwan Strait, is a major commercial shipping avenue. Taiwan had been annexed to and occupied by the Japanese from 1895 until 1945 when it was returned to China. When the decades-long Chinese civil war culminated in a communist victory over the mainland in 1949, remnants of the US-supported Nationalists (Kuomintang or KMT) escaped to the island and established their own government, the Republic of China (ROC). From its inception, the ROC was intended to be a temporary solution. The Nationalists argued that they were the sole legitimate government of China and insisted that they would some day reconquer the mainland. Meanwhile the PRC made plans to reclaim Taiwan after it had consolidated power on the mainland. What prevented this invasion was the US interest in balancing Chinese aggression in light of the Korean War.

Throughout the 1950s and 1960s, Taiwan became the cornerstone in the US Cold War containment strategy in Asia. The USA sent naval forces into the Taiwan Strait several times in response to Chinese provocations; it supplied the ROC with economic aid; and it signed a mutual defence treaty with it in 1954. This Cold War context changed by the early 1970s, however, as China had by then developed a mutual interest with the USA in counterbalancing the Soviet Union, and the USA and China explored the possibility of improved relations. In 1979 the USA established full diplomatic relations with the PRC, terminated its 1954 mutual security pact with Taiwan and reaffirmed the one-China principle that there is only one China and Taiwan is a part of it. Simultaneously, however, the USA adopted the 1979 Taiwan Relations Act, which declared that the USA has a commitment to Taiwan's security and is obligated to sell sophisticated defensive arms to it. The USA has also consistently argued it has a right to protect Taiwan from the PRC, and in 1996 it dispatched two aircraft-carrier groups to the region in response to Chinese military activities in the strait.

The triangular relationship between the USA, the PRC and the ROC is replete with strategic deterrent calculations. The USA attempts to pacify China with regards to Taiwan while also containing China and protecting Taiwan from it. The PRC attempts to intimidate Taiwan while preventing direct US involvement in their bilateral conflict. And the ROC seeks to maintain and increase its independence from China while being careful not to alienate American support. This trilateral structural relationship can also be examined from a neo-classical realist perspective, which focuses on the domestic politics of these states. Competing subgroups within the USA, the PRC and the ROC emphasise either cooperative economic linkages or militaristic policies in their relationships with one another. The extent to which any of these particular subgroups are in ascendance results from electoral competition in the USA and the ROC and internal bureaucratic struggles in the PRC.[6] Taiwan's development into a full-fledged democracy in the 1990s has increased hostilities between the ROC and the PRC, because democratisation allowed the main pro-independence political party, the Democratic Progressive Party (DPP), to gain control over and utilise state power in the pursuit of its nationalist policies.

Given neo-classical realism's concern with non-systemic variables, the impact of identity formation on intra-state politics in Taiwan is particularly important. The DPP and other pro-independence groups are intimately linked to a Taiwanese identity that sees itself as distinct from that of mainland China. These Taiwanese, who emigrated from mainland China before the Second World War and may be divided into two groups (Hoklos and Hakkas) based on linguistic differences, constitute 85 per cent of the population (Song 2002: 228). 'Mainlanders' are the Mandarin-speaking KMT who retreated to Taiwan after the Second World War; they constitute only 14 per cent of the population. As long as the Nationalists prevailed electorally, Taiwan pursued a foreign policy with China that subtly mixed accommodation (including the public acceptance of the one-China principle) and resistance (such as pursuing sovereign membership in international governmental organizations [IGOs]). Under the DPP, on the other hand, Taiwan has declared its intention to become a full-fledged sovereign nation-state within the next ten years; something the PRC has consistently indicated it will use force to prevent. These internal developments make conflict between the PRC and the ROC even more likely than international structural considerations alone would have done. Given US strategic interests in the region, the Taiwan Strait is, as David Lampton, Director of China Studies at John Hopkins observes, 'the only probable place [...] where two big nuclear powers could come into conflict.'[7]

Postmodern recognition and expressions of doubt

From a postmodern perspective, power is already at play in the ways in which a realist analysis describes and discusses what it has supposedly objectively framed as a potentially dangerous flashpoint (Ashley 1987). But how can postmodernism maintain that power is implicit in the very act of describing the realist version of 'reality'? Can this exercise of power be drawn out and made visible? The key lies in explicating the postmodern claim that not only is IR a discursive process, but that it is 'a process of knowledge as power' (George 1994: 216). Starting from this perspective, power is understood in terms of its relational context. Power relations are made known where attempts are made to bring ambiguity under control, where a privileged interpretation emerges, or where conduct is disciplined and discourse limited (Ashley 1988). Thus, when we choose to comprehend the world in a certain way, we thereby impose an order on it which must inevitably be held in place by power, a power which simultaneously produces us as 'knowers' of the world and disciplines us to know the world in accordance with an established mode of certitude.[8]

Realism is the established mode of certitude through which we have come to know the international, and it centres on national security as power politics. According to Taiwan's 'Guidelines for National Unification' issued in 1991, for example, any timeframe for the unification of Taiwan and China must 'respect the rights and interests of the people in the Taiwan area, and *protect their security and welfare*' (Cooper 1999: 178; emphasis added). Realism's national security power/knowledge grid establishes the order whereby security and welfare are conflated with the state and deployed to justify the use (or threat) of violence in order to maintain that discursive equation of state and security/welfare. It is this frame of sovereign certitude that a postmodern analysis seeks to disrupt.

It is not, as George suggests, that postmodernists are attempting to somehow move beyond power but rather that they are attempting to shift the focus of the knowledge/power grid through which we represent the world of IR (1994). In order to radically question the singular, irreducible version of reality imposed on the world via realist politics, we need to look to the various marginal sites and be attentive to what Ashley refers to as the 'reality of human struggles to make life go on' (1996: 244). We need to look at the various local sites where identity and territoriality have been thrown into radical doubt. This recognition of radical doubt opens a space for individuals to question and resist those who would marshal the forces of violence in the name of territorial certitude (see Ashley and Walker 1990a; 1990b). This recognition shifts us from relations of power that define security in terms of national security, to relations of power that exceed the limited purview of states.

One site to deconstruct is the representation of two titanic foes, the USA and China, squaring off in a primordial contest between good and evil. Such a dichotomous representational frame oversimplifies myriad complexities and also encourages political practices which necessarily categorise actions, words and thoughts as either/or. Framing China as a 'looming menace' scripts a scenario whereby cross-strait relations become denoted as one of the most dangerous sites in global politics. This script easily roles over into an attitude of resignation like that clearly expressed by Kurt Campbell, Director of the Center for Strategic and International Studies, when he admits that it appears as if almost inexorable forces are at work in the straits area.[9] Disrupting this realist representation of reality entails drawing out counter-narratives.

Certainly one marginal site where acts of resistance and transgression are transpiring is in the movement of Taiwan's indigenous peoples for recognition and cultural survival. There are currently eleven major indigenous peoples in Taiwan who make up less than 2 per cent of the total population. Prejudice, pressures to assimilate and a general underprivileged status constitute the context within which they struggle to make life go on. It is here, in their marginal existence, that the power deployed to construct an overarching, unified, national Taiwanese identity becomes visible. Many of these groups have become politically active at both the local and national levels in order to promote the welfare of their communities and to maintain their expression of difference.[10] They fear the narrative power of Taiwanese national identity, which threatens to subsume and eventually erase their cultural and historical memory.[11]

These are marginalised sites of difference, yet they locate a possibility that contests the inevitability of a move toward the solidification of one homogenising national Taiwanese identity. In these sites of struggle, security issues are also of paramount concern, but the security issues here are qualitatively different than those glimpsed from the triangulation of US, Chinese and Taiwanese representations of national security. These sites are fraught with doubt, contingency and chance, and they expose how focusing on titanic struggles between competing national identities and strategic foes is merely an attempt to impose a simplistic order on the complexity of life itself. It is not that the state is irrelevant to postmodern concerns, but, in order to problematise discourses that presume the inevitability and historical necessity of the state, we must locate sites of contestation that do not conflate state security and survival with that of individuals or communities. It is the rupture between these paradoxical positions that postmodernism seeks to explore.[12]

Realism is what states do

It is not that change is not possible in realism, or that alternative sites of struggle are not important, but the parameters of and sites of struggle for change highlighted by postmodernism seem analytically misplaced. If 'realism' is not simply explanation by ivory-tower academics but is what states and policy-makers do (it is, after all, Chinese and US officials who designate one another as menaces, and it is Taiwanese state officials who equate national security and welfare in their own documents), then why study the marginalised instead of the states and policy-makers involved? Why not talk about change within the context of state–society politics and among state policy-makers? The state is one of the ultimate sites of political, economic and social struggle and power in contemporary world politics, and it seems counter-productive to look for and promote change in representative practices while simultaneously ignoring the state and its relationship to these alternative sites of representation. If change is both possible and afoot in our representations of the world, shouldn't it be recognisable in the politics of and struggle over the state and its functions in society?

The fact that many states, such as the USA and the ROC, are democracies underscores this point, since they have been institutionally designed to respond to majorities and minorities within their societies. Even China's totalitarian regime responds to multiple interests emanating from its society. Hence, it is not clear to realists why a discussion of the marginalised does not also involve understanding the structural mechanisms whereby doubt and uncertainty are translated into political practice. Conversely, while there is a great deal of radical doubt in the world, not all of it matters to individual security or territorial violence and competition among nation-states. If the radical doubt engendered by the marginalised (in this case, 2 per cent of Taiwan's population) is not realised through state structures, then studying them won't get us any closer to understanding change and stasis in the China–Taiwan relationship. Wouldn't our understanding of change in this triangular relationship be better served by examining how the majority and the minority interact within the political structures, parties and interest groups of the USA, the PRC and the ROC and, in so doing, effect the politics and behaviour of the other states involved?

Postmodern responsibility to otherness

Such realist queries go to the heart of alterity in postmodern analysis. There is, in the continued realist focus on the state, an underlying presumption that there is a necessity for stability and order that can only be maintained with the perpetuation of a state-centric system. Perhaps most problematic are the effects of a realist perspective that would marshal all of its power in an effort to discipline and limit the individual's prospects for 'self-making in a register of freedom.'[13] Ashley and Walker describe freedom as that which exists prior to the imposition of limitations, necessity and need. On one level then, freedom finds its expression in a register or space which provides an opening to contemplate new ethical modes of behaviour in the conduct of international politics. Thus self-making in a register of freedom becomes possible amid the recognition of the contingency, chance and ambiguity of life.

Yet, this process of self-making does not transpire in a relational vacuum, nor is it a freedom in which anything goes. According to Ashley and Walker, all those engaged in questioning boundaries and resisting the imposition of limitations share the problem of freedom. And while no one's paradigm for questioning, resisting and/or transgressing boundaries should become the universal or standard paradigm for others to replicate, such freedom enacts an ethics that 'does discipline the active labor of self-making, orienting that labor not only to respect the uncertainties of every immediate locality but also to explore the connections across localities upon which the struggle for freedom depends' (Ashley and Walker 1990b: 394). Thus, postmodernism offers its version of a deterritorialised ethics, which draws its power from an engagement between individuals across locales who struggle to resist the sovereign imperative of exclusion in all its various guises.[14]

An interesting vantage point from which to view this 'open-ended, always hazardous contest among plural cultural possibilities' is within the contentious debate over the construction and content of Taiwanese literature (Ashley 1995: 98). This debate has engaged scholars on both sides of the straits and has profound implications for future cross-strait relations because at its heart lies issues of self-reflexivity and identity. Nativists advocate the creation of a Taiwanese national literature distinct from other Asian literary expressions and traditions. As Tang notes, these scholars and writers exemplify a 'willingness and desire to identify with and represent the land of Taiwan' (1999: 386). However, this representation trades on the positing of a nativist identity in opposition to an oppressive Chinese other. Tang confirms that the nativist 'objective is to institute and fortify a new sense of collective identity often through instilling a victim consciousness, so as to lend cultural and moral legitimacy to the pursuit for political self-determination' (1999: 391). Nativist literature thus reiterates the binding tie between people and territory while relying on the identification of China as a looming, ominous threat.

This literary debate is the site of disagreement and contest where issues of identity intersect with issues of originality (self-determination), particularity (authenticity) and subjectivity (national sovereignty) (Tang 1999: 406). The impulse of some within the nativist camp is to reduce these cross-cutting currents to a simple juxtaposition between separatists and unificationists, delineating the choice as an either/or determination between those Taiwanese who are pro-independence and those who favour eventual reunification with China. For instance, Chen Wanyi criticises the more exclusionary aspects of nativism and espouses the development of a literary tradition that includes 'literature written in the Taiwanese dialect', 'Hakka literature', 'literature of the indigenous people', and 'military compound literature' (Tang 1999: 399). Ultimately, what Tang advocates is encouraging a fluid exchange of ideas that keeps alive the play of difference and ambiguity. The point, then, is to open up possibilities for cross-strait discussions and the exploration of connections that would recognise the struggles for freedom occurring across these various locales. From a postmodern perspective, the crucial activity is to question, test and expose the power that lies behind the impulse to construct and impose an exclusionary version of either Chinese or Taiwanese identity that would demarcate itself as a bounded, sovereign territorial space compelled to defend the certitude of its identity by the threat, or actual use, of force.

Realist identity and reinforcing structures

It is precisely the equation between the state and order that leads realism, in turn, to question the possibility of such a deterritorialised postmodern ethics. The postmodern notion of 'self-making in a register of freedom' suggests that individuals can and want to be free to remake their identity but that they are prevented from doing so by the state. The problem with such a formulation from a realist perspective is that individuals do not want freedom from settled identity; and in any case it is the nation, not the state, that is the chief oppressor in this regard. Human beings are social creatures whose humanity is only realizable within the context of a group, and, as a result, human beings do not embrace identity ambiguity (Bloom 1990; Mercer 1995; Sterling-Folker 2002: Chapter 3). They will form groups even when there is no rational reason to do so, and group formation means the demarcation of identity difference from other human beings. What binds a collective of individuals is *always* the opposition to something normatively different, external and less desirable, because without this juxtaposition the members of a collective cannot know who they are and they cannot function as a collective. The need for order and stability is not a function of the state, then, it is a function of human sociability that derives, in turn, from the anarchic conditions of species evolution.

Postmodernism is correct to argue that the act of identity-settling is never complete and the content of identity contestable. This is what allows for identity manipulation, imposition and subjugation in the name of a greater collective good. But realism counter-proposes that the human need for a settled identity is stronger than the desire for contestability, and the voices offering ambiguity and contingency cannot prevail against those offering clarity of identity difference instead. In contemporary world politics, the most pertinent group identity is the nation, which subsumes other forms of group identity and is married to the state as a type of social institution and process for determining intra-group resource decisions.[15] Individual identity is intimately linked to the state as the primary decision-making structure for the national collective. A refusal to engage in this link analytically means an analytical failure to recognise how important the state remains for intra-national quarrels over identity and resource allocation. And to encourage the identity ambiguity while refusing engagement with the state is to play into the hands of the forces that postmodernists wish to counter-act: the builders of territorially defined nation-states.

It is no accident, then, that the ROC's development into a full-fledged democracy gave pro-independence forces access to the Taiwanese state and the opportunity to enact policies that encourage nationalist identity difference. Early pro-independence movements were as much about secession from China as they were opposition to the KMT's authoritarian rule over Taiwan between 1949 and 1989, and there was an ethnic link between China and the KMT that was in opposition to the island's Taiwanese majority. For many Taiwanese, 'they belong to a separate nation that has no more enduring connections to China than it does to Japan or even the Netherlands, its former colonial rulers' (Kahn 2004a: A8). This has proven to be electorally significant, and the DPP candidate, Chen Shui-bien, won the presidency in 2000 and 2004 on a party platform that aligns pro-independence with Taiwanese ethnicity. Taiwanese ethnic identity began 'enjoying a tailwind of popular support' during Chen's first term, and the 2004 presidential election was cast 'as a choice between subjugation to Communist China and Taiwanese nationalism' (Kahn 2004a: A1, A8).

Conversely, the political identity of the Taiwanese Nationalists is rife with ambiguity, which works to the political advantage of the DPP. Voting margins from the last two presidential elections, in which Chen won by 39 per cent and 50 per cent, suggest to electoral strategists that the Nationalists will need to embrace native Taiwanese nationalism, and downplay their Mandarin Chinese ethnic identities, if they wish to prevail electorally.[16] Meanwhile, Chen and the DPP show every sign of pursuing the nation-state-building agenda of their campaign, which includes revising the Taiwanese constitution, restructuring its government, redefining Taiwan's territory and changing the ROC's name to the Republic of Taiwan. According to Yan Xuetong, a foreign-policy expert at Beijing's Quingha University, Chen 'is determined to be the founding father of a new nation by 2008' (quoted in Kahn 2004b: A6); something which China has vowed to prevent with force if necessary.

Competitive elections over control of the state are a driving force in the upsurge in Taiwanese nationalism, because the state remains the primary resource allocating institution of contemporary global politics. Hence, access to and control over it ensures the ability to pursue and obtain specified preferences and agendas, and so it is a site where struggles over resource control and identity differentiation come together. Failure to examine the political and national struggles over state control that occur on a daily basis around the globe, and a preference for the study of the marginalised and ambiguous instead, will get us no closer to understanding or realising individual identity or security; either globally, or in the Chinese–Taiwanese relationship specifically. And to suggest to individuals and subgroups within China and Taiwan that their cause will be furthered by embracing identity ambiguity while simultaneously refusing participation in the state, is not simply unrealistic; it is an ethical abdication in its own right, as there is no surer way to marginalise oneself from the sites of and exercise of power.

Difference and ambiguity as postmodern political resources

The realist insistence that power is something that has a specific location and can be possessed is precisely the problem from a postmodern perspective. Postmodern power is not rooted in material capabilities, in access to institutional assets, nor in expressions of violent governmental force, it is rooted in doubt, uncertainty and vulnerability. In opposition to the centrality of order and unity in a realist analysis, the role of uncertainty and doubt are crucial to postmodern power.

Power constrains and limits, but it can also be said to constitute and produce certain modes of subjectivity. Where knowledge is expressed as certitude and order, as in the modern concept of sovereignty, power functions to produce docile and disciplined subjects. Knowledge claims imbued with doubt spawn resistant subjects because uncertainty and multiplicity encourage 'the undecidability of being and the proliferation of meaning as effective techniques of power' (Ashley 1995: 125). For Foucault, there can be no exercise of power without resistance because power operates within a relational web.[17] If there were no possibility for resistance, then a totalitarian order would emerge which would foreclose all possibilities for active, political resistance and all possibility for political relationships. Hence, power functions to produce subjects who are free to create themselves. Doubt gives those confronted with knowledge claims pause to rethink their presumptions, assumptions and conclusions. Such a pause opens the space to think things anew and it also provides a space for a multiplicity of views to emerge. Together, doubt and multiplicity operate as political resources to resist and transgress current modes of subjectivity.

The postmodern conceptualisation of power ultimately relies upon the ability of individual thought to 'present it [power] to oneself as an object of thought and question it as to its meaning, its conditions, and its goals' (Foucault, quoted in Norris 1994: 179). Thought is capable of creating a critical space between itself and external events, and this is the space where postmodern power becomes visible. This power is a power immanent only in the present and in the possibility inherent in the exercise of self-creative freedom. Power is productive in the immanently local moment wherein the individual exercises their capacity for critical thought, and they are empowered to challenge power's disciplinary order because they too can access power's productive capability.[18] Thus, the expression of difference opens the space wherein the individual can confront the existing web of power relations with an expression of that which it (the existing set of power relations) has yet to know, yet to discipline within its established set of practices. Proliferating sites of difference are the immanent conditions of possibility for expressions of freedom and self-making.

Difference and ambiguity are political resources that could serve to move the discussion beyond the confines of nationalist ideology and realist certitude by drawing attention to the ways in which the constructs of 'Taiwan' and 'China' function as absolute signifiers. To return to the example of Taiwanese literature, nativist discursive framings are open to disruption by calling attention to the island's varied mix of Malayo-Polynesian, Japanese Chinese, Dutch, Spanish, American, and other cultural legacies; the struggle of the indigenous peoples for social justice amid assimilationist pressures; the rise of consumer, environmental, labour, women's, students, Aboriginal, and human-rights social movements; and the gay and lesbian counter-culture movements.[19] The simple dichotomisation that would reduce these complex and varied expressions of identity down to an either or choice between Taiwaneseness or Chineseness would miss the complexity and nuance of these other contentious identity debates. Thus, Peng Ruijin, who served as editor of *Literary Taiwan*, cautioned the nativists, who are striving to establish a new literary tradition for Taiwan, that they 'do not have the right to restage a historical tragedy, to manufacture the authenticity of Taiwan literature and monopolise the right of interpretation' (Tang 1999: 401).

What has been transpiring within Taiwanese politics constitutes a paradigmatic expression of the postmodern play of power. It involves a struggle between competing iterations of foundational origins, collective memories and memoralisations that reveal an active and engaged struggle to attach meaning to the noun 'Taiwan' and its correlate, 'Taiwanese'. This is a struggle over definition and signification that is shot through with power. Within this struggle we can witness the contention and competition among a proliferation of different voices from various social, political and economic sites. Will this polyphonic discourse succumb to the pressures of homogenisation and uniformity, or will it remain indeterminately open? How power coalesces around these two trajectories will inevitably shape not only Taiwan's identity but also its relationship with China. In other words, how will the knowledge/power nexus play out? Will the play of power in Taiwanese politics open up possibilities for the emergence of a new form of subjectivity?

Postmodernism analyses these possibilities and indicates that the key to a new form of subjectivity lies within the practices of creativity, tolerance and self-transformation. Tang advises those involved in the debate over the concept of Taiwanese literature to recognise the play of ambiguity and difference in their own discussions and to be open to the ambiguity, difference and contestation that is also playing itself out in China (1999: 401). He refuses attempts to impose a monolithic identity on either China or Taiwan.[20] Sebastian Hsien-hao Liao advocates the cultivation of Taiwan's internal hybridity as a resource in order to negotiate cross-strait relations. He argues that the cultural drive for a pure and totalising expression of Taiwanese identity requires the positing of a contaminated, impure and threatening other. Thus Hsien-hao Liao concludes, 'If Taiwan's being contaminated by China were no longer considered a problem, China would not be perceived as a monolith. Then, and only then, could (the threat of) "China" be "dissolved" [...] through constructive cross-strait dialogues on the basis of a recognition of the multiple temporalities inherent in all socioscapes' (H. Liao 2000: 177). In sum, the recognition of ambiguity and difference within one's own position, as well as that of the other, is a tactical resource that has the potential to rescript the possibilities for politics across the region.

A postmodern approach to cross-strait relations seeks to locate sites of disruption where discourses that emphasise territorial integrity and political sovereignty are laid open to ambiguity and uncertainty. The point is to isolate those ongoing discussions and disagreements over the composition of national identity, history and political and cultural legitimacy, in order to expose the contingency of all national, territorial security discourses. It is in the exposure of those contingencies that change becomes possible.

Zero-sum interests and the realist state

Granting that postmodernism is seeking out the sources for radical change in and of the Westphalian sovereign system, how else are sources for rescripting to become translated into change in the Chinese–Taiwanese relationship except via the nations of China and Taiwan, their respective states and the strategic relationship they share with the USA? Doesn't the Taiwanese state also protect identity difference from Chinese repression? Collective identities may be socially constructed, but their content can still be zero-sum. What would it have meant for the individuals of Taiwan in the

1970s to have refused the national, territorial security discourses of realism and to have embraced identity tolerance with China instead?

Certainly, the latter could only have been achieved by embracing China on its own terms, and so it would have involved the political and economic subjugation of the Taiwanese people to Beijing. The vast majority of Taiwanese were already victims of identity intolerance at the hands of the Nationalist KMT, but they were neither Mandarin-speaking, nor did they identify with the Chinese mainland. Although the KMT were initially welcomed by the Taiwanese population as liberators from the Japanese occupation, Song notes that 'the expectation that Taiwanese could now share power with their "mainland brothers" was crushed by the KMT' (Song 2002: 232). Clashes and civil unrest ensued over KMT authoritarianism, corruption and favouritism, and in 1947 the KMT declared martial law. The formation of political parties was banned, the military was given considerable legal and censorship powers, thousands of opponents were executed, and for the next thirty-five years Taiwan became a virtual police state dominated by mainlanders who insisted that Mandarin be the official language.

While the KMT remained obsessed with returning to mainland China, it was not a goal shared by many Taiwanese. Those who dreamt of Taiwanese independence from China developed underground or overseas movements that later evolved into the DPP. There was little desire among the majority of Taiwanese to embrace identity tolerance with China on the latter's terms. Simultaneously, there was the possibility of greater participation in the political institutions of Taiwan itself. For the Taiwanese, at that moment, to have refused the national, territorial security discourses of IR in favour of ambiguity and tolerance would have been to refuse the very identity and goals that distinguished them from the KMT and mainland Chinese (and for which many of them had suffered). It would have meant a refusal of themselves, which hardly seems likely or even desirable. As Elshtain puts it, 'we are dealing with identities, remember, not easily sloughed off external garments' (1995: 349). To say that if the Taiwanese stop thinking of China as a problem then tensions will dissolve is true in an abstract sense but not in any practical sense for the vast majority of people who live these identities.

It was the Taiwanese desire to embrace statehood and the parameters of the Westphalian system that, along with US strategic deterrence, prevented a Chinese invasion of Taiwan. To argue that the individuals of Taiwan would be safer if they refused statehood is to ignore the Chinese commitment since 1949 to subjugate Taiwan according to its own identity parameters. It is also to ignore the desire of the vast majority of Taiwanese not to be subjugated according to those parameters. The ROC would not even exist if it had not been for classic balance-of-power politics between two nation-states, the USA and China, in the context of the early Cold War. Its evolution into a democracy is just as indebted to its relationship with the USA, since it was the US decision to improve its relations with China in the 1970s that forced the KMT to pursue democratisation as means of national consciousness. Simultaneously, the goal of Taiwanese nation-state-building was to confirm for other nation-states that the ROC had a legitimate claim to sovereignty (in opposition to China's claim that it is only a province), because the ROC government has the legitimate support of its population.

Hence, the increasing identity tolerance between Taiwan and China has only been realised *through* the avenues and mechanisms of national identity politics and the governing institutions of China and Taiwan, not outside or beyond them. Certainly nations have the option of refusing to become nation-states, but it would make little sense for nations and the individuals who comprise them to do so, when those parameters promise control over a specified territory via intra-national decision-making institutions. This is why civil wars are endemic to the Westphalian system and why nations will pursue statehood even when they are, in relative terms, politically and eco-nomically comfortable. If we don't examine particular, historical contexts, identities and institutions – that is, if we insist upon, in Morgenthau's words, the 'neglect of the contingencies of history and of the concreteness of historical situations' (1995: 40) – then we will miss the way in which radical ideas work through and shape existing institutions and practices, and are in turn shaped by them. Thus we will miss the most essential link between that which changes (namely, history) and what remains the same (namely, structure).

Postmodernism's structural critiques

Postmodernism refuses to concede that constitutive structures cannot or do not change. The strength of a postmodern analytic of power lies precisely within its ability to critique and expose how structural constraints operate at all levels, from the global to the individual. These points of critique reveal the traces of human design and, thus, our implication in the perpetuation and maintenance of those structures. Revealing their con-structedness and the points of contestation as structural constraints settle into place is potentially one of postmodernism's key analytical insights. Post-modernism's conception of power is ultimately much more comprehensive than that of realism because it recognises both the 'solidity' of our structural designs, in terms of their complexity and differential impact on people's lives, while also revealing the contingent and unforeseen points at which human actions reveal and/or result in breaches of structural constraints.

For example, Dirlik reveals how discourses among new left and liberal Chinese intellectuals are constrained within a China–West frame of reference 'that reifies both China and the West, even among confirmed deconstructionists and postmodernists' (2004: 137). His point is to draw attention to the powerful structural interplay between colonial legacies and ideological hegemony and how these operate to implicate 'many Chinese intellectuals [...] in the fetishization of Euro-America and the legitimization of the power relationships they would criticize' (Dirlik 2004: 130). By drawing attention to the complex interplay of speaking within and against the frame of the nation-state, postmodernism acknowledges both the complexity and the difficulty involved by revealing the points of our complicity in the perpetuation of those very same structural constraints which we are attempting to alter.[21] This is ultimately a very nuanced view of the interplay of power, which is anything but zero-sum. Realists would like to constrain us within this idiomatic logic, but doing so is both an abdication and refusal to acknowledge the political nature of power.

Observations about a realist–postmodern dialogue

Both realism and postmodernism have a problematic relationship with their conceptualisations of power and its implication in the possibilities for structural stasis and historical change. For neo-classical realism, there is no other way to understand contemporary global politics except through the institutions and mechanisms that national groups continue to rely upon to make resource-allocation decisions. Those who control such institutions will have at their disposal material resources (such as weapons or currency reserves) and ideational resources (such as the moral legitimacy to ask individuals to die on behalf of group survival). These can be utilised to pursue particular agendas and interests, and those pursuits involve choices both within and between national groups over who will be allocated what. Small wonder, then, that the state remains the primary site of struggle in world politics according to realism, since to those who control the group mechanisms of resource allocation go the spoils.

Conversely, postmodern attempts to understand global politics inevitably devolve into a study of conflicts from within their local, contingent and historicised locations, because postmodernists operate on the assumption that there is no universal rationality that can uniformly comprehend and evaluate the entirety of global politics. However, the power to elude, resist or alter realist representational practices of power politics is always already present within the emergent moment of thought and action. What else then can postmodernism rely upon except anecdotal instances of individual/collective acts of resistance and transgression to illustrate the emergence of new forms of international subjectivity? There is no one mode of being or form of subjectivity that can be deployed as a measure of teleological progression. There is no one conception of freedom that can be relied upon to evaluate expressions of self-making. There is no final arbiter, no final measure upon which determinations of success can come to rest.

It is also interesting to observe that there is something eerily similar in the conclusions of realism and postmodernism juxtaposed here. The realist position cautions us to look at the particulars of historical structure, while the postmodern position draws our attention to the necessity of thinking more expansively about the structure of historical possibility. Thus, in our dialogue, the realist and the postmodernist have traded places; shifting the analytical divide so that in order to understand stasis and change, the realist insists we study the particulars of history, while the postmodernist insists we study power as an overarching, structurally encompassing phenomenon. And whether one deploys the realist term 'power' or its postmodern variant 'power relations', both ultimately rely upon an understanding of power that is rooted in struggle.

Thus we realise that our dialogue serves as an analytic of power within which difference can be recognised and respected, without being absorbed into a unifying totality. Both realists and postmodernists discursively fill the content of the 'empty space of power' with referents such as order, discipline, vulnerability, survival, uncertainty, and indeterminacy. And in this sense the two positions can be viewed as mirror images. Postmodernism, as discussed by Ashley and Walker, is not an anarchical stance where anything goes but a process whereby difference can be expressed, negotiated and recognised within the disciplined effort of listening, questioning and speaking. Similarly, realism, as discussed by Morgenthau and Bull, is not a position whereby violence is sanctioned and recommended. Rather it seeks to understand how human difference can exist and be protected if structural continuity is demanded by human sociability itself. This is not, in either case, a valorisation of totalising chaos or violence.

This recognition of otherness is further implicated in a larger contextual struggle involving the tactical and symbolic content that we ascribe to the concept of power. Drawing upon Newman's notion of the 'empty place of power' enables us to open up the spaces within which power is rendered visible and determined to be at work (2004: 155). These sites are the sites of identity/difference, security/insecurity, order/disorder, self/other, vulnerability/invulnerability, and uncertainty/certainty. Security is inextricably linked to power, which both realists and postmodernists would concede, but what is the content of the security/power nexus? Power is already always implicated in the struggle to make life go on, but security is the rationale, which underlies both realist and postmodern reasons for the desire to exercise, resist or transgress power in the first place.

Realism and postmodernism share a similar recognition that life involves struggle and that the concept of power serves as both a means and a site of struggle. But how we view this struggle is where we part company and resume our agonistic postures. Postmodernists view struggle in terms of an agonism, where individual's 'constitute themselves as contending identities', whereas realists conceive of it as an essential antagonism reflective of timeless modes of human nature (Connolly 1991a; Morgenthau 1946). Thus we have returned to a point of discursive incommensurability in our attempt to conceptualise power's productive capacity for ushering in structural change within the movement and construction of history. For postmodernists, the admission and recognition of vulnerability serves as a tactical way to resist and/or transgress realist power politics, whereas for realists power can mitigate or lessen vulnerability. Postmodernists focus on the survival of people in the broadest definition of the term 'security', while realists focus on the survival and security of the state, which they link to the survival of the nation and its people. But this return to an incommensurable difference is precisely the point of our discussion, because 'once historical contingency and diversity enter the analysis, opportunities for critique and creativity in discussions of political possibility increase' (Walker 1987: 267).

Notes

1 This article relies upon Foucault's understanding of disciplinary power as that which separates, analyses and differentiates individuals while also training them to become useful, orderly and docile elements of the system (1979: 170, 216).

2 The term 'structure' is used here in reference to patterns of 'transtemporal transpatial abstract universalisms' that would be 'distinguished from the mere succession of events' (Walker 1987: 75). Walker observes that structuralism is 'guided by a fundamental attachment to the principles of identity and resemblance', so, for example, 'by ignoring diversity and particularity, it is possible to establish uniformity and universality in, say, all human myths' (76–7). Thus, if one assumes that universalisms will be manifest in the collective knowledge practices that constitute stable social structures, the differences in historical collective knowledge practices and social structures become relatively unimportant.

3 While Guzzini (1993; 2000), Schmidt (2005) and Baldwin (1979) argue that contemporary realists rely on material rather than relational perspectives of power, realists always assume that knowledge of material power has relational effects. For example, Mearsheimer clearly intends power to have relational effects when he asserts that 'states pay close attention to how power is distributed among them' (2001: 34).

4 Campbell has discussed Foucault's understanding of power as an attempt by one person to control another (1998: 510).

5 For overviews of neo-classical realism, see Rose (1998); Walt (2002).

6 Interviews with Kurt Campbell, David Sanger, Joseph Wu, PBS (2001).

7 David Lampton, interview, PBS (2001).

8 Ashley (1996) discusses sovereign certitude; Shapiro (1989) discusses intertextuality; Bleiker (2001) discusses aesthetic knowledge practices.

9 Kurt Campbell, interview, PBS (2001).

10 One group in particular, the Ping-Pu Ketagalan people, led by Chen Kimman and Lin Sheng-yi, have accused the Taiwanese Government of carrying out a genocide policy against them. See Pan (2004).

11 Darby (2004) has cautioned against over-valorising the local as a site of resistance and the global as a site of domination. I agree with his observation but disagree with his conclusion that postmodernists are unaware of this dynamic. There is a great deal of ambiguity involved in processes of domination and resistance, which is precisely why I draw attention to issues of identity where closure is being deferred. The point is politicisation, which implies recognition of historical contingency and the relationality of identity in conjunction with an attitude of agonistic respect. Identity is fundamentally paradoxical because any attempt to establish identity necessarily denies difference and yet identity is radically dependent upon difference for its existence. I am arguing that as long as the situation is fluid, power remains relational and the content of freedom remains open to politicisation. See also Connolly (1991a).

12 My intent is not to replay the arguments deconstructing the state and sovereignty but to focus on the more productive and transformative possibilities within a postmodern analytic of power. See Connolly (1991b); Shapiro (1991); Walker and Mendlovitz (1990); Walker (1991); Bartelson (1995); Weber (1995).

13 Ashley and Walker (1990b: 391). Self-making in a register of freedom transpires on the margins and in the lived experiences of everyday existence. A register of freedom emerges where individuals confront the lack of a universal or totalising narrative that would help them choose between competing and overlapping identities and/or to permanently secure them. Self-making becomes possible in the space wherein we recognise the 'constructedness' of all our identities. Hutchings describes a register of freedom as a celebration of 'the instability of discursively constructed boundaries' (1999: 78).

14 Campbell (1998) discusses the radical interdependence of being and our inescapable responsibility to the other.

15 See works as diverse as Anderson (1991); Druckman (1994); Smith (1991); Wilmer (2002).

16 For example, Liao Dai-chi, a political expert at National Sun Yat-sen University of Kaohsiung argues, 'any politician has to stand with "Taiwan identity" to win election' (quoted in Kahn 2004a: A8). It is not surprising, then, that during the 2004 campaign even the Nationalist candidate, Lien Chan, used Minnanese, the Taiwanese dialect, stressed his ethnic Taiwanese background and rarely mentioned reunification.

17 See Foucault's 'The Subject and Power', where he discusses how practices of insubordination are implicated in power relations, in Faubion (2000: 326–48).

18 Dumm (1996) argues that practices of freedom are enabled by power relations; and Norris (1994) explores possibilities for autonomy, freedom and self-determination within Foucault's essay 'What is Enlightenment?' See also Joseph's (2004) discussion of the productive aspects of power as creating the conditions of possibility for freedom; Faubion's (2000) examination of how will and freedom are central to provoking power relationships; Simmons' (1995) explanation of how limits imposed within power relations provide opportunities for acts and moments of transgression.

19 Buruma (2001) discusses the 2–28 Incident, the Kaohsiung Incident and their role as foundational myths of democratic Taiwan; Tu (1996) examines the multilayered and synchronic nature of Taiwan's cultural scene; Gold (1996) examines Taiwan's rapid social and political changes and the social cleavages and movements they have spawned; S. Liao (2000) provides a postmodern argument against a purified and totalising conception of 'Tawainess'; P. Liao (2000) examines the cultural implications of Taiwan's move from the periphery of China to the margins of international politics.

20 For an examination of ambiguity, contestation and difference relating to the construction of mainland Chinese identity and the writing of history, see Dirlik (1996); Guo and He (1999); Yang (2000).

21 Litzinger (1999) discusses the interplay between Chinese governmental structural pressures and local Yao cultural practices.

15 Theory meets practice

Facets of power in the 'War on Terror'[1]

M. J. Williams

Strategy depends for success, first and most, on a sound calculation and co-ordination of the end and the means. The end must be proportioned to the total means, and the means used in gaining each intermediate end which contributes to the ultimate must be proportioned to the value and needs of that intermediate end – whether it be to gain an objective or to fulfil a contributory purpose. An excess may be as harmful as a deficiency.

B. H. Liddell Hart, October 1928

'Power' is central to the discipline of international relations (IR), but thinking about power takes place in the realm of policy as well, with governments operating in all three dimensions – winning conflicts, dominating agendas and shaping normality. At the time of writing, winning conflicts is once again at the top of the agenda. The world is observing a struggle between different political positions, crudely speaking a conflict between Islamic fundamentalists who want to impose their vision of government upon the Middle East and the 'West' which, at the very least, wants to maintain the status quo and, at best, to cultivate liberal democratic regimes in the region. In the debate on what this conflict is about, some say the core issues are development and social mobility, which cannot be achieved with guns and bombs. Others believe that the use of military force is an important component in defeating what they see as an overtly 'military' threat, the new 'fascism' of the twenty-first century.

For all of the discussion, it is widely held that this conflict is ultimately about winning 'hearts and minds', particularly within the Islamic world. This is, in some respects, a facile point. While the US National Strategy for Combating Terrorism asserts that the war on terror is 'both a battle of arms and ideas', this is no different from many previous wars (White House 2006). The Cold War was embedded in a war over ideas (communism vs. democracy), as was the Second World War (fascism vs. democracy). Looking further back, the American Revolution was a war over ideas as well. The so-called 'War on Terror' is, therefore, not the first, nor will it be the last conflict that is both a 'battle of arms and ideas'.[2] What seems clear, however, is that the current conflict is one that falls outside the boundaries of the Westphalian state system and fails to fit the traditional profile of 'war' as known in the West. This is important because many conflicts in the West over political ideas during the course of the past 300 years ended up being settled by total war, with the most notable exception being the Cold War. The 'War on Terror' is a 'war' in name only.[3] It is certainly not a war that any Western military general – from Schwarzkopf to Jackson and Zhukov to Clausewitz – would recognise. These differences in this latest war of ideas pose serious challenges to traditional scholarly and policy conceptions of power in world politics.

While most of the reflections in this volume on the meaning of power are rather abstract, these reflections are of relevance to the 'real' world. It can be safely assumed that, as Keohane and Nye noted some time ago, 'academic pens leave marks in the minds of statesmen with profound results for policy' (Keohane and Nye 1989: 4–5). While many policy-makers might feel that they need not pay heed to the theoretical debates of ivory-tower academics, in one way or another they are touched by these debates as ideas filter into, and guide their thinking: 'We carry around in our heads maps of agents' power [...] usually as tacit knowledge, which allows us some measure of prediction and control' (Lukes 2005: 65). In this regard, the insights of this volume have much to offer current understandings of world politics, including the struggle between Western liberal democracies and radical Islamic fundamentalists. To that end, this conclusion will pick up a topic dear to realists, namely the link between power and war.[4] More precisely, by linking war and power through strategy, it will suggest how some of the insights made by the contributors help to make sense of how different conceptions of power lead to different strategies employed in this 'War on Terror', and how some of them seem more successful than others.

Deconstructing the Western way of war

War is not a neutral concept – it has cultural baggage. Within the West there is a specific understanding of war. The Western Way of Warfare is a delineated concept with specific cultural features; namely, that (i) war is engaged in by states; (ii) it occurs in a specific 'theatre' – generally a pitched battlefield; (iii) the units that wage war fight against reciprocal units (infantry vs. infantry, navy vs. navy); and (iv) the opposing sides utilise similar equipment to wage war and study the same strategic thought (Keegan 1993, Coker 2002). The principles of military strategy in the West are nearly universal. Every study of strategy will recognise the eight concepts of: objective, offence, cooperation, concentration (mass), economy, manoeuvre, surprise, security, and simplicity.[5] Armed conflict in the West was, for all intents and purposes, 'symmetrical.'[6] Within the West, war came to be highly instrumental because of the social institutions such as the nation-state that developed first in the West (Coker 2002). War was the default setting for relations under a condition of Hobbesian anarchy to settle political disputes that could not be resolved with diplomacy. Clausewitz's oft-quoted 'War is a continuation of politics by other means' illustrates this nicely.

This type of conflict, and the strategic wisdom devised for it, rested on a specific understanding of the conflicting parties and their 'power'. As Brian Schmidt has illustrated, the birth of IR in the 1920s and 1930s was driven by a perceived neglect related to the study of power. While early scholars such as Carr and Morgenthau talked both about relational power and differentiated elements of national power, in the Western Way of War, power became equated with the aggregate of military expenditure, the gross national product (GNP), the size of the armed forces, the size of territory and population. This preference essentially casts aside Morgenthau's caution against supplanting political power with military or pseudo-military power, in favour of Carr's belief that military power was the most important form of power. While Schmidt outlines the variety of opinions regarding the nature of power within the realist camp, the simple reading prevailed. In the Cold War, opponents were measured and strategy devised around some 'great power' indicators, which, as Joseph Grieco has shown in this volume, remained rather inaccurate.

It is within this understanding of war and power that the USA responded to the events of 9/11. For the American Administration, the events of that September day and, indeed, previous attacks against US targets such as the World Trade Center attack in 1993 and the bombing of the USS *Cole* in Yemen in 2000 were acts of war.[7] The response to these unconventional attacks by unconventional actors were conventional military invasions of Afghanistan and Iraq. Although a great number of realists argued against the eventual invasion of Iraq in 2003 because the ideological agenda that drove Washington and London to embark on regime change in the Middle East is far removed from realist theories of IR, the understanding of power as military capabilities is shared by both neo-realism and neo-conservatism. Those who advocate other types of power and the pursuit of goals through the avoidance of war, argued neo-conservative Robert Kagan, did so because they were militarily weak and had no other choice (Kagan 2003). In turn, new security challenges are being pressed into familiar realist frameworks of IR:

> The problem of weapons of mass destruction, for example becomes the problem of Saddam Hussein and what to do about Iraq. The problem of ballistic missiles becomes the problem of Iran, Iraq, North Korea and China. Terrorism becomes the problems of 'rogue states' like Sudan and Afghanistan.
>
> (Toal 1996: 121–2)

As it now turns out, realist and neo-conservative strategic thinking about the 'war on terror' fell victim to what Nye and Keohane referred to as 'inappropriate images and ill-conceived perceptions of world politics' (Keohane and Nye 1989: 4–5). The principal reason that military force fails to bring about a solution to these security challenges and a 'victory' in the ongoing 'war on terror' is that the opponent is very different from a state actor and chooses to act outside of the state system and the traditional understanding of war and power held in most Western capitals. Furthermore, their grievances cannot be addressed or eliminated through armed conflict. Rather than the linear progression of politics in the Westphalian system – political dispute, diplomacy, diplomatic failure, war, negotiations, conclusion of disagreement (or postponement until the next war) – this ongoing political dialogue is non-linear, combining facets of war with facets of politics, and blurring Clausewitz's line where war is a continuation of politics by other means. Liddell-Hart's prediction that 'In the future it is likely that, to an increasing extent, war will be waged by suggestion – by words and not by weapons, propaganda replacing the projectile' has more or less come true (Liddell Hart 1999: 176).

Of course, the shift from projectiles to propaganda is not an entirely new or recent phenomenon. There has always been a psychological aspect to war, and Carr and Morgenthau both discussed the ability to shape opinions. But never before have Western governments been engaged in a war of this exact nature.[8] As Geoffrey Parker argues, because 'high technology wars, with their emphasis on arduous training, massive logistical back-up, and copious state-of-the-art weaponry, make demands few societies can meet' (Parker 2005: 421), less conventionally powerful actors will choose a strategy that seeks to exploit alternative forms of power. In the West, this type of warfare is often called 'irregular warfare' and has generally been viewed as savage because it runs counter to the tendency towards 'humane warfare' prevalent within Western societies in the late twentieth and early twenty-first centuries (Coker 2001). Practitioners such as British General Sir Rupert Smith phrase it without the normative undertones: 'war as cognitively known to most non-combatants, war as a battle in a field between men and machinery, war as a massive deciding event in a dispute in international affairs: such war no longer exists' (Smith 2005: 1).

The traditional image of the enemy and its capabilities remains strong within the conception of war and 'victory' in Washington. No one will soon forget the image of President Bush landing on the USS *Abraham Lincoln* to deliver a speech on the US victory in Iraq under a large banner proclaiming 'Mission Accomplished', which highlights the lack of understanding by some in Washington about the nature of modern war and the ability of military force to effect political change. US policy-makers have slowly come to realise that a quick victory in a classic ground war does not equal a long-term political victory. The traditional Western way of war and its associated concepts of victory and power are less useful in understanding the nature of conflict within the current 'War on Terror'.[9] An analysis of the deconstruction of the Western Way of War by Islamic fundamentalists illustrates that Islamists grasped the necessity to utilise appropriate means, in line with their capabilities, to effect goals. Radical fundamentalists correctly assessed the situation and employed a strategy that would maximise their 'power' relative to the USA, while at the same time reducing the advantages on the USA in terms of traditional power resources.

The rise of the 'virtual' battlefield

> I make the enemy see my strengths as weaknesses and my weaknesses as strengths while I cause his strengths to become weaknesses and discover where he is not strong.
>
> Sun Tzu

Due to its status as the 'lonely superpower', it is fair to say that the USA can most likely prevail in a direct military engagement with any state on the planet. For this reason, in 1999, the Chinese military leadership allegedly argued to the country's leaders that China could not engage the USA within the traditional Western context of war, but should instead use a combination of 'terrorism, drug trafficking, environmental degradation and computer virus propagation' to achieve their strategic objectives (*Washington Post*, 8 August 1999, p. 1). If this is the tack the Chinese military leadership has taken for the time being, it is not surprising that the terms of confrontation chosen by Al Qaida's leadership circumvent the military and economic superiority of the USA as well. Non-state 'actors' like Al Qaida have to challenge the traditional form of conflict in the West if they are to score victories in a Westphalian system that is inherently disempowering them, to adapt Erik Ringmar's argument to this argument. Rather than pursuing objectives solely through violence, the Al Qaida leadership coupled violent acts with media savvy, drawing on soft-power resources and using 'discourse as capability' (Holzscheiter 2005). To understand such capability, according to Holzscheiter, one needs to look at how language alters social structures and how the alteration of structures can empower or disempower non-state actors to achieve their goals. Her view is that non-governmental organisations 'stand out as those participants in global governance whose credibility, respect and influence is to a large part founded on nonmaterial power resources and their successful enactment' (Holzscheiter 2005: 726). This view can be readily applied to the Al Qaida movement. To understand how, one first needs to acknowledge the political rationale of the Al Qaida cause.

A great deal has been written on the history and development of Al Qaida and the rise of fundamentalist Islamic radicals. It is therefore sufficient to say that the ultimate goal of the Al Qaida movement is the restoration of the Islamic caliphate (Kepel 2004; Devji 2005; Burke 2004). Barring this, the Al Qaida leadership would at least like to see Muslim states across the Greater Middle East under the rule of Islamic law. Islamic fundamentalists have tried for years to effect political change in the region through a variety of means, but they have not been successful. Previous attempts to create political change in the Middle East dealt the radicals two lessons. The first lesson drawn from this experience was that to effect political change the radicals would have to win the 'hearts and minds' of Muslims to harness broad support for their goals. The second lesson was that to address the issue of the 'near enemy' (corrupt Arab states) the fight must be taken to the 'far away enemy' (the USA) that supports these Arab states in the interest of regional stability (Brachman and McCants 2006; Kepel 2004). To achieve this end, a strategy was required that would reduce the power of the USA to support current Arab governments, while at the same time drawing upon the strengths of Al Qaida.

Without a state to ascribe blame to, it is more difficult for policy-makers working within a Cold War paradigm to use diplomatic prowess, economic power or military might to address terrorism. Al Qaida managed to negotiate and alleviate some of the bias in the system through the creation of an alternative narrative. The USA responded to 9/11 by invading Afghanistan, in line with the Western narrative of war, but the intervening years have illustrated the futility of this approach. Weak Islamic fundamentalist groups only further reduced the power of the USA by turning the Western way of warfare on its head, marginalising the military superiority of America. While the Al Qaida movement uses 'irregular' military force, the jihad is not premised on the use of military force alone. There is no engagement of like units using similar tactics and military force is not used in a specific area, but globally. All of these tenets make it extremely difficult for the USA and its allies to counter Islamic fundamentalists using military means. In turn, Bin Laden and his followers successfully empowered, via discursive practices, a group of individuals in a fight against a global superpower despite an international system that is structurally biased against such acts. In this strategy of empowerment, the military means are only one small ingredient in a much larger recipe tailored to win on the virtual battlefield.

While propaganda has always been a part of war, it has been an accessory rather than the principle focus. The rise of the virtual battlefield began in earnest during the Vietnam era. Although the media has always been able to comment on wars, the Vietnam War represented a watershed, as it was the first conflict to be widely televised – thereby affording it the capability of shaping perceptions in a way never before encountered. This early, and by comparison primitive, 'virtual war' only had one major front – the US domestic audience. The reporting was intended for an American audience. Although the USA was winning the war on the ground, US domestic support continued to plummet as the violence was brought home day after day in Technicolor on the evening news. The US leadership, even after extensive time in the field, failed to appreciate that the application of conventional military power to the conflict in Vietnam would not work against the irregular tactics of the Viet Cong. Washington overlooked the basic political nature of the situation and the fact that the weaker North Vietnamese would not fight on Western terms – making the conflict an inevitable loss given the strategy employed by the USA. Finally, the Americans did not fully understand the psychological side of the war and the effect the war would have on the domestic population's willingness to endure casualties (Johnson and Tierney 2006). As a result, the US developed the infamous 'body bag' syndrome – that is, the US public became intolerant of casualties in 'unnecessary' wars, which ultimately led to the collapse of domestic support for US policy in Vietnam.

The virtual battlefield became more advanced during the 1990s, with the rise of the CNN effect – the ability for twenty-four-hour news broadcasts to shape world politics. No longer were cameras and reporters just on the battlefield, they were also beaming footage back in real-time. This development made it even more pressing for governments to recognise the best way to remedy conflicts with as few casualties (on both sides) as possible. Humane warfare became increasingly important in this all-access information age (Coker 2001). The atrocities of yesteryear could not be tolerated or covered up in an age of real-time global media. With the information revolution of the late 1990s, this brief monopoly of accredited news agencies ended. Not only do non-Western broadcasters such as Al Jazeera International (AJI) challenge coverage of world events by CNN or BBC, but practically anyone can enter and affect the information world (Tatham 2006; Gowing 2006). The dominance of the state has been further reduced by the entry of the individual into the global narrative – the mass resources of the state or even a media corporation are no longer necessary. In an era of email, blogs, youtube, blackberries, digital cameras, cell phones, palm-sized video recorders, talk radio, and twenty-four-hour news, as well as a network to link all of these various components in real-time, it is now impossible to even attempt to control the flow of information or disinformation. As Nik Gowing has written, 'The new matrix of real-time recording and uplink technology means that even the most remote, hostile and (in theory) operationally secure locations are transparent' (Gowing 2006: 16). This point has not eluded policy-makers. Donald Rumsfeld highlighted this issue in early 2006 during a speech to the Council on Foreign Relations where he stated that the US Government still functions 'as a five and dime store in an eBay world' (Rumsfeld 2006). To fight this kind of war, the USA would need to adapt. Yet whereas the USA framed the conflict in line with its overwhelming military capabilities, Al Qaida's strategy is not reliant on victory through military force but via a discursive and pictorial narrative aimed at discrediting the legitimacy of the USA in the Middle East. To do this, its strategists effectively exploited the information revolution to wage the world's first cyber-jihad.

Power via narrative on the 'virtual' battlefield

Without the use of twenty-first-century information technologies, it is doubtful that Al Qaida would have been able to franchise out its basic ideology to the extent it has. Irregular warfare would have made victory difficult for America and her allies no matter what, but technology has made the ideology and the global insurgency self-perpetuating in a way never before seen. The Internet has been utilised for three main reasons: recruitment and fundraising, training/instruction and operational planning. Beyond these practical applications, the Internet allows Al Qaida to perpetuate a specific narrative that it then bolsters with footage from the conflicts in Iraq and Afghanistan. This narrative is based around three points. First, the West is 'implacably' hostile to Islam; second, 'the only way to address this threat and the only language the West understands is violence'; and, finally, that jihad is therefore the only option (Hoffmann 2006). Here one can see that what nineteenth-century anarchists called the 'propaganda of the deed' is crucial (Conrad 1963). This is where the symbolic component comes into play. 'The felling of the twin towers in New York and the filmed slaughter of "infidels" in Iraq have been Al Qaeda's force multipliers' (Stevens 2006: 15). Al Qaida not only humiliated America but also utilised the military response to advance its own purpose (see Saurette 2003). The images of British troops abusing Iraqis, of Americans burning bodies in Afghanistan and of Islamic radicals avenging Muslim deaths by beheading Americans all serve to perpetuate a skewed view of the insurgency in Iraq and Afghanistan in favour of the cause. This phenomenon is, according to Audrey Kurth Cronin, the new *levée en masse* (Cronin 2006). Islamic radicals use the Internet and other media outlets as a form of cyber-mobilisation. They are able to get new recruits into the theatre of war to wage an insurgency that perpetuates new material for their media campaign. Not only does this campaign animate disaffected Muslims to act against the Anglo-American coalition in a violent manner, it also undermines domestic support in the USA and UK for the military operations.

Whether Al Qaida followed a clear strategy or creatively adapted to given dynamics, it certainly appeared to set the agenda in the virtual battlefield. Whereas US policy-makers, aided by the mass media, constructed an image of Al Qaida as irrational and evil 'cavemen' (Ling and Agathangelou 2005), these very 'cavemen' coordinated and continue to inspire sophisticated attacks against the 'symbolic capital' (see Hassdorf, this volume) of the USA by entangling it in a web of conflict. The Al Qaida movement achieves this by tapping into memories of colonial victimhood, rhetoric about a clash of civilisations and an allegedly anti-Muslim West. Rhetoric affects not just social understanding – how Muslims, both radical and non-radical – have come to see the West but also how increasing numbers act vis-à-vis the West. Jihad, as Faisal Devji wrote, becomes a site of sociability. 'For most Muslims, as for most people, the jihad site is experienced visually, as a landscape initially made available by way of the international media and then redacted in conversation, posters, literature, art-work and the like' (Devji 2005: 93). Rather than jihad being an abstract phenomenon that occurs elsewhere, the information revolution has allowed participants far beyond the actual 'battlefield' to become participants in the action. The empowerment of the Al Qaida cause has occurred on the heels of the information revolution and the subsequent ability to make the conflict virtual and accessible to the world. This empowerment is now more crucial than ever because the Al Qaida 'organisation' as it existed pre-9/11 is no more. The destruction of the Al Qaida training camps in Afghanistan and the disruption of its organisational structure through a variety of military and non-military methods by the USA and its allies, however, has not meant the dissolution of Al Qaida but merely its reincarnation as a movement or ideology, a 'franchise' rather than a single outlet (Simpson 2006; see also Burke 2004). To use John Gaventa's terminology, the Al Qaida leadership successfully created a new participatory space open to a large number of sympathisers sharing no more than a religious conviction and anti-American sentiment.

Janice Bially Mattern's question, 'What makes an idea attractive or appealing in the first place?' remains unanswered. This is a question that Washington must answer if it is to devise a proper strategy for confronting the Al Qaida ideology. Are the radicals' ideas really that appealing, or are they just coming off better in light of their ability to create discord and insecurity, which is amplified through a sophisticated media campaign (*Los Angeles Times* 2006)? The question of how to win 'hearts and minds' has moved to the centre of attention and is echoed by Steven Lukes when he asks 'exactly how do agents succeed in wining the hearts and minds of those subject to their influence – by wielding power over them or by contributing to their empowerment?' For those involved in a war of ideas, these are important questions as between the lines there seems to be an overly self-confident bias in much of the soft-power literature that overlooks what is attractive and why. While Westerners may see values like democracy, human rights and individual opportunities as deeply seductive, it is questionable as to their appeal outside of the West. One might argue that Al Qaida fits the description of an 'ethical' actor within the global civil society described by Ronnie Lipschutz (this volume), it just happens to have other ethics than the West (see also Behnke 2004). If radical Islamists can create a normative framework akin to the kind that Europe is trying to create, as examined in the contribution by Manners and Diez, there is serious cause for concern among Western nations. War (however defined) and conflict may have lost their appeal in much of the Western world (certainly in Europe), but it is not difficult to see how partaking in a symbolic confrontation with the world's military hegemon is an empowering experience for those who buy into the Al Qaida ideology. As Chris Hedges pointed out, 'war is a force that gives us meaning' (Hedges 2002).

> The enduring attraction of war is this: Even with its destruction and carnage it can give us what we long for in life. It can give us purpose, meaning, a reason for living [...] war is an enticing elixir. It gives us resolve, a cause. It allows us to be noble. And those who have the least

meaning in their lives, the impoverished refugees in Gaza, the disenfranchised North African immigrants in France, even the legions of
young who live in the splendid indolence and safety of the indus-
trialized world are all susceptible to war's appeal.

(Hedges 2002: 3–4)

There can be no doubt as to the extent of latent power within the communities of disenfranchised Muslims that has been unleashed by the discursive
constructions of the Al Qaida movement and new norms this discourse has
created. The current narrative legitimises the fundamentalist struggle that
sees actions outside of the state, the killing of innocents and the destruction
of property as acceptable norms. It is a direct challenge to domestic and
international politics norms of the Westphalian system, but it is not of the
same magnitude as the challenge presented by Nazi Germany, as some
White House officials would like one to believe.

While most of this discussion has centred on how virtual war animates
believers in Al Qaida, the virtual war not only takes place in the so-called
'Muslim world' but in Western populations as well. Former UK Secretary of
State for Defense John Reid noted this, saying, 'Al Qaida's view is that the
western media is a virtual battleground where the swaying of public opinion
away from support for our campaigns could lead to a swift victory and a quick
way of undermining our public morale'.[10] The insurgents have time on their
hands and they will use this time against the West in the true tradition of
Mao's protracted warfare. It is a tactic that has served past insurgents well, and
it works. Democracies can only wage war for a certain period of time, particularly if the war is not seen as a core threat to the security of the nation.
Public support for the war in Iraq in the USA has dropped from 86 per cent in
2003 to 28 percent in May 2006. Furthermore, in Britain, 55 per cent of the
population thinks that troops should leave the country within the next twelve
months.[11] During the May 2005 UK General Election, Tony Blair's Labour
Party suffered at the polls, in large part because of his decision to invade Iraq.
US President George W. Bush saw a rollback of the Republican domination of
Congress that began in 1994, losing both the House and the Senate to the
Democrats during the 2006 mid-term elections. A staggering percentage voted
for Democrats to voice their discontent with the war (Nagourney and Thee
2006: A1). By April 2007, the Democratic-controlled Congress was in the
process of putting legislation to the President that mandates a withdrawal of
US forces over the course of two years. The virtual war undermined support at
home and it animated support of the insurgents.

Future strategy and power

Strategy is too often considered to comprise merely military factors, to
the overshadowing of the political and economic, with which it is
interwoven. The fallacy has been responsible for incalculable damage to

the fabric of warring nations. When such critics speak of strategy, they are thinking almost solely of the military pieces on the chessboard of war. Between logistical strategy and chess there is a distinct analogy. But on a higher plane, and with a far wider scope, is grand strategy.

B. H. Liddell Hart, October 1925

Military capabilities have not lost their effect. The question is, rather, whether their effect is beneficial if the conflict in which they are employed involves a relationship where power is measured, and works, in another dimension. What is apparent in this current conflict is that Western strategists seem to have forgotten that the fungibility of power resources is low and that the 'power to' invade Baghdad has little bearing on holding 'power over' Al Qaida. As Steven Lukes has pointed out; 'merely possessing or controlling the means of [military] power is not the same as being powerful' (Lukes 2006). It would certainly behove policy-makers to take to heart the view of the ancient Greeks put forward by Ned Lebow in this volume. The 'benign hegemony' of the USA and the power that position confers, is linked to authority derived from honour. This status is not obtained through the size of the armed forces alone. An overreliance on military power and a desire to 'control' world politics has come off as exceedingly ineffective against an opponent who may only operate on the third dimension of power but, to use Gaventa's typology, who does so on various levels, local to global, and by creative use of popular spaces held together by anti-American, West-versus-Islam narrative. This shows a distinct awareness of Luke's third dimension of power, 'to shape, influence or determine others' beliefs and desires, thereby securing their compliance' (Lukes 2005, Brachman and McCants 2006). While Washington gradually realised that US actions were 'misunderstood' when seen in a different context, Al Qaida has also been effective in catching US 'public diplomacy' off guard. While many analysts are now quick to point out that the USA needs to use more soft power, one must take seriously Joseph Nye's reminder in this volume that incorporating soft power into strategy is difficult.

Perhaps American and British policy-makers and academics should spend more time looking at how the 'war on terror' came into existence. While the US chose to frame the events of 9/11 as an opening volley of what is now the 'Long War', this was not an inevitable decision. While the 'war on terror' narrative might have empowered Washington to act in a specific way, allowing military force to retaliate against Afghanistan and pursue terrorists (from Kabul to Baghdad) using tanks and tomahawks, it also helped create the perfect foil for the narrative constructed by Bin Laden and the Al Qaida movement. In that sense, by misreading the power relationship they were being placed in, the USA and its allies became participants in, and strengthened, the contours of a space of which they were not sufficiently aware. The declaration of war may have brought meaning into a post-9/11 world, yet it has ultimately proved rather disempowering for the USA. That is the paradox of power in the twenty-first century that needs careful consideration by scholars and policy-makers alike.

Acknowledgement

I would like to thank Felix Berenskoetter, Stephanie Carvin, Kate Clouston, Christopher Coker, Michael Cox and Bastian Giegerich for their helpful feedback on this chapter.

Notes

1 This chapter will use the term 'War on Terror', rather than 'War on Terrorism' as the former is the choice term of the Bush White House. However, the terminology is not shared by most Europeans, who prefer to call it a 'fight'. See Berenskoetter and Giegerich (2006).
2 An important clarification is necessary here. The 'War on Terror' is not the first large scale war that is both 'a battle of arms and ideas', but this is not to undermine the fact that 'winning hearts and minds' is necessary for success in the on-going counter-insurgency campaigns in Afghanistan and Iraq. The uniqueness of counter-insurgency tactics should not be confused with the more generic similarities of the strategic level comparison.
3 See Reid (2004) for an interesting discussion of Foucault's view on power and the relationship to Clausewitzian strategic thought.
4 Many of these points do overlap with other forms of war, but this list is *sui generis* of the West.
5 It is important that here the West is defined along the lines of 'Western Civilisation' rather than the East–West conflict of the Cold War. The Cold War was, at its core, a conflict of Western civilisation over shared political ideologies – i.e., Marxism vs. Liberalism. The Soviets engaged in the same type of war as the 'West' of NATO reflecting this shared culture.
6 Based on interviews with US officials in London and Washington between September 2003 and August 2006.
7 While many are tempted to draw comparisons to Vietnam, such comparisons overlook the multitude of differences between the two conflicts: (i) the campaign in Vietnam against the USA was led by a hierarchical, Maoist style organisations; (ii) the combatants shared the same end goals; (iii) the tactics of the Viet Cong were overtly irregular military tactics – there was no coordinated media/information campaign. In the War on Terror (including Iraq) there is (i) no hierarchically organised opponent; (ii) there is no shared end goal among the various groups; (iii) the tactics are a collection of irregular military operations coupled with strategic communications. Even if the outcome may be similar (US failure), the reasons are very different (see Record and Terrill 2004).
8 This piece does not posit the end of the Western Way of Warfare or demise of state-based warfare but merely a shift on the current strategic environment away from such conflicts towards more irregular conflicts. This does not mean such wars will not one day return.
9 Poll: Most Still Think Iraq War a Mistake, CNN International, http://www.cnn.com/2006/US/06/12/iraq.poll/index.html.
10 Available online at http://www.mod.uk/DefenceInternet/DefenceNews/DefencePolicyAndBusiness/WeMustBeslowerToCondemnQuickerToUnderstandTheForcesJohnReid.htm.

Bibliography

Ackerman, J. (2004) 'Co-Governance for Accountability: Beyond "Exit" and "Voice"', *World Development*, 32 (3): 447–63.

Adamson, W. L. (1987–88) 'Gramsci and the Politics of Civil Society', *Praxis International* 7 (Winter): 320–9.

—— (1980) *Hegemony and Revolution*, Berkeley, Calif.: University of California Press.

Adler, E. (1987) *The Power of Ideology*, Berkeley, Calif.: University of California Press.

—— (2002) 'Constructivism and International Relations', in W. Carlsnaes, T. Risse and B. A. Simmons (eds) *Handbook of International Relations*, London: Sage, pp. 95–118.

Adler, E. and Barnett, M. N. (eds) (1998) *Security Communities*, Cambridge: Cambridge University Press.

Adler, E., Crawford, B., Bicci, F., and Del Sarto, R. (eds) (2006) *The Convergence of Civilizations?*, Toronto: University of Toronto Press.

Aeschylus (2003) *The Oresteia*, trans. A. Shapiro and P. Burian, Oxford: Oxford University Press.

Agathangelou, A. (2004) *The Global Political Economy of Sex*, New York: Palgrave Macmillan.

Agathangelou, A. and Ling, L. M. H (2005) 'Power and Play through Poisies: Reconstructing Self and Other in the 9/11 Commission Report', *Millennium*, 33 (3): 826–55.

Agnew, J. (2003) *Geopolitics*, 2nd edn, London: Routledge.

Allison, J. W. (1979) 'Thucydides and Polypragmosyne', *American Journal of Ancient History*, 4: 10–22.

Alvesson, M. and Sköldberg, K. (2000) *Reflexive Methodology*, London: Sage.

Amato, J. D., Morris, S. and Chin, H. S. (2002) 'Communication and Monetary Policy', paper prepared for the OXREP issue on Games and Coordination, October. Online. Available at http://www.nuff.ox.ac.uk/users/Shin/PDF/OXREP fin.pdf (accessed 14 October 2004).

Anderson, B. (1991) *Imagined Communities*, London: Verso.

Arendt, H. (1958) *The Human Condition*, 2nd edn, Chicago, Ill.: University of Chicago Press.

—— (1970) *On Violence*, London: Penguin.

Aron, R. (1966) *Peace and War*, London: Weidenfeld & Nicolson.

—— (1986/1964) 'Macht, power, puissance: prose démocratique ou poésie démonaique?', *Archives européennes de sociologie* (European Journal of Sociology), 5: 25–51, reprinted in S. Lukes (ed.) *Power*, Oxford: Blackwell, pp. 253–77.

Aronoff, M. J. (1998) 'The Politics of Collective Identity', *Reviews in Anthropology*, 27: 71–85.

Arquilla, J. and Ronfeldt, D. (1999) *The Emergence of Noopolitik*, Santa Monica, Calif.: RAND.

Art, R. J. (1999) 'Force and Fungibility Reconsidered', *Security Studies*, 8 (4): 18–89.

Ashley, R. K. (1986) 'The Poverty of Neorealism', in R. Keohane (ed.) *Neorealism and its Critics*, New York: Columbia University Press, pp. 255–300.

—— (1987) 'The Geopolitics of Geopolitical Space: Towards a Critical Social Theory of International Politics', *Alternatives*, 12 (4): 403–34.

—— (1988) 'Untying the Sovereign State: A Double Reading of the Anarchy Problematique', *Millennium*, 17 (2): 227–62.

—— (1989a) 'Imposing International Purpose: Notes on a Problematic of Governance', in E.-O. Czempiel and J. N. Rosenau (eds) *Global Changes and Theoretical Challenges*, Lexington, Mass.: Lexington Books, pp. 251–90.

—— (1989b) 'Living on Border Lines: Man, Poststructuralism, and War', in J. Der Derian and M. Shapiro (eds) *International/Intertextual Relations*, New York: Lexington Books, pp. 259–321.

—— (1995) 'The Powers of Anarchy: Theory, Sovereignty, and the Domestication of Global Life', in J. Der Derian (ed.) *International Theory Critical Investigations*, New York: NYU Press, pp. 94–128.

—— (1996) 'The Achievements of Post-structuralism', in S. Smith, K. Booth and M. Zalewski (eds) *International Theory: Positivism and Beyond*, Cambridge: Cambridge University Press, pp. 240–53.

Ashley, R. K, and Walker, R. B. J. (1990a) 'Speaking the Language of Exile: Dissident Thought in International Studies', *International Studies Quarterly*, 34 (3): 259–68.

—— (1990b) 'Reading Dissidence/Writing the Discipline: Crisis and the Question of Sovereignty in International Studies', *International Studies Quarterly*, 34 (3): 367–416.

Avineri, S. (1972) *Hegel's Theory of the Modern State*, London: Cambridge University Press.

Axelrod, R. (1984) *The Evolution of Cooperation*, New York: Basic Books.

Bachrach, P. and Baratz, M.S. (1962) 'The Two Faces of Power', *American Political Science Review*, 56 (4): 947–52.

—— (1963) 'Decisions and Nondecisions: An Analytical Framework', *American Political Science Review*, 57 (3): 641–51.

—— (1970) *Power and Poverty: Theory and Practice*, New York: Oxford University Press.

Baker, K. M. (1990) *Inventing the French Revolution*, Cambridge: Cambridge University Press.

Bakhtin, M. (1984) *Problems of Dostoevsky's Poetics*, Minneapolis, Minn.: University of Minnesota Press.

Baldwin, D. (1979) 'Power Analysis and World Politics: New Trends versus Old Tendencies', *World Politics*, 31 (2): 161–94.

—— (1985) *Economic Statecraft*. Princeton, NJ: Princeton University Press.

—— (1989) *Paradoxes of Power*. New York: Basic Blackwell.

—— (ed.) (1993) *Neorealism and Neoliberalism*. New York: Columbia University Press.

—— (1999) 'Force, Fungibility, and Influence', *Security Studies*, 8 (4): 173–83.

—— (2002) 'Power and International Relations', in W. Carlsnaes, T. Risse and B. Simmons (eds) *Handbook of International Relations*, London: Sage, pp. 177–91.

Balfour, R. (2006) 'Principles of Democracy and Human Rights', in S. Lucarelli and I. Manners (eds) *Values and Principles in European Union Foreign Policy*, London: Routledge, pp. 114–29.

Balibar, E. (2003) 'Europe: Vanishing Mediator', *Constellations*, 10 (3): 312–38.

Barberis, N. and Thaler, R. (2002) 'A Survey of Behavioral Finance', NBER Working Paper 9222, Cambridge, Mass.: National Bureau of Economic Research.

Barkin, S. J. (2004) 'Time Horizons and Multilateral Enforcement in International Cooperation', *International Studies Quarterly*, 48 (2): 363–82.

Barnes, B. (1988) *The Nature of Power*, Cambridge: Polity Press.

Barnett, M. and Duvall, R. (2005a) 'Power in International Politics', *International Organization*, 59 (1): 39–75.

—— (eds) (2005b) *Power in Global Governance*, Cambridge: Cambridge University Press.

Barnett, M. and Finnemore, M. (2004) 'The Politics, Power, and Pathologies of International Organizations', *International Organization*, 53 (4): 699–732.

Baron, M. (2003) 'Manipulativeness,' *Proceedings and Addresses of the American Philosophical Association*, 77 (2): 37–54.

Barry, B. (ed.) (1976) *Power and Political Theory*, London: John Wiley.

—— (1988) 'The Uses of Power', in B. Barry (ed.) *Democracy, Power and Justice*, Oxford: Clarendon Press, pp. 307–21. First published 1987.

Bartelson, J. (1995) *A Genealogy of Sovereignty*, Cambridge: Cambridge University Press.

Batliwala, S. (2002) 'Grassroots Movements As Transnational Actors: Implications for Global Civil Society', *Voluntas: International Journal of Voluntary and Non-profit Organizations*, 13 (4): 393–409.

Batliwala, S. and Brown, D. L. (eds) (2006) *Transnational Civil Society*, Bloomfield: Kumarian Press.

BBC News (2002) 'Jordan Praises US Stance', 1 February. Available at <http://news.bbc.co.uk/1/hi/world/middle_east/1796265.stm> (accessed 31 March 2005).

Beck, U. (2000) *What is Globalisation?*, Cambridge: Polity Press.

—— (2005) *Power in the Global Age*, Cambridge: Polity Press.

Bendix, R. (1960) *Max Weber: An Intellectual Portrait*, London: Heinemann.

Benedetti, F. and Washburn, J. L. (1999) 'Drafting the International Criminal Court Treaty: Two Years to Rome and an Afterword on the Rome Diplomatic Conference', *Global Governance*, 5 (1): 1–37.

Bennett, D. S., Gelpi, C. and Huth, P. (1992), 'System Uncertainty, Risk Propensity, and International Conflict among the Great Powers', *Journal of Conflict Resolution*, 36 (3): 504–6.

—— (1993), 'The Escalation of Great Power Militarized Disputes: Testing Rational Deterrence Theory and Structural Realism', *American Political Science Review*, 87 (3): 609–23.

Bennett, D. S. and Stam, A. C. (2004) *The Behavioral Origins of War*, Ann Arbor, Mich.: University of Michigan Press.

Berenskoetter, F. (2005) 'Mapping the Mind Gap: A Comparison of US and European Security Strategies', *Security Dialogue*, 36 (1): 71–92.

Berenskoetter, F. and Giegerich B. (2006) 'What 'War on Terror' Are We Talking About? A Response to Alistair Shepherd', *International Politics*, 43 (1): 93–104.

Best, J. (2003) 'From the Top-Down: The New Financial Architecture and the Re-embedding of Global Finance', *New Political Economy*, 8 (3): 263–384.

Beinhart, L. (2004) 'The "War on Terror" Badly Needs a Total Rewrite', *Newsday*, Long Island, New York. 1 October.

Beyers, M. (1999) *Custom, Power, and the Power of Rules*, Cambridge: Cambridge University Press.

Bially Mattern, J. (2005) *Ordering International Politics*, New York: Routledge.

Biernacki, R. (2000) 'Language and the Shift from Signs to Practices in Cultural Inquiry', *History and Theory*, 39 (3): 289–310.

Blair, A. (2002) *Saving the Pound?* London: Prentice Hall.

Blau, P. (1964) *Exchange and Power in Social Life*, New York: John Wiley & Sons.

Bleiker, R. (2000) *Popular Dissent, Human Agency, and Global Politics*, Cambridge: Cambridge University Press.

—— (2001) 'The Aesthetic Turn in International Political Theory', *Millennium*, 30 (3): 509–33.

Bloom, W. (1990) *Personal Identity, National Identity, and International Relations*, Cambridge: Cambridge University Press.

Blyth, M. (2002) *Great Transformations*, Cambridge: Cambridge University Press.

Bordo, S. (2003) *Unbearable Weight*, Berkeley, Calif.: University of California Press.

Bourdieu, P. (1968) 'Structuralism and Theory of Sociological Knowledge', *Social Research*, 35 (4): 681–706.

—— (1977) *Outline of a Theory of Practice*, trans. Richard Nice, Cambridge: Cambridge University Press.

—— (1984) *Homo academicus*, Paris: Les Éditions de Minuit.

—— (1989) *Noblesse d'état: grandes écoles et esprit de corps*, Paris: Les Éditions de Minuit.

—— (1990) *The Logic of Practice*, trans. Richard Nice, Stanford, Calif.: Stanford University Press.

—— (1992) *The Logic of Practice*, Palo Alto, Calif.: Stanford University Press.

—— (1993) *Language and Symbolic Power*, Cambridge, Mass.: Harvard University Press.

Bourdieu, P. and Passeron, J.-C. (1977) *Reproduction in Education, Society and Culture*, London: Sage Publications.

—— (1979) *The Inheritors: French Students and their Relation to Culture*, Chicago, Ill.: University of Chicago Press.

Bourdieu, P. and Wacquant, L. J. D. (1992) *An Invitation to Reflexive Sociology*, Chicago, Ill.: University of Chicago Press.

Bozeman, A. B. (1960) *Politics and Culture in International History*, Princeton, NJ: Princeton University Press.

Brachman J. M. and McCants, W. F. (2006) 'Stealing Al Qa'ida's Playbook', Combating Terrorism Centre, US Military Academy West Point, February. Available online at http://www.ctc.usma.edu/Stealing%20Al-Qai'da's%20Playbook%20–%20CTC.pdf (accessed 10 November 2006).

Bremer, S. and Singer, J. D. (1972) 'Major Power War, 1820–1965', in B. R. Russett (ed.) *Peace, War, and Numbers*, Beverly Hills, Calif.: Sage Publications.

Bretherton, C. and Vogler, J. (2006) *The European Union as a Global Actor*, 2nd edn, London: Routledge.

Brock, K., Cornwall, A. and Gaventa, J. (2001) 'Power, Knowledge and Political Spaces in the Framing of Poverty Policy', IDS Working Paper 143, Brighton: Institute of Development Studies.

Brock, K., McGee, R. and Gaventa, J. (eds) (2004) *Unpacking Policy*, Kampala: Fountain Press.

Brookes, P. (2006) *Iran: Our Military Options*, Washington, DC: Heritage Foundation.

Brooks, S. G. (1997) 'Dueling Realisms', *International Organization*, 51 (3): 445–77.

Brooks, S. G. and Wohlforth, W. C. (2000–1), 'Power, Globalization and the End of the Cold War', *International Security*, 25 (3): 5–53.

—— (2002) 'American Primacy in Perspective', *Foreign Affairs*, 81 (4): 20–33.

—— (2005) 'Hard Times for Soft Balancing', *International Security*, 30 (1): 72–108.

Brown, A. (1996) *The Gorbachev Factor*, Oxford: Oxford University Press.

Brown, C. (2002) *Sovereignty, Rights, and Justice*, Cambridge: Polity Press.

Brubaker, R. (1985) 'Rethinking Classical Theory: The Sociological Vision of Pierre Bourdieu', *Theory and Society* 14 (6): 745–75.

Bukovansky, M. (2002) *Legitimacy and Power Politics*, Princeton, NJ: Princeton University Press.

Bulmer, M. (1979) 'Concepts in the Analysis of Qualitative Data', *Sociological Review*, 27 (4): 651–77.

Burke, A. (2002) 'Aporias of Security', *Alternatives*, 27 (1): 1–27.

Burke, J. (2004) *Al Qaeda the True Story of Radical Islam*, London: I. B. Tauris.

Buruma, I. (2001) *Bad Elements*, New York: Random House.

Bush, G. W. (2001) Address to a Joint Session of Congress and the American People, 20 September.

Butler, J. (1997) *The Psychic Life of Power*, New York: Routledge.

Buzan, B. (1996) 'The Timeless Wisdom of Realism?', in K. Booth, S. Smith and M. Zalewski (eds) *International Theory: Positivism and Beyond*, Cambridge: Cambridge University Press, pp. 47–65.

Buzan, B., Wæver, O. and de Wilde, J. (1998) *Security: A New Framework for Analysis*, Boulder, Col.: Lynne Rienner.

Byman, D. and Pollack, K. (2001) 'Let Us Now Praise Famous Men: Bringing the Statesman Back In', *International Security*, 25 (4): 107–46.

Caillois, R. (2001) *Man and the Sacred*, Urbana, Ill.: University of Illinois Press. First published 1939.

Callaghy, T. M., Kassimir, R. and Latham, R. (2001) *Intervention and Transnationalism in Africa*, Cambridge: Cambridge University Press.

Campbell, D. (1998a) 'Why Fight: Humanitarianism, Principles, and Post-structuralism', *Millennium*, 27 (3): 497–521.

—— (1998b) *Writing Security*, 2nd edn, Minneapolis, Minn.: University of Minnesota Press.

Carporaso, J. (1978) 'Dependence, Dependency, and Power in the Global System: A Structural and Behavioral Analysis', *International Organization*, 32 (1): 2–43.

Carr, E. H. (1964) *The Twenty Years' Crisis*, New York: Harper & Row.

—— (2001) *The Twenty Years' Crisis*, with an introduction by M. Cox, Basingstoke: Palgrave. First published 1945.

Cashore, B., Auld, G. and Newsome, D. (2004) *Governing through Markets*, New Haven, Conn.: Yale University Press.

Cerny, P. G. (2001) 'Structuring the Political Arena: Public Goods, States and Governance in a Globalizing World', in R. Palan (ed.) *Global Political Economy: Contemporary Theories*, London: Routledge, pp. 21–35.

Chaloupka, W. (2003) 'There Must Be Some Way Out of Here: Strategy, Ethics and Environmental Politics', in W. Magnusson and K. Shaw (eds) *A Political Space:*

Reading the Global through Clayoquot Sound, Minneapolis, Minn.: University of Minnesota Press, pp. 67–90.

Chandler, D. (2004) 'Building Global Civil Society "From Below?"', *Millennium*, 33 (2): 313–39.

Checkel, J. (1999) 'Social Construction and Integration', *Journal of European Public Policy*, 6 (4): 545–60.

Christensen, T. J. (2001) 'Posing Problems without Catching Up: China's Rise and Challenges for US Security Policy', *International Security*, 25 (4): 5–40.

—— (2002) 'The Contemporary Security Dilemma: Deterring a Taiwan Conflict', *Washington Quarterly*, 25: 7–21.

Christiansen, T., Jörgensen, K. E. and Wiener, A. (eds) (2001) *The Social Construction of Europe*, London: Sage.

Claude, I. (1966) 'Collective Legitimization as a Political Function of the United Nations', *International Organization*, 20 (3): 367–79.

Clausewitz, C. von (1976) *On War*, trans. M. Howard and P. Paret (eds), Princeton, NJ: Princeton University Press.

Clegg, S. R. (1989) *Frameworks of Power*, London: Sage Publications.

Coelho, V. (2006) 'Brazilian Health Councils: Including the Excluded?' in A. Cornwall and V. Coelho (eds) *Spaces for Change?* London: Zed Books.

Cohen, B. J. (1993) 'The Triad and the Unholy Trinity: Lessons from the Pacific Region', in R. Higgott, R. Leaver and J. Ravenhill (eds), *Pacific Economic Relations in the 1990s*, Boulder, Col.: Lynne Rienner, pp. 133–58.

Cohen J. and Arato, A. (1992) *Civil Society and Political Theory*, Cambridge, Mass.: MIT Press.

Coker, C. (2001) *Humane Warfare*, London: Routledge.

—— (2002) *Waging War without Warriors*, Boulder, Col.: Lynne Rienner.

Colas, A. (2002) *International Civil Society*, Cambridge: Polity.

Collier, D. and Levitsky, S. (1997) 'Democracy with Adjectives: Conceptual Innovation in Comparative Research', *World Politics*, 49 (3): 430–51.

Collier, D. and Mahon, J. (1993) 'Conceptual "Stretching" Revisited: Adapting Categories in Comparative Research', *American Political Science Review*, 87 (4): 845–55.

Collins, J. L., Gariyo, A. and Burdon, T. (2001) 'Jubilee 2000: Citizen Action across the North-South Divide', in M. Edwards and J. Gaventa (eds) *Global Citizen Action*, Boulder, Col.: Lynne Rienner.

Connolly, B. (1995) *The Rotten Heart of Europe*, London: Faber & Faber.

Connolly, W. E. (1974) *The Terms of Political Discourse*, Oxford: Martin Robertson.

—— (1991a) *Identity/Difference*, Ithaca, NY: Cornell University Press.

—— (1991b) 'Democracy and Territoriality', *Millennium*, 20 (3): 463–84.

Conrad, J. (1963) *The Secret Agent: A Simple Tale*, London: Penguin Books.

Cooper, J. M. (1999) 'Socrates and Plato in Plato's Gorgias', in J. M. Cooper (ed.) *Reason and Emotion*, Princeton, NJ: Princeton University Press, pp. 29–75.

Cooper, R. (2003) *The Breaking of Nations*, London: Atlantic Books.

—— (2005) 'Economic Power', unpublished paper, Harvard University.

Copeland, D. C. (1996) 'Neorealism and the Myth of Bipolar Stability: Toward a New Dynamic Realist Theory of Major War', in B. Frankel (ed.) *Realism: Restatements and Renewal*, London: Frank Cass, pp. 29–88.

—— (2000) *The Origins of Major War*, Ithaca, NY: Cornell University Press.

Copper, J. (1999) *Taiwan Nation-State or Province?* 3rd edn, Boulder, Col.: Westview Press.

Cornwall, A. (2002) 'Making Spaces, Changing Places: Situating Participation in Development', IDS Working Paper 170, Brighton: Institute of Development Studies.

Cornwall, A. and Coehlo, V. (eds) (2004) 'New Democratic Spaces?', IDS Bulletin, 35.2, Brighton: Institute of Development Studies. See also Citizenship DRC website http://www.drc-citizenship.org (accessed 14 September 2006).

—— (eds) (2006) *Spaces for Change?* London: Zed Books.

Cox, A., Furlong, P. and Page, E. (1985) *Power in Capitalist Society*, Brighton: Harvester Press/Wheatsheaf Books.

Cox, M. (2003) 'The Empire's Back in Town: or America's Imperial Temptation – Again', *Millennium*, 32 (1): 1–27.

Cox, R. (1981) 'Social Forces, States and World Order: Beyond International Relations Theory', *Millennium*, 10 (2): 126–55.

—— (1987) *Production, Power and World Order*, New York: Columbia University Press.

Crawford, N. C. (2002) *Argument and Change in World Politics*, Cambridge: Cambridge University Press.

Cronin, A. K. (2006) 'Cyber-Mobilization: The New Levée en Masse', *Parameters*, 36 (2): 77–87.

Cruz, C. (2000) 'Identity and Persuasion: How Nations Remember Their Pasts and Make their Futures', *World Politics*, 52 (3): 275–312.

Dahl, R. A. (1957) 'The Concept of Power', *Behavioral Science*, 2 (3): 201–15.

—— (1961) *Who Governs?* New Haven, Conn.: Yale University Press.

—— (1968) 'Power', in David L. Sills, (ed.) *International Encyclopedia of the Social Sciences*, Vol. XII, New York: Free Press, pp. 405–15.

—— (1976) Modern Political Analysis, London: Prentice Hall.

Darby, P. (2004) 'Pursuing the Political: A Postcolonial Rethinking of Relations International', *Millennium*, 33 (1): 1–32.

Deakin, M. B. (2005) 'Wielding our Power', *UU World*, 28 (6): 26–8.

Dean, M. (1991) *Governmentality: Power and Rule in Modern Society*, London: Sage.

Deutsch, K. (1967) 'On the Concepts of Politics and Power', *Journal of International Affairs*, 21 (2): 232–41.

De Goede, M. (2001) 'Discourses of Scientific Finance and the Failure of Long-Term Capital Management', *New Political Economy*, 6 (2): 149–70.

De Grauwe, P. (1996) *International Money*, 2nd edn, Oxford: Oxford University Press.

—— (1997) *The Economics of Monetary Integration*, Oxford: Oxford University Press.

Della Porta, D. and Tarrow, S. (2005) *Transnational Protests and Global Activism*, New York: Rowan and Littlefield.

Der Derian, J. (1997) 'Post-Theory: The Eternal Return of Ethics in International Relations', in M. Doyle and J. Ikenberry (eds) *New Thinking in International Relations Theory*, Boulder, Col.: Westview Press, pp. 54–76.

Devji, F. (2005) *Landscapes of the Jihad: Militancy, Morality, Modernity*, London: Hurst.

DeWinter, R. (2001) 'The Anti-Sweatshop Movement: Constructing Corporate Moral Agency in the Global Apparel Industry', *Ethics and International Affairs*, 15 (2): 99–115.

Diez, T. (2001) 'Speaking "Europe": The Politics of Integration Discourse', in T. Christiansen, T., K. E. Jörgensen, and A. Wiener (eds) *The Social Construction of Europe*, London: Sage, pp. 85–100. First published in 1999 in *Journal of European Public Policy*, 6 (4): 598–613.

—— (2004) 'Europe's Others and the Return of Geopolitics', *Cambridge Review of International Affairs*, 17 (2): 319–35.

—— (2005) 'Constructing the Self and Changing Others: Reconsidering 'Normative Power Europe', *Millennium* 33 (3): 613–36.

Diez, T., Stetter, S. and Albert, M. (2006) 'The European Union and Border Conflicts: The Transformative Power of Integration and Association', *International Organization*, 60 (3): 563–93.

Diez, T. and Wiener, A. (2004) 'Introducing the Mosaic of Integration Theory', in T. Diez and A. Wiener (eds) *European Integration Theory*, Oxford: Oxford University Press, pp. 1–21.

Dillon, M. and Reid, J. (2000) 'Global Governance, Liberal Peace and Complex Emergencies', *Alternatives*, 25 (1): 117–43.

Dirlik, A. (1996) 'Reversals, Ironies, Hegemonies: Notes on the Contemporary Historiography of Modern China', *Modern China*, 22 (July): 243–84.

—— (2004) 'China's Critical Intelligentsia', *New Left Review*, 28 (July/August): 137.

Donnelly, J. (2000) *Realism and International Relations*, Cambridge: Cambridge University Press.

Dowding, K. (1991) *Rational Choice and Political Power*, Aldershot: Edward Elgar.

—— (1996) *Power*, Minneapolis, Minn.: University of Minnesota Press.

Doyle, M. (1997) *Ways of War and Peace*, New York: W.W. Norton.

Drahos, P. and Braithwaite, J. (2004) *Information Feudalism: Who Owns the Knowledge Economy?* New York: The New Press.

Drezner, D. (2000) 'Bargaining, Enforcement, and Multilateral Sanctions: When is Cooperation Counterproductive?' *International Organization*, 54 (1): 73–102.

Druckman, D. (1994) 'Nationalism, Patriotism, and Group Loyalty: A Social Psychological Perspective', *Mershon International Studies Review*, 38: 43–68.

Duchêne, F. (1971) 'A New European Defense Community', *Foreign Affairs*, 50 (1): 69–82.

—— (1972) 'Europe's Role in World Peace', in R. Mayne (ed.) *Europe Tomorrow: Sixteen Europeans Look Ahead*, London: Fontana, pp. 32–47.

—— (1973) 'The European Community and the Uncertainties of Interdependence', in M. Kohnstamm and W. Hager (eds) *A Nation Writ Large?* London: Macmillan, pp. 1–21.

Dufresne, J. (1998) 'Soft Opposition to Soft Domination', *Technology in Society*, 20 (3): 327–34.

Dumm, T. (1996) *Michel Foucault and the Politics of Freedom*, Thousand Oaks, Calif.: Sage Publications.

Dunn, F. S. (1948) 'The Scope of International Relations', *World Politics*, 1 (1): 142–6.

Dunne, T. and Schmidt, B. C. (2005) 'Realism', in J. Baylis and S. Smith (eds) *The Globalization of World Politics*, 3rd edn, Oxford: Oxford University Press, pp. 141–61.

Dyson, K. (1994) *Elusive Union*, Harlow: Longman.

—— (2000) 'Europeanization, Whitehall Culture and the Treasury as Institutional Veto Player: A Constructivist Approach to Economic and Monetary Union', *Public Administration*, 78 (4): 897–914.

Edwards, M. and Gaventa, J. (2001) *Global Citizen Action*, Boulder, Col.: Lynne Reinner.

Ehrenberg, V. (1947) 'Polypragmosyne: A Study in Greek Politics', *Journal of Hellenic Studies*, 67: 46–67.

Eisenstein, E. L. (1983) *The Printing Revolution in Early Modern Europe*, Cambridge: Cambridge University Press.

Elshtain, J. B. (1995) 'Feminist Themes and International Relations', in J. Der Derian (ed.) *International Theory Critical Investigations*, New York: NYU Press, pp. 340–60.

English, R. D. (2000) *Russia and the Idea of the West*, New York: Columbia University Press.

Enloe, C. (1989) *Bananas, Beaches, and Bases*, Berkeley, Calif.: University of California Press.

—— (1996) 'Margins, Silences, and Bottom Rungs: How to Overcome the Underestimation of Power in the Study of International Relations' in S. Smith, K. Booth and M. Zalewski (eds) *International Theory*, Cambridge: Cambridge University Press, pp. 186–203.

Erlich, A. (1967) *The Soviet Industrialization Debate 1924–1928*, Cambridge, Mass.: Harvard University Press.

Esbenshade, J. (2004) *Monitoring Sweatshops*, Philadelphia, Penn.: Temple University Press.

Etzioni, A. (2004) 'The Capabilities and Limits of Global Civil Society', *Millennium*, 33 (2): 341–53.

Euben, J. P. (1990) *The Tragedy of Political Theory*, Princeton, NJ: Princeton University Press.

European Union (2003) 'A Secure Europe in a Better World: European Security Strategy', Brussels, Council, 12 December.

Eyben, R., Harris, C. and Pettit, J. (2006) 'Exploring Power for Change', IDS Bulletin 37.6, Brighton: IDS.

Faber, K. G., Ilting, K. H. and Meier, C. (1982) 'Macht, Gewalt', in O. Brunner, W. Conze and R. Koselleck (eds) *Geschichtliche Grundbegriffe*. Band 3, Stuttgart: Klett-Cotta, pp. 817–935.

Fabian, J. (1994) 'Ethnographic Objectivity Revisited: From Rigor to Vigor', in A. Megill (ed.), *Rethinking Objectivity*, Durham, NC: Duke University Press, pp. 81–108.

Farr, J. (1989) 'Understanding Conceptual Change Politically', in T. Ball, J. Farr and R. L. Hanson (eds) *Political Innovation and Conceptual Change*, Cambridge: Cambridge University Press, pp. 24–49.

Faubion, J. (ed.) (2000) *Michel Foucault Power*, New York: The New Press.

Fearon, J. (1995), 'Rationalist Explanations for War', *International Organization*, 49 (3): 379–414.

Ferguson, A. (1995) *An Essay on the History of Civil Society*, ed. F. Oz-Salzberger, New York: Cambridge University Press.

Ferguson, N. (2001) *The Cash Nexus*, London: Allen Lane.

—— (2003) 'Think Again: Power', *Foreign Policy*, (March/April): 18–24.

Ferguson, Y. H. and Barry Jones, R. J. (ed.) (2002) *Political Space*, Albany, NY: State University of New York Press.

Fierke, K. (1998) *Changing Games, Changing Strategies: Critical Investigations in Security*, Manchester: Manchester University Press.

Finley, J. H. (1938) 'Euripides and Thucydides', *Harvard Studies in Classical Philology*, 49: 23–68.

Finnemore, M. and Sikkink, K. (1998) 'International Norm Dynamics and Political Change', *International Organization*, 52 (4): 887–918.

Finnemore, M. and Troope, S. (2001) 'Alternatives to "Legalization": Richer Views of Law and Politics', *International Organization*, 55 (3): 743–58.

Florini, A. (ed.) (2000) *The Third Force: The Rise of Transnational Civil Society*, Washington DC: Carnegie Endowment for International Peace.

Forster, A. (2002) *Euroscepticism in Contemporary British Politics*, London: Routledge.

Fossum, J. E. (2006) 'Conceptualizing the European Union through Four Strategies of Comparison', *Comparative European Politics*, 4 (1): 94–123.

Foucault, M. (1972) *The Archeology of Knowledge and the Discourse on Language*, New York, Pantheon.

—— (1980) *Power/Knowledge*, trans. Colin Gordon, New York: Pantheon.

—— (1988) *History of Sexuality*, 3 vols, New York: Vintage Books.

—— (1995) *Discipline and Punish*, 2nd edn, New York, Vintage Books.

—— (2002) *Power: Essential Works of Foucault, 1954–84*, ed. J. Faubion, London: Penguin.

—— (2004a) 'Governmentality', in P. Rabinow and N. Rose (eds) *The Essential Foucault*, New York: The New Press, pp. 229–45.

—— (2004b) 'Truth and Power', in P. Rabinow and N. Rose (eds) *The Essential Foucault*, New York: The New Press, pp. 300–18.

—— (2004c) 'The Subject and Power', in P. Rabinow and N. Rose (eds) *The Essential Foucault*, New York: The New Press, pp. 126–44.

Frankel, B. (1996) 'Restating the Realist Case: An Introduction', *Security Studies*, 5 (3): xiv–xx.

Frei, D. (1969) 'Vom Mass der Macht', *Schweizer Monatshefte*, 49 (7): 642–54.

Freres, C. (2000) 'The European Union as a Global 'Civilian Power': Development Cooperation in EU-Latin American Relations', *Journal of Interamerican Studies and World Affairs*, 41 (2): 63–86.

Freyberg-Inan, A. (2004) *What Moves Man*, Albany, NY: SUNY Press.

Friedman, M. and Friedman, R. (1980*) Free to Choose*, New York: Harcourt Brace Jovanovich.

Frisch, M. (1954) *Stiller*, Frankfurt: Suhrkamp.

Fuchs, D. (2005) 'Commanding Heights? The Strength and Fragility of Business Power in Global Politics', *Millennium*, 33 (3): 771–802.

Funabashi, Y. (1999) *Alliance Adrift*, New York: Council on Foreign Relations.

Fung, A. and Wright, E. O. (2003) *Deepening Democracy*, London: Verso.

Gadamer, H. (1980) 'Plato and the Poets', in *Dialogue and Dialectic*, trans. P. C. Smith, New Haven, Conn.: Yale University Press, pp. 39–72.

—— (1989) *Truth and Method*, 2nd edn, trans. J. Weinsheimer and D. G. Marshall, New York: Crossroad.

—— (1997) 'Reflections on My Philosophical Journey', in L. E. Hahn (ed.) *The Philosophy of Hans-George Gadamer*, Chicago, Ill.: Open Court.

Galtung, Johan (1969): 'Violence, Peace, and Peace Research', Journal of Peace Research, 6 (3): 167–91.

—— (1971): 'A Structural Theory of Imperialism', Journal of Peace Research, 8 (2): 81–117.

Gambetta, D. (2004) 'Reason and Terror', Boston Review, April/May 2004.

Garthoff, R. L. (1985) *Détente and Confrontation*, Washington, DC: Brookings Institution.

—— (1994) *The Great Transition: American Soviet Relations and the End of the Cold War*, Washington, DC: Brookings Institution.

Garton Ash, T. (2004) 'Are There Moral Foundations of European Power?', Adam von Trott Memorial Lecture, Mansfield College, Oxford. Available at http://www.sant.ox.ac.uk/esc/esc-lectures/von Trott.pdf.

Gaventa, J. (1980) *Power and Powerlessness*. Oxford: Clarendon Press.

—— (1999) 'Citizen Knowledge, Citizen Competence and Democracy Building' in S. Elkin (ed.) *Democracy and Citizen Competence*, University Park, Penn.: Penn State Press, pp. 49–67.

—— (2004) 'Towards Participatory Governance: Assessing the Transformative Possibilities', in S. Hickey and G. Mohan (eds) *From Tyranny to Transformation*, London: Zed Books, pp. 25–41.

—— (2006) 'Reflections on the Uses of the "Power Cube" Approach for Analyzing the Spaces, Places and Dynamics of Civil Society Participation and Engagement', prepared for I. Guijt, (ed.) *Assessing Civil Society Participation as Supported In-Country by Cordaid, Hivos, Novib and Plan Netherlands 1999–2004*, The Hague: MFP Breed Netwerk.

—— (2006a) 'Finding the Spaces for Change: A Power Analysis', in R. Eyben, C. Harris and J. Pettit (eds) 'Exploring Power for Change', *IDS Bulletin* 37 (6), Brighton: Institute of Development Studies, pp. 23–33.

—— (2006b) 'Triumph, Deficit or Contestation? Deepening the "Deepening Democracy" Debate', IDS Working Paper 264, Brighton: Institute of Development Studies.

George, J. (1994) *Discourses of Global Politics*, Boulder, Col.: Lynne Rienner.

Giddens, A. (1979) *Central Problems in Social Theory*, London: Macmillan.

—— (1984) *The Constitution of Society*, Berkeley, Calif.: University of California Press.

—— (1987) *The Nation-State and Violence*, Berkeley, Calif.: University of California Press.

Gill, B. and Huang, Y. (2005) 'The Dragon's Underbelly: Assessing China's Soft Power', CSIS unpublished paper.

Gill, S. R. (1995) 'The Global Panopticon? The Neoliberal State, Economic Life, and Democratic Surveillance', *Alternatives*, 2 (1): 1–50.

—— (2003) *Power and Resistance in the New World Order*, Basingstoke: Palgrave Macmillan.

Gill, S. R. and Law, D. (1989) 'Global Hegemony and the Structural Power of Capital', *International Studies Quarterly*, 33 (4): 475–99.

Gilpin, R. (1981) *War and Change in World Politics*, Cambridge: Cambridge University Press.

Glasius, M. (2003) 'How Activists Shaped the Court', *Crimes of War Project Magazine*. Online. Available at http://www.crimesofwar.org/icc_magazine/icc glasius.html#top (accessed 28 February 2005).

Gold, T. (1996) 'Taiwan Society at the Fin de Siècle', Special Issue: Contemporary Taiwan, *The China Quarterly*, 148 (December): 1091–114.

Gordon, C. (2002) 'Introduction' in M. Foucault, *Power*, ed. J. Faubion, London: Penguin, pp. xi–xli.

Gorgias (1956) in H. Diels and W. Kranz (eds), *Die Fragmente der Vorsokratiker*, 7th edn, Berlin: Weidmannsche Verlagsbuchhandlung.

Gortzak, Y., Haftel, Y. Z. and Sweeny, K. (2005), 'Offense-Defense Theory: An Empirical Assessment', *Journal of Conflict Resolution*, 49 (1): 67–89.

Gowing, N. (2006) 'Real Time Crises: New Real Time Information Tensions', in M. Joyce (ed.), *Transformation of Military Operations on the Cusps*, London: RUSI, pp. 16–20.

Gramsci, A. (1971) *Selections from Prison Notebooks*, New York: International Publishers.

—— (1971) 'State and Civil Society', in *Selections from the Prison Notebooks*, trans. and ed. Q. Hoare and G. N. Smith, New York: International Publishers, pp. 206–46.

Gray, J. (1983) 'Political Power, Social Theory and Essential Contestability', in D. Miller and L. Siedentop (eds), *The Nature of Political Theory*, Oxford: Clarendon Press, pp. 75–101.

Grieco, J. (1997) 'Realist International Theory and the Study of World Politics', in M. W. Doyle and G. J. Ikenberry (eds), *New Thinking in International Relations Theory*, Boulder, Col.: Westview Press, pp. 163–201.

—— (1999) 'Realism and Regionalism: American Power and German and Japanese Institutional Strategies During and After the Cold War', in E. Kapstein and M. Mastanduno (eds) *Unipolar Politics*, New York: Columbia University Press, pp. 319–53.

Guijt, I. (2005) 'Assessing Civil Society Participation as Supported In-Country by Cordaid, Hivos, Novib and Plan Netherlands 1999–2004', *Synthesis Report of Dutch CFA Programme Evaluation*, The Hague: MFP Breed Netwerk.

Guo, Y. and He, B. (1999) 'Reimagining the Chinese Nation: The "Zeng Guofan Phenomenon"', *Modern China*, 25 (April): 142–70.

Guzzini, S. (1993) 'Structural Power: the Limits of Neorealist Power Analysis', *International Organization*, 47 (3): 443–78.

—— (1994) 'Power Analysis as a Critique of Power Politics', unpublished Ph.D. Thesis, Florence, European University Institute.

—— (1998) *Realism in International Relations and International Political Economy*, London, New York: Routledge.

—— (2000a) 'A Reconstruction of Constructivism in International Relations', *European Journal of International Relations*, 6 (2): 147–82.

—— (2000b) 'Strange's Oscillating Realism: Opposing the Ideal – and the Apparent', in T. C. Lawton, J. N. Rosenau and A. C. Verdun (eds) *Strange Power*, Aldershot: Ashgate, pp. 215–28.

—— (2000c) 'The Use and Misuse of Power Analysis in International Theory', in R. Palan (ed.) *Global Political Economy*, London: Routledge, pp. 53–66.

—— (2001) 'The Significance and Roles of Teaching Theory in International Relations', *Journal of International Relations and Development*, 4 (2): 98–117.

—— (2004a) '"The Cold War Is What We Make of It": When Peace Research Meets Constructivism in International Relations', in S. Guzzini and S. Jung (eds) *Contemporary Security Analysis and Copenhagen Peace Research*, London: Routledge, pp. 40–52.

—— (2004b) 'Constructivism and International Relations: An Analysis of Niklas Luhmann's Conceptualisation of Power', in M. Albert and L. Hilkermeier (eds) *Observing International Relations*, London: Routledge, pp. 208–22.

—— (2004c) 'The Enduring Dilemmas of Realism in International Relations', *European Journal of International Relations*, 10 (4): 533–68.

—— (2006) 'From (alleged) unipolarity to the decline of multilateralism? A power-theoretical critique', in Edward Newman, Ramesh Thakur, and John Tirman, eds, *Multilateralism Under Challenge? Power, International Order and Structural Change*, Tokyo: United Nations University Press, pp. 119–138.

Haas, E. (1953) 'The Balance of Power: Prescription, Concept, or Propaganda?' *World Politics* (5) 4 (4): 442–77.

—— (1964) *Beyond the Nation State*, Stanford, Calif.: Stanford University Press.

—— (1990) *When Knowledge Is Power*, Berkeley, Calif.: University of California Press.

Habermas, J. (1979) 'Legitimation Problems in the Modern State' in *Communication and the Evolution of Society*, trans. T. McCarthy, Boston, Mass.: Beacon Press.

—— (1981) *Theorie des kommunikativen Handelns*, Vol. I, Frankfurt: Suhrkamp.

—— (1984–7) *The Theory of Communicative Action*, 2 vols, trans. T. McCarthy, Boston, Mass.: Beacon Press.

—— (1990) *Moral Consciousness and Communicative Action*, trans. C. Lenhardt and S. W. Nicholsen, Cambridge, Mass.: MIT Press.

Hacking, I. (1986) 'Making up People' in T. Heller, M. Sosna and D. Wellbery (eds), *Reconstructing Individualism*, Stanford, Calif.: Stanford University Press, pp. 222–36.

—— (1999) *The Social Construction of What?* Cambridge, Mass.: Harvard University Press.

Haftendorn, H., Keohane, R. O. and Wallander, C. (eds) (1999) *Imperfect Unions*, Oxford: Oxford University Press.

Hajer, M. and Wagenaar, H. (2003) *Deliberative Policy Analysis*, Cambridge: Cambridge University Press.

Hale, J. R. (1977) *Renaissance Europe*, Berkeley, Calif.: University of California Press.

Hall, P. A. and Taylor, R. (1996) 'Political Science and the Three New Institutionalisms', *Political Studies*, 44: 936–57.

Hall, R. B. (1999) *National Collective Identity*, New York: Columbia University Press.

Halperin, S. (2004) *War and Social Change in Modern Europe: The Great Transformation Revisited*, Cambridge: Cambridge University Press.

Hardt, M. and Negri, A. (2000) *Empire*, Cambridge, Mass.: Harvard University Press.

Hardy, R. (2002) 'Jordan Steps up Drive Against Militants', BBC News, 14 November. Available at http://news.bbc.co.uk/1/hi/world/middle_east/2477393.stm (accessed 31 March 2005).

Harmes, A. (1998) 'Institutional Investors and the Reproduction of Neoliberalism', *Review of International Political Economy*, 5 (1): 92–121.

—— (2001) 'Institutional Investors and Polanyi's Double Movement: A Model of Contemporary Currency Crises', *Review of International Political Economy*, 8 (3): 389–437.

Hart, Jeffrey (1976) 'Three Approaches to the Measurement of Power in International Relations', *International Organization*, 30 (2): 289–305.

Hassdorf, W. (2003) 'Is Rationalist Institutionalism Correct? Markets and Domestic Structures in the 1992/93 ERM Crisis', unpublished Ph.D. thesis, London School of Economics, London.

Haugaard, M. (ed.) (2002) *Power: A Reader*, Manchester: Manchester University Press.

Havel, V. (1986) 'The Power of the Powerless', in V. Havel (ed.) *Living in Truth*, London: Faber & Faber, pp. 36–122.

Hay, Colin (1997): 'Divided by a Common Language: Political Theory and the Concept of Power', *Politics*, 17 (1): 45–52.

Hayek, F. A. (1988) *The Fatal Conceit: The Errors of Socialism*, London: Routledge.

Hayward, C. R. (1998) 'De-Facing Power', *Polity*, 31 (1): 22–34.

—— (2000) *De-Facing Power*, Cambridge: Cambridge University Press.

Hedges, C. (2002) *War Is a Force That Gives Us Meaning*, Oxford: Public Affairs.

Hegel, G. W. F. (1942) *Philosophy of Right*, trans. T. M. Knox, Oxford: Clarendon Press.

Held, D. and McGrew, A. (eds) (2003a) *The Global Transformations Reader*, Cambridge: Polity Press.

—— (2003b) *Governing Globalization*, Cambridge: Polity Press.

Henning, C. R. (1994) *Currencies and Politics in the United States, Germany, and Japan*, Washington, DC: Institute for International Economics.

Herman, M. (1996) *Intelligence Power in Peace and War*, Cambridge: Cambridge University Press.

Herrmann, R. K. and Lebow, R. N. (eds) (2004) *Ending the Cold War*, New York: Palgrave.

Hill, C. (1990) 'European Foreign Policy: Power Bloc, Civilian Model – or Flop?', in R. Rummel (ed.) *The Evolution of an International Actor*, Boulder, Col.: Westview Press, pp. 31–55.

Hindess, B. (1986) *Discourses of Power*, Oxford: Blackwell.

Hirschman, A. O. (1977) *The Passions and the Interests*, Princeton, NJ: Princeton University Press.

—— (1985) *Shifting Involvements*, London: Blackwell.

Hitchens, C. (1990) *Blood, Class, and Nostalgia*, New York: Farrar, Strauss & Giroux.

Hoffmann, J. (1988) *State, Power and Democracy*. Brighton: Wheatsheaf Books.

Hoffmann, S. (1959) 'International Relations: The Long Road to Theory', *World Politics*, 11 (3): 346–77.

Hofstadter, R. (1969) *The Idea of a Party System*, Berkeley, Calif.: University of California Press.

Hollis, M. and Smith, S. (1990) *Explaining and Understanding in International Relations*, Oxford: Oxford University Press.

Holquist, M. and Clark, K. (1984) *Mikhail Bakhtin*, Cambridge, Mass.: Harvard University Press.

Holzscheiter, A. (2005) 'Discourse as Capability', *Millennium*, 33 (3): 723–46.

Honneth, A. (1991) *The Critique of Power*, Cambridge, Mass.: MIT Press.

Hooker, T. J. (1974) 'Charis and arête in Thucydides', *Hermes*, 102 (1): 164–9.

Hopf, T. (1998) 'The Promise of Constructivism in International Relations Theory', *International Security*, 23 (1): 171–200.

Hume, D. (1998) *An Inquiry Concerning the Principles of Morals*, ed. T. L. Beauchamp, New York: Oxford University Press.

—— (2000) *A Treatise of Human Nature*, ed. D. F. Norton and M. Norton, Oxford: Oxford University Press.

Huntington, S. P. (1993) 'The Clash of Civilizations?', *Foreign Affairs*, 72 (3): 22–42.

—— (1999) 'The Lonely Superpower', *Foreign Affairs*, 78 (2): 35–49.

Hurt, S. (2006) 'Institutionalizing Food Power: U.S. Foreign Policy, Intellectual Property Law, and the Origins of Agricultural Biotechnology, 1969–1994', unpublished Ph.D. dissertation, The New School.

Hutchings, K. (1999) *International Political Theory*, London: Sage.

Huysmans, J. (1998) 'Security! What Do You Mean? From Concept to Thick Signifier', *European Journal of International Relations*, 4 (2): 226–55.

Ignatieff, M. (2003) 'The American Empire: The Burden', *The New York Times Magazine*, 5 January. Online. Available at http://www.ksg.harvard.edu/cchrp/pdf/NYTimesJan03Burden.pdf (accessed 21 April 2006).

Ikenberry, G. J. (2001) *After Victory*, Princeton, NJ: Princeton University Press.

Ioakimidis, P. (2003) 'Is Europe an "Emerging Superpower"?', International Dialogue Article, Greek Presidency of the European Union. Online. Available at http://www.eu2003.gr/en/articles/2003/5/28/2918.

Jackson, P. T. and Nexon, D. H. (1999): 'Relations Before States: Substance, Process and the Study of World Politics', *European Journal of International Relations*, 5 (3): 291–332.

Jenkins, P. (2003) *Images of Terror*, New York: Aldine de Gruyter.

Jervis, R. (1976) *Perception and Misperception in International Politics*, Princeton, NJ: Princeton University Press.

—— (1999) 'Realism, Neoliberalism, and Cooperation', *International Security*, 24 (1): 42–64.

Jileva, E. (2004) 'Do Norms Matter? The Principle of Solidarity and the EU's Eastern Enlargement', *Journal of International Relations and Development*, 7 (1): 3–23.

Joffe, J. (1995) 'Bismarck or Britain? Toward an American Grand Strategy after Bipolarity', *International Security*, 19 (4): 94–117.

Johnson, D. and Tierney, D. (2006) 'The Wars of Perception', *New York Times*, Editorial, 28 November.

Jones, E. (2003) 'New Dynamics of "Old Europe"', *French Politics*, 1 (2): 233–42.

Joseph, J. (2004) *Social Theory: An Introduction*, New York: NYU Press.

Jouvenel, B. de (1952) *Power: The Natural History of its Growth*, London: Batchworth Press.

—— (1972) *Du pouvoir*, Paris: Hachette.

Jullien, F. (2000) *Detour and Access*, New York: Zone Books.

Juncos, A. (2005) 'The EU's Post-Conflict Intervention in Bosnia and Herzegovina: (Re)Integrating the Balkans and/or (re)Inventing the EU?', *Southeast European Politics*, 6 (2): 88–108.

Jünemann, A. (2003) 'Repercussions of the Emerging European Security and Defence Policy on the Civil Character of the Euro-Mediterranean Partnership', *Mediterranean Politics*, 8 (2–3).

Just Associates, Institute of Development Studies, Knowledge Initiative Action Aid International (2006) *Making Change Happen: Citizen Engagement and Global Economic Power*, http://www.ids.ac.uk/ids/Part/docs/MCH2.pdf

Kabeer, N. (1994) *Reversed Realities*, London: Verso.

—— (2005) *Inclusive Citizenship*, London: Zed Books.

Kagan, R. (2003) *Of Paradise and Power*, New York: Knopf.

Kahn, J. (2004a) 'Taiwan Voters Weighing How Far to Push China', *New York Times*, 18 March, pp. A1, A8.

—— (2004b) 'Election Fallout: Mounting Tension', *New York Times*, 22 March, p. A6.

Kang, D. C. (2003) 'Getting Asia Wrong: The Need for New Analytic Frameworks', *International Security*, 27 (4): 57–85.

Kantorowitz, E. (1957) *The King's Two Bodies*, Princeton, NJ: Princeton University Press. First published 1951.

Kasner, S. D. (1985) *Structural Conflict*, Berkeley, Calif.: University of California Press.

Keane, J. (2003) *Global Civil Society?* Cambridge: Cambridge University Press.

Keck, M. and Sikkink, K. (1998) *Activists Beyond Borders*, Ithaca, NY: Cornell University Press.

Keegan, J. (1993) *History of Warfare*, New York: Penguin.

Kenen, P. B. (1995) *Economic and Monetary Union in Europe*, Cambridge: Cambridge University Press.

Kennedy, P. (1987) *The Rise and Fall of the Great Powers*, New York: Random House.

Kenny, A. J. P. (1975) *Will, Freedom and Power*, Oxford: Blackwell.

Keohane, R. O. (1983) 'Theory of World Politics: Structural Realism and Beyond', in A. W. Finifter (ed.) *Political Science: The State of the Discipline*, Washington, DC: APSA, pp. 503–40.

—— (1989) 'International Relations Theory: Contributions of a Feminist Standpoint', *Millennium*, 18 (2): 245–55.

—— (ed.) (1986) *Neorealism and its Critics*, New York: Columbia University Press.

Keohane, R. O. and Nye, J. (1977) *Power and Interdependence*, Boston, Mass.: Little Brown.

—— (1989) *Power and Interdependence*, 2nd edn, Glenview, Ill.: Foresmen and Company.

—— (eds) (2000) *Governing in a Globalizing World*, Cambridge: Visions of Governance for the 21st Century.

Kepel, G. (2004) *The War for Muslim Minds*, trans. P. Ghazaleh, Cambridge, Mass.: Harvard University Press.

King, G., Keohane, R. O. and Verba, S. (1994) *Designing Social Inquiry*. Princeton, NJ: Princeton University Press.

Kinnvall, C. (2004) 'Globalization and Religious Nationalism: Self, Identity, and the Search for Ontological Self', *Political Psychology*, 25 (5): 741–67.

Kirshner, J. (1995) *Currency and Coercion*, Princeton, NJ: Princeton University Press.

Kirste, K. and Maull, H. (1996) 'Zivilmacht und Rollentheorie', *Zeitschrift für Internationale Beziehungen*, 3 (2): 283–312.

Knorr, Klaus (1975) *The Power of Nations*, New York: Basic Books.

Knox, B. (1970) *Oedipus at Thebes*, New York: Norton.

—— (1982) *The Heroic Temper: Studies in Sophoclean Tragedy*, New York: Cambridge University Press.

Kolk, A. (2005) 'Corporate Social Responsibility in the Coffee Sector: The Dynamics of MNC Responses and Code Development', *European Management Journal*, 23 (2): 228–36.

Koselleck, R. (1979) *Vergangene Zukunft. Zur Semantik geschichtlicher Zeiten*, Frankfurt: Suhrkamp Verlag.

—— (1988) *Critique and Crisis: Enlightenment and the Pathogenesis of Modern Society*, Cambridge, Mass.: MIT Press. First published 1959.

Krasner, S. D. (1983) *International Regimes*, Ithaca, NY: Cornell University Press.

Kratochwil, F. (1989) *Rules, Norms and Decisions*, Cambridge: Cambridge University Press.

—— (2000) 'Constructing a New Orthodoxy? Wendt's "Social Theory of International Politics" and the Constructivist Challenge', *Millennium*, 29 (1): 73–101.

Kraus, C. (2006) 'Canada to Shield 5 Million Forest Acres', *New York Times*, 7 February. Online. Available at http://www.nytimes.com/2006/02/07/international/americas/07canada.html (accessed 13 February 2006).

Krause, K. (1991) 'Military Statecraft: Power and Influence in Soviet and American Arms Transfer Relationships', *International Studies Quarterly*, 35 (3): 313–36.

Krauthammer, C. (1990–1) 'The Unipolar Moment', *Foreign Affairs*, 70 (1): 23–33.

Kristeva, J. (1982) *Powers of Horror*, New York: Columbia University Press.

—— (1991) *Strangers to Ourselves*, New York: Columbia University Press.

Kubik, Jan (1994) *The Power of Symbols against the Symbols of Power*, University Park, Penn.: Pennsylvania State University Press.

Kuhn, T. (1970) *The Structure of Scientific Revolutions*, Chicago, Ill.: University of Chicago Press. First published 1962.

Kuisong, Y. (2000), 'The Sino-Soviet Border Clash of 1969: From Zhenbao Island to Sino-American Rapprochement', *Cold War History*, 1 (1): 21–52.

Kurlantick, J. (2006) *China's Charm: Implications of Chinese Soft Power*, Washington, DC: Carnegie Endowment.

Lakoff, G. and Johnson, M. (2003) *Metaphors We Live By*, Chicago, Ill.: University of Chicago Press. First published 1980.

Laïdi, Z. (2005a) 'Peut-on prendre la puissance européenne au sérieux?', *Cahier européen*, no. 05. Online. Available at http://www.portedeurope.org/IMG/pdf/Cahier_europeen_ZAKILAIDI.pdf.

—— (2005b) *La norme sans la force*, Paris: Presses de Sciences Po.

Lamont, N. (1999) *In Office*, London: Little, Brown and Company.

Lamy, P. and Laïdi, Z. (2002) 'A European Approach to Global Governance', *Progressive Politics*, 1 (1): 56–63.

Laplanche, J. (1993) *Seduction, Translation and the Drives*, New York: Ica Editions.

Lasswell, H. D. (1936) *Politics: Who Gets What, When, How*, New York: McGraw-Hill/P. Smith.

—— (1958) *Politics: Who Gets What, When, How*, Cleveland, Ohio: Meridian Books.

Lasswell, H. D. and Kaplan, A. (1950) *Power and Society*. New Haven, Conn.: Yale University Press.

Lau, D. C. (1970) *Mencius*, New York: Penguin.

Laursen, F. (1991) 'The EC in the World Context: Civilian Power or Superpower?', *Futures*, 23 (7): 747–59.

Layne, C. (1993), 'The Unipolar Illusion: Why New Great Powers Will Arise', *International Security*, 17 (4): 5–51.

—— (1997), 'From Preponderance to Offshore Balancing: America's Future Grand Strategy', *International Security*, 22 (1): 86–124.

Leander A. (2002) 'The Cunning of Imperialist Reason: Using a Bourdieu Inspired Constructivism in IPE', Copenhagen Peace Research Institute, December. Online. Available at http://www.socsci.auc.dk/institut2/nopsa/arbejdsgruppe13/annaleander.pdf (accessed 25 April 2006).

—— (2000) 'A Nebbish Presence: Undervalued Contributions of Sociological Institutionalism to IPE', in R. Palan, (ed.), *Global Political Economy: Contemporary Theories*, London and New York: Routledge, pp. 184–97.

—— (2005) 'The Power to Construct International Security: On the Significance of Private Military Companies', *Millennium*, 33 (3): 803–26.

Lebow, R. N. (2005) 'Power, Persuasion and Justice', *Millennium*, 33 (3): 551–81.

—— (2001) 'Thucydides the Constructivist', *American Political Science Review*, 95 (3): 547–60.

—— (2003) *The Tragic Vision of Politics*, Cambridge: Cambridge University Press.

Lefebvre, H. (1991) *The Production of Space*, London: Verso.

Legro, J. W. and Moravcsik, A. (1999) 'Is Anybody Still a Realist?', *International Security*, 24 (1): 5–55.

Lennon, A. T. (ed.) (2003) *The Battle for Hearts and Minds*, Cambridge, Mass.: MIT Press.

Lévesque, J. (1997) *The Enigma of 1989: The USSR and the Liberation of Eastern Europe*, trans. K. Martin, Berkeley, Calif.: University of California Press.

Levy, D. L. and Newell, P. J. (eds) (2005) *The Business of Global Environmental Governance*, Cambridge, Mass.: MIT Press.

Levy, J. S. (2002): 'Balances and Balancing: Concepts, Propositions, and Research Design', in J. Vasquez and C. Elman (eds), *Realism and the Balancing of Power*, London and Upper Saddle River, NJ: Prentice Hall, pp. 128–53.

Liao, H. (2000) 'Becoming Cyborgian: Postmodernism and Nationalism in Contemporary Taiwan', in A. Dirlik and X. Zhang (eds), *Postmodernism and China*, Durham, NC: Duke University Press, pp. 175–202.

Liao, P. (2000) 'Postmodern Literary Discourse and Contemporary Public Culture in Taiwan', in A. Dirlik and X. Zhang (eds), *Postmodernism and China*, Durham, NC: Duke University Press, pp. 68–88.

Lieber, K. and Alexander, G. (2005) 'Waiting for Balancing: Why the World Is Not Pushing Back', *International Security*, 30 (1): 109–39.

Lightfoot, S. and Burchell, J. (2004a) 'Green Hope or Greenwash? The Actions of the European Union at the World Summit on Sustainable Development', *Global Environmental Change*, 14 (4): 337–44.

—— (2004b) 'Leading the Way? The European Union and the WSSD', *European Environment*, 14 (6): 331–41.

—— (2005) 'The European Union and the World Summit on Sustainable Development: Normative Power Europe in Action?', *Journal of Common Market Studies*, 43 (1): 75–95.

Lindblom, C. E. (1976) *Politics and Markets*, New York: Basic Books.

Link, W. (1988) *Der Ost-West-Konflikt*, 2nd edition, Stuttgart: Kohlhammer.

Linklater, A. (2005a) 'Dialogic Politics and the Civilising Process', *Review of International Studies*, 31 (1): 141–54.

—— (2005b) 'A European Civilising Process?', in C. Hill and M. Smith (eds) *International Relations and the European Union*, Oxford: Oxford University Press, pp. 367–87.

Lipschutz, R. D. and Mayer, J. (1996) *Global Civil Society and Global Environmental Governance*, Albany, NY: State University of New York Press.

—— (2002) 'The Clash of Governmentalities: The Fall of the UN Republic and America's Reach for Imperium', *Contemporary Security Policy*, 23 (2): 214–31.

—— (2004) 'Global Civil Society and Global Governmentality: or, the Search for Politics and the State Amidst the Capillaries of Social Power', in M. Barnett and R. Duvall (eds), *Power in Global Governance*, Cambridge: Cambridge University Press, pp. 229–48.

—— (ed.) (2006) *Civil Society and Social Movements*, Aldershot: Ashgate.

Lipschutz, R. D. and Rowe, J. K. (2005) *Globalization, Governmentality, and Global Politics*, New York: Routledge.

Lipset, S. M. (1996) *American Exceptionalism: A Double-Edged Sword*, New York: W. W. Norton & Company.

Little, R. (1989): 'Deconstructing the Balance of Power: Two Traditions of Thought', *Review of International Studies*, 15 (2): 87–100.

Litzinger, R. (1999) 'Reimagining the State in Post-Mao China', in J. Weldes, M. Laffey, H. Gusterson, and R. Duvall (eds) *Cultures of Insecurity*, Minneapolis, Minn.: University of Minnesota Press, pp. 293–318.

Locke, J. (1988) *Two Treatises of Government*, ed. Peter Laslett, Cambridge: Cambridge University Press.

—— (1948) *The Second Treatise on Civil Government and a Letter Concerning Toleration*, ed. J. W. Gough, Oxford: Blackwell. First published 1660.

Lodge, J. (1993) 'From Civilian Power to Speaking with a Common Voice: The Transition to a CFSP', in J. Lodge (ed.) *The European Community and the Challenge of the Future*, 2nd edn, London: Pinter, p. 235.

Lucarelli, S. and Manners, I. (eds) (2006) *Values and Principles in European Union Foreign Policy*, London: Routledge.

Luce, E. and Sevastopulo, D. (2006) 'The Real Costs to the US Are Yet to Surface from War's Murky Depths', *Financial Times*, 22 November.

Luhmann, N. (1975) *Macht*, Stuttgart: Ferdinand Enke Verlag.

—— (1990a) *Die Wissenschaft der Gesellschaft*, Frankfurt: Suhrkamp.

—— (1990b) *Political Theory in the Welfare State*, Berlin: de Gruyter. First published 1981.

Luke, T. W. (2003) 'On the Political Economy of Clayoquot Sound: The Uneasy Transition from Extractive to Attractive Models of Development', in W. Magnusson and K. Shaw (eds) *A Political Space*, Minneapolis, Minn.: University of Minnesota Press, pp. 91–112.

Lukes, S. (1977) 'Power and Structure', in S. Lukes (ed.), *Essays in Social Theory*, New York: Columbia University Press, pp. 3–29.

—— (1979) 'Power and Authority', in T. Bottomore and R. Nisbet (eds) *History of Sociological Analysis*, London: Heinemann, pp. 633–76.

—— (2005) *Power: A Radical View*, 2nd edn, Basingstoke: Palgrave Macmillan. First published 1974.

—— (2006) 'Reply to Comments', *Political Studies Review*, 4 (2): 164–73.

Lynch, M. (2000) 'The Dialogue of Civilisations and International Public Spheres', *Millennium*, 29 (2): 307–30.

Lynn-Jones, S. M. (1998) 'Realism and America's Rise: A Review Essay', *International Security*, 23 (2): 157–82.

Lynn-Jones, S. M., Miller, S. E. and Van Evera, S. (eds) (1991) *Military Strategy and the Origins of the First World War*, Princeton, NJ: Princeton University Press.

Lyotard, J.-F. (1979) *The Postmodern Condition: A Report on Knowledge*, Minneapolis, Minn.: University of Minnesota Press.

McGee, R. (2004) 'Unpacking Policy: Actors, Knowledge and Spaces', in K. Brock, R. McGee and J. Gaventa (eds), *Unpacking Policy*, Kampala: Fountain Publishers.

MacIntyre, A. (1984) *After Virtue*, 2nd edn, Notre Dame, Ind.: Notre Dame University Press.

McNamara, K. R. (1998) *The Currency of Ideas*, Ithaca, NY: Cornell University Press.

Macpherson, C. B. (1962) *The Political Theory of Possessive Individualism: Hobbes to Locke*, Oxford: Oxford University Press.

Magnusson, W. and Shaw, K. (eds) (2003) *A Political Space: Reading the Global Through Clayoquot Sound*, Minneapolis, Minn.: University of Minnesota Press.

Major, J. (1999) *John Major: The Autobiography*, London: HarperCollins.

Maley, W. (2003) 'Asylum-Seekers in Australia's International Relations', *Australian Journal of International Affairs*, 57 (1): 187–202.

Mann, M. (1986) *The Sources of Social Power*, Vol. I, Cambridge: Cambridge University Press.

—— (1993) *The Sources of Social Power*, Vol. II, Cambridge: Cambridge University Press.

—— (1997) 'Has Globalization Ended the Rise and Rise of the Nation-State?' *Review of International Political Economy*, 4 (3): 472–96.

Manners, I. (2000) 'Normative Power Europe: A Contradiction in Terms?' Copenhagen Peace Research Institute, Working Paper 38.

—— (2002) 'Normative Power Europe: A Contradiction in Terms?' *Journal of Common Market Studies*, 40 (2): 235–58.

—— (2006a) 'Normative Power Europe Reconsidered: Beyond the Crossroads', *Journal of European Public Policy*, 13 (2): 182–99.

—— (2006b) 'European Union "Normative Power" and the Security Challenge', in C. Kantner, A. Liberatore and R. Del Sarto (eds) 'Security and Democracy in the European Union', *European Security*, 15 (4): 405–21.

—— (2006c) 'European Union, Normative Power, and Ethical Foreign Policy', in David Chandler and Volker Heins (eds) *Rethinking Ethical Foreign Policy*, London: Routledge, pp. 116–36.

—— (2007) 'Another Europe is Possible', in K. E. Jörgensen, M. Pollack and B. Rosamond (eds) *Handbook of European Union Politics*, London: Sage.

Manners, I. and Whitman, R. (1998) 'Towards Identifying the International Identity of the European Union', *Journal of European Integration*, 21 (2): 231–49.

—— (2003) 'The "Difference Engine"', *Journal of European Public Policy*, 10 (3): 387–91.

Mansfield, E. D. (1992) 'The Concentration of Capabilities and the Onset of War', *Journal of Conflict Resolution*, 36 (1): 3–24.

—— (1994) *Power, Trade, and War*, Princeton, NJ: Princeton University Press.

Marx, K. and Engels, F. (1970) *The German Ideology*, New York: International Publishers.

Mastanduno, M. (1997) 'Preserving the Unipolar Moment: Realist Theories and U.S. Grand Strategy after the Cold War', *International Security*, 21 (1): 86–124.

Mattei, U. (2003) 'A Theory of Imperial Law', *Global Jurist Frontiers* 3 (2): 1. Online. Available at http://www.bepress.com/gj/frontiers/vol3/iss2/art1 (accessed 13 February 2006).

Mattingly, G. (1955) *Renaissance Diplomacy*, London: Cape.

Maull, H. (1990) 'Germany and Japan: The New Civilian Powers', *Foreign Affairs*, 69 (5): 91–106.

Mayo, M. (2005) *Global Citizens*, London: Zed Books.

Mayr, O. (1986) *Authority, Liberty and Automatic Machinery in Early Modern Europe*. Baltimore, Md.: Johns Hopkins University Press.

Mead, W. R. (2004) *Power, Terror, Peace and War*, New York: Knopf.

Mearsheimer, J. J. (2001) *The Tragedy of Great Power Politics*, New York: W.W. Norton.

Meiggs, R. (1972) *The Athenian Empire*, Oxford: Oxford University Press.

Menon, A., Nicolaïdis, K. and Welsh, J. (2004) 'In Defence of Europe: A Response to Kagan', *Journal of European Affairs*, 2 (3): 5–14.

Mercer, J. (1995) 'Anarchy and Identity', *International Organization*, 49 (2): 229–52.

Merlingen, Michael (2007) 'Foucault and World Politics: Promises and Challenges of Extending Governmentality Theory to the European and Beyond', *Millennium*, 35 (2): 181–196.

Merritt, R. L. and Zinnes, D. A. (1989) 'Alternative Indexes of National Power', in R. J. Stoll and M. D. Ward (eds), *Power in World Politics*, Boulder, Col.: Lynne Rienner, pp. 11–28.

Miller, P. (1987) *Domination and Power*, London: Routledge & Kegan Paul.

Milliken, J. (1999) 'The Study of Discourse in International Relations', *European Journal of International Relations*, 5 (2): 225–54.

Ministry of Defense (2006) 'We must be "slower to condemn, quicker to understand" the Forces – John Reid', *Defense News*, 20 February. Available online at http://www.mod.uk/DefenceInternet/DefenceNews/DefencePolicyAndBusiness/

WeMustBeSlowerToCondemnQuickerToUnderstandTheForcesJohnReid.htm (accessed 10 November 2006).

Mitrany, D. (1943) *A Working Peace System*, London: Royal Institute of International Affairs.

Mitzen, J. (2006) 'Ontological Security and World Politics: State Identity and the Security Dilemma', *European Journal of International Relations*, 12 (3): 341–70.

Mohan, G. and Stokke, K. (2000) 'Participatory Development and Empowerment: The Dangers of Localism', *Third World Quarterly*, 21 (2): 247–68.

Mokken, R. J. and Stokman, F. N. (1976) 'Power and Influence as Political Phenomena', in B. Barry (ed.), *Power and Political Theory*, Bath: The Pitman Press, pp. 33–54.

Morgenthau, H. J. (1933) *La Notion du 'politique' et la théorie des différends internationaux*, Paris: Sirey.

—— (1946) *Scientific Man vs. Power Politics*, Chicago, Ill.: University of Chicago Press.

—— (1948) *Politics Among Nations*, 1st edn, New York: Knopf.

—— (1954) *Politics Among Nations*, 2nd edn, Chicago, Ill.: University of Chicago Press.

—— (1960) *Politics Among Nations*, 3rd edn, New York: Knopf.

—— (1967) 'Common Sense and Theories of International Relations', *Journal of International Affairs*, 21: 207–14.

—— (1982) *In Defense of the National Interest*, Lanham, Md.: University Press of America.

—— (1995) 'The Intellectual and Political Functions of Theory', in J. Der Derian (ed.) *International Theory: Critical Investigations*, New York: NYU Press.

Morriss, P. (1987) *Power: A Philosophical Analysis*, Manchester: Manchester University Press.

—— (2002): *Power: A Philosophical Analysis*, 2nd edn, Manchester: Manchester University Press.

Mouffe, C. (2000) *The Democratic Paradox*, London: Verso.

Nagel, J. H. (1975) *The Descriptive Analysis of Power*, New Haven, Conn.: Yale University Press.

Nagourney, A. and Thee, M. (2006) 'The 2006 Campaign: With Iraq Driving the Election, Voters Want New Approach', *New York Times*, 2 November, p. A1.

Neumann, I. B. (1999) *Uses of the Other*, Minneapolis, Minn.: University of Minnesota Press.

—— (2002) 'Returning Practice to the Linguistic Turn: The Case of Diplomacy', *Millennium*, 31 (3): 627–51.

Newman, S. (2004) 'The Place of Power in Political Discourse', *International Political Science Review*, 25 2): 139–57.

Nicolaídis, K. (2004) 'The Power of the Superpowerless', in T. Lindberg (ed.) *Beyond Paradise and Power*, London: Routledge, pp. vi, 245.

Nicolaídis, K. and Howse, R. (2002) '"This is my EUtopia...": Narrative as Power', *Journal of Common Market Studies*, 40 (4): 767–92.

Nielsen, K. (1995) 'Reconceptualizing Civil Society for Now', in M. Walzer (ed.) *Toward a Global Civil Society*, Providence, RI: Berghahn Books, pp. 41–68.

Norris, C. (1994) 'What is Enlightenment?' in G. Gutting (ed.) *Cambridge Companion to Foucault*, Cambridge: Cambridge University Press, pp. 159–96.

Notes from Nowhere (2003) *We Are Everywhere: The Irresistible Rise of Global Anti-Capitalism*, London: Verso.

Nove, A. (1976) 'Was Stalin Really Necessary?' *Problems of Communism*, 25 (4): 49–62.

—— (1982) *An Economic History of the Soviet Union*, rev. edn, Harmondsworth: Penguin.

Nye, J. S., Jnr. (1990) *Bound to Lead*, New York: Basic Books.

—— (1999) 'The Challenge of Soft Power', *Time Magazine*, Online Edition.

—— (2002) *The Paradox of American Power*, Oxford: Oxford University Press.

—— (2003a) 'Propaganda Isn't the Way: Soft Power', *International Herald Tribune*, 10 January.

—— (2003b) *Understanding International Conflicts*, 4th edn, New York: Longman.

—— (2004a) 'Leverage on Soft Power to Fight Terrorism', *The Straits Times. Taiwan*.

—— (2004b) *Soft Power*, New York, Public Affairs.

—— (2004c) 'The Decline of America's Soft Power: Why Washington Should Worry', *Foreign Affairs*, 83 (3): 16–20.

—— (2004d) 'When Hard Power Undermines Soft Power', *New Perspectives Quarterly*, 21 (3): 13–15.

—— (2004e) 'Hard and Soft Power', in J. Nye, *Power in the Global Information Age*, London: Routledge, pp. 1–9.

Nye, J. S., Jnr. and Owens, W. (1996) 'America's Information Edge', *Foreign Affairs*, 75 (2): 20–34.

Oguzlu, T. (2002) 'The Clash of Security Identities', *International Journal*, 57 (4): 579–603.

—— (2003) 'An Analysis of Turkey's Prospective Membership in the European Union from a "Security" Perspective', *Security Dialogue*, 34 (3): 285–99.

Onishi, N. (2006) 'For China's Youth, Culture Made in South Korea', *New York Times*.

Onuf, N. G. (1989) *World of our Making*, Columbia, SC: University of South Carolina Press.

Oppenheim, F. E. (1976) 'Power and Causation', in B. Barry (ed.) *Power and Political Theory*, Bath: The Pitman Press, pp. 103–16.

—— (1981) *Political Concepts: A Reconstruction*, Oxford: Basil Blackwell.

Orford, A. (2000) 'Positivism and the Power of International Law', *Melbourne University Law Review*, 24: 502–29.

Organski, A. F. K. (1967) *World Politics*, 2nd edn, New York: Knopf.

Organski, A. F. K. and Kugler, J. (1980) *The War Ledger*, Chicago, Ill.: University of Chicago Press.

Orwell, G. (1949) *1984: A Novel*, New York: Harcourt.

Orwin, C. (1994) *The Humanity of Thucydides*, Princeton, NJ: Princeton University Press.

Padoa-Schioppa, T. (2004) *Europe, a Civil Power*, London: Federal Trust for Education and Research.

Pagden, A. (1987) 'Dispossessing the Barbarians', in A. Pagden, (ed.) *The Languages of Political Theory in Early-Modern Europe*, Cambridge: Cambridge University Press, pp. 79–98.

Palan, R. and Blair, B. (1993) 'On the Idealist Origins of the Realist Theory of International Relations', *Review of International Studies*, 19 (4): 385–99.

Pan, J. (2004) 'Ketagalan People Promote Revival of Culture, Traditions', *Taiwan News*, 9 August. Available at http://www.etaiwannews.com/Taiwan/2004/08/09 (accessed 10 August 2004).

Pape, R. (2005) 'Soft Balancing against the United States', *International Security*, 30 (3): 7–45.

Parker, G. (2005) 'The Future of Western Warfare', in G. Parker (ed.), *The Cambridge History of Warfare*, Cambridge: Cambridge University Press, pp. 413–33.

Paul, T. V. (2005) 'Soft Balancing in the Age of U.S. Primacy', *International Security*, 30 (3): 46–71.

Payne, R. A. (2001) 'Persuasion, Frames, and Norm Construction', *European Journal of International Relations*, 7 (1): 37–61.

PBS (2001) 'Frontline Special Dangerous Straits, Exploring the Future of US-China Relations and the Long Simmering Issue of Taiwan (October)'. Available at http://www.pbs.org/wghb/pages/frontline/shows/china/interviews (accessed 14 August 2004).

Pearce, J. and Vela, G. (2005) 'Colombia Country Report for the Dutch CFA Programme Evaluation', prepared for I. Guijt (ed.), *Assessing Civil Society Participation as Supported In-Country by Cordaid, Hivos, Novib and Plan Netherlands 1999–2004*, The Hague: MFP Breed Netwerk.

Pelham, N. (2002) 'Jordan's Peaceful Image Shattered', *BBC News*, 19 November. Available at http://news.bbc.co.uk/1/hi/world/middle_east/2489777.stm (accessed 31 March 2005).

Pieterse, J. (1997) 'Globalisation and Emancipation', *New Political Economy*, 2 (1): 79–92.

Pijpers, A. (1988) 'The Twelve Out-of-Area', in A. Pijpers, E. Regelsberger, W. Wessels, and G. Edwards (eds), *European Political Cooperation in the 1980s*, Dordrecht: Martinus Nijhoff.

Plato (1996) *Republic*, trans. and ed. I. A. Richards, Cambridge: Cambridge University Press.

Polanyi, K. (1944) *The Great Transformation*, Boston, Mass.: Beacon Press.

—— (2001) *The Great Transformation*, 2nd edn, Boston, Mass.: Beacon Press.

Polsby, N. W. (1963) *Community Power and Political Theory*, New Haven, Conn.: Yale University Press.

—— (1980) *Community Power and Political Theory*, 2nd edn, New Haven, Conn.: Yale University Press.

Pomfret, S. J. (1999) 'China Ponders New Rules of "Unrestricted Warfare"', *Washington Post*, 8 August, p. 1.

Powers, W. (2005) *Blue Clay People: Seasons on Africa's Fragile Edge*, New York: Bloomsbury.

Price, R. (1998) 'Reversing the Gun Sights', *International Organization*, 52 (3): 613–44.

Record, J. and Terrill, W. A. (2004) *Iraq and Vietnam: Differences, Similarities, and Insights*, Carlisle, Penn.: US Army War College.

Reid, J. (2003) 'Focault on Clausewitz: Conceptualizing the Relationship between War and Power', *Alternatives* 28 (1): 1–28.

Reus-Smit, C. (2004) *American Power and World Order*, London: Polity.

Rhodes, E. (2003) 'The Imperial Logic of Bush's Liberal Agenda', *Survival*, 45 (1): 131–54.

Ringmar, E. (2005) *Surviving Capitalism*, London: Anthem.

—— (2007a) 'The Self-Actualisation of Modernity', in R. Mole (ed.) *Language, Discourse and Identity*, London: Palgrave, forthcoming.

—— (2007b) *Why Europe Was First*, London: Anthem, forthcoming.

Risse, T. (2000) '"Let's Argue!": Communicative Action in World Politics', *International Organization*, 54 (4): 1–40.

—— (2002) 'Transnational Actors and World Politics' in W. Carlsnaes, T. Risse and B. A. Simmons (eds) *Handbook of International Relations*, London: Sage, pp. 255–74.

Robin, C. (2004) *Fear: The History of a Political Idea*, New York: Oxford University Press.

Rose, A. K. and Svensson, L. E. O. (1995) 'Macroeconomic and Political Determinants of Realignment Expectations', in B. Eichegreen, J. Frieden and J. von Hagen (eds) *Monetary and Fiscal Policy in an Integrated Europe*, Berlin: Springer, pp. 91–117.

Rose, G. (1998) 'Neoclassical Realism and Theories of Foreign Policy', *World Politics*, 51 (1): 144–72.

Rosenau, J. (2002) 'Governance in the Twenty-First Century' in R. Wilkinson (ed.) *The Global Governance Reader*, London: Routledge, pp. 45–67.

Rosenberg, J. (1994) *The Empire of Civil Society*, London: Verso.

Ross, R. S. (1995) *Negotiating Cooperation: The United States and China, 1969–1989*, Stanford, Calif.: Stanford University Press.

Rowden, R. and Irama, J. O. (2004) *Rethinking Participation*, Washington, DC: ActionAid International USA and Kampala: ActionAid International Uganda.

Rowe, J. K. (2006) 'Rethinking Politics, Rethinking Theory', *Theory and Event*, 9 (2).

Rueschemeyer, D. (1991) 'Different Methods – Contradictory Results? Research on Development and Democracy', *International Journal of Comparative Sociology*, 32 (1–2): 9–38.

Ruggie, J. G. (1975): 'International Responses to Technology: Concepts and Trends', *International Organization*, 29 (3): 557–83.

—— (1982) 'International Regimes, Transactions, and Change', *International Organization*, 36 (2): 379–415.

—— (1993) 'Territoriality and Beyond: Problematizing Modernity in International Relations', *International Organization*, 47 (1): 139–74.

—— (2004) 'Reconstituting the Global Public Domain', *European Journal of International Relations*, 10 (4): 499–531.

Rumelili, B. (2004) 'Constructing Identity and Relating to Difference', *Review of International Studies*, 30 (1): 27–47.

Russell, R. L. (2000) 'The 1996 Taiwan Strait Crisis', Case 231, Institute for the Study of Diplomacy, Washington, DC: Georgetown University School of Foreign Service, pp. 3–6.

Sabine, George (1969): 'What is a Political Theory?', in J. A. Gould and V. V. Thursby (eds), *Contemporary Political Thought*, New York: Rinehart & Winston, pp. 7–20. First published 1931.

Sagan, S. D. (1994), 'From Deterrence to Coercion to War: The Road to Pearl Harbor', in A. George and W. Simons (eds), *The Limits of Coercive Diplomacy*, 2nd edn, Boulder, Col.: Westview Press.

Said, E. (1979) *Orientalism*, New York: Vintage.

Sandholtz, W. and Stone Sweet, A. (1998) *European Integration and Supranational Governance*, Oxford: Oxford University Press.

Sandilands, C. (2003) 'Between the Local and the Global', in W. Magnusson and K. Shaw (eds), *A Political Space*, Minneapolis, Minn.: University of Minnesota Press, pp. 139–68.

Sartori, A. (2002) 'The Might of the Pen: A Reputational Theory of Communication in Disputes', *International Organization*, 56 (1): 121–49.

Sartori, G. (1970) 'Concept Misformation in Comparative Politics', *American Political Science Review*, 64 (4): 1033–53.

Sassen, S. (2002) 'Global Cities and Diasporic Networks: Microsites in Global Civil Society', in H. Anheier, M. Glasius and M. Kaldor (eds), *Global Civil Society*, Oxford: Oxford University Press, pp. 217–40.

Saurette, P. (2006) 'You Dissin' Me? Humiliation and Post 9/11 Global Politics', *Review of International Studies*, 32 (3): 495–522.

Schelling, T. C. (1966) *Arms and Influence*, New Haven, Conn.: Yale University Press.

Schmidt, B. C. (2004) 'Realism as Tragedy', *Review of International Studies*, 30 (3): 427–41.

—— (2005) 'Competing Realist Conceptions of Power', *Millennium*, 33 (3): 523–50.

Schmitt, C. (1985) *Political Theology: Four Chapters on the Concept of Sovereignty*, trans. G. Schwab, Cambridge, Mass.: MIT Press.

—— (1996) *The Concept of the Political*, Chicago, Ill.: University of Chicago Press. First published 1932.

Scholte, J. A. (2002) 'Civil Society and Democracy in Global Governance' in R. Wilkinson (ed.), *The Global Governance Reader*, London: Routledge, pp. 322–40.

Schoppa, L. J. (1999) 'The Social Context in Coercive International Bargaining', *International Organization*, 53 (2): 307–42.

Schuman, F. S. (1933) *International Politics: An Introduction to the Western State System*, New York: McGraw Hill.

Schwarzenberger, G. (1941) *Power Politics: An Introduction to the Study of International Relations and Post-War Planning*, London: Jonathan Cape.

Schweller, R. L. (1996) 'Neorealism's Status-Quo Bias: What Security Dilemma?', *Security Studies*, 5 (3): 90–121.

—— (1998) *Deadly Imbalances*, New York: Columbia University Press.

—— (2003) 'The Progressiveness of Neoclassical Realism', in C. Elman and M. F. Elman (eds), *Progress in International Relations Theory*, Cambridge, Mass.: MIT Press, pp. 311–47.

—— (2004) 'Unanswered Threats: A Neoclassical Realist Theory of Underbalancing', *International Security*, 29 (2): 159–201.

Scott, J. C. (1990) *Domination and the Arts of Resistance*, New Haven, Conn.: Yale University Press.

—— (1998) *Seeing Like a State*, New Haven, Conn.: Yale University Press.

Searle, J. R. (1995) *The Construction of Social Reality*, New York: The Free Press.

Seldon, A. (1998) *Major: A Political Life*, London: Phoenix.

Sellin, V. (1978) 'Politik', in O. Brunner, W. Conze and R. Koselleck (eds), *Geschichtliche Grundbegriffe*, Vol. IV, Stuttgart: Klett-Cotta, pp. 789–874.

Shapiro, M. (1989) 'Representing World Politics: The Sport/War Intertext', in J. Der Derian and M. Shapiro (eds), *International/Intertextual Relations*, New York: Lexington Books, pp. 69–96.

—— (1991) 'Sovereignty and Exchange in the Orders of Modernity', *Alternatives*, 16: 447–77.

Shefrin, H. (2000) *Beyond Greed and Fear*, Cambridge, Mass.: Harvard Business School Press.

Shiller, R. J. (2000) *Irrational Exuberance*, Princeton, NJ: Princeton University Press.

Shonfield, A. (1973) *Europe: Journey to an Unknown Destination*, London: Allen Lane.

Simmons, J. (1995) *Foucault and the Political*, New York: Routledge.

Simon, H. A. (1997) *Models of Bounded Rationality*, Vol. I, Cambridge, Mass.: MIT Press.

Simpson, J. (2005) 'Battling the Al-Qaeda Franchise', BBC Online, 3 October. Available online at http://news.bbc.co.uk/2/hi/asia-pacific/4304516.stm (accessed 10 November 2006).

Siniavski, A. (1988) *La Civilisation soviétique*, Paris: Albin Michel.

Sjöstedt, G. (1977) 'The Exercise of International Civil Power: A Framework for Analysis', *Cooperation and Conflict*, 12 (1): 23–4.

Sjursen, H. (2004) 'Changes to European Security in a Communicative Perspective', *Cooperation and Conflict*, 39 (2): 107–28.

—— (ed.) (2006) 'What Kind of Power? European Foreign Policy in Perspective', *Journal of European Public Policy*, 13 (2), Special Issue: 169–81.

Skinner, Q. (1989) 'Language and Political Change', in T. Ball, J. Farr and R. L. Hanson (eds), *Political Innovation and Conceptual Change*, Cambridge: Cambridge University Press, pp. 6–23.

—— (2002) *Visions of Politics*, Vol. I: *Regarding Method*, Cambridge: Cambridge University Press.

Skocpol, T. (1979) *States and Social Revolutions*, Cambridge: Cambridge University Press.

Smith, A. (1982) *The Wealth of Nations*, ed. A. Skinner, Harmondsworth: Penguin.

Smith, A. D. (1991) *National Identity*, Reno, Nev.: University of Nevada Press.

Smith, K. E. (2000) 'The End of Civilian Power EU: A Welcome Demise or Cause for Concern?' *International Spectator*, 35 (2): 11–28.

—— (2001) 'The EU, Human Rights and Relations with Third Countries: "Foreign Policy" with an Ethical Dimension?' in K. Smith and M. Light (eds), *Ethics and Foreign Policy*, Cambridge: Cambridge University Press, pp. 185–203.

—— (2005) 'Beyond the Civilian Power EU Debate', *Politique Europeénne*, 17: 63–82.

Smith, M. A. (1998) 'The European Union and the United States in a Superpower Context', *European Security*, 7 (1): 66–73.

Smith, R. (2005) *The Utility of Force*, London: Allen Lane.

Smith, S. (1995) 'The Self-Images of a Discipline: A Genealogy of International Relations Theory', in K. Booth and S. Smith (eds), *International Relations Theory Today*, Cambridge: Polity Press, pp. 1–36.

Smyth, R. (2001) 'Mapping US Public Diplomacy in the 21st Century', *Australian Journal of International Affairs*, 55 (3): 421–44.

Snyder, A. (1995) *Warriors of Disinformation*, New York: Arcade Publishing.

Soja, E. (1996) *Third Space: Journeys to Los Angeles and Other Imagined Places*, Cambridge, Mass.: Blackwell.

Song, X. (2002) 'Intellectual Discourses in the Taiwan Independence Movement', in B. Coppieters and M. Huysseune (eds), *Secession, History and the Social Sciences*, Brussels: Brussels University Press.

Sophocles (1999) 'Antigone', in D. Slavitt and P. Bovie (eds), *Sophocles*, 2, trans. K. Cherry, Philadelphia, Penn.: University of Pennsylvania Press.

Spirtas, M. (1996) 'A House Divided: Tragedy and Evil in Realist Theory', *Security Studies*, 5 (3): 385–423.

Spykman, N. J. (1942) *America's Strategy in World Politics: The United States and the Balance of Power*, New York: Harcourt, Brace & Co.

Stanley, A. D. (1998) *From Bondage to Contract: Wage Labor, Marriage and the Market in the Age of Slave Emancipation*, Cambridge: Cambridge University Press.

Stavridis, S. (2001) '"Militarising" the EU: The Concept of Civilian Power Europe Revisited', *International Spectator*, 36 (2): 43–50.

Stephens, P. (1997) *Politics and the Pound*, London: Macmillan.

Sterling-Folker, J. (2002) *Theories of International Cooperation and the Primacy of Anarchy*, Albany, NY: SUNY Press.

Stevens, P. (2006) 'The Paradox of Being Insecure in a Far More Peaceful World', *Financial Times*, 15 September, p. 15.

Strange, S. (1987) 'The Persistent Myth of Lost Hegemony', *International Organization*, 41 (4): 551–74.

—— (1988) *States and Markets*, New York: Basil Blackwell.

—— (1990): 'Finance, Information and Power', *Review of International Studies*, 16 (3): 259–74.

—— (1996) *The Retreat of the State*, Cambridge: Cambridge University Press.

Swartz, D. (1997) *Culture and Power: The Sociology of Pierre Bourdieu*, Chicago, Ill.: University of Chicago Press.

Taliaferro, J. W. (2000/1) 'Security Seeking Under Anarchy', *International Security*, 25 (3): 128–61.

Tang, X. (1999) 'On the Concept of Taiwan Literature', *Modern China*, 25 (4): 386.

Tarrow, S. (2005) *The New Transnational Activism*, Cambridge: Cambridge University Press.

Tatham, S. (2006) *Losing Arab Hearts and Minds*, London: Hurst & Company.

Tellis, A.J. (1996) 'Reconstructing Political Realism: The Long March to Scientific Theory', in B. Frankel (ed.) *Roots of Realism*, London: Frank Cass, pp. 3–104.

Telò, M. (2005) *Europe: A Civilian Power?* Basingstoke: Palgrave.

Tewes, H. (1997) 'Das Zivilmachtskonzept in der Theorie der Internationalen Beziehungen', *Zeitschrift für Internationale Beziehungen*, 4 (2): 361–88.

Thatcher, M. (1997) 'Speech to the Conservative Party Conference, Brighton, 10 October 1980', in R. Harris (ed.), *The Collected Speeches of Margaret Thatcher*, London: HarperCollins, pp. 112–16.

Thompson, H. (1996) *The British Conservative Government and the European Exchange Rate Mechanism, 1979–1994*, London: Pinter.

Thucydides (1972) *History of the Peloponnesian War*, trans. R. Warner, New York: Viking-Penguin.

Tickner, J. A. (1988): 'Hans Morgenthau's Principles of Political Realism: A Feminist Reformulation', *Millennium*, 17 (3): 429–40.

Toal, G. (1999) 'Understanding Critical Geopolitics: Geopolitics and Risk Society', *Journal of Strategic Studies*, 22 (2/3): 107–24.

Tocqueville, A. de (1966) *Democracy in America*, trans. and ed. G. Lawrence, J. P. Mayer and M. Lerner, New York: Harper & Row.

Tonra, B. (2003) 'Constructing the Common Foreign and Security Policy: The Utility of a Cognitive Approach', *Journal of Common Market Studies*, 41 (4): 731–56.

Traub, J. (2005) 'The New Hard-Soft Power', *New York Times Magazine*, 30 January.

Treacher, A. (2004) 'From Civilian Power to Military Actor: The EU's Resistible Transformation', *European Foreign Affairs Review*, 9: 49–66.

Tsakaloyannis, P. (1989) 'The EC: From Civilian Power to Military Integration', in J. Lodge (ed.) *The European Community and the Challenge of the Future*, London: Pinter, pp. 241–55.

Tu, W. (1996) 'Cultural Identity and the Politics of Recognition in Contemporary Taiwan', *China Quarterly* Special Issue: Contemporary Taiwan, 148: 1115–40.

Tucker, N. B. (1995–6), 'China as a Factor in the Collapse of the Soviet Empire', *Political Science Quarterly*, 110 (4): 501–18.

Tully, J. (1980) *A Discourse on Property*, Cambridge: Cambridge University Press.

—— (1988) 'The Pen Is a Mighty Sword', in J. Tully (ed.), *Meaning and Context: Quentin Skinner and his Critics*, Cambridge: Polity Press, pp. 7–25.

Twitchett, K. (1976) *The External Relations of the Common Market*, New York: St. Martin's Press.

Tyson, A. S. (2002) 'Where The Anti-Terror Doctrine Leads', *Christian Science Monitor*, 7 February.

Van Rooy, A. (2004) *The Global Legitimacy Game*, Basingstoke: Palgrave MacMillan.

Veblen, T. (1898) 'The Beginnings of Ownership', *American Journal of Sociology*, 4 (3) (November): 352–65.

VeneKlasen, L. and Miller, V. (2002) *A New Weave of People, Power and Politics*, Oklahoma City, Okla.: World Neighbors.

Vico, G. (1986) *The New Science of Giambattista Vico*, 3rd edn, Ithaca, NY: Cornell University Press. First published 1744.

von Wright, G. H. (1971) *Explanation and Understanding*, Ithaca, NY: Cornell University Press.

Wæver, O. (1995) 'Securitization and Desecuritization', in Ronnie Lipschutz, (ed.) *On Security*, New York: Columbia University Press, pp. 46–86.

—— (1996) 'European Security Identities', *Journal of Common Market Studies*, 34 (1), 103–32.

—— (1998) 'Insecurity, Security and Asecurity in the West European Non-war Community', in E. Adler and M. Barnett (eds) *Security Communities*, Cambridge: Cambridge University Press, pp. 69–118.

Walker, R. B. J. (1987) 'Realism, Change, and International Political Theory', *International Studies Quarterly* 31 (1): 65–86.

—— (1991) 'On the Spatiotemporal Conditions of Democratic Practice', *Alternatives*, 16: 243–62.

—— (1993) *Inside/Outside*, Cambridge: Cambridge University Press.

—— (1995) 'International Relations and the Concept of the Political', in K. Booth and S. Smith (eds) *International Relations Theory Today*, Cambridge: Polity, pp. 306–27.

—— (2003) 'Polis, Cosmopolis, Politics', *Alternatives*, 28: 267–87.

Walker, R. B. J. and Mendlovitz, S. (eds) (1990) *Contending Sovereignties, Redefining Political Community*, Boulder, Col.: Lynne Rienner.

Walsh, J. I. (2000) *European Monetary Integration and Domestic Politics: Britain, France and Italy*, Boulder, Col.: Lynne Rienner.

Walt, S. (2002) 'The Enduring Relevance of the Realist Tradition', in I. Katznelson and H. V. Milner (eds) *Political Science: The State of the Discipline*, New York: Norton, pp. 197–230.

—— (2005) *Taming American Power*, New York: Norton.

Waltz, K. N. (1959) *Man, the State, and War*, New York: Columbia University Press.

—— (1964), 'The Stability of a Bipolar World', *Daedalus*, 93 (3): 881–909.

—— (1967), 'International Structure, National Force, and the Balance of World Power', *Journal of International Affairs*, 21: 215–31.

—— (1979) *Theory of International Politics*, New York: Random House.

—— (1986) 'Reflection on Theory in International Politics: A Response to My Critics', in R. O. Keohane (ed.), *Neorealism and its Critics*, New York: Columbia University Press, pp. 322–45.

—— (1989) 'The Origins of War in Neorealist Theory', in R. Rotberg and T. K. Rabb (eds) *The Origin and Prevention of Major Wars*, Cambridge: Cambridge University Press, pp. 39–52.

—— (1990) 'Realist Thought and Neorealist Theory', *Journal of International Affairs*, 44 (1): 21–37.

—— (1993) 'The Emerging Structure of International Politics', *International Security*, 18 (2): 44–79.

—— (2000), 'Structural Realism after the Cold War', *International Security*, 25 (1): 5–41.

Weber, C. (1994) 'Good Girls, Little Girls and Bad Girls: Male Paranoia in Robert Keohane's Critique of Feminist International Relations', *Millennium*, 23 (2): 337–49.

—— (1995) *Simulating Sovereignty: Intervention, the State and Symbolic Exchange*, Cambridge: Cambridge University Press.

Weber, M. (1947) *The Theory of Social and Economic Organization*, New York: The Free Press.

—— (1976) *Wirtschaft und Gesellschaft. Grundriss der Verstehenden Soziologie*, Tübingen: J. C. B. Mohr (Paul Siebeck). First published 1921–2.

—— (1992) *Soziologie: Universalgeschichtliche Analysen Politik*, Stuttgart: Alfred Kröner.

—— (1999) *Politik als Beruf*, Stuttgart: Reclam. First published 1919.

Webster, N. and Engberg-Pedersen L. (eds) (2002) *In the Name of the Poor*, London: Zed Books.

Weiss, Linda (2005) 'Michael Mann, State Power, and the Two Logics of Globalization', *Millennium*, 34 (2): 529–41.

Wendt, A. (1992) 'Anarchy is What States Make of it: The Social Construction of Power Politics', *International Organization*, 46 (2): 391–425.

—— (1998) 'On Constitution and Causation in International Relations', *Review of International Studies*, 24 (special issue): 101–17.

—— (1999) *Social Theory of International Politics*, Cambridge: Cambridge University Press.

Wendt, A. and Duvall, R. (1989) 'Institutions and International Order', in J. Rosenau and E. O. Czempiel (eds) *Global Changes and Theoretical Challenges*, Lexington, Ky.: Lexington Books, pp. 51–74.

Wertsch, J. (1991) *Voices of the Mind*, Cambridge, Mass.: Harvard University Press.

White, H. (1987a) *The Content of the Form*, Baltimore, Md.: Johns Hopkins University Press.

—— (1987b) *The Value of Narrativity in the Representation of Reality: The Content of the Form*, Baltimore, Md.: Johns Hopkins University Press.

White, J. B. (1984) *When Words Lose Their Meaning*, Chicago, Ill.: University of Chicago Press.

—— (1985) *Heracles' Bow: Essays on the Rhetoric and Poetics of the Law*, Madison, Wisc.: University of Wisconsin Press.

White House (2006) 'National Strategy for Combating Terrorism'. Available online at http://www.whitehouse.gov/nsc/nsct/2006/nsct2006.pdf (accessed 10 November 2006).

Whitman, R. (1998) *From Civilian Power to Superpower?* Basingstoke: Macmillan.

Wiebe, R. H. (1967) *The Search for Order: 1877–1920*, New York: Hill & Wang.

Wildmaier, W. W. (2003) 'Constructing Monetary Crises: New Keynesian Understandings and Monetary Cooperation in the 1990s', *Review of International Studies*, 29 (1): 61–77.

Williams, M. J. (2005a) *On Mars and Venus*, Berlin: LIT Verlag.

—— (2005b) 'Revisiting Established Doctrine in an Age of Risk', *RUSI Journal*, 150 (5): 48–52.

Wilmer, F. (2002) *The Social Construction of Man, the State, and War*, New York: Routledge.

Wohlforth, W. C. (1993) *The Elusive Balance*, Ithaca, NY: Cornell University Press.

—— (1999) 'The Stability of a Unipolar World', *International Security*, 24 (1): 5–41.

Wolf, M. (2005) 'Soft Power: The EU's Greatest Gift', *Financial Times.*

Wolfers, A. (1962) *Discord and Collaboration*, Baltimore, Md.: Johns Hopkins University Press.

—— (1951) 'The Pole of Power and the Pole of Indifference', *World Politics*, 4: 39–63.

Wolin, S. (1996) 'Fugitive Democracy', in S. Benhabib (ed.) *Democracy and Difference*, Princeton, NJ: Princeton University Press, pp. 31–45.

Wood, E. M. (1995) *Democracy against Capitalism: Renewing Historical Materialism*, Cambridge: Cambridge University Press.

—— (2002) *The Origins of Capitalism*, London: Verso.

Wrong, D. H. (1988) *Power: Its Forms, Bases and Uses*, Oxford: Basil Blackwell. First published in 1979.

Yang, X. (2000) 'Whence and Whither the Postmodern/Post-Mao-Deng', in A. Dirlik and X. Zhang (eds) *Postmodernism and China*, Durham, Md.: Duke University Press, pp. 379–98.

Youngs, Richards (2004) 'Normative Dynamics and Strategic Interests in the EU's External Identity', *Journal of Common Market Studies*, 42 (2): 415–35.

Zaharna, R. S. (2000) 'Intercultural Communication and International Public Relations', *Communication Quarterly*, 48 (1): 85–100.

Zakaria, F. (1998) *From Wealth to Power*, Princeton, NJ: Princeton University Press.

Zehfuss, M. (2001) 'Constructivism and Identity: A Dangerous Liaison', *European Journal of International Relations*, 7 (3): 315–48.

—— (2002) *Constructivism in International Relations*, Cambridge: Cambridge University Press.

Zhao, S. (ed.) (1999) *Across the Taiwan Strait*, New York: Routledge.

Zielonka, J. (1998) *Explaining Euro-Paralysis*, Basingstoke: Macmillan. Adapted from Michael Barnett and Raymond Duvall (eds.) (2005) *Power in Global Governance,* Cambridge: Cambridge University Press, p. 12.

Index